The Śūraṅgama Sūtra

On Respecting Sacred Books

In the Buddhist tradition, sutras are understood to contain the teachings of Buddhas and greatly enlightened masters. As guidebooks to the path to awakening, sutras are treated with reverence. It is customary to keep sutra volumes in a clean place, either above or apart from secular works; to handle them with respect; and to read them only while sitting upright or standing.

The Śūraṅgama Sūtra

With Excerpts from the Commentary
by the Venerable Master Hsüan Hua

A New Translation

Buddhist Text Translation Society

The Śūraṅgama Sūtra.
Newly translated from the Chinese by the Śūraṅgama Sūtra Translation Committee of the Buddhist Text Translation Society: Rev. Bhikṣu Heng Sure (certifier); Bhikṣu Jin Yan, Bhikṣu Jin Yong, Novice Jin Jing, Novice Jin Hai, Ron Epstein, David Rounds, Joey Wei, Fulin Chang, and Laura Lin.

The Buddhist Text Translation Society is an affiliate of the Dharma Realm Buddhist Association, 4951 Bodhi Way, Ukiah, California 95482 (707) 462-0939, bttsonline.org.

ISBN 978-0-88139-962-2

Library of Congress Cataloguing-in Publication Data:

Tripitaka. Sutrapitaka. Surangamasutra. English.
    The Surangama sutra : a new translation / with excerpts from the commentary by the venerable master Hsüan Hua.
        p. cm.
    Translated from Chinese originally written in Sanskrit.
    Includes bibliographical references and index.
    I. Hsüan Hua, 1918-1995. II. Buddhist Text Translation Society.
    III. Title.
    BQ2122.E5B84 2009
    294.3'85--dc22

                                    2009002694

09 10 11 12 13 / 5 4 3 2 1

Printed in the United States of America.

Table of Contents

V: Instructions for Practice

VI: Twenty-Five Sages

VII: Four Clear and Definitive Instructions on Purity

VIII: The Śūraṅgama Mantra

IX: Levels of Being

The Buddha Śākyamuni in meditation posture, Gal Vihara, Polonnaruwa, Sri Lanka, twelfth century. Photograph copyright by John C. and Susan L. Huntington, reprinted by permission of the Huntington Archive of Buddhist and Related Art.

The Venerable Master Hsüan Hua on the occasion of Śākyamuni Buddha's Birthday, in the Buddha-Hall at the City of Ten Thousand Buddhas, Talmage, California, May 1990. Photo courtesy of Soohoong Liung.

The Thousand-Hand Thousand-Eye Bodhsattva Who Hears the Cries of the World, at the City of Ten Thousand Buddhas, Talmage, California. Camphor wood, twentieth century. Photo courtesy Dharma Realm Buddhist Association archive.

A Buddhist disciple kneeling, probably the Venerable Ānanda. Lacquer on wood, Burmese, nineteenth century. Photo by Christian Maillard

Acknowledgements

The members of the Śūraṅgama Sūtra Translation Committee would like to gratefully acknowledge with special thanks the important work of Bhikṣuṇī Heng Chih, who was the primary translator for the Buddhist Text Translation Society's first edition of this Sutra. Her translation opened the way for this new translation and made the task much easier than it would otherwise have been.

We would like further to thank Bhikṣuṇī Heng Yin, Madalena Lew, Martin Verhoeven, and Doug Powers for their advice; Bhikṣuṇī Jin Xiang for proofreading the Sanskrit; Anne Cheng for her work in assuring the publication of this book; Stan Shoptaugh for book design; Laura Lin for copyediting; Dennis Crean for book and cover design, pagemaking, copyediting, and advice; Roger Kellerman and Susan Rounds for proofreading; Ruby Grad for indexing; and Mark Vahrenwald for his rendering of the Wheel of Dharma.

Foreword

When Tripitaka Master Hsüan Hua moved to San Francisco to teach the Dharma to Westerners, his first project was to explain the Śūraṅgama Sūtra in detail. During the summer of 1968, he convened a ninety-day meditation retreat that focused not only on meditation but also on the Śūraṅgama Sūtra.

Beginning in 1980, the Buddhist Text Translation Society published Master Hua's lectures from that summer session, and for the first time a complete Mahāyāna meditation manual was available to Western readers. Earlier English translations of the Śūraṅgama were incomplete and often came without explanation. Master Hua's presentation placed the Sutra at the heart of the contemplative life, thereby opening a road into actual cultivation of the Dharma for those who desired to follow the Buddha's path. From Master Hua's perspective, the Śūraṅgama is not obscure or intimidating, nor is it lofty beyond reach. He explained the text as a *kalyāṇamītra,* a good and wise spiritual friend. He was not alone in doing so. Throughout the centuries in China, Japan, Korea, and Vietnam, meditation teachers and monks such as Master Han Shan of the Ming Dynasty, Master Yuanying of the Republic era, and Master Hua's own teacher Master Xuyun respected and endorsed the Śūraṅgama Sūtra's instructions and used the Sutra as a reliable yardstick of proper samādhi.

Over the years, when I have needed advice in cultivation, I have referred to the Śūraṅgama Sūtra for authoritative information. I go to the "Fifty Demonic States of Mind" (part 10) to check on strange states in meditation. I go to the "Twenty-Five Sages" (part 6) for encouragement on the path from the voices of Bodhisattvas. I go to the "Four Clear and Definitive Instructions on Purity" (part 7) for clarity on interaction with the world; for example, there I find the Buddha's reasons for advocating a harmless, plant-based diet.

In carrying on the perspective of the past, Master Hua emphasized the real-life interaction between the Buddha and his students. I am drawn to the Buddha's voice as it appears in the Sutra. His tone is at all times both wise and kind. For example, a noble king converses with the Buddha about his childhood alongside the Ganges River. After answering the Buddha's skillful questions, the king experiences the serenity of his intrinsic nature and loses his fear of death.

The king hears the Dharma and gradually understands; but even before that conversation, a young courtesan meets the Buddha and immediately wakes up. She has fallen in love with Ānanda, but upon hearing the Dharma, she adjusts her priorities, abandons the pursuit of pleasure, and discovers samādhi and wisdom. She becomes an Arhat on the spot, before Ānanda does. Her story illustrates the lack of gender or class bias in the Buddha's teaching as found in Mahāyāna sutras.

In the dialogue between the Buddha and his cousin Ānanda, we find the framework of the narrative and the full expression of the Buddha's range of teaching skills. The Buddha patiently guides Ānanda through the landscape of his mind as he progresses from book-learning to actual experience.

The Buddha's teaching in the Sutra came alive for me because at Gold Mountain Monastery as a young monk, I observed Master Hua respond with the same measure of unerring kindness to the variety of faithful Chinese devotees, university professors, and truth-seeking hippies who passed through the door of the monastery. Each received the appropriate measure of Dharma-water to nourish their *bodhi* sprouts.

Nearly thirty years have passed since the Buddhist Text Translation Society first published the Śūraṅgama Sūtra in English. This new translation adds tools for scholarly investigation, including helpful footnotes, a more systematic treatment of technical terms, and lucid prose that has benefited from three decades of practice. The devotion of the disciples who worked on the Śūraṅgama Sūtra (who, I might point out, worked entirely as unpaid volunteers) shows on every page. These individuals — monastics and laity alike — follow Master Hua's model in keeping alive this jewel of wisdom and making it available for our use. The Dharma came to the West only a short time ago, but the appearance of this new edition shows the deepening of its roots.

I congratulate the many volunteers of the Buddhist Text Translation Society who have given so generously of their time and effort. May their wisdom and virtue become full and continue to benefit all sentient be-ings so that together we might leave behind the sense-limitations and knots of the mundane world and experience the Buddha's description of how things are at root. There in the bright realm of the Thus-Come One's Treasury, infused with the Buddha's majestic spirit, may we master the three practices that end outflows and realize patience with the state of mind in which no mental objects arise.

Rev. Heng Sure, Ph.D.
President, Dharma Realm Buddhist Association
Director, Berkeley Buddhist Monastery
February 2009

Introduction

1. Overview

For over a thousand years, the Śūraṅgama Sūtra — the "Sutra of the Indestructible"[1] — has been held in great esteem in the Mahāyāna Buddhist countries of East and Southeast Asia. In China the Sutra has generally been considered as important and has been as popular as the Lotus Sūtra,[2] the Avataṁsaka Sūtra,[3] the Mahāyāna Mahāparinirvāṇa Sūtra,[4] the Heart Sūtra,[5] and the Diamond Sūtra.[6] The appeal of the Śūraṅgama Sūtra lies in the broad scope of its teachings and in the depth and clarity of its prescriptions for contemplative practice. Because of its wealth of theoretical and practical instruction in the spiritual life, it was often the first major text to be studied by newly ordained monks, particularly in the Chan school. Many enlightened masters and illustrious monastic scholars have written exegetical commentaries on it.[7] To this day, for both clergy and laity in the Chinese Buddhist tradition, the Śūraṅgama Sūtra continues to be the object of devout study, recitation, and memorization.

---

[1] The Sutra (T. 945) is generally known in Chinese as the *Dafoding shoulengyanjing*, 大佛頂首楞嚴經, often shortened to *Lengyanjing*, 楞嚴經; the complete title is *Dafoding rulai miyin xiuzheng liaoyi zhu pusa wanheng shoulengyan jing* 大佛頂如來密因修證了義諸菩薩萬行首楞嚴經. The Sanskrit word *śūraṅgama* roughly means "indestructible"; it combines the words *śūram* (greatly, absolutely) and *gama* (durable, solid). The Chinese text transliterates the two Sanskrit words as *shou leng yan* 首楞嚴.

This Sutra is not to be confused with the Śūraṅgamasamādhi-sūtra (T. 642), translated by Étienne Lamotte as *La concentration de la marche héroïque* (*Śūraṃgamasamādhisūtra*) (Paris: Institut belge des hautes études chinoises, 1965). His French translation has been rendered into English by Sarah Boin-Webb (Richmond, UK: Curzon Press, 1998).

[2] Skt. Saddharmapundarika Sūtra, Ch. *Miaofa lianhua jin*I 妙法蓮華經.

[3] Ch. *Huayan jing* 華嚴經.

[4] Ch. *Da Niepan jing* 大涅槃經.

[5] Skt. Hṛdaya Sūtra, Ch. *Xin jing* 心經.

[6] Skt. Vajracchedikā Sūtra, Ch. *Jingang jing* 金剛經.

[7] Commentators have included the late–Ming dynasty master Hanshan Deqing, and more recently the Venerable Masters Xuyun, Yuanying, and Hsüan Hua (Xuanhua). At least 127 Chinese commentaries were written on the Sutra between 767 CE and 1968. A list of commentaries is available online at http://online.sfsu.edu/%7Erone/Buddhism/Shurangama/Ron%20Epstein%20Diss%201975%20SS%20Commentary%20List.pdf.

More specifically, the Śūraṅgama Sūtra has traditionally been regarded as a complete and practical manual for spiritual practice that will eventually lead to enlightenment. It gives instruction in the correct understanding of the Buddha-nature, which is the potential within all beings for becoming a Buddha. The Sutra explains how and why this true nature is hidden within our ordinary experience of ourselves and of the world, and it shows how we can uncover this nature and recognize that it is our own true mind. The Sutra also explains that personal integrity and purity of conduct are essential prerequisites for spiritual awakening. It presents the general principles of Buddhist meditation, introduces several specific meditation methods, and recommends which methods are the most effective and the easiest to practice. Further, a considerable portion of the Sutra is devoted to guidelines for discerning what understandings and practices are correct and which deviate into wrong ones. It explains how our own intentional acts, whether physical, verbal, or mental, directly result in our experiences, including our future rebirths at various levels of being, both human and nonhuman. It shows how correct action can also lead to initial awakenings and eventually to the perfect enlightenment of the Buddhas.

Much of the Sutra is devoted to the Buddha Śākyamuni's instructions to the monk Ānanda, whose personal story provides a narrative frame for the entire discourse. Joined by several of his enlightened disciples, the Buddha shows Ānanda how to turn the attention of his sense-faculties inward in order to achieve a deeply focused state of meditation known as samādhi.[8] He tells Ānanda that by practicing a particular form of samādhi, the Śūraṅgama Samādhi, he and anyone else who also maintains purity of conduct and develops right understanding can gain an awakening that is equal to the awakening experienced by all Buddhas.

At the heart of the Sutra is the Śūraṅgama Mantra. The Sutra promises that the practice of reciting this mantra, in the context of the other practices taught in the Sutra, can succeed in eliminating whatever internal or external obstacles may lie in the way of spiritual progress. To this

---

[8] See below "A Brief Explanation of Some Important Technical Terms," p. xlv.

day, monks and nuns in the Chinese Buddhist tradition, as well as many practitioners among the laity, recite the mantra every morning as an essential aspect of daily practice.

2. The Sutra's Literary Style

Despite its importance in Buddhist tradition, and despite its intrinsic value as a masterpiece of spiritual writing, the Śūraṅgama Sūtra continues to be little known in the West. The reason for the Sutra's relative obscurity outside of Asia is in part due to aspects of the Chinese text itself. In the first place, no Indic original of the Śūraṅgama Sūtra survives. It is preserved only in its eighth-century translation into Chinese,[9] and this translation, while widely appreciated among Chinese readers for its literary elegance, is also well known as being unusually difficult to understand. The text is expressed in a succession of four-character phrases.[10] in what amounts to a metered prose — a format that imbues the entire discourse with a vigorous and stately rhythm. But to maintain the four-character meter, the Chinese translators were often forced to omit characters necessary to the meaning, and this resulted not infrequently in an extreme terseness of expression. For such passages, the exegetical tradition is essential for understanding. In addition, the Chinese translators resorted frequently to rare characters, often allowed themselves ambiguities of grammar and word usage, made allusions to doctrines without explaining them, and left many technical terms in a transliterated Sanskrit. The result has been that even devout and erudite Chinese readers are sometimes puzzled as to the meaning of the text. It is perhaps not surprising, then, that relatively few attempts have been made to produce even a partial English translation.[11]

---

[9] The year of the translation is recorded in the colophon as 705. A complete Tibetan translation was made of the Chinese translation during the Qing dynasty.

[10] The four-character pattern is broken occasionally to accommodate proper names; and three sets of verses are spoken in the Sutra, one in seven-character lines (part 3.6 of the present translation) and two in five-character lines (parts 5.3 and 6.3).

[11] Previous to the present volume, the only complete translation in English has been that by the Buddhist Text Translation Society, with the complete commentary by the Venerable Master Hsüan Hua, first published in an eight-volume edition between 1977 and

In undertaking this new English rendering of the complete text of the Śūraṅgama Sūtra, the present translators' first priority has been to ensure that the difficulties of the text are reduced as far as possible for the Western reader. To that end we have striven for clarity, transparency, and naturalness of expression. We have been ready to sacrifice any attempt to emulate the complex literary elegance of the Chinese whenever it seemed to us that to do so would interfere with a plain statement of the meaning in English. We have translated many of the Sanskrit technical terms that the Chinese translators left in Sanskrit. We have also interpolated chapter and sub-chapter headings and have occasionally inserted numbering to mark the succession of topics in the Sutra's argument.[12] Further, we have provided interlinear explanatory commentary wherever we judged that it might be helpful in clarifying the meaning of the text. To this end we have chosen excerpts from a commentary that was redacted from lectures given in 1968 by the Venerable Master Hsüan Hua (1918–95),[13] an eminent Chinese monk and teacher who was a pioneer in bringing the Buddhist tradition of scriptural exegesis to Western

1986. A revised edition was published between 2000 and 2005 as *The Shurangama Sūtra with Commentary by the Venerable Master Hsüan Hua,* trans. Buddhist Text Translation Society (Burlingame, CA: Buddhist Text Translation Society, 2000–05). The first translation into English, of only the first four of the ten rolls, was made by Samuel Beal and included in *A Catena of Buddhist Scriptures from the Chinese* (London: Trubner, 1871), 284–369. A very small portion of the first roll of the Sutra was translated by Reverend Joseph Edkins as the first chapter of his *Chinese Buddhism: A Volume of Sketches, Historical, Descriptive, and Critical,* 2nd ed. (London: Trubner, 1893), 289–301. In 1938, in conjunction with Bhikshu Wai-tao, Dwight Godard included a rough translation of about a third of the Sutra in his *A Buddhist Bible* (New York: Dutton, 1938), 108–275. Most of the text was translated by Lu K'uan Yü (Charles Luk), together with an abridged translation of the commentary by Chan Master Hanshan Deqing, as *The Śūraṅgama Sūtra* (London: Rider, 1966). Regrettably, by omitting the Śūraṅgama Mantra and the section that describes the proper practice of the mantra, Luk's volume in effect leaves out the Sutra's heart. (This section is part 8 of the present volume.)

[12] Chinese editions of the text also interpolate section headings. All the section and sub-section headings in the present translation were added to the text by the translators. There are no section headings in the original Chinese text.

[13] See the appendix.

audiences. Finally, we have added explanatory footnotes to supplement the present introduction and commentary. The footnotes also provide occasional references to other commentaries. In most cases, without giving special notice, we have followed the interpretations given in his commentary by the Venerable Master Hsüan Hua.

Fortunately, the difficulties imposed by the Chinese translators' rhetorical choices are somewhat mitigated by the manner in which the Sutra unfolds. Much of the discussion of samādhi is presented in the form of a dramatic dialogue between the Buddha Śākyamuni and his young cousin and attendant Ānanda. To the Western reader, the Sutra's dialogic format suggests a rough similarity to the dialogues of Plato. But Plato's manner of uncovering truth by means of Socrates' sly cross-examinations of his hapless interlocutors is in fact very different from the pattern we encounter in the Śūraṅgama Sūtra. For much of the first part of the Sutra, both the Buddha and Ānanda make use of the syllogism as it later came to be used in the tradition of Buddhist logical argument.[14] In constructing a syllogism, mere reasoning was not considered to be sufficient. It was necessary to establish a proposition's truth by citing, as an instance or example, some evidence of the proposition at work in the ordinary experience of daily life. The presence of these examples is a significant aspect of the Sutra's distinctive style. As the argument progresses from point to point, the reader is given a series of glimpses into the daily routines of the monastic community and the life of ordinary citizens of the nearby city of Śrāvastī.[15] We read of the monks seated with their almsbowls, busy eating food with their fingers in the Indian manner. We hear of householders digging wells for new dwellings and local healers holding up bowls to the full moon to collect dew that they will mix into their herbal potions. We meet a monk who has spent his life repairing potholes in the public roads and a king who despairs because he is growing old. However abstract or subtle the discourse may sometimes seem, then, it is always deeply colored

---

[14] For more on the syllogism, see section 9 of the introduction below.

[15] The capital city of the ancient kingdom of Kosala, on the Ganges Plain, in what is now Uttar Pradesh.

with a sense of time and place, with the sights and sounds and people of Northern India as it was some twenty-five hundred years ago.

3. A Synopsis of the Sutra

Prologue: The Occasion for the Teaching

As the Sutra opens, Ānanda is alone on the road, making the traditional monastic almsround. Passing unwittingly by a house of courtesans, he is confused by a young woman's recitation of a spell. She attempts to seduce him, and he is soon on the brink of breaking his vow of celibacy. The Buddha Śākyamuni senses from a distance his cousin's distress. He thereupon causes a Buddha to appear seated above his head, and this Buddha proceeds to recite the Śūraṅgama Mantra.[16] The Buddha Śākyamuni then sends the Bodhisattva Mañjuśrī[17] to wield the mantra's powers in order to defeat the young courtesan's spell. The Bodhisattva Mañjuśrī then returns to the monastic grounds with both Ānanda and the courtesan. Amidst the assembly of monks and a throng of lay adherents, Ānanda now finds himself face to face with the Buddha. Deeply mortified by his own behavior, Ānanda requests instruction so that he can avoid further error. This is the "request for Dharma" with which most of the Buddha's discourses begin.

Part I: The Nature and Location of the Mind

In responding to his cousin's request, the Buddha makes clear that Ānanda's error lay not only in his jeopardizing of his practice of celibacy. Equally serious was his laxity in his practice of meditation and of samādhi. Because of this laxity, his mental focus was not firm enough to resist the influence of the courtesan's spell. It is this failure that the

---

[16] The mantra is given in full below in part 8 of the text. The Chinese translators did not translate the mantra but rather transliterated the syllables of the original Indic language into Chinese characters. It is in this form that the mantra is still recited in monasteries that follow the Chinese Buddhist tradition. The present translation gives a transliteration of the sound of the Chinese characters using the pinyin system of romanization.

[17] In the Mahāyāna tradition the Bodhisattva Mañjuśrī embodies wisdom.

Buddha will address in his teaching. He undertakes first to show Ānanda what might be involved in transcending the conditioned world — that is, in transcending the stream of sense-impressions that we take to be our external environment and the stream of inner thoughts that we cherish as characteristic of our identity.

To approach this topic, the Buddha begins by asking Ānanda to consider where his mind is located. Ānanda offers the evident answer that his mind is to be found in his body. The Buddha, with his superior command of logical argument, quickly disposes of this widely held supposition and of six other possibilities that Ānanda offers. Ānanda is left with the bewildering conclusion that his mind is neither inside his body, nor outside it, nor somewhere between, nor anywhere else. The Buddha then compounds his cousin's confusion by stating that there are fundamentally two kinds of mind — first, the ordinary mind of which we are aware and which is entangled, lifetime after lifetime, in the snare of illusory perceptions and deluded mental activity; and second, the everlasting true mind, which is our real nature and which is identical to the fully awakened mind of all Buddhas. The Buddha adds that it is because beings have lost touch with their own true mind that they are bound to the cycle of death and rebirth.

Part II: The Nature of Visual Awareness

Now that the existence of a true mind has been established, the Buddha undertakes next to explain, in dialogue with Ānanda, a way of practicing samādhi that leads to the true mind. The Buddha begins by bringing our attention to the simple fact that we are aware. Taking visual awareness as the paradigm, he examines awareness through a series of illustrative vignettes, several of them involving other speakers. He demonstrates that, though things move in and through and out of the field of our visual awareness, the essence of our awareness itself does not move. Our awareness teems with objects but is not itself an object. Even blindness, strictly speaking, does not mean that there is no visual awareness at all. Ask any blind person what he sees, the Buddha suggests to Ānanda, and the blind person will answer that he sees darkness. In short, the essence of our visual awareness is unchanging. It does not arise and disappear in response to visible objects that enter its scope. The same may be said of our awareness of sounds, odors, flavors, tangible objects, and also of our awareness of the thoughts in our minds. The Buddha explains later that the essential capacity to hear is never absent, no matter whether there is sound or silence.[18] The logical implication is that, given that our various awarenesses exist independent of their objects, it ought to be possible to disentangle those awarenesses from their objects. Then we will be free to redirect our attention inward, separate ourselves from the conditioned world, and establish ourselves in the highest level of samādhi, that is, in the Śūraṅgama Samādhi.

Part III: The Matrix of the Thus-Come One[19]

The question remains: why would we want to stop paying attention to the conditioned world? The answer is twofold: first, our involvement in that world is fraught with dissatisfaction and suffering; and second, that world is not real. It is this second point that the Buddha now turns to. He begins by declaring:

> Fundamentally, everything that comes and goes, that comes into being and ceases to be, is within the true nature of the Matrix of the Thus-Come One, which is the wondrous, everlasting understanding — the unmoving, all-pervading, wondrous suchness of reality.[20]

He then undertakes to demonstrate the truth of this proposition by means of a series of syllogisms. He shows one by one that each of the elements of the physical world and each of the elements of our sensory apparatus is, fundamentally, an illusion. But at the same time, these illusory entities and experiences arise out of what is real. That matrix from which all is produced is the Matrix of the Thus-Come One. It is identical to our own true mind and identical as well to the fundamental nature of the universe and to the mind of all Buddhas. It is beyond the psychological

[18] Part 5.3.
[19] The Tathāgata-garbha. See p. xxxi.
[20] Part 3.1, p. 89.

concatenation we call the self and beyond the mirage of sense-data that we call the world.

Part IV: The Coming into Being of the World of Illusion

Now Pūrṇamaitrāyaṇiputra, a senior disciple, poses questions of his own. If, as the Buddha's logic has just shown, the primary elements of the psycho-physical world and the constituent elements of perception are illusory in the form we experience them, while nevertheless being fundamentally identical with the Matrix of the Thus-Come One, how is it that they come into being as separate, illusory entities? How is it that we forget our grounding in true reality and become lost in the maze of illusion? In dialogue with Pūrṇamaitrāyaṇiputra, the Buddha explains that everything flows from our initial error of dividing reality into self and other. This process begins with what the Buddha calls "adding understanding to understanding," and it leads to a division of what was originally a unified awareness into an observer who is separate from what is observed. Our fundamental unity with the Matrix of the Thus-Come One is obscured, as a bright sky is obscured by clouds. To emphasize how unnecessary the division into self and other is, the Buddha relates a parable. A villager named Yajñadatta runs through his village looking for his head, which he foolishly thinks he has lost. His head, of course, has been on his shoulders all along, just as our own true mind, which we have forgotten, is, even so, always accessible within us.

Part V: Instructions in Practice

The Buddha has now built the conceptual basis for instruction in the Śūraṅgama Samādhi. The sense-faculties — eyes, ears, nose, tongue, body, and cognition — are obstacles that keep us from our home in true reality. But if the direction of these faculties' attention is reversed so that they are focused inward rather than outward, then they become the means of our return to reality. The Buddha reminds Ānanda that freeing the mind from its involvement in perceived objects is possible because our awareness of the world is independent of the world it perceives. He once again demonstrates that independence by instructing his son, Rāhula, to sound a bell. The Buddha shows that when the sound of the bell dies away, our power of hearing remains intact, since we are aware first of silence and then of the sounding of the bell once again. The Buddha says:

> All that you need to do is not to allow your attention to be diverted by the twelve conditioned attributes of sound and silence, contact and separation, flavor and the absence of flavor, openness and blockage, coming into being and perishing, and light and darkness. Next, extricate one faculty by detaching it from its objects. Redirect that faculty inward so that it can return to what is original and true. Then it will radiate the light of the original understanding. This brilliant light will shine forth and extricate the other five faculties until they are completely free.[21]

Part VI: Twenty-Five Sages

Ānanda now asks the Buddha to instruct him as to which of the faculties of perception he should focus on in his practice. He expects that the Buddha will transmit an answer to him privately in a direct mind-to-mind transmission, but instead the Buddha turns Ānanda's question over to the audience. He asks the sages who are present to volunteer to explain how their spiritual practice allowed them to enter samādhi and then to break through illusion and become enlightened. In response, twenty-five sages stand up one by one in the midst of the assembly to tell their enlightenment stories. Seventeen of the sages tell of practices involving one of the constituent elements of perception, and seven other sages tell of their enlightenment through contemplation of one of the primary elements.

The most extensive of these narratives is given by the twenty-fifth sage, the Bodhisattva Who Hears the Cries of the World.[22] The practice that led to the enlightenment of this Bodhisattva focused on reversing the attention of the faculty of the ear. Having told his story, the Bodhisattva Who Hears the Cries of the World discusses the powers that his hear-

---

[21] Part 5.2, p. 182.

[22] Skt. Avalokiteśvara, Ch. Guanshiyin 觀世音. More explanation of this name is given in part 6, note 48.

ing practice has brought him. He specifies how he can fulfill the wishes of thirty-two types of human and nonhuman beings, how he protects people in dangerous situations so that they will have nothing to fear, and how he appears in various forms to teach beings and protect them.

The Buddha then asks the Bodhisattva Mañjuśrī to recommend to Ānanda one of the twenty-five paths to enlightenment just described by the twenty-five sages. Speaking in verse, Mañjuśrī endorses the practice of listening within as it was described by the Bodhisattva Who Hears the Cries of the World. This practice, Mañjuśrī concludes, is the practice most suitable for Ānanda and for beings of the future.[23]

Part VII: Four Clear and Definitive Instructions on Purity

The Buddha next describes a second aspect of the practice of samādhi. Reversing the attention of the ear-faculty is not enough. One cannot make proper progress in any spiritual practice unless one's moral behavior is correct. The Buddha insists on purity in four spheres of conduct, which in Buddhist tradition are addressed by the first four of the five moral precepts: one must not kill, steal, commit sexual misconduct, or speak either falsely or in a manner which may cause harm to others.[24] Here the Buddha explains that in order to practice samādhi in the correct manner it is not enough to refrain from killing, stealing, sexual misconduct, and false speech; one must erase any thoughts of such actions from the mind.

Part VIII: The Śūraṅgama Mantra

At Ānanda's request, the Buddha explains in great detail how to set up a "place for awakening"[25] devoted to the practice of the Śūraṅgama Mantra, and then he recites the mantra for everyone in the assembly to hear. Next he explains how reciting the mantra, especially from memory, as

---

[23] The passage on the powers of the Bodhisattva Who Hears the Cries of the World recalls a similar account in the celebrated chapter 25 of the Lotus Sūtra, "On the Universal Gateway." The Śūraṅgama Sūtra, unlike the Lotus Sūtra, explains how the Bodhisattva gained these powers.

[24] The fifth of these basic Buddhist precepts is abstaining from intoxicants.

[25] Skt. *bodhimaṇḍa*, Ch. *dao chang* 道場.

well as simpler acts of devotion to the mantra, can bring many benefits to the practitioner, including safety from harm and more rapid progress in spiritual practice. Finally, numerous beings in the assembly of listeners rise to vow that they will protect anyone who undertakes the Śūraṅgama Mantra practice.

Part IX: Levels of Being

In this section, the Buddha responds to Ānanda's wish to learn about the levels of being. The Buddha first divides beings into twelve classes organized according to the manner of their birth. He then briefly summarizes sixty stages through which Bodhisattvas pass on their way to the full awakening of the Buddhas. Finally, he describes at greater length the sufferings of the beings consigned to the hells, and then more briefly six other destinies: ghosts, animals, humans, ascetic masters,[26] gods at their twenty-eight celestial levels, and finally *asuras.*[27] In describing the stages of the Bodhisattva, the Buddha offers Ānanda a roadmap to follow in his future practice. In describing the hells and the other destinies, he warns his listeners of the dangers of committing intentional acts that entail negative consequences. Here again he refers to the prohibitions that he has emphasized repeatedly in this text: do not kill, do not steal, do not commit sexual misconduct, and do not speak falsely.

Part X: Fifty Demonic States of Mind

In this final section of the Sutra, the Buddha once again speaks without a request for teaching, as he did in Part III. Here he undertakes to warn practitioners to be on their guard against fifty demonic states of mind that can arise during the period in which the practitioner is breaking his attachments to the five aggregates.[28] Ten such states of mind are described for each of the five aggregates. The Buddha explains that if practitioners dismiss these states as of no importance, the states will disappear

---

[26] Skt. *ṛṣi,* Ch. *xian* 仙. See p. xl and part 9.10.

[27] Beings addicted to violence. See part 9.12.

[28] Skt. *skandha,* Ch. *yun* 蘊. An explanation of the five aggregates — form, sense-perception, cognition, mental formations, and consciousness — is given at pp. xlvi ff.

of their own accord. But if practitioners fall under the influence of these states, they may become stuck. They may even face insanity or demonic possession, or they may simply stray from the Path. The practitioner may lead others into error as well. In describing people whose practice has taken a wrong turn, this section also serves as a warning against falling under the influence of spiritual charlatans and their cults. The warning is as relevant today as it was when it was spoken.

For each of these fifty states of mind, a vivid description is given of the mental phenomena experienced by the practitioner. In essence, what is presented is a unique method of cataloguing and classifying spiritual experiences, together with an indication of what causes lead to such experiences. Although the fifty states of mind described are by no means an exhaustive list of all possible states, the text offers a framework for the classification of all spiritual experience, both Buddhist and non-Buddhist.

Finally, in dialogue with Ānanda, the Buddha describes the immense amount of merit that is earned by those who teach others about the Śūraṅgama Sūtra and the Śūraṅgama Mantra.

4. The Meaning of the Title

The Śūraṅgama Sūtra is an abbreviated title. A longer but still partial title in widespread use is the "Sūtra on the Śūraṅgama Mantra That Is Spoken from above the Crown of the Great Buddha's Head." The full title is the "Sūtra on the Śūraṅgama Mantra That Is Spoken from above the Crown of the Great Buddha's Head, and on the Hidden Basis of the Thus-Come Ones' Myriad Bodhisattva-Practices That Lead to Their Verifications of Ultimate Truth." This full title conflates two of the titles which the Buddha himself suggests in a brief passage near the end of the Sutra.[29]

In the Buddhist tradition, a sutra is a discourse that contains the teachings of the Buddha Śākyamuni or the teachings of other Buddhas or enlightened beings.

A Buddha is a fully enlightened being who has developed perfect wisdom and universal compassion. The particular Buddha whose teachings

---

[29] Part 9.5.

were spoken for the benefit of beings of this planet and this age, and who lived in northern India during the sixth and fifth centuries B.C.E.,[30] was the Prince Siddhārtha Gautama, who upon attaining full awakening, became the Buddha Śākyamuni. He is sometimes referred to as the "historical Buddha." It is he who gives the teachings contained in this Sutra.

"Great" describes the true nature of a Buddha — not his physical body but his fully awakened mind, which fills the entire universe. This aspect of a Buddha is sometimes symbolically represented as the Buddha Vairocana, who is the "Great Buddha" referred to in the title.

The "Hidden Basis of the Bodhisattva's Practices" is the Śūraṅgama Mantra and the Śūraṅgama Samādhi.

"Thus-Come One" is an honorific name used to address a Buddha.

The word "Bodhisattva" can be translated as "awakening being." Bodhisattvas devote themselves to the awakening of all beings, while at the same time they engage in the "Myriad Practices" that will lead to their own full awakening.

When one becomes a Buddha, which is the goal of the myriad Bodhisattva-practices, one can verify through one's own experience the nature of ultimate truth.

5. Levels of Teaching

The Buddha taught at two different levels: he taught the unchanging, true Dharma, which applies to all circumstances at all times, and he taught provisional Dharma, which he tailored to the needs of his audience and fitted to the context and circumstances. The Śūraṅgama Sūtra was spoken in response to the disastrous error of judgment and behavior that Ānanda almost made while on his almsround, making plain his need to develop the power of samādhi, as recounted in the Sutra's prologue.

The Buddha's provisional teachings vary because his audiences varied in their aspirations, in their level of accomplishment, in their practice of meditation, and in their capacity for understanding. Some of the records of his teachings contain several levels of instruction in the same document,

---

[30] The dates of the Buddha Śākyamuni's lifetime are a subject of scholarly controversy.

while other records confine themselves to a single type of teaching. All of his teachings are not necessarily appropriate for everyone at all levels.

Further, during a career of almost fifty years, as his audiences matured in their practice, his teachings progressed gradually from the introductory to the advanced. In some cases, the later teachings substantially critique the earlier ones, replacing provisional teachings with ultimate ones. Such critiques are a feature of this Sutra, as are critiques of non-Buddhist teachings that existed in India during and before the Buddha's time.

Buddhist tradition holds that, after the Buddha's nirvana, the general level of understanding and practice of the Buddhist teachings slowly declined. The first major sign of that decline occurred roughly five hundred years after his nirvana; this was the schism that divided Buddhism into the Mahāyāna ("Great Vehicle") or Northern Buddhism, which subsequently spread to China, Korea, Java, Vietnam, and Tibet; and the Theravada ("Teaching of the Elders") or Southern Buddhism. This southern form spread to Sri Lanka and Southeast Asia. The Mahāyāna itself divided further into various sub-schools, among them the Emptiness school (Mādhyamaka); the Consciousness-Only school (Yogācāra); the Pure Land teachings; the Matrix of the Thus-Come One (Tathāgatagarbha) teachings; and the Esoteric teachings (called Vajrayāna in Tibet). The Śūraṅgama Sūtra contains teachings that are consonant with all of these schools, while placing particular emphasis on the Matrix of the Thus-Come One teachings and on the Esoteric teachings, both of which were flourishing in India before being introduced into China in the late seventh and eighth centuries.

Another approach given in the traditional commentaries to an understanding of the levels of teaching in the Śūraṅgama Sūtra enumerates and explains four successive gateways of inquiry and understanding: 1) intellectual inquiry into the meaning of the Sutra text; 2) meditation on the coming into being of phenomena from our own making of distinctions, as elaborated by the Consciousness-Only school; 3) a noumenal approach that directly fathoms the true nature of phenomena, which is that they are empty of any real essence and have no independent existence, as elaborated by the Emptiness school; and 4) the realization of the unobstructed interrelationship of noumenon and phenomena, as found in the Matrix of the Thus-Come One teachings and later elaborated in the Chinese Huayan School.

6. The Reasons for the Teaching

Traditional commentators have identified six concerns that are addressed by the Buddha's teachings in the Śūraṅgama Sūtra. They may be summarized as follows:[31]

1) The first is the importance of balancing learning and meditation practice. Ānanda was considered to have the keenest memory of all the Buddha's disciples. But he made the false assumption that he could rely solely on his intelligence and his special relationship with the Buddha; as a result, he neglected his practice. Consequently, he did not have sufficient samādhi to ward off the spell that the courtesan cast on him.

2) The second is the danger of charlatans who pose as teachers and whose wrong views are a consequence of their own mental derangement. The Sutra condemns self-described spiritual teachers who brag of advanced spiritual accomplishments and who violate the rules of moral behavior. The Buddha warns against such people in three places in the text: in Part VII and Part IX.3B, in which he discusses purity, and in Part X, in which he describes the demonic states associated with the five aggregates.

3) The third is the need for a proper understanding of the difference between one's true mind and one's distinction-making consciousness, since this understanding is a prerequisite for right practice. Since what people generally consider to be their mind is not their true mind, the early portion of the Sutra systematically explores wrong presuppositions about the mind in order to reveal the nature of the true mind.

4) The fourth is that correct understanding must be followed by meditation practice that is grounded in the true mind. Once we commit ourselves to following a path to awakening, we need to learn the practice necessary to make progress. This includes learning the proper medita-

---

[31] This section is based on the discussion of these six concerns by the Venerable Master Hsüan Hua in his introduction to *The Shurangama Sūtra*, v. 1, 24–36.

tion techniques, choosing those meditation practices that are grounded in our deepest being, and avoiding meditation practices that will not lead to full awakening. In the Venerable Master Hsüan Hua's words:

> There are many gateways to the Dharma in the practice of samādhi, and there are other samādhis not taught in Buddhism. But in cultivating samādhi, if you begin in a direction that is wrong even by the width of a hair, you will end up missing your target by a thousand miles. Therefore it is necessary to cultivate proper samādhi. . . . People who take a wrong path do not develop proper samādhi because they work among the branches rather than applying themselves to the roots. They work on this body, which is a false shell. They take the ordinary thinking mind, the sixth consciousness, to be the true mind. As a result, their practice gives them a little of the experience of stillness, but what they experience is not genuine. They force themselves to keep their thoughts from arising, but they haven't dug out the root of their deluded thinking, so they can't put an end to death and rebirth. It is like trying to stop grass from growing by placing a rock on it. When the rock is removed, the grass grows right back.[32]

5) The fifth is that, in order to practice meditation correctly, one must know how to get rid of distortions in one's mental processes. Proper meditation techniques, once learned, must be used to systematically eliminate both the coarse and the subtle cognitive processes that are obstacles to progress on the Path. Those mental activities are often likened to dust on the mirror of our true mind. The Sutra exhorts us to make a commitment to purifying our minds.

6) The sixth is that, in order to teach others, we must not only realize the true nature of our minds but also learn the various skillful means necessary to help others along the Path. The provisional teachings make use of skillful means to bring people into the Dharma.

---

[32] *The Shurangama Sūtra,* v. 1, 41–2.

7. Correspondence of Teachings in the Sutra to Schools of Mahāyāna Buddhism

Several of the essential Mahāyāna teachings represented in the Śūraṅgama Sūtra were later systematized by specific schools. Knowledge of these schools can therefore be useful in gaining a clearer understanding of the teachings of the Sutra, particularly when the Sutra alludes to a teaching but does not explain it in detail. For this reason, a brief summary is given here of some of the relevant teachings of the Consciousnness-Only (Yogācāra) school, the Matrix of the Thus-Come One (Tathāgata-garbha) school, and the Esoteric school.

The Consciousness-Only School

Although the eight consciousnesses doctrine of the Consciousness-Only school of Mahāyāna Buddhism is not explicitly taught in the Śūraṅgama Sūtra, traditional commentators have found this doctrine to be useful in explaining the meaning of the text.

The Consciousness-Only school describes the mind as a system of seven active consciousnesses (*vijñāna*), all of which develop out of an eighth, the "storehouse consciousness." The latter is passive and contains the potentials, or "seeds" (*bija*), for the development and activity of the first seven consciousnesses. The seventh consciousness, or "individuating consciousness" (*manas*), contains the innate sense of self. The sixth consciousness contains the learned sense of self and is a perceptual and cognitive processing center. It makes distinctions among the data sent to it from the first five consciousnesses, which are the perceptual awarenesses of eyes, ears, nose, tongue, and body. The sixth consciousness also makes distinctions about cognitive objects, such as thoughts and emotions.

Once the first seven consciousnesses have emanated out of the eighth consciousnesses, they are usually experienced as separate and distinct, but these faculties remain fundamentally one.

The eight consciousnesses account for the full range of mental processes. In this system there is no need for the notions of a real, permanent self or of real, permanent external (and internal) phenomena. All actual and potential realms of experience are shown to be contained within the transformations of consciousness. They appear as manifestations of the distinction-making mind. What truly exists is consciousness only, that is, the purified eighth consciousness.

Nevertheless, because of our attachment to and belief in the reality of self and in the reality of the phenomena that we perceive and understand to be the external world, the true nature of the world and of ourselves is obscured, so much so that we are entirely unaware of it.

The Matrix of the Thus-Come One Teachings

These teachings focus on the nature of ultimate reality and the potential that all beings have to awaken to that reality. Through correct Buddhist practice, we can bring forth from our spiritual wombs[33] the embryonic Buddha that is found within every sentient being. The eight consciousnesses described in the Yogācāra doctrine are considered to be real only provisionally. Ultimately they are illusory, as the Buddha explains in Part III. Our world of illusion arises from the Tathāgata-garbha, the Matrix of the Thus-Come One (other equivalent terms include the Buddha-nature, the Dharma-body, and the true mind). This essential spiritual reality is inherent in all beings, and the work of spiritual practice is to remove the dross of illusion that covers it. The Matrix of the Thus-Come One school emphasized the presence of this spiritual essence in all sentient creatures, and from this arose an emphasis on vegetarianism, which appears in this Sutra in Part VII.

In Part IV, the Buddha explains how the illusory world of mental and physical phenomena — of me, you, and things — comes to appear from the first appearance of ignorance in the enlightened mind. This explanation, which is consonant with the Tathāgata-garbha teachings, is not meant to be historical or temporal. It is more an exposition of the layers of our

---

[33] *Tathāgata-garbha* literally means "the womb of the Thus-Come One," the ultimate reality from which all appearances spring. The English word "matrix" is used here in its proper meaning of "womb" and "that which gives form, origin, or foundation to something enclosed or imbedded in it" (*Webster's New International Dictionary,* 2nd ed., 1961).

experience or awareness. The implication is that we are living on the surface of our consciousness. What we are actually aware of is merely the surface of a deeper mind or potential consciousness. Even though we may be entirely content to live on that surface, we have the potential to deepen our awareness. Buddhist practice is concerned with this deepening, which involves a reversal of the direction of our awareness, away from the world of illusion and toward our original mind, which is identical to the mind of all Buddhas.

Esoteric Teachings

The Esoteric teachings, also known as Buddhist tantra or Vajrayāna, include various methodologies of meditation and other practices that are often privately transmitted from teacher to disciple in formal transmissions or empowerment rituals. They include the recitation of mantras, sometimes in coordination with mudras (ritual dispositions of the hands) and the use of ritual implements, and also teachings about the visualization of deities, the ritual creation of sacred spaces (mandalas), and the making of elaborate offerings. The central chapter of the Śūraṅgama Sūtra (Part VIII) describes certain of these practices in detail. Moral purity is an essential prerequisite for all of the Esoteric practices, as is the case for all Buddhist practice, and the Sutra contains strong warnings about the dangers of moral impurity, which became widespread in many of the early Indian Buddhist tantric circles.[34] Since that time, failure to recognize the necessity of moral purity has been a frequent pitfall for a significant number of teachers and students of the esoteric teachings, both in Asia and the West.

8. The Syllogism and the Tetralemma

Many readers may be surprised by how much logical argumentation they encounter in the first half of the Śūraṅgama Sūtra. In fact, Buddhism and other Indian religions developed highly elaborated systems of formal logic. In this Sutra, both the Buddha and Ānanda make use of syllogisms

---

[34] See Ronald M. Davidson, *Indian Esoteric Buddhism: A Social History of the Tantric Movement* (New York: Columbia University Press, 2002).

that are advanced as proof of propositions. These syllogisms largely conform to the system of logical inference developed by Buddhist logicians in India and known as *hetu-vidyā*.[35] Occasionally, too, one encounters an example of fourfold negation (the tetralemma).

The Syllogism

According to the ancient Indian formal logic,[36] the truth of a proposition can be demonstrated in a five-step syllogism:

1) A proposition (*pratijñā*) is stated;

2) The reason (*hetu*) that the proposition is claimed to be true is stated;

3) One or more instances (*dṛṣṭānta* or *udāharaṇa*) of the proposition that can be found in ordinary life are given;

4) These instances are applied (*upanaya*) to the proposition, showing how they demonstrate its truth;

5) The conclusion (*nigamana*) reiterates the proposition, now demonstrated.

These five steps were later reduced to three, in effect leaving out the last two of the five:

1) Proposition,

2) Reason,

3) Instances:

   a) positive instance,

   b) negative instance.

In the Śūraṅgama Sūtra, the Buddha uses elements of both the three-step and the five-step procedures.

What is perhaps most striking to a Western reader is the importance given to instances. In effect, specific cases of a proposition, provided that they are precisely applicable, are considered to be demonstrative of the truth of the proposition in general. Debate therefore centers on whether an instance is in fact an applicable case, that is, whether the truth of the

---

[35] Ch. *yin ming* 因明, clarification of causes.

[36] See, for example, S. S. Barlingay, *A Modern Introduction to Buddhist Logic* (Delhi: National Publishing House, 1965), 107 ff.

proposition can indeed be inferred from it.[37] This pattern of inference by instance is a dominant rhetorical element in the first half of the Sutra. The following example, drawn from the beginning of Part II, may be helpful in following the many occurrences of this pattern:

1) Proposition: it is the mind, not the eyes, that see (in the text this step is implicit rather than stated);

2) Reason: our visual awareness is active even if nothing is being seen;

3) Instance drawn from ordinary life: In the Buddha's words, "If you asked a blind man on the street, 'Do you see anything?'" he would no doubt answer, 'All I see is darkness.'"

4) Application of the instance: "Reflect upon what that might mean. Although the blind man sees only darkness, his visual awareness is intact."

5) Conclusion: "The eyes themselves simply reveal visible objects; it is the mind that sees, not the eyes."[38]

The Fourfold Negation (Tetralemma)

In the logic of ancient India, statements could be affirmed, negated, neither affirmed nor negated, and both affirmed and negated. The founder of the Emptiness (Mādhyamaka) school of Buddhism, the Bodhisattva Nāgārjuna, popularized the logical negation of these four possibilities as a way of showing the emptiness of anything that might be construed as a real, permanent self or phenomenon or as an attribute of a real, permanent self or phenomenon. In this fourfold negation, sometimes called the "tetralemma," (catuṣkoṭi), a proposition is asserted to be neither true, nor not true, nor both true and not true, nor neither true nor not true. This formula can serve as a reminder in our practice that all we perceive is empty of any attribute, and so nothing definitive can be asserted about the world and the contents of the mind. There are numerous instances of the tetralemma in this Sutra.

---

[37] See Barlingay, 144 ff.
[38] Part 2.1.

9. Aids to Reading

The Commentarial Tradition

In Asian wisdom traditions, sacred texts have generally been studied with the aid of commentaries that were either written or spoken by esteemed spiritual teachers. The usual pattern has been that each passage of text is followed by interpretive comment, sometimes quite lengthy. The Buddhist sutras are no exception. Around the Śūraṅgama Sūtra in particular, a rich commentarial tradition has flourished. As mentioned above,[39] one search found reference to 127 Chinese commentaries on this Sutra, including fifty-nine in the Ming dynasty (1368–1644) alone, when the Sutra was especially popular.

For serious students of this Sutra, the commentarial exegeses are essential. The present translators have closely consulted two recent commentaries in particular: that by the Venerable Master Hsüan Hua and that by the Venerable Master Yuanying (1877–1953).[40] In addition, the translators also made use of the Ming dynasty commentary by Venerable Master Jiaoguang Zhenjian (fl. 1600)[41] and occasionally the commentaries by the celebrated Ming dynasty Chan Master Hanshan Deqing (1546–1623)[42] and the Qing dynasty Venerable Master Xufa.[43]

Engagement with Sutras as Spiritual Practice

In the Buddhist tradition, sutras are understood to contain the teachings of the Buddhas and greatly enlightened masters. They function as guidebooks to the Path to awakening. For those reasons, they are treated with reverence. It is customary to keep sutras in a clean place, either above or

---

[39] See note 7.

[40] Yuanying 圓瑛, *Shoulengyan jing jiangyi* 大佛頂首楞嚴經講義 (Shanghai: Shanghai shi fo jiao xie hui 上海市佛教協會, 1933).

[41] Zhenjian 眞鑑, *Dafoding shoulengyan jing zhengmai shu* 大佛頂首楞嚴經正脈疏 (Taipei: *Taiwan shang wu yin shu guan* 臺灣 商務 印書館, 1968).

[42] Hanshan 憨山, *Dafoding shoulengyan jing tongyi* (Nanjing: Jinling ke jing chu 金陵刻處, 1894).

[43] Xufa 續法, *Shoulengyan jing guandingshu* 首楞嚴經灌頂疏 (Yangzhou: Yangzhou cang jing yuan 揚州藏經院,1929). For a complete list of traditional commentaries, see n. 7.

apart from secular works; to handle them with respect; and to read them only while one is sitting upright or standing — never while one is lying down or in a slouching position.

Sutras — like sacred texts in other religious traditions — can themselves be the focus of a spiritual practice. Some practitioners read a particular text, such as the Śūraṅgama Sūtra, for a certain period of time each day. Others commit a text to memory and recite it. Yet another practice is to bow in reverence to it; one bows to each word or character in turn until one has bowed through the entire text. Such practices can develop faith, loosen the ties to self, and lead to personal transformation and spiritual growth.

The Sutras as Practical Guides

The Buddha should not be understood as a philosopher who was trying to develop a systematic philosophical system, complete with its own epistemology, metaphysics, and cosmology. Nor was he engaging in early scientific thinking. His teachings do not speculate about the nature of what seems to us to be the external world. Rather, his goal was to teach beings to understand their experience in such a way that they would be able to eliminate suffering and the fundamentally unsatisfactory quality of their lives. When we read in the sutras statements that seem to be abstract philosophical claims or excursions into neuroscience or cognitive psychology, we should realize that the purpose and meaning of these statements is to be understood and evaluated in light of their utility in advancing spiritual practice.

In a celebrated passage from the Middle Length Discourses of the Buddha, the Buddha compared himself and his teachings to a surgeon who removes a poisoned arrow from a man's body in order to save his life. The surgeon instructs the man how to care for his wound so that it will heal quickly, but he gives him no extraneous medical information that would not be germane to his healing.

> Suppose that a man were wounded by an arrow thickly smeared with poison, and his friends and companions, his kinsmen and relatives, brought a surgeon. The surgeon would cut around the

open wound with a knife, then he would probe for the arrow with a probe, then he would pull out the arrow and would expel the poisonous humour without leaving a trace of it behind. Knowing that no trace was left behind, he would say: "Good man, the arrow has been pulled out from you; the poisonous humour has been expelled with no trace left behind, and it is incapable of harming you. Eat only suitable food; do not eat unsuitable food or else the wound may suppurate. From time to time wash the wound and from time to time anoint its opening, so that pus and blood do not cover the opening of the wound. Do not walk around in the wind and sun or else dust and dirt may infect the opening of the wound. Take care of your wound, good man, and see to it that the wound heals."

The man would think: "The arrow has been pulled out from me; the poisonous humour has been expelled with no trace left behind, and it is incapable of harming me." He would eat only suitable food, and the wound would not suppurate. From time to time he would wash the wound and from time to time he would anoint its opening, and pus and blood would not cover the opening of the wound. He would not walk around in the wind and sun, and dust and dirt would not infect the opening of the wound. He would take care of the wound and would see to it that the wound heals. Then, both because he does what is suitable and because the foul poisonous humour has been expelled with no trace left behind, the wound would heal, and because it had healed and was covered with skin, he would not incur death or deadly suffering.

So, too, Sunakkhatta, it is possible that some *bhikkhus*[44] here might think thus: "Craving has been called an arrow by the Recluse; the poisonous humour of ignorance is spread about by desire, lust, and ill will. That arrow of craving has been pulled out from me; the poisonous humour of ignorance has ben expelled. I am one who is completely intent on Nibbāna." Being one who really is intent on Nibbāna, he would not pursue those things unsuitable for one

---

[44] The Pali form of *bhikṣu,* a fully ordained Buddhist monk.

completely intent on Nibbāna. He would not pursue the sight of unsuitable forms with the eye, he would not pursue unsuitable sounds with the ear, unsuitable odours with the nose, unsuitable flavours with the tongue, unsuitable tangibles with the body, or unsuitable mind-objects with the mind. Because he does not pursue the sight of unsuitable forms with the eye . . . unsuitable mind-objects with the mind, lust does not invade his mind. Because his mind is not invaded by lust, he would not incur death or deadly suffering.

Sunakkhatta, I have given this simile in order to convey a meaning. This is the meaning here: "Wound" is a term for the six internal bases.[45] "Poisonous humour" is a term for ignorance. "Arrow" is a term for craving. "Probe" is a term for mindfulness. "Knife" is a term for noble wisdom. "Surgeon" is a term for the Tathāgata, the Accomplished One, the Fully Enlightened One.[46]

In his teachings, the Buddha starts from the worldviews and beliefs of the people he is teaching. He only leads them to question their views and beliefs to the extent necessary for his teaching and to the degree necessary for their liberation.

10. The Early History of the Sutra and the Issue of Authenticity

The Śūraṅgama Sūtra in India

The period in India just prior to the Sutra's transmission to China at the beginning of the eighth century was one of social upheaval, political fragmentation, and severe social strain. The country was divided into many feudal kingdoms, with a good share of extremely violent rulers and a resurgence of tribal influence. Buddhism was in danger of losing its traditional social supports and was facing new challenges from the Hindu Śaivite tantrism that was spreading from south India. This was the context of the initial flourishing of Indian esoteric Buddhism along with its *siddha* traditions. Moral challenges and confusion arose both in secular

---

[45] That is, the six faculties.

[46] Majjhima Nikāya 105, "Sunakkhatta Sutta," in *The Middle Length Discourses of the Buddha,* Bhikkhu Ñāṇamoli and Bhikkhu Bodhi, trans. (Boston: Wisdom Publications, 1995), 866–7.

society and within Buddhist communities. Powerful sorcerers — tribal, Śaivite, and self-described Buddhist — flaunted their psychic powers and tried to overturn the fundamental precepts of the monastic life.[47] Given this atmosphere, it must have been quite plain at the time that the teachings of the Śūraṅgama Sūtra directly addressed the problems that Indian society was experiencing. Perhaps that was why, according to the traditional accounts, the Sutra was considered a state treasure.

Concerns about the Sutra's Authenticity

The authenticity of the Śūraṅgama Sūtra has been challenged by some modern scholars on the grounds that, since no Indic original is extant, the text must be no translation at all but rather an original composition in the Chinese. The date of the translation has been questioned, and textual anomalies that might suggest the interpolation of purely Chinese cultural elements have been identified. There are strong reasons to believe, however, that the original text can only be Indian.[48] It is true, for example, that during Buddhism's earliest centuries in China, spurious or corrupted Buddhist texts were circulated; but by 705 C.E., when the translation of the Sutra was completed, Chinese monastic scholars had become sufficiently skilled to recognize inauthentic texts.[49]

Further, while some details in the text do seem to arise from a Chinese context, these could merely represent choices made by the translators to substitute Chinese equivalents or analogues for unfamiliar Indian elements that were present in the original.[50] A prime example is the appearance of ascetic masters in Part IX, among the lists of categories of

---

[47] See Davidson, *Indian Esoteric Buddhism.*

[48] A brief summary of modern scholarly claims of inauthenticity and of a refutation of them can be found in Ronald Epstein, "The Surangama-Sūtra (T. 945): A Reappraisal of Its Authenticity," 1976. http://online.sfsu.edu/~rone/Buddhism/authenticity.htm; this is a summary of an unpublished monograph of the same title (T.S., 223 pp.).

[49] Beginning with Dao An in the fourth century.

[50] For example, the references to parahelial phenomena and other malign astrological influences, and the mention of housewives' use of metal mirrors to focus light on tinder to make fire. In other cases, what may seem Chinese turns out, on further investigation, to be

beings. The Chinese uses the character *"xian"* 仙 for these ascetic masters. This *"xian,"* often translated as "Immortal," is the Chinese character for the long-lived spiritual masters of the Chinese Daoist tradition. The appearance of such a clearly Daoist word has led some scholars to suggest that the passage is evidence that the Śūraṅgama Sūtra was composed in China. A much more plausible explanation is also the simpler one: that the Indic original was "ṛṣi," which referred to the ascetic Hindu saints.[51] The Chinese translators sensibly chose to render "ṛṣi" as "xian," supposing the two kinds of ascetics to be, if not precisely equivalent, then at least occupants of similar spiritual niches in their respective societies.

The presence of two indisputably Indian elements that play leading roles in the text also point to an Indian origin. One of these, already mentioned here, is the presence of Indian Buddhist logic in the many syllogisms and the use of the fourfold negation. The other is the Śūraṅgama Mantra, which the Chinese text leaves untranslated and which lies at the heart of the Sutra's instructions for spiritual practice.

Having considered the authenticity of the Śūraṅgama Sūtra from the point of view of the historical criticism of religious texts, it is important to consider it as well from the point of view of the Sutra's own tradition. Whatever the historical origin and provenance of this text may ultimately be shown to be — if indeed the questions about it can ever be definitively answered — one fact is not in dispute: the Śūraṅgama Sūtra has been widely accepted in China as canonical for well over a thousand years. Such acceptance reflects the view that a religious text's authoritativeness must be measured by its effectiveness as a guide to moral and spiritual practice. From this pragmatic and orthopraxic point of view, the Śūraṅgama Sūtra may be correctly deemed to be authentic simply because generations of advanced practitioners and their students and

---

Indian as well. For example, in Part IX.2, the Buddha cites an owl that lays its eggs on the ground; this could easily be the grass owl, which is found in both India and China.

[51] According to the *Monier Williams Sanskrit-English Dictionary*, "The ṛṣis were regarded by later generations as patriarchal sages or saints . . . and constitute a peculiar class of beings in the early mythical system, as distinct from gods, men, asuras."

disciples have revered this text, have followed its instructions, and have explained it to others as a trustworthy prescription for moral purification and spiritual advancement towards enlightenment.[52] In the minds of its many admirers, then, the Sutra's validity and importance do not depend on whether the text actually represents a verbatim record of words spoken by the Buddha Śākyamuni in the Magadhan dialect of Sanskrit in what is now Uttar Pradesh sometime in the fifth century B.C.E. From this point of view, uncertainty about the Sutra's textual history is not a cause for any uncertainty about its ethical and spiritual truth.

[52] See Hanshan Deqing, in his *Autobiography,* in the entry for his thirty-first year (1576–7): "After my great awakening, having no one to confirm and testify to it, I opened the Śūraṅgama Sūtra to verify my experience. I had not listened previously to lectures on this Sūtra and so did not know its meaning. Now by using the power of the direct reasoning of the nondiscriminating mind and without even the slightest use of its consciousness since there was no room for thinking, I gained after eight months a complete comprehension of its profound meaning without having a single doubt left." Translated by Charles Luk, in *Practical Buddhism* (London: Rider, 1971), 83.

Martin Verhoeven, in his article "Glistening Frost and Cooking Sand: Unalterable Aspects of Purity in Chan Buddhist Meditation," has called attention to the importance of the Śūraṅgama Sūtra as a guide to and standard for correct meditation practice in the life of the famous enlightened Chan Master Xuyun (1840–1959). In discussing that master's great awakening, Verhoeven comments: "He credits the Shurangama-sutra with instilling in him the importance of purity and the consequent dispassion it instills. 'If I had not remained indifferent to both favorable and adverse situations,' he reflected, 'I would have passed another life aimlessly and this experience would not have happened.'" In *Purity of Heart and Contemplation: A Monastic Dialogue between Christian and Asian Traditions* (New York/London: Continuum, 2001), 85ff.

See also Ven. Hsüan Hua: "Where the Śūraṅgama Sūtra exists, then the Proper Dharma exists. If the Śūraṅgama Sūtra ceases to exist, then the Proper Dharma will also vanish. If the Śūraṅgama Sūtra is inauthentic, then I vow to fall into the Hell of Pulling Tongues to undergo uninterrupted suffering." In "On the Authenticity of the Śūraṅgama Sūtra" (http://online.sfsu.edu/~rone/Buddhism/Shurangama/Shurangama%20Sūtra%20Is%20Definitely%20Authentic.htm).

Dōgen, in his *Nihon Shisō Taikei,* says of the Sutra, "Even if it were a forgery, if the Buddhas and Bodhisattvas have taken it up, it is a true Buddha-sutra, a true Patriarch Sutra, a traditional Dharma wheel of the Buddhas and Bodhisattvas." Translated by Carl Bielefeldt, in Terada and Mizono, eds., *Dōgen,* vol. 2, 229.

The Traditional Account of Its Transmission to China

The Venerable Master Hsüan Hua has summarized the traditional account of the transmission of the Sutra from India to China as follows:

> The king of one of the regions of India had proclaimed the Śūraṅgama Sūtra to be a national treasure because it was one of the Sutras that the Bodhisattva Nāgārjuna had brought back from the Dragon (*nāga*) Palace.[53] After the proclamation, no one was permitted to take the Sutra out of the country. At that time, Bhikṣu Paramiti was intent upon getting the Sutra out of India into other countries, especially China. He set out for China carrying a copy of the Sutra, only to be stopped by customs officials who would not permit him to carry the Sutra across the border. He returned home and tried to think of a way to get the Sutra out of the country. Finally, he thought of a way. He wrote out the Sutra in minute characters on extremely fine silk, rolled it up, and sealed it with wax. Then he cut open his arm and placed the small scroll inside his flesh. Next he applied medicines to the wound and waited for it to heal. (Some people say he put the Sutra in his leg, but I think that since it would not have been respectful to place the text below the waist, he probably chose some fleshy place on the upper part of his body and put the Sutra there.) When the wound healed, he again set out for China and passed the border guards without incident. Eventually, he arrived in Guangdong, where he happened to meet the court official Fang Yong, who invited him to reside at a temple in Guangdong while he translated the Sutra.[54]

11. A Brief Explanation of Some Important Technical Terms

For those who are new to Buddhist teachings, we offer here brief explanations of important terms and concepts mentioned in the Sutra.

---

[53] According to the Mahāyāna tradition, many of the major Mahāyāna sutras were initially stored in a dragon-king's palace at the bottom of the ocean. The tradition credits the Bodhisattva Nāgārjuna with bringing these sutras back to India.

[54] *The Shurangama Sūtra*, vol. 1, 68.

No-Self

The teaching of no-self[55] is fundamental to Buddhism. The Buddha did not teach that we do not exist, but he did teach that suffering is caused by our clinging to a self, an individuality that is illusory and does not exist. What "self" is it that does not exist? It is not merely the personality, or ego, that identifies itself in terms of social roles and interactions. Buddhism denies the existence of a basic self that is identified with our physical being, including our gender, and also the existence of what is called the "soul" and other levels of spiritual self. The existence of a self of cosmic consciousness that is identified with the universe is also denied. All these "selves" are constructed, conventional designations that only contribute to our attachment to illusion. The true reality that does exist, and that is who we really are, lies beyond our attachment to a duality of self and other and a duality of existence and nonexistence.

Enlightenment or Awakening

In this volume we use the English terms "enlightenment" and "awakening" as synonyms. In Buddhism, when these terms are used in a formal sense, they do not connote a temporary experience but rather a complete and irreversible transformation of one's fundamental way of being in the world. Only the enlightenment of a Buddha is perfect and complete. Bodhisattvas, Solitary Sages,[56] and Arhats[57] have awakened but have not

---

[55] Skt. *anātman*. For explanations of this and many other technical terms and lists mentioned in the Sutra, the reader who is not familiar with Buddhist teachings may find the following publication a helpful aid: *Buddhism A to Z*, Ronald B. Epstein, comp. (Burlingame, CA: Buddhist Text Translation Society, 2003). Many excellent introductory books about Buddhism are available and can provide useful background for the teachings of this Sutra. A short selection of these is listed online under the title "A Short Introductory Reading List on Buddhism," http://online.sfsu.edu/~rone/Buddhism/ introbuddhistbibiog.htm.

[56] Skt. *pratyekabuddha*. Solitary Sages are beings who achieve enlightenment on their own without the aid of the Buddha's Dharma or who became enlightened through contemplation of the twelve-fold conditioned arising (Skt. *pratītyasamutpāda*). See part 4, note 18.

[57] Arhats become enlightened through contemplation of the Four Noble Truths. There are four stages of Arhat: the *srota-āpanna* (one who has entered the stream of the sages), the *sakṛdāgāmin* (one who must be reborn only once more), the *anāgāmin* (one who does not

perfected their awakening. All enlightened beings have three accomplishments in common: they have seen through the illusion of self; they have achieved permanent release from the cycle of death and rebirth; and as a byproduct of their enlightenment, they possess spiritual powers. The Sanskrit word "bodhi," which we have translated as "full awakening," refers in this text to the awakening or enlightenment of a Buddha.

Dharma and Dharmas

In Buddhism, "Dharma" no longer has its Hindu meaning of religious duty according to one's class. In Buddhist usage the word has several meanings, as follows:

1) It is a general term for the Buddha's teachings as a whole (the Dharma, or the Buddha's Dharma), and it also may designate a particular teaching, usually a method of practice leading to enlightenment.

2) It signifies the reality that one realizes upon one's enlightenment — that is, the fundamental reality that is immanent in the entire universe (the Dharma-Realm[58]).

3) It is a term for the individual components of a teaching, often as an item in a list. Among them are the lists of the various divisions of the mental and physical world. We sometimes translate "dharmas" in this sense as "phenomena."

4) It is also a term both for the sense-data that enter our minds through our faculties of perception and for the thoughts and emotions that arise in our minds and are identified by the faculty of cognition. We translate "dharmas" in this sense as "mental objects" or "objects of cognition."[59]

---

need to be reborn again); and the Arhat (one who has ended all outflows and needs no further instruction). The term "Arhat" may refer to all four stages or only to the fourth stage. At the outset of this Sutra, Ānanda is an Arhat at the first stage.

[58] *Dharmadhātu,* Ch. *fa jie* 法界. In a related usage, the "ten Dharma-Realms" consist of the four levels of the sage (Buddhas, Bodhisattvas, Solitary Sages, and Arhats) together with six destinies of the unenlightened (gods, asuras, humans, animals, ghosts, and denizens of the hells).

[59] In the present translation, we capitalize "Dharma" when it represents the first and second of these meanings and do not capitalize it when it carries the other two meanings.

Samādhi

Samādhi is "a concentrated, self-collected, intent state of mind and meditation, which, concomitant with right living, is a necessary condition to the attainment of higher wisdom and emancipation."[59]

There are four distinct senses in which the word "samādhi" is used. First, it designates the correct mental focus or concentration that is a necessary preliminary to the deeper meditative states. Second, samādhi indicates those deeper levels of mental concentration and stability which may be reached through correct practice. These levels include the four *dhyānas,* which correspond to the states of mind of the gods in the heavens of the realm of form, and the four *samāpattis,* which correspond to the states of mind of gods who abide on the planes of formlessness. Third, there are even more profound levels of samādhi that are experienced by enlightened beings. Fourth, "samādhi" may also refer specifically to the Śūraṅgama (Indestructible) Samādhi, which is the state of mind of all Buddhas and which is discussed at length in this Sutra.

Emptiness

There are at least three ways in which the idea of emptiness can be understood: on the intellectual level, in practice, and as a description of enlightenment.

On the intellectual level, it can be said that emptiness[61] means that all dharmas — all phenomena, mental and physical — lack an independent existence of their own and exist only through reliance on other phenomena. All dharmas lack real, permanent, essential attributes that distinguish them from all other phenomena. In other words, everything in the world, both physical and mental, is interdependent. Nothing exists entirely on its own, separate, and with no causal relation to anything else. Thus all dharmas are empty of any individual, inherent being.[62]

---

[60] T. W. Rhys Davids and William Stede, eds., *Pali Text Society's Pali-English Dictionary* (London: Pali Text Society, 1972).

[61] Skt. *śūnyatā,* Ch. *kong* 空.

[62] Skt. *svabhāva,* Ch. *zixing* 自性.

An intellectual understanding of emptiness can be extended into a method of practice and a way of life that empties our experience in every moment. To "empty our experience" means, first, to remove "me" and "mine" from every thought that arises in our consciousness. Sustained contemplation of the emptiness of the self can extricate us from ego-centered experience and liberate us from the prison of selfishness. We learn to see ourselves and our concerns, our desires and fears, as empty — like a mirage or a dream, as ephemeral as a bubble or a flash of lightning. The Diamond Sūtra says,

> As stars, a fault of vision, as a lamp,
> A mock show, dew-drops, or a bubble,
> A dream, a lightning-flash or cloud,
> So should one view what is conditioned.[63]

Emptying ourselves opens us up to the fullness of the world.

Emptying experience also entails eliminating the boundaries that we have drawn to cope with the world — the walls we erect to protect ourselves, the turf we stake out to rule, and the fantasies of future conquests that we map in our minds. Emptying ourselves must lead to the emptying of the "other," the "no-self," so that self and other are no longer two. When the line that divides them is erased, then there is no conflict, no longer anything to fear or to gain.

With enlightenment comes the realization that true emptiness is identical to the fullness of wondrous existence. It can be reached through the hard work of becoming aware of every single thought and emptying them one by one.

The Five Aggregates

The word "aggregate" renders the Sanskirt word "skandha," which means "heap," "pile," or "aggregation." (The Buddha once illustrated his teaching about the aggregates with five small piles of different grains.)

---

[63] "The Diamond Sūtra," in Edward Conze, *Buddhist Wisdom Books* (London: George Allen and Unwin, 1956), 68.

The five aggregates — form, sense-perception, cognition, mental formations, and consciousness — are general categories that together include everything that we experience in the psycho-physical world. Thus they can be an effective tool for understanding the teaching of no-self. If one analyzes all aspects of what one feels to be one's self, one finds that all fall within the scope of the five aggregates.

More specifically, the aggregate of form comprises what we perceive as our bodies and the rest of the physical world. The aggregate of sense-perception comprises the first five faculties of perception — eyes, ears, nose, tongue, and body — and their intake of the five corresponding categories of sense-data — visible objects, sounds, odors, flavors, and tactile objects. We respond to these perceptions as pleasant, unpleasant, or neutral.

The aggregate of cognition includes the function of identifying sense-data and making distinctions concerning the data. It also involves differentiating between mental contents; thus it includes the higher perceptual functions and thinking processes, for example the use of language.

The aggregate of mental formations refers to both conscious and non-conscious volitional forces, including conscious intentions or acts of will; innate predispositions resulting from karma created during previous lives; and unconscious forces having to do with basic life functions, nourishment, and growth.

The aggregate of consciousness is the subtle basis of the aggregates of sense-perception, cognition, and mental formations. It consists of a subtle distinction-making awareness that distinguishes awareness from the objects of awareness.

The Eighteen Constituents

The eighteen constituents are the six faculties, the six kinds of perceived objects, and the six consciousnesses. The six faculties are the eyes, ears, nose, tongue, body, and mind. The six kinds of perceived objects are visible objects, sounds, odors, flavors, tactile objects, and objects of cognition. The six faculties and the six kinds of perceived objects are together known as the "twelve sites." They are the sites for the coming into being of the six consciousnesses. That is, contact between the faculties and their objects is a necessary condition for the coming into being of eye-consciousness, ear-consciousness, nose-consciousness, tongue-consciousness, body-consciousness, and mind-consciousness (seeing, hearing, smelling, tasting, tactile sensation, and cognition).

Like the five aggregates, the eighteen constituents provide an analysis of the entire psycho-physical world and an aid to breaking attachments to that world. Everything that we experience can also be subsumed within the eighteen constituents. The first five groups of perceived objects — visible objects, sounds, odors, flavors, and tactile objects — together with the first five faculties that perceive these objects comprise the entire physical world. The faculty of cognition and objects of cognition in the mind, together with the six consciousnesses, comprise the world of mind. All mental experience and the entire physical world lie within these eighteen; therefore, no notion of a permanent soul or self is needed to describe and account for any experience.

Seven Primary Elements

The seven primary elements are earth, which represents solidity; water, which represents what is liquid; fire, which represents warmth; wind, which represents motion; space; visual awareness; and consciousness. These primary elements are the qualities of matter-energy as they are distinguished in the mind. It may be helpful to think about the primary elements on three different levels: first, their identity with the Matrix of the Thus-Come One, which is the enlightened mind and the primary elements' true nature; second, their pure and essential qualities, which we do not usually experience directly; and third, the primary elements as we experience them in their state of mixture with each other in various proportions in our bodies and in the world.

12. Notes on This Translation

We have already mentioned[64] some of the challenges involved in undertaking to translate into modern English the formal eighth-century Chinese of

---

[64] See p. xv.

the Śūraṅgama Sūtra. Perhaps the most difficult challenge came from the constraints the Chinese translators imposed upon themselves in choosing the pattern of four-character phrases in which the greater part of the Chinese translation is written. Not infrequently, in order to preserve the four-character meter, the translators found it necessary to omit one or more characters even though the characters to be omitted were essential to the meaning. An example that the reader of the Chinese text frequently encounters involves the list of the six faculties of perception, or the list of their six objects. Although in each case all six are clearly meant, two are routinely omitted so that the remaining four fit the four-character meter. (A further complication is that the same two are not always omitted.) In general, wherever such terseness might inhibit understanding, we have either added clarifying words, included an explanatory excerpt from the commentary of the Venerable Master Hsüan Hua, or identified the missing meanings in a footnote.

Second, the Chinese text often proceeds in patterned paragraphs, and the resulting repetition sometimes tempted the Chinese translators to enliven the repeated text with a variety of synonyms. The opposite is also true: the Chinese translators often used one character to indicate quite different meanings — sometimes in the same sentence or even in the same four-character phrase. In both cases we have chosen clarity over literary flourish. Several characters that mean the same thing we have generally rendered with one English word, and single characters with multiple meanings we have generally translated into several English words.

Third, the abundance of Sanskrit terms, represented in the text by specialized transliteration characters, is one of the features that most challenges the reader of the Chinese text. We chose not to pass on this difficulty to readers of the English version. We have, in general, left in the Sanskrit only those words that are already familiar to English readers (such words as "Dharma," "karma," "nirvana," and "Bodhisattva") or those words that we expect will become English words as Buddhist texts become more and more familiar to Westerners. When we have translated Sanskrit terms that the Chinese text merely transliterates, we have noted the Sanskrit original in the footnotes.

Fourth, although the original Sanskrit text is no longer extant, almost all of the many technical Buddhist terms and concepts appearing in this Sutra also appear in other sutras, including many of the sutras that survive in the Sanskrit. Thus, for these terms and concepts, the Sanskrit originals are well known. In all such cases, in translating the Śūraṅgama Sūtra, where we could confidently identify the Sanskrit words or phrases that lay behind the Chinese renderings, we have relied on the Sanskrit to determine a correct translation into English.

In preparing the present volume it was necessary for the translators to decide whether to include a commentary, in the manner that is tradition-al in Asia. Most Western translations of sacred texts, unless the texts are short, have not included traditional commentaries. The Buddhist Text Translation Society has been an exception, having issued numerous texts with the full commentaries given by the Venerable Master Hsüan Hua. The length of these commentaries has meant that the translations of the longer sutras, with commentary, have run into multiple volumes — nine for the Buddhist Text Translation Society's 2000–05 edition of this Sutra. One of the primary intents of this new translation has been to present the Śūraṅgama to an audience literate in English in the convenient and ac-cessible form of a single volume. Still, to the translators it seemed unac-ceptable to omit commentary altogether given the difficulty of the text. It was decided, therefore, to preserve the traditional format of interlinear exegesis and to draw excerpts from the Venerable Master Hsüan Hua's commentary when passages of text clearly called for elucidation.

The Venerable Master Hsüan Hua's commentary to the Sutra was given in the form of lectures delivered over a period of four months in the sum-mer and fall of 1968 at the Buddhist Lecture Hall in San Francisco. The lectures were later transcribed and edited, and they have been published in full as part of the Buddhist Text Translation Society's nine-volume edition of this Sutra. Besides explaining the Sutra text itself, the lectures were the occasion of many lessons in personal conduct, spiritual prac-tice, monastic discipline, and general Buddhist doctrine. These lessons, often given in the form of stories, are of very great value to anyone who undertakes a spiritual practice or who simply wishes for a better life. We

1

include some of these instructions in the present volume. For the most part, however, and with some reluctance, we quote in this single-volume translation only those passages of the Venerable Master Hsüan Hua's commentary which directly present explanations of the Sutra text itself. Thus, the commentary excerpted for this translation is by no means a substitute for the full commentary and is only partly representative of the commentary's scope and depth. Fortunately, the complete record of these lectures remains easily available in the Buddhist Text Translation Society's earlier translation.

A word concerning gender-neutrality of language is appropriate here. Where possible we have resorted to the gender-neutral plural pronouns "they," "them," and "their." But most often this escape from the gender bias of English pronouns was not feasible. First, the bulk of the Sutra consists of dialogue between two male speakers, the Buddha Śakyamuni and his cousin Ānanda. Second, as translators we strove to avoid anachronistic language, that is, language that might weaken the Sutra's ties to its time and place. We did not wish to portray the Buddha speaking in a way that, it seemed to us, he would not have spoken; thus we did not use words derived from modern science or technology, technical terms of European philosophy, or twenty-first-century casual speech. It was our wish to find a voice for these speakers that would be formal, precise, and natural, both time-specific and timeless. It was there that our quandary lay. English speakers have been engaged for the last quarter-century in making an overdue transition to gender-neutral speech — above all by the use of the phrase "he or she" and by the heretofore ungrammatical use of "they" forms in the singular. But in translating a document that has come down to us over many centuries, we found that repeated use of these contemporary gender-neutral usages struck a dissonant tone of anachronism that tended to distract from the naturalness and authority of the speakers' voices. We therefore resigned ourselves to the unsatisfactory use of masculine pronouns when both genders are meant. Our decision to do so was entirely editorial, not doctrinal.

All this does not mean that the Śūraṅgama Sūtra holds male gender to be an advantage in spiritual practice. There is no such teaching in the

Sutra. In fact, the courtesan who casts her spell upon Ānanda at the opening of the Sutra and who accompanies Ānanda and the Bodhisattva Mañjuśrī back to the Buddha's assembly becomes enlightened during the course of the dialogue, reaching a level of awakening higher than Ānanda's level.[66] The enlightenment of Yaśodarā, who had been the Buddha Śākyamuni's wife when he was still a prince, is also mentioned.[67]

Finally, a few words about our translation process. As with other texts produced by members of the Buddhist Text Translation Society, the present translation was made in four distinct steps. First, a primary translation was accomplished by a committee that included both native speakers of Chinese and native speakers of English. The second step consisted of reviews of the entire text to check for accuracy. Next came editorial polishing to ensure naturalness and consistency of English style, and finally, certification that the translation faithfully presents the Buddha's teachings. In all this effort we relied on the pioneering work of the previous translators. Without their labors, making this translation would have been far more difficult and the result far more subject to error. Nevertheless, despite the effort of many people during a period of six and a half years, we recognize that our translation can hardly be free of mistakes, and we request that the students, scholars, practitioners, and general readers who undertake to read this translation will kindly point out any errors to us so that we may correct them in any future printing.

We join our colleagues in dedicating any merit accrued in the making of this translation to world peace and to the enlightenment of all beings.

Ron Epstein and David Rounds,
Co-Chairs, Śūraṅgama Sūtra Translation Committee,
Buddhist Text Translation Society

---

[66] At the end of part 4.
[67] Ibid.

Sūtra on the Śūraṅgama Mantra That Is Spoken from above the Crown of the Great Buddha's Head, and on the Hidden Basis of the Thus-Come Ones' Myriad Bodhisattva-Practices That Lead to Their Verifications of Ultimate Truth

Translated into Chinese during the Tang Dynasty
by the Elder Monk Parāmiti of Central India

Reviewed by the Elder Monk Meghaśikha of Uḍḍiyāna

Verified by the Elder Monk Huaidi
of Nanlou Monastery on Mt. Luofu

Edited by Attending Minister, Court Regulator,
and Former State Censor Fangyong of Qingho,
a Disciple of the Buddha
and Follower of the Bodhisattva Precepts

Prologue

The Occasion for the Teaching[1]

Thus have I heard:[2] at one time the Buddha was staying in the city of Śrāvastī in a sublime abode in Prince Jetri's Grove,[3] together with a gathering of great monks,[4] twelve hundred fifty in all. These disciples of the Buddha were all great Arhats, free of outflows:[5] they abided in the Dharma and upheld it. They had completely transcended all existence, and their perfect demeanor inspired awe in every place they went. They followed the Buddha in turning the Wheel of Dharma,[6] supremely worthy of what he had bestowed upon them. Stern and pure in their adherence to the monastic code,[7] they were great exemplars for beings in the three realms of existence.[8] To liberate beings they appeared in countless bodies in response to what those beings required, and in the future they would rescue other beings, who thereby would transcend the burden of their attachment to sense-objects.

The Arhats' leaders were Śāriputra, great in wisdom, and Mahā-Maudgalyāyana, Mahā-Kauṣṭhila, Pūrṇamaitrāyaṇīputra, Subhūti, Upaniṣad, and others. Innumerable Solitary Sages,[9] who needed no further

[1] As noted in the introduction, this and all other headings and sub-headings have been added by the present translators as an aid to understanding.

[2] "I" refers to Ānanda, the Buddha Śākyamuni's cousin and attendant, who recited the Buddha's teachings to the assembly of enlightened disciples after the Buddha's nirvana. He is both protagonist and narrator of this Sutra.

[3] The grove was donated to the Buddha's order by Prince Jetri (Skt. Jetṛ). It was part of a park called the Garden of the Benefactor of Orphans and the Childless; the park itself was donated to the Buddha by the Buddhist layman Anāthapiṇḍada.

[4] Skt. bhikṣu, Ch. biqiu 比丘, a fully ordained Buddhist monk. The Sanskrit for nun is bhikṣuṇī, Ch. biqiuni 比丘尼.

[5] Skt. anāsrava. "Outflows" refers to the flowing out of vital energies toward the objects one perceives, including objects of desire.

[6] That is, teaching using the words of the Buddha.

[7] Skt. vinaya.

[8] The realm of desire, the realm of form, and the realm beyond form. See part 9.11.

[9] Skt. Pratyekabuddhas. See the introduction, note 56 and part 4, note 18.

instruction,[10] as well as other beings who had only recently made a resolve to attain full awakening,[11] also came to the place where the Buddha
and the monks were staying. It was during the Days of Unburdening[12] at
the conclusion of the summer retreat. Bodhisattvas from all ten directions[13] were gathered there as well; they desired counsel to resolve their
doubts.[14] All were respectful and obedient to the awe-inspiring, compassionate Thus-Come One as they prepared themselves to understand his
hidden meaning.

> People who have become enlightened are free of outflows: the outflows of
> desire, the outflows of existence, and the outflows of ignorance. Because they
> are free of outflows, they do not fall into the realm of desire, the realm of forms,
> and the realm beyond form. We people now dwell in the realm of desire. . . . It
> is called the realm of desire because the people in it have desires for material
> things and for sex, desires which they cannot put a stop to. . . . The outflows of
> existence are suffered by beings who are beyond these desires and who dwell
> in the heavens of the realm of forms. . . . These beings still cannot control their
> desire for bodily existence. . . . Beyond these two outflows, and the greatest
> of the three, is the outflow of ignorance, which is the source of all afflictions.
> When this outflow is ended, the other two are ended also. (I, 99–100)[15]

[10] Skt. *aśaikṣa*, Ch. *wu xue* 無學. Those who need no further instruction are the Solitary
Sages and the Arhats at the fourth stage, as opposed to *śaikṣa* (Ch. *you xue* 有學) Arhats,
who are at the first three stages and who still need instruction — including Ānanda, who at
the outset of the Sutra is at the first stage.

[11] Skt. bodhi, Ch. *pu ti* 菩提, full awakening.

[12] Skt. *pravāraṇa*, the final days of the monastic retreat during the rainy season.

[13] The ten directions are north, south, east, west, northeast, northwest, southeast,
southwest, above, and below.

[14] They did not yet understand the "Hidden Basis" mentioned in the Sutra title.

[15] This is the first of the excerpts from the Ven. Master Hsüan Hua's commentary quoted
in the present volume. To ensure a clear distinction between the passages of the Sutra text
and the passages of commentary, the commentary excerpts are indented and are set in a
contrasting typeface. The references, given in parentheses at the end of each passage or
paragraph of commentary, cite the volume and page number at which the excerpts may
be found in the Buddhist Text Translation Society's 2003 edition of this Sutra. The excerpts
have been edited for brevity and conformity with the present translation.

The Thus-Come One,[16] having arranged his seat, sat quietly and peacefully, and then, for the sake of everyone assembled there, spoke of the profound and mysterious. The assembly, pure in mind and body, learned at that banquet of Dharma what they had not known before. The Immortal's voice was like the call of the *kalaviṅka* bird,[17] and it could be heard in worlds throughout all ten directions. As many Bodhisattvas as there are sand-grains in the Ganges gathered at that place for awakening, with Mañjuśrī as their leader.

King Prasenajit, on the anniversary day of mourning for his father, the late king, had arranged a vegetarian feast in the banquet hall of the palace. He had invited the Buddha, and he welcomed the Thus-Come One in person to a meal of savory delicacies. He also invited in the great Bodhisattvas. Meanwhile, in the city, elders and other laity had also prepared meals for the Sangha,[18] and they stood waiting for the Buddha to come receive their offerings. The Buddha directed Mañjuśrī to designate Arhats and Bodhisattvas to accept the pure vegetarian food that the donors were offering.

> When donors make offerings to the Three Treasures — the Buddha, Dharma, and Sangha — they plant seeds that grow and ripen into blessings in the future. Thus, people who have entered the monastic life are called "fields for blessings." People who enjoy the reward of many blessings are entirely content. Those who feel their blessings are not sufficient should make more offerings to the Three Treasures. (I, 130)

Only Ānanda was late for this assigning of the Sangha. Earlier he had traveled for some distance to accept a special invitation and had not yet returned. No senior monk[19] was accompanying him as his teacher; he was returning on the road alone.

---

[16] Skt. Tathāgata, Ch. *ru lai* 如來, an honorific title for the Buddha.

[17] The kalaviṅka is an Indian bird with a pure and penetrating call. The "Immortal" is the Buddha.

[18] The Sanskrit word *sangha* means "community." Here, and most often in the Buddhist traditions of Asia, "Sangha" refers specifically to the monastic community of monks and nuns, both fully ordained and in training.

[19] Skt. *ācārya*, an exemplar in following the monastic regulations.

Ānanda is about to run into trouble, and the reason is that he was alone. He had accepted a special invitation. . . . Basically, monks should not accept special invitations. . . . The rule in Buddhism is that all the members of the Sangha in a particular monastic community should be invited as a group. . . . Furthermore, members of the Sangha should always travel at least in pairs, although someone whose samādhi is strong may do things on his or her own.
(I, 126–8)

So far that day Ānanda had received no offerings. At the appropriate time, therefore, he took his almsbowl out, and as he walked through the town he accepted alms in sequential order.[20] While receiving alms from his first to his last donor,[21] he thought to himself that he would accept pure food from everyone, not only from Kṣatriyas[22] of honorable family and others from the purer classes, but also from Caṇḍālas[23] and others who were considered impure. While practicing impartiality and compassion, he would not favor the humblest people only; he was determined to assist all beings in creating merit beyond measure. Ānanda knew that the Thus-Come One, the World-Honored One,[24] had admonished the Arhats Subhūti and Mahākāśyapa for being prejudicial on their almsrounds. Ānanda revered the Thus-Come One's instruction: let alms be received impartially so that people will not be led to doubt or slander.

Why did Ānanda want to practice impartiality and compassion during his alms-round? Earlier, he had heard the Buddha scold Subhūti and Mahākāśyapa about their manner of receiving alms. . . . It was Subhūti's opinion that he should receive alms exclusively from the rich, on the grounds that people with money should create more merit . . . because if they don't make offerings now, they won't have any money in the next life. . . . Mahākāśyapa, on the other hand, received alms exclusively from the poor. He thought: "People without any money should create merit through good deeds, so that in the next life

---

[20] That is, not skipping any households on his route.

[21] Skt. dānapati, almsgiver.

[22] The royal and warrior class of ancient Indian society.

[23] A tribe of outcastes in ancient Indian society.

[24] Skt. Bhagavān, Ch. shi zun 世尊, an honorific title of a Buddha.

they can be wealthy and honored. If I don't help them out by receiving alms from them, then in the next life and on into the future, they will continue to be poor." . . . I believe there was another reason underlying their behavior. It seems fairly certain that Subhūti liked to eat good food, and Mahākāśyapa, foremost among the disciples in his practice of asceticism, ate what others couldn't bear to eat and endured what others couldn't endure. (I, 130–1)

Having crossed the city moat, Ānanda walked slowly through the outer gates, his manner stern and proper as he followed strictly and respectfully the rules for accepting offerings of pure food. Because he was receiving alms sequentially, he soon chanced to pass a house of courtesans, and there he was waylaid by a powerful artifice. Wielding a spell that Kapila[25] had obtained from a god of the Brahma Heavens,[26] a young Mātaṅga woman[27] seduced Ānanda onto her bed. Then she caressed him lasciviously, until the power of his vows[28] was on the verge of being broken.

Knowing that Ānanda was succumbing to the carnal influence of the spell, the Thus-Come One ended his meal immediately and returned to the monastic grounds. The king, his senior ministers, the elders, and the other laity, desiring to hear the essentials of the Dharma, followed after the Buddha. Then from the crown of his head[29] the World-Honored One poured forth invincible light which was as dazzling as a hundred gems. The Buddha Śākyamuni made appear within that light a Buddha who, seated in full-lotus posture on a thousand-petaled sacred lotus, proclaimed a spiritually powerful mantra.[30]

---

[25] An ancient Indian sage who was the founder of the Sāṅkhya School.

[26] The Brahma Heavens belong to the realm of form and correspond to the level of single-minded meditation known as the first dhyāna. See part 9.11b.

[27] The Mātaṅga were a non-Aryan tribal people.

[28] Ch. *jie ti* 戒體. The phrase indicates the moral fortitude that arises from receiving and following the Buddhist precepts.

[29] At the crown of the Buddha's head is a fleshy prominence (Skt. *uṣṇīṣa*), which is the first of the thirty-two hallmarks that are distinctive characteristics of the bodies of all Buddhas.

[30] The Śūraṅgama *Mantra*, see part 8. In general, mantras are spoken phrases whose primary meanings are not cognitive but whose meanings and powers lie on a spiritual level that transcends ordinary verbal understanding.

The Śūraṅgama Mantra is the king of the kings of mantras. It is extremely important. Students of the Buddha's Dharma who can learn this mantra in their present lives will not have been born as a human in vain. (I, 97–8)

The Buddha instructed Mañjuśri to go to Ānanda and protect him with the spiritually powerful mantra and, once the evil spell had been defeated, to give support to Ānanda and also to the young Mātaṅga woman, and to encourage both to return with him to where the Buddha was.

I
The Nature and Location of the Mind

1
The Request for Dharma

When Ānanda saw the Buddha, he bowed and wept in sorrow. He regretted that, since time without beginning, he had devoted himself to erudition but had not fully developed his practice on the Path. Respectfully and repeatedly he asked the Buddha to explain for him the elementary steps that lead to attainment in the wondrous practices of calming the mind, contemplative insight, and meditation in stillness[1] — practices through which the Thus-Come Ones from all ten directions had become fully awakened.

Meanwhile, as many Bodhisattvas as there are sand-grains of the River Ganges, along with the great Arhats, Solitary Sages, and others from the ten directions, all eagerly wished to listen. They sat down and waited silently to hear instruction from the Sage.

Then the World-Honored One, before the great assembly, extended his golden-hued arm, circled his hand on the crown of Ānanda's head,[3] and said to Ānanda and to all gathered there, "There is a samādhi called 'The Great and Royal Śūraṅgama that Is Spoken from above the Crown of the Buddha's Head and that Is the Perfection of the Myriad Practices.' It is a wondrous and magnificent Path, the unique portal through which the Buddhas in all ten directions have passed in order to transcend the conditioned world. You should all now listen attentively." Ānanda humbly bowed and waited for compassionate instruction.

Why was Ānanda unable to resist the evil spell, even though he was already a first-stage Arhat? He had been practicing samādhi with his conscious mind.[2] . . . For instance, when he listened to sutras, he remembered the principles that the Buddha spoke of. But the conscious mind which remembers the principles cannot lead to the fundamental solution, and so when Ānanda

[1] Skt. *śamatha, samāpatti, dhyāna.*

[2] Skt. *citta,* Ch. *xin* 心, the mind in which distinctions are made based on ignorance.

[3] A gesture giving comfort and blessing. The teacher places his hand on the crown of the disciple's head and then rubs the disciple's head in a circling motion.

encountered a demonic influence, he failed to recognize it. . . . The conscious
mind is subject to coming into being and ceasing to be and is not ultimate. . . .
If instead one bases one's practice on the true nature which neither comes
into being nor ceases to be, one can develop a samādhi which neither comes
into being nor ceases to be. That is a genuine samādhi, one that cannot be
affected by outside forces. . . . The power of such a samādhi can be victorious
in any set of circumstances, agreeable or disagreeable. In the midst of them
all, one can remain "still and just as one is, fully and forever luminous." That is
genuine samādhi. If happy situations make you happy and sad events make
you sad, you're being influenced by circumstances. If you keep jumping from
joy to anger to sorrow to happiness, you're being influenced by circumstances.
Instead, you should be like a mirror, which reflects what appears in it and then
is still. . . . That is to have genuine wisdom. (I, 146–7)

The Buddha said to Ānanda, "You and I are members of the same family,[4] and we share the affection that is natural among relatives. At the
time you first made the resolve to become enlightened, what excellent
attributes did you see in my Dharma that immediately led you to reject
the deep familial affection and conjugal love found in the world?"

Ānanda said to the Buddha, "I saw the thirty-two hallmarks[5] of the
Thus-Come One, which were so supremely wondrous and incomparable
that his entire body shone like crystal, with an interreflecting radiance.
I often thought to myself that a body with such hallmarks could not be
the consequence of an act of sexual love. Why? The energies of desire are
coarse and murky. Foul and putrid intercourse results in a turbid merging of procreative substances; such things as that cannot generate a body
with such a wondrous, pure, magnificent, and brilliant concentration of
purple-golden light. That is why I admired the Buddha and why I let the
hair fall from my head[6] so I could follow him."

---

[4] Ānanda and the Buddha were paternal first cousins.

[5] See the prologue, note 29.

[6] Buddhist monks and nuns shave their heads upon entering the monastic life. The
practice continues to this day.

The Buddha said, "Excellent, Ānanda! All of you should know that since time without beginning, all beings have been undergoing death and rebirth over and over simply because they have not been aware of the pure understanding which is the essential nature of the everlasting true mind. Instead, the workings of their minds are distorted, and because the workings of their minds are distorted, they are bound to the cycle of death and rebirth.

"Now you all wish to inquire about unsurpassed enlightenment and to discover the truth of your own nature. You should answer my questions straightforwardly, because that is the path that the Thus-Come Ones everywhere throughout the ten directions have taken as they freed themselves from death and rebirth. Their minds and their words were straightforward, and therefore, at every point in their progress from the first stage to the last, they were never in the least evasive.

"Now, Ānanda, I ask you this: when, in response to the thirty-two hallmarks of the Thus-Come One, you first made the resolve to attain full awakening, just what was it that saw those hallmarks, and who was it that took delight in them and loved them?"

Ānanda said to the Buddha, "World-Honored One, I delighted in them and loved them with my mind and eyes. Because I saw with my eyes the excellent hallmarks of the Thus-Come One, my mind admired and delighted in them. In this way I became resolved to extricate myself from death and rebirth."

The Buddha said to Ānanda, "It is as you say: your mind and eyes were the reason for your admiration and delight. Someone who does not know where his mind and eyes are will not be able to overcome the stress of engagement with perceived objects.[7] Consider, for example: when bandits invade a country and the king sends forth his soldiers to drive them out, the soldiers must first know where the bandits are. It is the fault of your mind and eyes that you are bound to the cycle of death and rebirth. I am now asking you: precisely where are your mind and eyes?"

[7] Ch. *chen lao* 塵勞. This is the first mention of a theme to which the Buddha returns frequently in the Sutra: the stress and weariness that inevitably results from immersion in the world of the senses. The theme is developed in full below in Parts IV and V.

2
The Location of the Mind

A. Ānanda Proposes That the Mind Is in the Body

"World-Honored One," Ānanda then said to the Buddha, "The ten classes of beings[8] in all the worlds believe that the conscious mind dwells in the body; and as I regard the blue-lotus eyes of the Thus-Come One, I know that they are part of the Buddha's face. Clearly they are also part of his body. It is evident that those physical organs which respond to four kinds of perceived objects[9] are part of my face, and so, my conscious mind, too, is surely found within my body."

The Buddha said to Ānanda, "Now as you sit in the Dharma Hall of the Thus-Come One, you can see Prince Jetri's Grove. Where is the grove?"[10]

"This great and sacred Dharma Hall, with its many stories, World-Honored One, is in the Garden of the Benefactor of Orphans and the Childless, and the Prince Jetri's Grove is outside the hall."

"Ānanda, what is the first thing that you see from your place in the hall?"

"World-Honored One, here in the hall I am looking first at the Thus-Come One. I can also see the great assembly; then, as I gaze out, I see the grove in the park."

"Why is it, Ānanda, that when you look out, you can see the grove in the park?"

---

[8] In part 9.2 below, the Buddha describes twelve kinds of beings according to the manner of their birth.

[9] Eyes, ears, nose, and tongue, responding respectively to visible objects, sounds, odors, and flavors. The other two pairs — the body and objects of touch and the cognitive faculty and objects of cognition — are understood to be included.

[10] Following the conventions for stating a syllogism (see section 8 of the introduction), the Buddha now suggests an apt instance drawn from orginary life to demonstrate the truth of what he is proposing, which is that Ānanda is wrong to suggest that the mind is located outside the body. He applies the instance to his proposition in the sentence beginning "Then if your mind that sees . . ." and states his conclusion in the sentence beginning "In this way you can know. . . ." This pattern is repeated to refute each of Ānanda's propositions concening the location of the mind.

"World-Honored One, since the doors and windows of this great hall have been thrown open wide, I can be in the hall and yet see into the distance."

The Buddha said to Ānanda, "It is as you say. Someone in the hall can see far into the grove and park when the doors and windows are open wide. Now, could that person in the hall not see the Buddha and yet see outside the hall?"

Ānanda answered, "It would not be possible, World-Honored One, to be in the hall and be able to see the grove and fountains, and yet not be able to see the Thus-Come One."

"Ānanda, the same is true of you. You have the intelligence to understand everything clearly. If your mind, with its clear understanding, were inside your body, then the inside of your body would be what your mind would first come into contact with and have knowledge of. Are there beings that see the inside of their bodies first, before they can observe things outside?[11] Even if they could not see their heart, liver, spleen, or stomach, they still at least would detect the growing of their nails and hair, the twisting of their sinews, and the throbbing of their pulse. Why then are you not able to see these things? And since your mind is definitely not visually cognizant of what is inside your body, how can it have knowledge of what is outside your body? Thus you can know that when you say the mind that is aware and makes distinctions is inside the body, you state what is impossible."

B. Ānanda Proposes That the Mind Is Outside the Body

Ānanda bowed and said to the Buddha, "Now that I have listened to the Thus-Come One explain the Dharma in this way, I realize that my mind must be located outside my body instead. Why do I say this? For example, a lamp lit in a room will certainly illuminate the inside of the room first, and then its light will stream through the doorway and reach the recesses of the hall beyond it. Since beings do not see inside their

---

[11] According to Buddhist teaching, the cognitive faculty acts together with the eye-faculty in the process of visual perception of objects. The eye-faculty senses the objects and the mind recognizes what they are.

bodies but only see outside them, it is as if the lamp were placed outside the room, so that it cannot shed its light inside the room. This principle is perfectly clear and beyond a doubt; it conforms to the Buddha's ultimate teaching — and so it can't be wrong, can it?"[12]

The Buddha said to Ānanda, "The monks who followed me to Śrāvastī to receive their alms in sequential order have by now returned to Prince Jetri's Grove, and they are eating their meal with their fingers.[13] I have finished my meal, but consider the monks: can all of them be full when only one person has eaten?"

Ānanda answered, "No, World-Honored One. Why not? These monks are all Arhats, but their physical bodies, their own separate lives, are distinct. How could one person cause everyone to be full?"

The Buddha said to Ānanda, "Then if your mind that sees, is aware, discerns, and knows really were outside your body, your body and mind would be separate and unrelated to each other. The body would not be aware of what the mind has knowledge of, and the mind would have no knowledge of what the body is aware of. Now as I hold up my hand, which is as soft as cotton, does your mind distinguish it when your eyes see it?"

Ānanda said, "It does, World-Honored One."

The Buddha told Ānanda, "Then if your mind and eyes work together to perceive my hand, how can the mind be outside? In this way you can know that when you say the mind that is aware and makes distinctions is outside the body, you state what is impossible."

The Buddha shows that if the mind which is aware, knows, and makes distinctions were outside the body, then there would be no connection between them. . . . The body would not be aware of the mind or be influenced by it. If

[12] Here Ānanda offers a second proposition and he brings forth his own instance, which is, however, very similar to the one the Buddha proposed above. Ānanda has merely substituted the lamp and its light for himself and his vision. The Buddha refutes this second proposition in two steps: the first, by showing that Ānanda's example is logically flawed because it cannot be correctly applied to his proposition; the second, by offering the counter-example of the physical separateness of the monks seated at their meal.

[13] A traditional manner of eating in India.

your awareness were in your body, your mind would not have an awareness of it. . . . But if your mind knows what your eyes are seeing, how can you say that your mind is outside your body? . . . Note, though, that the Buddha does not say that the mind is inside the body. He has already made clear that that, too, is a mistake. . . . Ānanda only knows how to analyze the Buddha's teachings by means of his conscious mind, which comes into being and ceases to be. He is not aware of his everlasting true mind. (I, 179–81)

C. Ānanda Proposes That the Mind Is in the Eye-Faculty

Ānanda said to the Buddha, "World-Honored One, it is as the Buddha has said. Because I do not see inside my body, my mind is not located there, and because the body and the mind work together and are not separate from each other, my mind is not outside my body either. Now that I think of it, I know just where the mind is."

The Buddha said, "Where is it, then?"

Ānanda said, "Because the mind that discerns and is aware knows nothing of what is inside but can see what is outside, I believe, upon reflection, that the mind is hidden in the eyes. For instance, let us say that someone places transparent crystal cups over his eyes. Although the crystal cups cover his eyes, they will not obstruct his vision. In this way his eyes can see, and discernments are made accordingly. And so my mind that is aware and knows does not see inside because it is in the eye-faculty. It gazes at what is outside the body, seeing clearly and without impediment, for the same reason: the mind is hidden in the eyes."

Ānanda says, "I believe" and "upon reflection." It's still his ordinary mind at work. We reflect and consider with the ordinary mind, the mind that comes into being and ceases to be.

Ānanda does not yet understand what the Buddha is driving at. In general, people can't expect to understand the Śūraṅgama Sūtra having studied it only this far. You have to study the entire Sutra; then you will come to understand it. . . . There's no sense in saying to yourself, "I don't understand this Sutra, so I'm not going to study it." It's precisely because you don't understand it yet that you should study it. (I, 183)

The Buddha said to Ānanda, "Let us assume the mind is hidden in the eyes, as you assert in your instance of the crystals. When the person in your example places crystal cups over his eyes and looks at the mountains, the rivers, and all else on this great earth, does he see the crystal cups too?"

"He does, World Honored One. He sees the crystal cups when he places them over his eyes."

The Buddha said to Ānanda, "If in fact your mind can be compared to someone's eyes with crystals placed over them, then when you look at the world of perceived objects, why don't you see your own eyes? If you could see your eyes, your eyes would be part of your external surroundings. But then your mind and eyes could not work together to make distinctions. And since you cannot see your eyes, why did you say that the mind that is aware and makes distinctions is concealed within the eye-faculty, as in the example of the eyes with crystal cups placed on them? Know then that when you say the mind that is aware and makes distinctions is concealed in the eye-faculty, like eyes with crystal cups placed on them, you state what is impossible."

> The Buddha points out that if Ānanda could see his eyes, that would mean that his eyes would be outside of him, not part of his body. But if they were outside of his body, he would not be able to see, because the eyes need to be connected to the mind to complete the process of seeing. (I, 187)

D. Ānanda Reconsiders Seeing Inside and Seeing Outside

Ānanda said to the Buddha, "World-Honored One, I now offer this reconsideration. Our viscera are located inside our bodies, while our orifices are open to the outside. Our viscera lie concealed in darkness, but at the orifices there is light. Now, facing the Buddha, with my eyes open, I see light. Seeing that light I would call 'seeing outside.' Seeing darkness when I close my eyes I would call 'seeing inside.' How does that idea sound?"[14]

[14] Ānanda now proposes, in his fourth supposition, that what is dark is inside and what is light is outside, so that he can return to his first supposition, that the mind is located

Ānanda is more intelligent than we are. We couldn't think of so many ways to answer. How many options has he come up with already? He has one opinion after another. Whatever the Buddha asks, he has an answer. He's always got something to say; he's full of theories and arguments and thoughts and considerations. He was, after all, foremost among the disciples in learning. (I, 189)

The Buddha said to Ānanda, "Consider this question, then: when you close your eyes and see darkness, is that darkness in front of your eyes? If the darkness is in front of your eyes, how can it be inside? But if in fact it were inside, then if you were in a room that was completely dark because it was not lit by the sun or by the moon or by lamps, the darkness in the room would have to be the darkness of your own insides. Besides, if the darkness were not in front of you, how could you see it?[15] But suppose you did see inside in a way that is distinct from how you see outside. In that case — if we grant that closing your eyes and thus seeing darkness would be to see the inside of your body — then when you open your eyes and see light, why don't you see your own face? Since you can't see your own face, there can be no seeing inside, because if you could see your face, then your eyes and also your mind that knows and understands would be suspended in the air. How then could they be part of your body?[16]

---

inside the body. If the inside of the body is dark, the Buddha's objection that the mind should see the internal organs first is removed.

[15] The Buddha demolishes Ānanda's new position in two stages. He first analyzes the darkness that is seen when the eyes are closed. According to the Buddhist understanding of perception, what we see, including the darkness we see when our eyes are closed, must be before the eye-faculty in order for the eye-faculty to perceive it, and therefore it must be outside the body, not inside it. Then, taking up the case of the darkness that we see when our eyes are open, such as in a room that is completely dark, the Buddha points out that if darkness is internal, as Ānanda contends, then everything in a pitch-dark external environment must be inside of our bodies.

[16] If one sees internal darkness and external light, then although the face cannot be seen as part of the illuminated external world, it ought to be seen as an illuminated internal opposite. Or to put it the other way around, when one opens one's eyes and sees the illuminated external environment, one can't turn one's vision around to see one's face; why then should we suppose that when one's eyes are closed, one can turn one's vision around to see the darkness inside one's body? If one's own face could be seen — if it had become part of the normally seen external environment — it would have to be external to

The Buddha continues his questioning. . . . Ānanda argues that to see darkness is to see inside the body; then when one opens one's eyes to look outside, one ought to be able to see one's own face. . . . But if one can't see one's own face with one's eyes open, how could it be that upon closing one's eyes, one would see inside? What Ānanda has contended has no basis in fact. (I, 191)

"If your eyes and mind were actually suspended in the air, then it would follow that they would not be part of your body. If, however, they were part of your body and yet they were suspended in the air, then the Buddha, who now sees your face, would be part of your body as well. Thus, when your eyes became aware of something, your own body would be unaware of it. If you press the point and say the body and the eyes each have a separate awareness, then you would have two awarenesses so that you, one person, would eventually become two Buddhas. Therefore, you should know that when you say that to see darkness is to see inside, you state what is impossible."[17]

E. Ānanda Proposes That the Mind Comes into Being in Response to Conditions

Ānanda said to the Buddha, "I have heard the Buddha teach the four assemblies[18] that because a state of mind arises, various perceived objects

---

one's eyes and mind. Since the face is part of the body, the eyes and mind would then have to float in empty space, external to the body. The Buddha continues to explain to Ānanda that if his eyes and mind are not part of his body, then his body must be an external object like any other. Or vice versa: if Ānanda's mind and eyes are part of his body after all, despite their being suspended in space, then other people's minds and eyes, which are also external to Ānanda's body, should also be part of his body. Therefore, the Buddha concludes that it should be the case that "the Buddha, who now sees your face, would be part of your body as well."

[17] In the second part of his refutation the Buddha shifts his focus from what is seen to the one who sees. He points out that if the eyes and mind are separate from the body, then if awareness is located in the eyes and mind, the body is left without awareness. If both nevertheless have their own separate awareness, and accordingly two different stores of knowledge, then two different sets of consciousness are involved, and therefore two different people. Therefore, the Buddha concludes that "you, one person, would eventually become two Buddhas."

[18] That is, monks, nuns, laymen, and laywomen.

arise, and that because perceived objects arise, various states of mind arise. I am now thinking, and that very act of thinking, which is an instance of a state of mind arising in response to perceived objects, is my mind's true nature. Thus the mind comes into being by combining with perceived objects wherever they arise. It does not exist in just one of the three locations — inside, outside, and the middle."

Then the Buddha said to Ānanda, "Now you are saying that when perceived objects arise, various states of mind arise, and therefore that the mind comes into being by combining with those perceived objects wherever they arise. But such a mind as this would have no essential nature of its own, and so could not combine with anything. If, having no essential nature of its own, it still were able to combine with perceived objects, then there would be a nineteenth constituent element of perception, because such a mind would be combining with a seventh category of perceived object — and that is impossible.[19]

The Buddha refutes Ānanda's new proposition as follows. If the mind had location but no essential nature, it would lie outside of the eighteen constituent elements of perception. The eighteen constituents are the six perceptual faculties, the six kinds of perceived objects corresponding to the perceptual faculties, and the six consciousnesses.[20] . . .The Buddha points out that the logical extension of Ānanda's argument is that there is a nineteenth constituent, the place in which a supposedly insubstantial mind comes into being when it "combines with perceived objects." The objects the mind would combine with

[19] The Buddha discusses the ramifications of Ānanda's new proposition in terms of the essential nature and location of the mind. First, if the mind has no essential nature of its own, it either lacks a location or has a location. Second, if the mind indeed has no essential nature, then (a) to be in accord with conditions it must have a definite locus as it moves from one set of conditions to the next, and (b) it must be composed either of a single essential nature which pervades the body or of multiple essential natures. If the mind has no essential nature of its own, it makes no sense to talk about its uniting with something else. Were it to have a location without an essential nature, it would not be located within any of the eighteen constituent elements (Skt. *dhātu*, Ch. *jie* 界), which contradicts fundamental tenets of the Buddhist teaching.

[20] Contact between faculty and object is a necessary but not sufficient condition for the arising of one of the six consciousnesses.

would constitute a seventh category of perceived object. But there is no such category of object. (I, 195–6)

"Furthermore, if such a mind did have an essential nature of its own, then if you were to pinch yourself, where would your mind that has awareness of the pinch be coming from? Would it be coming forth from the inside of your body, or would it be coming in from outside? If it came out from inside, then once again, you would see the inside of your body. If it came in from outside, it would see your face first."[21]

Ānanda said, "It is the eyes that see. It is the mind, and not the eyes, that is aware. To suppose that the mind sees is not my idea."

The Buddha said, "If the eyes could see, then by analogy, when you were in a room, it would be the doorway, not you, that would see what is outside the room. Not only that: when someone has died with his eyes still intact, his eyes would see. But how could a dead person see?

"Ānanda, if your mind which is aware and knows and makes distinctions indeed has an essential nature of its own, then would it have a single essential nature or multiple essential natures? Would this essential nature pervade your body or wouldn't it? Suppose it were a single essential nature: then if you were to pinch one limb, wouldn't you feel that pinch in all four limbs? If you did, the feeling of the pinch would not be confined to one place. And if the feeling of the pinch were confined to one place, it would follow that your mind cannot have only one essential nature. But if your mind had multiple essential natures, you would be many people. Which of those essential natures would you be? Furthermore, if a single essential nature did pervade your body, then a single pinch — as in the previous instance — would be felt throughout your body. But if this mental essence does not pervade your body, then if

[21] By referring to the instance of someone pinching himself, the Buddha further shows that it is not logical to suppose that the mind has an essential nature and yet has no definite location. According to Ānanda's idea, the mind cannot exist until the necessary conditions arise. A pinch is located on the boundary between internal and external; therefore, before the mind can come into existence at the location of the pinch, the essential nature of the mind must be located either inside or outside the body — alternate possibilities that have already been refuted.

you touched your head and touched your foot at the same moment, you would feel the touch on your head but would not feel the touch on your foot. Yet that is not what your experience is.[22]

"Therefore, you should know that when you say the mind comes into being by combining with perceived objects wherever they arise, you state what is impossible."

F. Ānanda Proposes That the Mind Is in the Middle

Ānanda said to the Buddha, "World-Honored One, I have also listened when the Buddha was discussing true reality[23] with Mañjuśrī and other disciples of the Dharma-King. The World-Honored One then said that the mind is neither inside the body nor outside of it. And so I am now thinking that if the mind were inside, it would not see anything, and if it were outside, its awareness would be separate from the body. But since the mind is not aware of what is inside,[24] it cannot be inside; and since the awareness of the mind is not separate from the body, it makes no sense to say the mind is outside. Therefore, since the mind's awareness and the body's awareness are not separate, and since the mind does not see what is inside, the mind must be in the middle."

The Buddha replied, "You say that it is in the middle. A middle must be in some certain place. Propose a middle. Where is this 'middle' of yours?

---

[22] The Buddha asserts that if the mind is composed of a single essential nature which pervades the body, then the pinch should be discerned not only at its actual location but wherever the mind extends (i.e., over the entire body). On the other hand, if the mind is composed of more than one essential nature, then Ānanda would have to be two people, as the Buddha has just demonstrated in refuting Ānanda's fifth supposition. Were the mind to have a single essential nature that nevertheless did not pervade the body, then when one touched one's head and foot at the same time, one could not be aware of both at the same time.

[23] Ch. *shi xiang* 實相. The Sanskrit equivalent for this term is uncertain, perhaps *dharmatā* or *bhūtatathatā*. Numerous equivalents to this central concept are given in the text, including "true mind," "suchness of reality," "Matrix of the Thus-Come Ones," "Dharma-body," "Buddha-nature," "enlightened nature," and others.

[24] Ānanda is not saying that we cannot be aware of any internal sensations but that, in the case of seeing, which is being discussed, the mind has no visual data about the inside of the body to make distinctions about.

Is it outside the body or inside it? If your 'middle' were inside the body, it might exist at the surface of the body or else somewhere within it. If it existed at the surface, it would not be in the middle, and to be within it would be the same as to be inside it. Does this 'middle' have a location, then? If so, is there some indication of that location? If there were no indication of its location, then the middle would not exist. And even if there were some indication of its location, that location would be indefinite. Why? Suppose that someone were to place a marker to indicate the location of a middle. Seen from the east, it would be in the west; seen from the south, it would lie to the north. Such a marker would not mark a definite middle, and in the same way, it is unclear what it might mean for the mind to be located in a 'middle.'"

Ānanda said, "The middle I speak of is in neither of those places. For seeing to occur — as the World-Honored One has said — the eyes and visible objects are necessary conditions. The eyes record visual distinctions; the objects that are seen have no awareness. Between them, eye-consciousness is produced. The mind is there."[25]

The Buddha said, "If your mind were located between the eye-faculty and the objects it perceives, would the mind's essential nature be the same as the essential natures of the eye-faculty and of its objects, or would it not? If the mind's essential nature were the same as the essential natures of the eye-faculty and of its objects, it would be a confused combination of what is aware and what is not aware. That is contradictory. Where would this 'middle' be, then? And even if the mind's essential nature were not the same as the essential natures either of the eye-faculty or of its objects, then the mind would be neither aware nor unaware. Such a mind would have no essential nature at all. How then could it be in the middle?[26]

---

[25] In order to clarify his statement in this sixth supposition, Ānanda says that by "middle" he means between the faculty and its perceived object. He argues that since the Buddha taught that contact between faculty and perceived object is a necessary precondition of the arising of consciousness, then consciousness must arise in the "middle," between the two, and must constitute the location of the mind.

[26] The Buddha refutes Ānanda's argument by considering whether the mind's essential nature includes the essential nature of the eye-faculty and the essential natures of the

Therefore, you should know that it would be impossible for the mind to be in the middle."

G. Ānanda Proposes That the Mind Has No Specific Location

Ānanda said to the Buddha, "World-Honored One, when, along with Mahā-Maudgalyāyana, Subhūti, Pūrṇamaitrāyaṇīputra, and Śāriputra — four of the great disciples — I have listened to the Buddha as he turned the Wheel of Dharma, I have often heard him say that the mind that is aware and makes distinctions is not located inside or outside or in the middle; it is not located in any one of those places. That which has no specific location must be what is called the mind. Can what has no specific location be called my mind?"

> The aware, perceiving mind is not located anywhere at all. . . . Basically, Ānanda's view here would be acceptable from the point of view of ordinary people. But the mind the Buddha is speaking of is not the ordinary conscious mind. It is the everlasting true mind, not the mind of deluded mental process-es. Yet Ānanda still thinks his deluded mind is his true mind; he has mistaken a burglar for his child. (I, 208)

The Buddha said to Ānanda, "You say the mind that is aware and makes distinctions is not located in a specific place. However, the air, the lands, the waters, and the creatures that fly over them or move on them or in them — all things, in fact, existing in the world — do have specific locations.

"Then does the mind that you suppose has no specific location exist in some place, or else does it exist in no place? If it is located nowhere, then it is an absurdity — like a turtle with fur or a hare with horns. How can you speak of something that does not have a specific location? Suppose, how-ever, things could in fact exist without a definite location. Now, what does

visible objects that are perceived by it. Here the Buddha returns to an argument similar to one he made in response to Ānanda's fourth supposition, namely, that it would be impossible for the mind to consist of two different essential natures that are aware. But in the present case, one entity, the eye-faculty, is aware, and the other, the visual object, is not. If the mind includes both, then we are left with "a confused combination of what is aware and what is not aware."

not exist lacks attributes. What does exist has attributes. And whatever has attributes does have a location. How can you say then that the mind has no specific location?[27] Therefore, you should know that when you say the mind which knows and is aware has no specific location, you state what is impossible."

---

[27] The Buddha shows Ānanda that if having no specific location is an attribute of something that really exists, then by definition it must have a specific location, and that is contradictory. Therefore, nonattachment implies that something exists and has characteristics and therefore location. Having a definite location is a form of attachment, and so Ānanda's argument collapses.

3
The Conditioned Mind and the True Mind

Then Ānanda stood up in the midst of the great assembly. He uncovered his right shoulder, placed his right knee on the ground, put his palms together respectfully, and said to the Buddha, "The Buddha has bestowed his loving-kindness on me as his youngest cousin, but now that I have entered the monastic life, I have continued to presume upon his kindness, and as a result, all I have done is to become learned, and so I am not yet free of outflows.

> According to the customs of India, uncovering the right shoulder is a gesture of respect, especially in the Buddhist tradition. It represents the purification of the karma of the body. Putting the palms together represents the purification of the karma of the mind, and speaking to the Buddha represents the purification of the karma of speech. (I, 211–2)

"Since I could not resist the Kapila spell, I was lured into a house of courtesans, all because I did not know how to find the realm of true reality.[28] I only hope that the World-Honored One, out of pity and great kindness, will instruct us in the path of calming the mind, will guide people who have no trust in the Dharma,[29] and will counteract the wrong tendencies of the uncivilized."[30] When he had finished speaking, Ānanda bowed to the ground and, with the rest of the great assembly, prepared himself with keen anticipation to listen reverently to the teaching.

At that time, an array of lights as dazzling and as brilliant as a hundred thousand suns poured forth from the World-Honored One's face. Six kinds of quaking shook the lands of the Thus-Come Ones, and an infinite number of worlds appeared throughout all ten directions all at the same time. The Buddha's awe-inspiring spiritual power caused all these worlds to merge into a single world, and in that world, all the great Bodhisattvas

---

[28] Ch. *zhen ji* 真際, probable Skt. *bhūta-koṭi*.
[29] Skt. *icchantika*.
[30] Skt. *mleccha*.

— while remaining in their own lands — placed their palms together and listened.

Earthquakes occurred in their six aspects in all the billions of worlds in which there were Buddhas — not only in our Sahā world,[31] but all the others. Three of these aspects involve movement: quaking, erupting, and upward heaving. "Quaking" is the motion of the earth during an earthquake. "Erupting" refers to intermittent agitations which cause lava to little by little seep forth like water from a fountain. "Heaving upward" refers to continual, violent upward movements of the earth. . . . At present our planet earth is in the midst of changes brought about by the six aspects of earthquakes. The other aspects of earthquakes — cracking, roaring, and striking — involve sound. When there is cracking, whole sections of the earth are torn asunder. The earth splits apart and often rends whole buildings in the process. Roaring occurs when the earth emits strange sounds. Striking occur after the ground has split apart and the two faces of the crevasse strike against one another. (I, 218–9)

The Buddha used his awe-inspiring spiritual power to bring all the lands together into one. . . . Nowadays we can greatly enlarge a very small photograph and reduce a large photograph into a very small one. . . . In the same way, the Buddha, by means of his spiritual power, made distant places close, brought all the myriad lands throughout the universe into one, as if he were reducing a photograph. And yet, though the lands were united into one, each remained located in its respective position without being mixed up. . . . The Buddha brought these lands together so that everyone, including Bodhisattvas in every land, could listen as he spoke about the Great Śūraṅgama Samādhi. (I, 220–1)

The Buddha said to Ānanda, "Since time without beginning, all beings, because of the many distortions in their minds, have been creating seeds of karma, which then grow and ripen naturally, like a cluster of fruit on a *rūkṣa* tree.[32]

---

[31] In Buddhist cosmology, the Sahā world is the world-system we inhabit. The name is interpreted as "what must be borne."

[32] Ch. *e cha* 惡叉, *elaeocarpus ganitrus.* The berry-like fruit grows in tight clusters of three. The round seeds are used for recitation beads.

The rūkṣa represents delusion, intentional action, and the consequences of action, which are interconnected as if they were joined on a single stem. You can't say which precedes the other; they follow after one another in a continuing cycle, life after life, eon after eon. When would you say it all began? It has no beginning. It's an endless cycle as one is bound to the cycle of death and rebirth in the six destinies.[33] Each of us born here in the world is like a fine mote of dust which suddenly rises high and suddenly falls low. When your actions are meritorious, you are born higher. When you commit offenses, you fall. Therefore, we people should only do things that are good. Don't commit offenses, because the world runs on the principle of cause and effect, the principle of karma. The seeds of karma develop of their own accord, bringing you the appropriate consequences of whatever you have done, for good or for evil. (I, 225)

"People who undertake a spiritual practice but who fail to realize the ultimate enlightenment — people such as the Hearers of the Teaching[34] and the Solitary Sages, as well as celestial beings and others, such as demon-kings and members of the demons' retinues, who follow wrong paths[35] — all fail because they do not understand two fundamentals and are mistaken and confused in their practice. They are like someone who cooks sand, hoping to prepare a delicious meal. Even if the sand were cooked for eons[36] numberless as motes of dust, no meal would result from it.

People are born in a stupor and die in the midst of a dream. . . . With nothing to do, they go looking for something to do. They fail to recognize their pure and fundamental nature and devote themselves to deluded thinking instead. . . . They divide experiences into good and bad, right and wrong. . . . But in the Matrix

---

[33] That is, beings in the heavens, humans, asuras (beings addicted to anger and violence), animals, ghosts, and beings in the hells. See part 9, in which a seventh destiny, the ascetic masters, is listed as well. Which destiny beings are born into depends upon the karma they have created in previous lives.

[34] Skt. śrāvakas, Ch. sheng wen 聲聞, that is, practitioners who have become Arhats through hearing the Buddha teach.

[35] Ch. wai dao 外道.

[36] Skt. kalpa, Ch. jie 劫.

of the Thus-Come One[37] there are no such distinctions. In the Matrix of the Thus-Come One there isn't anything at all. It is absolutely pure. Our eyes may see the world of perceived objects, but they are simply manifestations of consciousness. When you really understand the truth that there isn't anything that comes into being and ceases to be, then you will understand that basically there isn't anything at all. But this principle is not easy to comprehend. We must come to understand its meaning gradually. (I, 224–5)

"Ānanda, what are the two fundamentals? The first is the mind that is the basis of death and rebirth and that has continued since time without beginning. This mind is dependent on perceived objects,[38] and it is this mind that you and all beings make use of and that each of you consider to be your own nature.

"The second fundamental is full awakening, which also has no beginning; it is the original and pure essence of nirvana.[39] It is the original understanding,[40] the real nature of consciousness. All conditioned phenomena arise from it, and yet it is among those phenomena that beings lose track of it. They have lost track of this fundamental understanding though it is active in them all day long, and because they remain unaware of it, they make the mistake of entering the various destinies.

"Ānanda, because you now wish to know about the path of calming the mind and wish to be subject to death and rebirth no longer, I will question you again." Then the Thus-Come One raised his golden-hued arm and bent his five fingers — each of them marked with lines in the shape of a wheel[41] — and he asked Ānanda, "Did you see something?"

Ānanda said, "I did."

---

[37] The Buddha's Dharma-body, which is immanent in all things. See part 3.

[38] Ch. pan yuan 攀緣.

[39] "Nirvana" here does not signify the passing of the Buddha into a state of cessation after the death of his body; it means simply the state of the enlightened mind.

[40] "Understanding" here and elsewhere renders the Ch. ming 明, which also carries the meaning of "light" and, at the esoteric level, the meaning of "illumination" as experienced in enlightenment.

[41] Lines in the shape of wheels on the pads of the fingers are among the thirty-two hallmarks that characterize the body of a Buddha.

The Buddha said, "What did you see?"

Ānanda said, "I saw the Thus-Come One raise his arm and bend his fingers into a fist that sends forth light, dazzling my mind and eyes."

> Why did the Buddha ask about such a simple matter? You may see it as simple now, but actually it is not. The more the Buddha's question is examined as the text continues, the deeper and more wonderful it becomes. It is just in the course of ordinary everyday matters that you can become fully aware of the Buddha that is inherent in you. The familiar places you come in contact with every day are the representations of the Buddha-nature. But you need to know that through your own experience; otherwise what is wrong seems right to you, and what is right seems wrong, and what is not lost seems lost. In fact, you haven't lost your Buddha-nature, but it seems lost to you. . . . Since time without beginning, the root of death and rebirth, which is the mind that is dependent on conditioned phenomena, has been too strong. If that mind were to disappear, you would become aware of your Buddha-nature in an instant. (I, 241–2)

The Buddha said, "When you saw my fist emit light, what did you see it with?"

Ānanda said, "All of us in the great assembly saw it with our eyes."

The Buddha said to Ānanda, "You have answered that the Thus-Come One bent his fingers into a fist that sent forth light, dazzling your mind and eyes. Your eyes can see my fist, but what do you take to be your mind that was dazzled by it?"

Ānanda said, "The Thus-Come One has just now been asking me about my mind's location, and my mind is what I have been using to determine where it might be. My mind is that which has the capability of making such determinations."

The Buddha exclaimed, "Ānanda! That is not your mind!"

Startled, Ānanda stood up, placed his palms together, and said to the Buddha, "If that is not my mind, what is it?"

The Buddha said to Ānanda, "It is merely your mental processes that assign false and illusory attributes to the world of perceived objects.[42]

---

[42] That is, the internal and external objects of awareness.

These processes delude you about your true nature and have caused you, since time without beginning and in your present life, to mistake a burglar for your own child — to lose touch with your own original, everlasting mind — and thus you are bound to the cycle of death and rebirth."

Ānanda said to the Buddha, "World-Honored One, I am the Buddha's favorite cousin. It was my mind that loved the Buddha and led me to enter the monastic life. That mind of mine has been responsible not only for my serving the Thus-Come One but also for my serving all Buddhas and all good and wise teachers throughout as many lands as there are sandgrains in the River Ganges. It has always been that mind that has marshaled great courage to practice every difficult aspect of the Dharma. If I were ever to slander the Dharma and forsake forever my good roots in it, that mind of mine would be the cause even of that. If this activity of comprehending is not the mind, then I have no mind, and I am the same as a clod of earth or a piece of wood, because nothing exists apart from my mind's awareness and its knowledge. Why does the Thus-Come One say that this is not my mind? Now I am genuinely alarmed and frightened; neither I nor anyone else here in the great assembly is free of doubt. I only hope that the Thus-Come One, with great compassion for us, will instruct all those among us who are not yet awake."

> Ānanda says that everyone who was also listening to his dialogue with the Buddha had doubts about what they had just heard, but in fact that too was a deduction Ānanda made with his conscious mind. . . . He didn't realize that the great Bodhisattvas who were present had already understood, although they hadn't said anything. (I, 251)

Then to Ānanda and the others in the great assembly the World-Honored One gave instruction in gaining patience with the state of mind in which no mental objects arise.[43]

> Before you understand, you think: "Oh no, nothing comes into being or ceases to be, and all the myriad mental objects vanish!" A fear arises in your heart;

---

[43] Skt. *anutpattikadharmakṣānti*, Ch. *wu sheng fa ren* 無生法忍.

you can't bear the idea of it. But if you actually experience the state of mind in which nothing comes into being or ceases to be, it will not seem at all un-usual, and you will be able to bear it because you will have gained patience with the state of mind in which no mental objects arise. . . . A special experi-ence occurs when you are about to become enlightened. When the special experience happens, the only thing you can do is cherish it in your heart. You yourself know, but you cannot tell people about it. It is inexpressible. That is patience with the state of mind in which no mental objects arise. When you can see that the entire world of perceived objects is within your essential na-ture, that the three realms of existence are made from the mind alone — when you can see that the entire world of perceived objects is the mind only, that the myriad phenomena are consciousness only — then mental objects will no longer come into being or cease to be. (I, 253)

From the Lion's Seat he reached out and circled his hand on the crown of Ānanda's head, saying to him, "The Thus-Come One has often ex-plained that all phenomena that come into being are nothing more than manifestations of the mind. All things that are subject to the principle of cause and effect — from the largest world to the smallest mote of dust — come into being because of the mind. If we examine the fundamental nature of each thing in the world, Ānanda, down to even the smallest wisps of grass, we will see that all have reality. Even space has a name and attributes. Given that, how could the clear wondrous, pure mind — the mind that truly understands and is the basic nature of all mental states — itself lack reality?

"But if, as you insist, that which makes distinctions and is aware of them, which knows and understands them is indeed the mind, then that mind would necessarily have its own essential nature independent of its involvement with objects — with visible objects, sounds, odors, flavors, and objects of touch. Yet now, as you listen to my Dharma, it is due to sounds that you can distinguish my meaning. Even if you were to with-draw into a state of quietude in which all seeing, hearing, awareness of tastes, and tactile awareness ceased, you still would be making distinc-tions among the shadowy objects of cognition in your mind.

In that kind of state you would still be making distinctions among the objects
of your mental awareness. A state of quietude is still just a function of the sixth
consciousness, the mind-consciousness. . . . Dreaming, for example, is a function of the mind-consciousness, as are psychotic states and also our ordinary
state of scattered thoughts and discriminations. A state of quietude, which the
Buddha mentions here, is another example. The first five consciousnesses
have ceased functioning, yet you still have thoughts. . . . You feel that what is
going on is very fine; but from the point of view of the Buddhist teaching, you
haven't even taken the first step. Don't feel satisfied; instead, you should continue to make progress. If you stop at that place, it is easy to fall into a void . . .
which is of no benefit in developing your skill in meditation. (I, 257–8)

"I am not demanding that you just accept that this distinction-
making capacity is not the mind. But examine your mind in minute detail
to determine if a distinction-making capacity exists independent of its
perceived objects of awareness. That would truly be your mind. If, on the
other hand, your distinction-making capacity does not have an essential
nature apart from its perceived objects, then it too would be a perceived
object — a shadowy mental object. Perceived objects are not permanent,
and when that mind ceased to exist such that it had no more reality than
a turtle with fur or a hare with horns, then your Dharma-body would
cease to exist along with it. Then who would be left to practice and to perfect patience with the state of mind in which no mental objects arise?"

At that point Ānanda and the others in the great assembly were utterly dumbfounded. They had nothing to say.

The Buddha said to Ānanda, "The reason why so many practitioners
in the world do not succeed in putting an end to outflows and becoming
Arhats — though they may have passed through all nine of the successive
stages of samādhi[44] — is that they are attached to distorted mental processes that come into being and then cease to be, and they mistake these

---

[44] Ch. *jiu zhu xin,* 九住心. Müller lists them as follows: "1) The mind holds deep
concentration upon one object with ease (安住心); 2) The mind, supposed to be concentrated
upon one object, drifts to other objects; a reaction occurs, and the mind promptly switches
back to its chosen object (攝住心); 3) The mind, concentrating upon an object for the

processes for what is real. That is why, even though you have become quite learned, you have not become a sage."

When Ānanda had heard that, he again wept sorrowfully. He then bowed to the ground, knelt on both knees, placed his palms together, and said to the Buddha, "Ever since I followed the Buddha and resolved to enter the monastic life, I have relied on the Buddha's awe-inspiring spirit. I have often thought, 'There is no reason for me to toil at spiritual practice,' because I just expected that the Thus-Come One would graciously transfer some of his samādhi to me. I never realized that in fact he simply could not stand in for me, in body or in mind. Thus I abandoned my original resolve, and though my body has indeed entered the monastic life, my mind has not entered the Path. I am like that poor son who ran away from his father.[45] Today I realize that, though I am learned, I might as well not have learned anything if I do not practice, just as someone who only talks of food never gets full.

"World-Honored One, we all are bound by two obstructions, and as a consequence we are unaware of the mind that is everlasting and still.[46] I only hope the Thus-Come One will take pity on us who are destitute and homeless, will disclose the wondrous mind that truly understands, and will open our eyes to the Path."

purpose of grasping its nature by analysis, drifts to other objects; a reaction occurs, and the mind instantly returns to its work (解住心); 4) The mind ceases to grasp the nature of things by analysis. When this occurs, the mind has entered deep concentration (轉住心); 5) The mind, after prolonged meditation, experiences a feeling of fatigue; a reaction occurs, and immediately the mind is revitalized (伏住心); 6) The inner mind becomes agitated, whereupon a reaction occurs, and the mind is quickly soothed (息住心); 7) When greed, desire, and attachment arise in the mind, a reaction occurs which eliminates them (滅住心); 8) When various temptations appear in the mind, distracting it, a reaction occurs, and the mind becomes cognizant that it is pure in nature. This realization enables the mind to function correctly again (性住心); 9) As the result of extended practice, the person is able to remain in meditation. The person is therefore in a blissful condition, which enables him to maintain virtue steadily and avoid falling into error (持住心)." Charles A. Müller, ed., *Digital Dictionary of Buddhism*, s.v. "Nine Stages of Meditation," www.buddhism-dict.net.

[45] A reference to the parable of the errant son in chapter four of the Lotus Sūtra.

[46] The two obstructions are the obstruction of affliction, which arises from attachment to self, and the obstruction of knowledge, which arises from attachment to phenomena and which leads to arrogance.

Then the Thus-Come One poured forth resplendent light from the symbol of purity[47] on his chest. The brilliant light, radiant with hundreds of thousands of colors, shone all throughout the ten directions simultaneously to illuminate Buddha-lands as many as motes of dust, and it shone upon the crowns of the heads of the Thus-Come Ones in every one of those radiant Buddha-lands. Then the light returned to shine upon the great assembly — upon Ānanda and all the others.

> Earlier in the Sutra the Buddha emitted light from his face — a blazing light as brilliant as a hundred thousand suns. That light represents the dispelling of delusions. Now he again emits light, this time from the symbol of purity on his chest. This light represents the disclosing of the true mind. (I, 268)

Thereupon the Buddha said to Ānanda, "I now will raise for all of you a great Dharma-banner so that all beings in all ten directions can gain access to what is wondrous, subtle, and hidden[48] — the pure and luminous mind that understands — and so that they can open their clear-seeing eyes."

---

[47] Skt. svastika. In contradistinction to its perverted use in the twentieth century, the svastika was in ancient India a symbol representing spiritual goodness and purity.

[48] A reference to the "Hidden Basis" in the Sutra's title.

II

The Nature of
Visual Awareness

1
It Is the Mind That Sees

"Ānanda, a moment ago you said you saw my fist send forth light. What caused my fist to send forth light? How did I make the fist? And what were you seeing it with?"

Ānanda replied, "The Buddha's body is the color of crimson-tinted gold from the River Jambu. His body is like a mountain of precious stones. It sends forth light because it is born of purity. With my own eyes I saw his hand when he held it up for us and made a fist by curling his wheel-imprinted fingers."[1]

The Buddha said to Ānanda, "Now the Thus-Come One will demonstrate a truth for you. Following the wise, who use analogies as aids to understanding, Ānanda, let us use my fist as an analogy. Without a hand, I couldn't make a fist. Without your eyes, would you be able to see? Are these two situations similar?"

Ānanda replied, "They are, World-Honored One, because without my eyes, I couldn't see. Therefore the Thus-Come One's making a fist can be compared to my using my eyes."

The Buddha said to Ānanda, "You say they are comparable; however, they are not. Why? A person with no hands will never make a fist. But one whose eyes do not function will not be entirely unable to see. Why? If you asked a blind man on the street, 'Do you see anything?' he would no doubt reply, 'All that I see in front of me is darkness — nothing more.' Reflect upon what that might mean. Although the blind man sees only darkness, his visual awareness is itself intact."

Ānanda replied, "It's true that all a blind man sees before his eyes is darkness, but can that really be what we call 'seeing'?"

The Buddha said to Ānanda, "Is there any difference between the darkness seen by the one who is blind and the darkness seen by sighted people when they are in a completely darkened room?"

---

[1] A lines on a Buddha's fingertips, his palms, and the soles of his feet form the shape of wheels.

"No, World-Honored One, there is no difference between the darkness seen by sighted people in a completely dark room and the darkness seen by the blind."

"Then suppose, Ānanda, that the blind person, who has been seeing only darkness, now sees before him a variety of objects because suddenly he has regained his sight. In such a case, you would say it is his eyes that see. Therefore, when a sighted person who has been seeing only darkness in the darkened room now sees before him a variety of objects because someone has suddenly lit a lamp, you'd have to say, by analogy, that it is the lamp that sees. Now if a lamp could see, it would no longer be what we would call a lamp. Moreover, if it were the lamp that sees, what would that have to do with that sighted person?

"Thus you should know that, in the analogy, the lamplight simply reveals visible objects; it is the eyes that see, not the lamp. In actuality, the eyes themselves simply reveal visible objects; it is the mind that sees, not the eyes."

2
Visual Awareness Does Not Move

Ānanda and the others in the great assembly had not understood what they had heard and so were silent. But they hoped that they would hear the Thus-Come One continue to proclaim the teaching. Putting their palms together, they cleared their minds and waited for the Buddha to compassionately instruct them.

> Why did they put their palms together? It represents their single-mindedness. They were of one mind, not two. When your hands are apart, it is said you have ten minds, and when your palms are together, it is said you have one mind, because when your palms come together, your mind also comes together and becomes one. (II, 9–10)

Then the World-Honored One stretched forth his arm and opened his shining, cotton-soft, finely webbed hand,[2] revealing the wheel-shaped lines on his fingers. To instruct Ānanda and the others in the great assembly, he said, "After my awakening, I went to the Deer Park, where, for Ājñātakauṇḍinya's sake and for the other four monks,[3] and also for all of you in the four assemblies, I said that beings in their multitudes have not become Arhats, nor have they become fully awake, because they are confused by afflictions that are like visitors and like dust. What in particular, at that time, caused the five of you to awaken and become sages?"

Then Ājñātakauṇḍinya stood up and said respectfully to the Buddha, "Of all the elders here in this great assembly, I was the one who was given the name 'Ajñāta,' meaning 'one who understands,' because I had come to realize what 'visitor' and 'dust' signify. It was in this way that I became a sage.

---

[2] Softness of the hands and fine webbing between the fingers are also among the thirty-two hallmarks that characterize of the body of a Buddha.

[3] The other four monks who were staying with Ājñātakauṇḍinya at the Deer Park were Aśvajit, Bhadrika, Daśabala-Kāśyapa, and Mahānāma. After becoming fully awakened, the Buddha went to the Deer Park, where he taught these five ascetics; they were awakened by his teaching and became his first disciples.

"World-Honored One, suppose a visitor stops at an inn for a night or for a meal. Once his stay is ended or the meal is finished, he packs his bags and goes on his way. He's not at leisure to remain. But if he were the innkeeper, he would not leave. By considering this example of the visitor, the one who comes and goes, and the innkeeper, the one who remains, I understood what the visitor signifies. He represents transience.

"Again, suppose the morning skies have cleared after a rain. Then a beam of pure light from the rising sun may shine through a crack in a door to reveal some motes of dust obscuring the air. The dust moves, but the air is still. Thus by consideration of this example — the dust, which as it moves obscures the air, and the air, which itself remains still — I understood what the dust may signify. It represents motion."

The Buddha said, "So it is."

When the sun has just come up, early on a clear fresh morning, a morning after rain, the sun shines though a crack in the door or perhaps a crack in the wall, and it displays the fine bits of dust bobbing up and down in space, moving all around in the sunshine. If the sun doesn't shine in the crack, you can't see the dust, although there is actually a lot of dust everywhere. But while the dust moves, bobbing up and down, space is still. It doesn't move. The ability to see the dust in the light that pours through the crack represents the attainment of the light of wisdom. When you reach the first stage of an Arhat and overcome the eighty-eight kinds of deluded awareness, you have the light of wisdom. Then you can see your ignorance, which moves like the dust in sunlight and which causes as many afflictions as there are sand-grains in the River Ganges. You will also see the unmoving stillness of your essential nature. (II, 17–8)

Thereupon the Thus-Come One, before the assembly, made a fist with his wheel-lined fingers, and having made the fist, he opened his hand again. Once his hand was open, he made the fist again and said to Ānanda, "What did you see just now?"

Ānanda said, "I saw the Thus-Come One, before the assembly, open and close his hand over his resplendent wheel-lined palm."

The Buddha said to Ānanda, "You saw me here before the assembly open and close my hand. Was it my hand that opened and closed, or did your visual awareness open and close?"

Ānanda said, "It was the World-Honored One's resplendent hand that opened and closed before the assembly. Although I saw his hand open and close, my visual awareness neither opened nor closed."

The Buddha said, "What moved and what was still?"

Ānanda said, "The Buddha's hand moved, but my awareness is beyond even stillness; how could it have moved?"

The Buddha replied, "So it is."

Then from his wheel-lined palm the Buddha sent forth a ray of resplendent light that flew past Ānanda to his right. Ānanda immediately turned his head and glanced to the right. Then the Buddha sent a ray of light to Ānanda's left. Ānanda turned his head again and glanced to the left. The Buddha said to Ānanda, "Why did you turn your head just now?"

Ānanda said, "I saw the Thus-Come One send forth a wondrous ray of shining light which flew past me on my right; then another ray flew past me on my left. My head moved as I looked to the right and to the left."

"Ānanda, when you glanced at the Buddha's light and moved your head to the right and left, was it in fact your head that moved, or else was it your visual awareness that moved?"

"World-Honored One, it was my head that moved. The nature of my visual awareness is beyond even stillness; how then could it have moved?"

The Buddha said, "So it is."

Stillness comes from movement. If there isn't any movement, then there isn't any stillness. So it is said that there is no emerging from the Great Śūraṅgama Samādhi and no entering it. That's the principle here. . . . Thus Ānanda said that his visual awareness, by which he sees the Buddha . . . is beyond the characteristics of movement and of stillness, its opposite. Without movement, there is no stillness; both are gone. They are fundamentally unattainable and nonexistent; they cannot be found. Then how could his awareness not be at rest? (II, 21–2)

Then the Thus-Come One told everyone in the assembly, "All beings need to understand that whatever moves is like the dust and, like a visitor, does not remain. Just now you saw that it was Ānanda's head that moved, while his visual awareness did not move. It was my hand that opened and closed, while his awareness did not open or close. How can you take what moves to be your body and its environment, since they come into being and perish in every successive thought? You have lost track of your true nature, and instead you act out of delusion. Therefore, because you have lost touch with your mind's true nature by identifying yourself with the objects you perceive, you keep on being bound to the cycle of death and rebirth."[4]

> Here the Buddha scolds the great assembly. He tells them that they are un-able to discern their own true awareness. They take their physical bodies and their bodies' environment to be real. . . . They cling tenaciously to the body and mind. . . . Yet every thought of the conscious mind is subject to coming into being and perishing. One thought arises and perishes, and then the next thought arises and perishes. . . . People concentrate their efforts exclusively on the realm of coming into being and perishing and have no real understand-ing of the true nature of their awareness. (II, 25–6)
>
> Because you conduct yourselves in confused ways, your true nature and your mind do not work together, and thus you lose track of your true nature. You mistake external states for your real selves. You take that inn of yours as your self. You shouldn't think of that inn as you. That would be to consider yourself a mere object. You create all kinds of attachments. You fail to see through things. You aren't clear about truth. And because of that, you cling to death and rebirth. If you weren't so confused, if you stopped mistaking a burglar for your own child by mistaking objects for yourself, you would be able to end death and rebirth.
>
> To end death and rebirth is easy. All you need to do is turn yourself around. If you go forward, you head right down the path of death and rebirth. If you turn around and go the other way, you end death and rebirth. It's not that dif-ficult, but it's up to you to do it. You simply turn around; you turn your head and pivot your body. That's all that's needed. It is said, "The sea of suffering is boundless; a turn of the head is the other shore." (II, 26–7)

[4] Skt. *saṃsāra,* the continuous undergoing of the suffering of repeated deaths and rebirths. It is contrasted with nirvana.

The Sutra says that the members of the assembly had renounced their fundamental minds and had relied only on their deluded minds, their conscious minds, their minds that make distinctions. They hadn't understood external states; they'd taken their distinction-making minds to be true and real. They had engaged in confused activities at the gates of the six faculties and hadn't the least bit of skill with regard to their true natures. . . . You need to understand that the mountains, the rivers, the vegetation, and all the rest of the myriad appearances on this earth are the Dharma-body of the Buddhas, which neither comes into being nor perishes. . . . You must recognize the pure, luminous essential nature of the everlasting true mind, and your mad distinction-making mind must cease. It is said, "The ceasing of the mad mind is full awakening." The mad mind's coming to a stop is the manifestation of our awakened mind. Because the mad mind exists and has not ceased, the awakened mind cannot come forth. The mad mind covers it over. The aim of this passage, and every other passage of the Sutra without exception, is to reveal everyone's true mind. (II, 29–30)

When Ānanda and the great assembly had heard the Buddha's teachings, their bodies and their minds were serene. They realized that since time without beginning they had strayed from the fundamental, true mind. Instead, they had been mistaken about the conditioned objects of perception and had made distinctions about what are in fact nothing but shadowy mental events.[5] Now they all had awakened, and each was like a lost infant suddenly reunited with its beloved mother. Putting their palms together, they bowed to the Buddha. They wished to hear the Thus-Come One reveal the contrasting qualities of body and mind — what is true and what is false about them, what is real and what is insubstantial, what comes into being and then ceases to be, and what neither comes into being nor perishes.

[5] That is, our experience of what seems to be an external world is in fact the experience of images produced in our minds.

3
Visual Awareness Does Not Perish

Then King Prasenajit stood up and said to the Buddha, "Before I was instructed by the Buddha, I met Kātyāyana and Vairāṭiputra.[6] Both of them said that after this body dies, we cease to exist and become nothing. That very nothingness itself is what they called nirvana. Now, though I have met the Buddha, I still have doubts that make me cautious. How can I come to realize the true and fundamental mind that neither comes into being nor perishes? All in this great assembly who have outflows wish to hear the answer."

The Buddha said to the king, "May I ask, is your body as indestructible as *vajra*,[7] or is it subject to decay?"

"World-Honored One, this body of mine will keep on changing till in the end it will perish."

The Buddha said, "Your Majesty, you have not perished yet. How is it that you know you will perish?"

"World-Honored One, my body is impermanent and subject to decay, although it has not perished yet. But now, upon reflection, I can see that each one of my thoughts just fades away, followed by a new thought which also does not last, like fire turning into ash, constantly dying away, forever perishing. By this I am convinced that my body, too, must perish."

The Buddha said, "So it is. Your Majesty, you are in your declining years. How do you look now, compared to when you were a boy?"

"World-Honored One, when I was a child, my skin was fresh and smooth, and I was full of vital energy when in my prime. But now in my later years, as old age presses upon me, my body has withered and is weary. My vital spirits are dulled, my hair is white, my skin is wrinkled. Not much time remains for me. How can all this compare to the prime of life?"

---

[6] Kātyāyana and Vairāṭiputra were contemporaries of the Buddha who taught forms of skepticism. This Kātyāyana is said to have been a fierce opponent of the Buddha; he is not to be confused with the Buddha's disciple Mahākātyāyana.

[7] A material of extreme hardness and durability.

The king has reached a point where his body no longer helps him out. His body is oppressive and nags at him to move somewhere else. It will soon be unlivable. (II, 36)

The Buddha said, "Your Majesty, your body's appearance cannot have deteriorated suddenly."

The king replied, "World-Honored One, the change has in fact been so subtle that I have hardly been aware of it. I've reached this point only gradually through the passing of the years. Thus when I was in my twenties, I was still young, but I already looked older than I did when I was ten. My thirties marked a further decline from my twenties, and now, at two years past sixty, I look back on my fifties as a time of strength and health.

"World-Honored One, as I observe these subtle transformations, I realize now that the changes wrought by this descent toward death are evident not only from decade to decade; they can also be discerned in smaller increments. Considering more closely, one can see that changes happen year by year as well as by the decade. In fact, how could they happen merely year by year? Such changes happen every month. And how could they occur from month to month only? These changes happen day by day. And if one contemplates this deeply, one can see that there is ceaseless change from moment to moment,[8] in each successive thought. Thus I can know that my body will keep on changing till it perishes."

The Buddha said to the king, "Observing these changes — these never-ceasing transformations — you know that you must perish. But do you also know that when you perish, something in you does not perish with you?"

Putting his palms together, King Prasenajit replied to the Buddha, "Indeed I do not know."

The Buddha said, "I now will reveal to you what it is that does not come into being and does not perish. Your Majesty, when you first saw the River Ganges, how old were you?"

---

[8] Skt. *kṣaṇa.*

The king replied, "I was three when my beloved mother took me to pay respects to the goddess Jīva.[9] When we went past a river, I knew that it was the Ganges."

The Buddha said, "Your Majesty, you said that when you were in your twenties, you had already aged compared to when you were ten. Year after year, month after month, day after day, in each successive thought there have been changes till you have reached your sixties. Consider, though: when you were three years old, you saw the river; ten years later, when you were thirteen, what was the river like?"

The king replied, "It looked the same when I was thirteen as it did when I was three, and even now, when I am sixty-two, it is still the same."

The Buddha said, "Now you are mournful that your hair is white and your face is wrinkled. Your face is certainly more wrinkled than it was when you were in your youth. But when you look at the Ganges, is your visual awareness any different from your visual awareness as it was when you saw the river in your boyhood?"

The king replied, "No different, World-Honored One."

The Buddha said, "Your Majesty, your face is wrinkled, but the essential nature of your visual awareness itself has not wrinkled. What wrinkles is subject to change. What does not wrinkle does not change. What changes will perish. But what does not change neither comes into being nor perishes. Then how could it be affected by your being born and dying? So you have no need to be concerned with what such people as Maskari Gośālīputra[10] say: that when this body dies, you cease to exist."

The king believed the words that he had heard, and he understood that when we leave this body, we go on to another. He and all the others in the great assembly were elated at having gained a new understanding.

---

[9] Skt. *jīva* means "the principle of life."

[10] The king mentioned above that the non-Buddhist teachers expressing this view were Kātyāyana and Vairāṭiputra. Here the Buddha mentions instead Maskāri Gośālīputra, presumably because Maskari was named first in a standard list of six major non-Buddhist teachers (Ch. *wai dao liu shi,* 外道六師) who were contemporaries of the Buddha.

4

The True Nature of
Visual Awareness Is Not Lost

Ānanda then stood up, bowed to the Buddha, knelt, put his palms together, and said to the Buddha, "World-Honored One, if our visual awareness and our awareness of sounds, too, indeed do not come into being and do not perish, why then did the World-Honored One say that we have lost track of our true nature and our actions are deluded — as if we were upside-down and not right-side-up? I hope the World-Honored One, out of kindness, will clear away the dust of our delusions."

At that time, bending his golden-hued arm so that his wheel-lined fingers pointed downward, the Thus-Come One said to Ānanda, "Here you see my hand as it forms a mudra.[11] Is it upside-down, or is it upright?"

Ānanda said, "Ordinary people would take it to be upside-down. I myself do not know what may be called upright and what is upside-down."

The Buddha said to Ānanda, "If ordinary people would take this to be upside-down, what then would people consider to be upright?"

Ānanda said, "They would call it upright if the Thus-Come One raised his arm so that his hand, which is a soft as cotton, was pointing upward in the air."

Then the Buddha raised his arm and said to Ānanda: "Ordinary people are deluded if they suppose that reversing the way my arm is pointing means that my arm itself has changed. And if, in the same way, we compare the bodies of ordinary people to the pure Dharma-body of the Thus-Come One,[12] we might describe the Dharma-body of the Thus-Come One as endowed with 'right and all-encompassing knowledge,'[13] and ordinary people's bodies as upside-down. But consider more carefully this

---

[11] A ritualized symbolic gesture, usually of one but sometimes of both of the hands, representing a particular aspect of the Buddha's teaching.

[12] The text here probably refers both to the body of the Buddha and to the Buddha's mind. The Dharma-body mentioned here is identical with the true mind of the Buddha.

[13] Ch. *zheng bian zhi* 正 偏 知, an honorific title of the Buddha.

comparison of the Buddha's body with your bodies, which are said to be upside-down. Where, exactly, might the characteristic 'upside-down' be found?"

At this point Ānanda and the others in the great assembly were dazed. They stared unblinking at the Buddha. They did not know where, in their minds and bodies, the characteristic "upside-down" might be.

The Buddha out of kindness took pity on Ānanda and on everyone else assembled there. He spoke to them in a voice that swept over them like the ocean-tide. "All you good people! I have often said that all phenomena with physical form,[14] all phenomena of mind,[15] the conditions under which they arise, as well as the phenomena that interact with the mind[16] and all other conditioned phenomena, are mere manifestations of true mind. Your bodies and your minds appear within the wondrous light of the true essence of that wondrous mind. How is it that you all have lost track of the wondrous nature of the fundamental, marvelously perfect, wondrously understanding and resplendent mind, so that your understanding of it is confused?

> Where do all phenomena come from — the mountains, the rivers, the vegeta-
> tion, and all the myriad things on this earth? They come forth from minds;
> all the myriad things are contained within the mind. It is not that these things
> contain the mind but rather the opposite: absolutely everything in the environ-
> ment, both natural and man-made, is contained in a single thought of the
> mind, and all are produced from the mind. If you recognize your original true
> mind, all these things cease to exist. . . . Then is there yet another mind above
> and beyond the conscious mind? No, but because people don't know how to
> use the wondrous mind, they think their conscious mind is their mind. Actu-

[14] The phrase "phenomena with physical form" refers to the perceived physical body and sights, sounds, odors, flavors, and tangible objects.

[15] "Phenomena of mind" refers to the various consciousnesses. In the Yogācāra teachings there are eight.

[16] In the Yogācāra teachings, there are fifty-one phenomena that interact with the mind, divided into six categories. See *Shastra on the Door to Understanding the Hundred Dharmas by Vasubandhu Bodhisattva, with Commentary of Tripitaka Master Hua* (Talmage, CA: International Institute for the Translation of Buddhist Texts, 1983).

ally, they are mistaking a burglar for their own child, and for that reason they become confused. . . . They think that they understand clearly about the wondrous nature of the fundamental, perfect, wondrously understanding mind, but they don't understand. They don't realize that they have a perfect, wondrously luminous mind, which is the precious light of our wondrous nature. They think the conscious mind they are aware of is their mind. But actually it is only confusion within confusion. (II, 51–2)

"Out of darkness, a mental void appears, and this dark void condenses to create a subtle object of mind.[17] What characterizes this distorting mental activity is that it leads to the coming into being of the embryonic body. An internal confluence of causes distorts this body and directs its attention outward. At this stage there is confused agitation, and we take this agitation to be the true nature of the mind. Once we take this initial confusion to be the mind, we are committed to the delusion that the mind is inside the physical body.

"What you do not know is that the true, wondrous, luminously understanding mind contains the body and everything outside the body — mountains, rivers, sky, the entire world. You are like someone who fails to see a boundless ocean a hundred thousand miles across and is aware only of a single floating bubble. You see that bubble floating there and think it is the vast tide that surges toward the farthest branchings of the sea. Within your confusion you are confused further, just as you were about my lowered arm. The Thus-Come One says you are to be pitied."

Most people think the mind is within the body. This is a great mistake. It is neither inside nor outside. It is not that our minds are within our bodies but that we are within the true mind. . . . Our mind encompasses empty space and the ten thousand things. It is not that empty space and the ten thousand things contain us. If you understand this doctrine, you have not lost track of your true mind. (II, 55)

[17] This very brief summary of how the world comes into being foreshadows a more detailed explanation given below in part 4.

5

Visual Awareness Is Not
Dependent upon Conditions

Clasping his hands, Ānanda wept, mindful that the Buddha had compassionately rescued him and had bestowed upon him a profound teaching. He said respectfully to the Buddha, "Having heard the Buddha speak these marvelous words, I comprehend that my wondrously understanding mind is perfect at its source and that it is the everlasting ground of my mind. I understand the Dharma that the Buddha has just spoken. I see that I have been revering the Buddha with my conditioned mind. But, because I have only just now learned about my wondrously understanding mind, I do not dare as yet to accept it as my mind's fundamental ground. May the Buddha in his all-pervading voice compassionately give further instruction about this in order to uproot my doubts and bring me back to the supreme Path!"

The Buddha said to Ānanda, "You and others like you still listen to the Dharma with conditioned minds, and therefore you fail to understand its real nature. Consider this example: suppose someone is pointing to the moon to show it to another person. That other person, guided by the pointing finger, should now look at the moon. But if he looks instead at the finger, taking it to be the moon, not only does he fail to see the moon, but he is mistaken, too, about the finger. He has confused the finger, with which someone is pointing to the moon, with the moon, which is being pointed to.

"Moreover, his mistake about the finger shows he has failed to distinguish light from dark, in that he has confused what is dark — the finger — with what is light — the moon. He does not know the difference between the nature of light and the nature of darkness. In this way, he is like you.

The moon represents the true mind. The Dharma which is spoken is the finger, since the Buddha speaks about the Dharma in order to point to the true mind. . . . The person in the example doesn't recognize either the finger or the moon for what they are, and so they seem lost, although they are still there.

He doesn't understand light and darkness; in other words, he doesn't know what is meant by "enlightenment" or what is meant by the "lack of enlightenment"; he doesn't know what is meant by "ignorance" and what is meant by "true understanding." . . . The Buddha speaks about the Dharma in order to point to the true mind, and it was Ānanda's mistake to suppose that the true mind was in the Dharma. The Buddha points that out to Ānanda by means of the example of the finger and the moon. (II, 61–3)

"If you understand your mind to be what makes distinctions when you hear me speak about the Dharma, then that mind of yours would necessarily exist on its own, apart from my speaking, which it is making distinctions about. By analogy, a traveler who stops at an inn may stay for a night; he then goes on his way. He does not live there all the time, unlike the innkeeper, who, as the host, does not go anywhere.

"In the same way, if what makes distinctions when you hear me speak were truly your mind, then it would not go anywhere. But could the nature of the mind be such that it makes distinctions about sound independently of sound? And the mind that makes distinctions about my voice also makes distinctions about my appearance. What makes distinctions about visible objects cannot do so independently of the visible objects it distinguishes. Your mind that makes distinctions does not exist independently of the objects that it distinguishes. And when the making of distinctions ceases such that neither space nor objects are distinguished — the state that Maskari Gośālīputra and the others wrongly call the 'truth of the unmanifested nature'[18] — even then, your mind does not have a distinction-making nature that exists independent of objects of mind. Thus each of your mental states is dependent on something else. They are not like the host of an inn."

Ānanda said, "If each of my mental states is dependent on something else, then is the fundamental, wondrously understanding mind of which the Thus-Come One speaks also dependent on something else? I only hope that the Buddha will take pity on us and explain."

[18] Skt. prakṛti. According to the Sāṅkhya school, which was founded by the sage Kapila, prakṛti was the origin of everything in the world that is not the cosmic person (Skt. puruṣa).

The Buddha said to Ānanda, "As you see me now, the fundamental, luminous essence of visual awareness is not the wondrous, essential, understanding mind; nevertheless, it can be compared to a second moon rather than to a reflection of the moon.[19]

"Listen attentively. I will now show you what does not depend on anything.

"This great lecture hall, Ānanda, opens to the east. Thus when the sun rises, the hall is flooded with light. But the hall is in darkness in the middle of the night if the moon has not risen or if the sky is obscured by clouds or fog. Further, one can see out through cracks in the doors and shutters, but the walls and roof block the view. Where the various objects are distinguished, we can perceive how they are related to one another, but where there are no objects, space is all that one sees. Where mists or clouds of dust are present, objects are obscured or distorted. Once the mist has dispersed or once the dust has settled so that the air is pure again, one can again see everything clearly.

"Ānanda, you have all observed how aspects of these phenomena will change. Now I will show you how the presence of each of them depends on a condition necessary to it. What are the conditions necessary to these changing phenomena, Ānanda? The sun is a necessary condition for sunlight, since there can be no sunlight without the sun. Therefore the sunlight is dependent upon the sun, which is a necessary condition for its presence. The moon's absence is a necessary condition for the darkness in the hall. Cracks in the doors and shutters are necessary conditions for your being able to see out. The walls and roof are necessary conditions for the view being blocked. Distinguishing the various objects is a necessary condition for observing how they are related to one another. The absence of objects is a necessary condition for seeing only space. Mists and clouds of dust are necessary conditions for obscuring or distorting our visual awareness of objects. Dispersal of the mist and the settling of the dust are

---

[19] The "essence of visual awareness" is the observing division of the eight consciousnesses, while the "wondrous, essential, understanding mind" is the true mind.

necessary conditions for seeing clearly again. And every act of seeing the changing phenomena of this world belongs to one of these types.

"Consider these eight types. What would you say is the necessary condition for the presence of the understanding nature that is the essence of your visual awareness? If the presence of light is a necessary condition for your visual awareness, then when light is absent so that it is completely dark, you would not be able to see the darkness which in fact you do see.[20] Your mind makes distinctions about light and darkness and the other phenomena, but the essence of your visual awareness does not make these distinctions. Clearly then, the mind that experiences these conditioned phenomena is not what is fundamentally you. But what is not these conditioned phenomena must be what is fundamentally you. If it is not you, what else could it be?

> Distinctions are being made when you perceive light and darkness, but not by your visual awareness; rather, they are made by your distinction-making mind that responds to circumstances. Don't take that to be the essential nature of your awareness. Your knowledge of light and dark is an activity of your mind. Your visual awareness sees everything impartially without making any distinction. The act of seeing is simply to see. . . . The distinctions you make are made by your distinction-making mind.
>
> This particular section of text explains these teachings extremely well in a few words. All transitory characteristics are dependent on something else. They are not part of you. What stays with you and does not go anywhere else, what is not dependent on anyone or anything else — if that is not you, who is it? . . . It is something you cannot give away. (II, 75)

"Know then that your mind is fundamentally wondrous, luminous, and pure. You have confused yourself and have lost track of what is fundamental. Constantly drifting and drowning, you have become submerged in the sea of death and rebirth. That is why the Thus-Come One says you are to be pitied."

---

[20] As the Buddha demonstrated in part 2.1 with the instance of the blind man in the street.

Our true mind is not dependent on anything, but we ourselves are confused. . . . It is something that belongs to us, but we don't realize that, so it seems to us that we have lost it. One who fails to understand the true mind will fall in life after life into the sea of suffering. Although we have not really lost our true minds, our falling is real enough. . . . Suffering one death and rebirth after another is like being tossed about on the open ocean and drowning. If you have not ended death and rebirth, then even if you can handle the water and swim, you will drown after being tossed about long enough. The waters of the sea of death and rebirth are composed of the karmic offenses you create. . . . You create karma because you do not recognize the true mind. It is said, "The sea of karma is vast." It has no shore. Sometimes you are tossed about on its surface, and sometimes you sink to the bottom. Being in the water of that ocean is dangerous. That is what makes Ānanda pitiable. . . . He has put all his effort into intellectual learning. He is able to come up with many questions, but he still doesn't understand, even when the explanations are repeated. (II, 77–80)

6
Visual Awareness Is Not a Perceived Object

Ānanda said, "Now I recognize that the nature of my visual awareness is that it does not depend on anything else. But how can I come to know that it is my true nature?"

The Buddha said to Ānanda, "I will continue to question you. Aided by the Buddha's wondrous power, you can now see clearly all the way to the heavens of the first dhyāna.[21] You do not yet have the purity of freedom from outflows, but Aniruddha,[22] who is free of outflows, sees the entirety of Jambudvīpa[23] as plainly as one might see an *amala* fruit placed in the palm of one's hand. Bodhisattvas at their various stages can see hundreds of thousands of worlds and more, and there is not one of the infinite numbers of Pure Lands[24] that the Thus-Come Ones in the ten directions do not see. Ordinary beings cannot see with such clarity as this, even for a fraction of an inch.

> The purity of freedom from outflows is the purest of purities. Nothing is defiled about it. It's easy to talk about, but it's a very difficult state of mind to attain. In that state, there are no outflows from the eyes, ears, nose, tongue, body, or mind. When ordinary people see something, their attention is diverted to it: that is an outflow. If you hear something and cannot apply the skill of reversing your hearing[25] but instead allow your attention to direct itself to the sound so that you listen, that too is an outflow. Your nose smells odors, your tongue

[21] The three heavens of the first dhyāna are the first three heavens of the realm of form: the Heaven of Brahma's Retinue, the Heaven of the Ministers of Brahma, and the Heaven of the Great Brahma. See part 9.11b.

[22] Aniruddha was foremost among the Arhat disciples of the Buddha in the power of the celestial eye.

[23] Jambudvīpa (the name means "Rose-Apple Island") in Buddhist cosmology is the southernmost of the four continents and the one on which we live.

[24] A pure land (Skt. *sukhāvatī*; Ch. *jing du* 淨土) is inhabited by a Buddha and other pure beings. The Pure Land, or Land of Ultimate Bliss, of Amitābha Buddha in the West is the focus of the Pure Land School of Buddhism.

[25] The recommended method of practice explained by the Bodhisattva Who Hears the Cries of the World (Skt. Avalokiteśvara). See part 6.3 below.

tastes flavors, your body comes in contact with tangible objects, your mind responds to objects of cognition: all these events involve outflows. It is like a glass bottle with a hole in the bottom. It leaks when water is poured into it. If people don't undertake spiritual practice and put an end to outflows, they become leaky bottles. They gradually pour themselves from the heavens to the realm of people. From the human realm they pour themselves into the animal realm and from there to the realm of hungry ghosts and on into the hells . . . depending on what kind of karma they have created. (II, 81–2)

When compared to the vision of sages or of the Buddhas, ordinary people can't see farther than a tenth of an inch or an inch at the most, even if they use all their power of sight. The Buddhas can see all the Pure Lands as numerous as fine motes of dust, but ordinary people can't see even an entire country or even an entire town. If they look to the left, they can't see what's on their right. If they look to the right, they can't see what's on their left. If they look ahead, they can't see what's behind them, and if they try to see behind themselves, they can't see what's in front of them. Ordinary people's vision is extremely limited. Although the essential nature of their visual awareness neither comes into being nor ceases to be, their physical bodies have limitations, and that is why their sight is obstructed. The Arhats, the Bodhisattvas, and the Buddhas all have the spiritual power of the celestial eye, and their visual awareness extends everywhere without impediment. But consider what ordinary beings can see: I can see you now, but if I hold a piece of paper up in front of my eyes, it stops me from seeing you. And the piece of paper is not even a tenth of an inch thick . . . . If you open the celestial eye, of course, there will be no obstruction, and you will be able see everything. Compared to the Buddha, we truly fall short. (II, 87)

"Ānanda, you and I can now see the palaces where the Four Celestial Kings reside. Between there and here, we can see forms and shapes that move on land, in the water, and through the air, in light and in shade. All these are perceived objects that you can distinguish as solid, and among them you should be able to distinguish what is you and what is not you. I am now asking you to choose, from all that lies within your visual awareness, what is essentially you and what are perceived objects. If you employ the power of your vision to its fullest extent, Ānanda, you will be able to see as far as the Sun Palace and Moon Palace. All that you will see are objects; they are not you. Carefully observe everything as far as the seven circular ranges of golden mountains; everything that you will see, even the various sources of light, will be an object; it will not be you. Again, step by step, observe the clouds in motion, the birds in flight, the wind blowing, the dust rising, the trees, the mountains, the rivers, the plants, the people, and the animals. All are objects of your perception. None of them is you.

> The Heaven of the Four Celestial Kings is the heaven closest to us, located half-way up Mount Sumeru. As explained in the Buddhist sutras, this heaven does not reach the peak of Mount Sumeru. There is a celestial king in the north of this heaven, one in the east, one in the south, and one in the west. The lifespan of beings in the Heaven of the Four Celestial Kings is five hundred years; after five hundred years, they are destined to die and be reborn in a lower destiny. . . .
> A day and a night in the Heaven of the Four Celestial Kings is equivalent to fifty years among people. "How can this be?" you ask. I'll give you an example to help you understand. If we feel very happy on a given day, the day passes without our even being aware of it. We feel the day was very short. Because it is blissful in the heavens, one day and one night there is equal to fifty years among people. Fifty years count for such a long time in the realm of people because people are subject to the unrelenting disturbance and affliction arising from their involvement with perceived objects. . . .
> Circling Mount Sumeru are seven ranges of mountains made of gold. A fragrant sea lies between each range. (II, 88–90).

"Ānanda, all these perceived objects, near and far, have their own distinctive nature; nevertheless, all are seen within the purity of the essence of your visual awareness. Each kind of object is distinguished as different from the others, but there are no such distinctions in the wondrous understanding of the essence of your visual awareness. This visual awareness is in fact the pure and wondrous understanding mind.

"If visual awareness were a perceived object, then would you not be able to see my visual awareness as an object? You may argue that you do see my visual awareness at the moment when we are both looking at the same thing. But when I am no longer looking at that thing, then would you still see my visual awareness? Even if you had been able to see my awareness when you and I were looking at the same thing, clearly you will not be able to see my awareness once I begin looking at something else.[26] And since you cannot see my awareness when you and I are looking at different things, clearly my visual awareness cannot be an object. Therefore, how could your own visual awareness not be what is fundamentally you?[27]

> The Buddha has told Ānanda that visual awareness is not an object, but Ānanda doesn't believe it yet, so the Buddha has to make it clearer to him. . . .
> If visual awareness were an object, then visual awareness would be visible. Therefore Ānanda should be able to see the Buddha's visual awareness, because if visual awareness were an object, it would have attributes which could be distinguished. In fact, however, visual awareness has no form or appearance. It is neither green, yellow, red, white, nor black; neither long, short, square, nor round. It isn't a thing, and so you can't see it.
> You say, "If visual awareness cannot be put in the category of objects, what is it then? What is it in the same category with?" You figure it out. Investigate it . . . as a meditation topic. . . . To ask, "Who is it who is mindful of the Buddha?" is to investigate this question. If you can recognize your visual awareness just at this point — if you can say, "Oh, basically my visual awareness does not come and does not go, basically does not come into being and does not perish" — if you understand this doctrine, then you understand the nature of your visual awareness. (II, 96–8)

---

[26] Commentaries are not in agreement as to the meaning of this sentence. The present translation follows the Ven. Master Hsüan Hua's interpretation.

[27] It is established in part 2.8 below that our visual awareness is not separate from the objects it is aware of (nor is it identical to them). The Buddha here argues that if awareness were an object, it should be visible, and it should above all be visible at the place where it is looking at something. If it is not looking at something, then it cannot be identified with the object it is no longer looking at (nor, by extension, can it be identified with any object). Therefore it cannot be an object.

"Otherwise, when you see an object, the object would see you as well.[28] If visual awareness and its objects were intermixed like that, you and I and everything else in the world would be immersed in chaos. But, Ānanda, when you are aware of something, it is you, not I, who are aware of it. The essential nature of your visual awareness pervades everything. If it is not yours, whose could it be? Why do you doubt that it is your true nature? Why don't you accept it as genuine and instead ask me what is true?"

[28] The Buddha extends his argument by pointing out that if our visual awareness were identified with the objects that it sees, then those objects would themselves become aware.

7
Visual Awareness Has Neither Shape Nor Extension

Ānanda then said respectfully to the Buddha, "World-Honored One, I accept that my visual awareness, with its capacity to understand, cannot be other than mine. The Thus-Come One and I are looking now at the halls of the Four Celestial Kings, which are adorned and resplendent with superb treasures; our glance has lingered on the Sun Palace and Moon Palace, and then our visual awareness has extended to fill the entire Sahā world. However, when we return our gaze to this pure hall and look upon this sanctuary only, we do not see beyond the roof and the walls.

"World-Honored One, that is how our visual awareness is. First it extended throughout a world; now it is confined to this one room we are in. Did our awareness contract to fit into the room, or did the walls and ceiling divide our awareness up, enclosing part of it and leaving the rest outside? At this point, I don't know which one of these alternatives is right. I hope that the World-Honored One will bestow his great kindness upon us and will explain this point to us."

> A balloon is big when it is filled with air, but when the air is released it becomes small. . . . Is visual awareness like a balloon? Ānanda is still making visual awareness into a thing. He still thinks, "Ah, awareness is a thing. I've got to think of a way to use an example in order to debate with the Buddha and win. I'm going to think of a way to invalidate his theory. I'm going to find a way to make my notion be right, and he'll have to acknowledge my achievement." That is what is going on in Ānanda's mind. "You say that everything I say is wrong. I'm definitely going to find something to say that's right and let you have a look at it." One suspects that Ānanda's attachment to self is particularly tenacious just now. (II, 103)

The Buddha said to Ānanda, "Everything visible in the world — whether large or small, whether inside this hall or outside of it, whatever kind of thing it is — may be an object of our visual awareness. Do not say your awareness itself expands and contracts.

"Let us consider an example: suppose you are looking at the space inside a square box. Let me ask you: is the space you see inside the box fixed there in a cubical shape, or is it not? If it is, then if it were transferred into a round box, it would not become round. If, on the other hand, it is not fixed in a cubical shape, then there can't have been a cube of space in the box in the first place.

"You said that you don't know which one of your alternatives is right. What you said about the nature of visual awareness can be compared to what I said about the space in the square box. In truth, neither the awareness nor the space can have a location.

"Do you want to say the space in the boxes is neither square nor round? Simply remove the boxes, and you'll see that the remaining space indeed has neither shape. You can't say that when the boxes are removed, you would still be able to remove a cube or a sphere of space.

"Besides, suppose your visual awareness does contract when you enter a room, as you suggest. Then why, when you look up at the sun, does your awareness not expand till it reaches the sun's surface? Suppose, again, your visual awareness does divide when walls and ceilings are interposed; then why, if someone drills a hole through one of the walls, will there be no evidence of a linkage created as your divided awareness expands through the hole to reconnect itself? These ideas of yours cannot be right.

"From time without beginning, all beings have mistakenly identified themselves with what they are aware of. Controlled by their experience of perceived objects, they lose track of their fundamental minds. In this state they perceive visual awareness as large or small. But when they're in control of their experience of perceived objects, they are the same as the Thus-Come Ones. Their bodies and minds,[29] unmoving and replete with perfect understanding, become a place for awakening. Then all the lands in the ten directions are contained within the tip of a fine hair."

[29] By "bodies and minds" the Buddha here refers to the Dharma-body and the enlightened mind. In his reply, however, Ānanda shows that he misunderstands the Buddha's meaning in that he supposes that the Buddha meant the physical body and the mind-faculty (Yuanying, 262).

8

Visual Awareness Is Both Separate
and Not Separate from Objects

Ānanda said respectfully to the Buddha, "World-Honored One, granted that my visual awareness is indeed my wonderful true nature; then this wonderful nature must be what appears before me. But if my visual awareness is in fact really my true nature, what is the mind that I experience in my body? The mind that I experience in my body is able to make distinctions, whereas my visual awareness does not make distinctions, even about my own body. But if my visual awareness is really my mind and is what causes me to see, then the essential nature of this visual awareness is what is truly me, and so my body is not me. Is not my objection, though, the same as the objection that the Thus-Come One made previously, namely, that perceived objects cannot see me?[30] Bestow upon us your great kindness and explain this to us who have not yet awakened."

> It can be said that Ānanda is confused, but it can also be said that he is not confused. He manifests the appearance of confusion in order to help others. He is acting as a model, showing others that even someone as confused as Ānanda pretends to be can become enlightened. . . . So as he and Śākyamuni Buddha investigate the nature of visual awareness, it is as if they are acting out a play, line by line, each in harmony with the other. (II, 116–8)

The Buddha said to Ānanda, "What you have just said — that your visual awareness is in front of you — is not correct. If it were actually in front of you, you would see it. In that case, your visual awareness would have a location which you could point to easily.

"As you and I are seated in Prince Jetri's Grove, we can see the Dharma hall, with trees and streams around it, and beyond them the River Ganges,

---

[30] Ānanda's argument here is that if his visual awareness is in front of him, it should be able to see him, and it should also itself be a perceived object; yet objects as objects lack sentience and therefore cannot see.

and both the sun and the moon above us. Now, you and I, from here at the Lion's Seat, could point to all these things: the shade cast by the trees, the shining sun, the walls that block our view, the trees themselves, the other plants, the space through which we see these things, some of them large, some as small as strands of hair — all are distinct from one another, but as long as they are visible, you can point to them. If your visual awareness were indeed in front of you, then as you point to these things you would be able to indicate which one of them is your awareness.

"Therefore, understand this: if your awareness were identical with space, how could space still be space? If your awareness were all these objects, how could they still be objects? Can you reveal, by means of a minute analysis of these many objects, the source that is the essential, pure, wondrously understanding awareness? Can you point it out to me in the same way that, with clarity and certainty, you can point out these objects?"

Ānanda said, "Looking from this many-storied Dharma hall as far as the distant Ganges and as far as the sun and the moon, I can point out all the things that my eyes observe, and all of them are perceived objects. None is my visual awareness. World-Honored One, it is as the Buddha said. Neither I nor any other Arhat who is at the first stage and still has outflows, nor even a Bodhisattva, could analyze the myriad objects and show us a visual awareness with a nature of its own that is distinct from all the objects."

The Buddha said, "So it is. So it is."

The Buddha continued, saying to Ānanda, "It is as you said. Our visual awareness does not have a nature of its own that is distinct from the myriad things. Thus your awareness is not something you can point out. I will explain this to you again. As you and I are seated here looking at Prince Jetri's Grove, let us look once more at the trees and garden and as far as the sun and moon. It is clear that not one of all the many different sights that you can point to is your visual awareness. But let us continue to explore this: are any of these things separate from your visual awareness?"

Ānanda said, "In fact, I do not think that anything I see, as I look around Prince Jetri's Grove, is separate from my awareness. Why? If the trees were separate from my awareness, how could I be seeing them? But if the trees were identical to my awareness, how could they still be trees? The same is true of every other perceived object and of space as well. If space were separate from my awareness, how could I be seeing it? But if it were identical to my awareness, how could it still be space? Having reexamined this — having considered in detail the myriad sights around us, I realize that not even the smallest of them is separate from my awareness."[31]

The Buddha said, "So it is. So it is."

The Buddha's words stunned everyone in the assembly who still needed instruction.[32] None of them had understood his meaning. Having lost what they had been relying on, they were distressed and fearful. The Thus-Come One took pity on them, knowing that their spirits were anxious and troubled, and he said in order to console Ānanda and the others in the great assembly, "Good people, the king of highest Dharma has been telling you the truth. He explains reality just as it is. He does not deceive or lie. What he has expounded for you is different from the four theories concerning what is everlasting[33] propounded by Maskari Gośālīputra and the others. Consider this carefully; in earnestly seeking instruction, be worthy of my sympathy."

Then Mañjuśrī, Prince of Dharma, taking pity on the four assemblies, stood up amidst the gathering. Having bowed at the Buddha's feet, he put his palms together in respect and said to the Buddha, "World-Honored One, the great assembly has not understood the two disclosures that the Thus-Come One has made: first, that the essence of our visual awareness and visible objects, and space as well, are identical; and, second, that they are not identical.

Mañjuśrī Bodhisattva stood up and then bowed down before the Buddha and held the Buddha's feet with his two hands. In India this was a gesture of utmost respect. People's feet are most unclean, and so to use one's hands to hold the

---

[31] The first of the Sutra's tetralemmas. See the introduction, page xxxiv.

[32] That is, unenlightened beings and Arhats at the first, second, and third stages.

[33] These four theories are described in more detail at part 5.5.

Buddha's feet indicates, "I am beneath your feet." So now when we bow to the Buddha, we turn our palms up, and in this position we should contemplate that our two hands are under the Buddha's feet. This represents purity in the karma of the body, because while showing respect in this way, we are not committing any offenses with the body. Placing our palms together in respect represents purity in the karma of the mind; placing the fingers together carefully side by side while placing our palms together represents single-minded respect. It means that your mind has returned to oneness and now gives undivided attention to revering the Buddha. . . . Finally, Mañjuśrī's speaking to the Buddha represents purity in the karma of speech. . . . He says that the great assembly has not understood. Did he himself not understand, then? He understood. He asked because no one else knew how to phrase the question. . . . We know that Mañjuśrī understood because the text says that he took pity on the four assemblies. But even without that phrase, we would know that he understood because he is the Bodhisattva of Great Wisdom. (II, 129–31)

"World-Honored One, if our visual awareness were identical to the conditions before us — space and visible objects — then we should be able to point to our awareness just as we can point to visible objects and to space. But if our awareness were separate from visible objects and from space, we would not be able to observe them. People in the assembly are alarmed because they do not understand the basis of this argument; it is not that their roots in the Dharma from their previous lives are shallow. Therefore, I hope that the Thus-Come One will compassionately reveal exactly what the essence of visual awareness is, what the essence of observed objects is, and what it means to say that the essence of visual awareness is neither identical nor not identical to the objects we observe."

Ānanda does not understand, but when Mañjuśrī Bodhisattva speaks, his reasoning is perfect. . . . He mentions that some people in the assembly are alarmed although their foundations in the Dharma are not weak. But they haven't understand the principle at all. Sometimes people whose foundations in the Dharma are slight will become very afraid when they undertake a spiritual practice. In that case, they should do more good deeds; this will strengthen their foundation, and then their samādhi will grow strong. (II, 131–3)

The Buddha said to Mañjuśrī and to the rest of the great assembly, "To the Thus-Come Ones of the ten directions and to the Great Bodhisattvas who dwell in samādhi, visual awareness and visible objects, and objects of mind as well, are like elaborate mirages that appear in space. They have no real existence of their own. Fundamentally, visual awareness and all its conditioned objects are the pure, wondrously understanding enlightenment itself. In enlightenment, how could there be identity or a lack of it? Mañjuśrī, I now ask you: you are Mañjuśrī; is there a Mañjuśrī about whom one can say, 'That is Mañjuśrī'? Or is there no such Mañjuśrī?"

How can identity and lack of identity be found within the true mind, which does not admit of duality? The true mind is not in the realm of opposites. (II, 134)

"Neither, World-Honored One. I am simply Mañjuśrī. There is no one about whom one can say, 'That is Mañjuśrī.' Why? If there were, there would be two Mañjuśrīs. Nor is it the case that there is no such Mañjuśrī. In fact, neither the affirmation nor the denial of the statement 'That is Mañjuśrī' is true."

The Buddha said, "The same is true of the wondrously understanding essence of our visual awareness and also of the objects we observe and of space. All are the wondrously understanding, supreme enlightenment — the pure, perfect, true mind. It is a mistake to consider them as separate — as observed objects, space, and visual awareness — or as awareness of sound and the other kinds of awareness.

There is no "is" or "not." . . . Space and objects, like our awareness, are the true mind. Later, it is explained that the four primary elements — earth, water, fire, and wind — are the Matrix of the Thus-Come One. . . . Identity and separation are relative concepts, but what is spoken of here is absolute. (II, 136–8)

"Similarly, in the analogy of the second moon,[34] which moon is the one about which one can say, 'That is the moon,' and which one is not in fact the moon? Actually, Mañjuśrī, there is really only one moon. We

[34] Cf. part 2.5, p. 56.

can neither affirm nor deny the statement, 'That is the moon.' Therefore, all your various interpretations of visual awareness and visible objects are nothing but delusion, and in the midst of delusion one cannot avoid thinking 'That is' and 'That is not.' Only from within the true, essential, wondrously understanding, awakened mind can one escape the error of trying to point to what 'is' and what 'is not.'"

9

Visual Awareness Arises
Neither on Its Own nor from Causes

"World-Honored One," Ānanda said respectfully to the Buddha, "It truly is as the Dharma-King has said. Our enlightened nature can be involved with things throughout all ten directions, and yet it remains clear and still. It is eternally present. It neither comes into being nor ceases to be.

"But how does what the Buddha has said in this regard differ from the 'truth of the unmanifested nature' as taught by the Brahmin Kapila,[35] or from the 'true self' as taught by the ascetics who smear ashes on themselves,[36] or by others who are not on the right path? Also, on Mount Laṅkā[37] the World-Honored One explained this principle to the Bodhisattva Mahāmati and to others, and he said then that those who are not on the right path are always speaking of things existing in and of themselves,[38] whereas the Buddha speaks of something else: he speaks of causes and conditions. But as I see it now, the enlightened nature exists in and of itself; it neither comes into being nor ceases to be; it far transcends all that is distorted and unreal. It seems it does not arise from causes and conditions; instead it seems that it exists in and of itself. I only hope that the Buddha will explain this to us so that we may realize our true and genuine mind, which is our wondrously understanding, enlightened nature, and avoid all the wrong paths."

The primary cause is like a seed, and the conditions are what aid the growth of a seed, such as soil, water, fertilizer, sunlight, etc. (II, 144)

[35] The same Kapila who taught the spell used against Ānanda earlier in the Sutra.

[36] The Buddha condemned nonbeneficial ascetic practices. The text here probably refers to an ascetic sect that later became known as the *paśupatas;* they were worshippers of the Hindu god Śiva. They smeared ashes on their bodies three times a day as part of their ritual purification practice.

[37] The mountain in Sri Lanka where the Buddha taught the Laṅkāvatāra Sūtra to the Bodhisattva Mahāmati and others.

[38] Ch. *ziran xing* 自然性. That is, arising of its own accord without an external cause and therefore having an independent existence.

The Buddha said to Ānanda, "Just now, by various means I have explained this to you in order that the truth would be made clear to you. But you have not understood, and you mistakenly suppose that the enlightened nature exists in and of itself.

"Ānanda, if the enlightened nature indeed exists in and of itself, as you say, then you should be able to discern what it essentially consists of. Consider your wondrously understanding visual awareness: what about it exists in and of itself? Does it consist of light that exists in and of itself? Does it consist of darkness that exists in and of itself? Does it consist of space that exists in and of itself? Does it consist of solid objects that exist in and of themselves? If it consisted of light that existed in and of itself, Ānanda, you would not be able to see when it is dark. If it consisted of space that existed in and of itself, you would not be able to see solid objects. In the same way, if it consisted of darkness that existed in and of itself, the essential nature of your visual awareness would cease to exist, and so you would not be able to see when it is light."

Ānanda said, "It must be then that the wondrously understanding nature of this visual awareness does not exist in and of itself after all. It now seems to me that it comes into being due to causes and conditions. But I do not understand this clearly yet. May I inquire of the Thus-Come One how this idea fits with the Buddha's teachings about causes and conditions?"

The Buddha said, "You are saying that the luminous nature of visual awareness comes into being from causes and conditions. I ask you to consider, then: what is the primary cause of your being aware of what you see before you? Is light the primary cause of your being aware of what you see before you? Is darkness the primary cause? Is space the primary cause? Are solid objects the primary cause?

"Ānanda, if light were the cause of your being aware of what you see before you, you could not see when it is dark. If darkness were the cause, you could not see when it is light. And what is true of light and darkness as causes is equally true of space and objects as causes.

"Moreover, Ānanda, is light or darkness a condition of your being aware of what you see before you? Are objects conditions? Is space a condition? If space were a condition of your being aware of what you see before you, Ānanda, then you could not see solid objects. If solid objects were a condition of your being aware of what you see before you, you would be unable to perceive space. And what is true of space and solid objects as conditions is equally true of light and darkness as conditions.

"Therefore, you should understand that the existence of the essential, wondrously understanding, enlightened visual awareness is not dependent for its existence on causes and conditions, nor does it exist in and of itself. Nevertheless, one cannot say that it does not exist in and of itself, nor can one say that it is independent of causes and conditions. Statements that account for its existence cannot be negated, yet one cannot say that they cannot be negated. Such statements cannot be affirmed, yet one cannot say that they cannot be affirmed. What is entirely beyond all defining attributes — that is the entirety of Dharma.

"In making all these distinctions, why have you resorted to terms used in the reckless fabrications of worldly discourse? You might as well try to seize a handful of space. However much you weary yourself in the attempt, space will forever elude your grasp."

10
True Visual Awareness

Ānanda said to the Buddha, "World-Honored One, if the wondrous enlightened nature is indeed not dependent on causes and conditions, why then has the Buddha often taught the monks that our visual awareness requires four conditions to be present: space, light, mind,[39] and the eye-faculty. What did you mean then?"

The Buddha said, "Ānanda, what I have said about causes and conditions as they function in the world is not an ultimate truth. I have another question for you, Ānanda. When ordinary people say, 'I see' or 'I do not see,' what do they mean by 'seeing' and 'not seeing'?"

Ānanda said, "Relying on the light of the sun, of the moon, or of lamps, ordinary people can see various objects. That is what they mean by 'seeing.' Without at least one of these three sources of light, they would not be able to see."

"Ānanda, if people cannot see when light is absent, they would have no visual awareness of total darkness. Since they are visually aware of total darkness, you cannot say that they cannot see in the absence of light. Further, if their inability to see light when they are in total darkness indeed means they cannot see when it is dark, then conversely, their inability to see darkness when it is light must also mean that they cannot see when it is light, since the cases are parallel and both involve instances of not seeing.

"Light and darkness are mutually exclusive; still, regardless of which one is present, your visual awareness does not lapse for an instant. Therefore you should understand that in both cases there is seeing. How can you say that there is not?[40]

"You should understand then that when people see light, their awareness of it does not come into being because of the light. When people see darkness, their awareness of it does not come into being because

---

[39] "Mind" here refers to the first, sixth, seventh, and eighth consciousnesses.
[40] The Buddha made a similar point above at the beginning of part 2.

of the darkness. When people see space, their awareness of it does not come into being because of the space, and when people see solid objects, their awareness of them does not come into being because of the solid objects.

"Now that we have arrived at the conclusion that visual awareness does not come into being because of any of these four, you should also understand that when you are able to use your true awareness to be aware of the essence of your visual awareness, you will know that your true awareness is not the same as the essence of your awareness. The two are quite separate from one another. The essence of awareness is not the equal of true awareness.[41] How can you still be speaking of the attributes of causes and conditions and of things existing in and of themselves, or even coming into being from inhering or combining?[42] You Hearers of the Teaching are deficient in knowledge; your views are narrow and your attainment limited. Because you have not yet been able to break through to true reality in its purity, I will now instruct you further. Consider well what I say. Do not become weary and lose heart on the road to the wonder of full awakening."

> "To break through" here means to understand. The Buddha tells the Arhats that at present their minds are too strongly attached, the distinctions they make are too numerous, for them to understand the teachings of the Mahāyāna, the Greater Vehicle, concerning the purity of true reality. . . . True reality has no attributes. That is the first explanation. Yet nothing is apart from true reality: that is the second explanation. All attributes are produced from within it. . . . The third explanation is that true reality has no attributes, and yet there is nothing which is not an attribute. All phenomena are born from true

---

[41] "True awareness" here is the true mind, while the "essence of awareness" refers to the observing division of the eighth consciousness, which contains a small amount of distortion. The Buddha explains the difference between true awareness and the essence of awareness in part 2.11. The difference has already been expressed in terms of the example of a "real moon" and "a second moon." The process by which our awareness becomes distorted is explained more fully in part 4.1.

[42] That inhering and combining cannot account for awareness is the subject of part 2.12 below.

reality, and so true reality is the essential nature of all phenomena. . . . What then is true reality ultimately like? You cannot see it. It has merely been given a name, "true reality." The idea is similar to the idea expressed in Laozi's saying, "The Way that can be spoken of is not the eternal Way." . . .

True reality is true emptiness, and it is also wondrous existence. Do you say that true emptiness is empty? It is not, because within it, all that exists comes into being. True emptiness is said to be true because it is not in fact empty, and all that exists is wondrous because it does not in fact exist. What exists within emptiness is wondrous existence. Emptiness therefore is not empty, and that lack of emptiness within emptiness is true emptiness. Since true emptiness is not empty, it is called "wondrous existence." Since wondrous existence does not exist, it is called "true emptiness." These two names are one. If you investigate this in detail, you will find, however, that even that "one" does not exist. . . . Fundamentally, there isn't anything at all. . . . To truly be apart from all attributes is to have real samādhi. If you can separate yourself from all attributes, Mt. Tai could come crashing down in front of you and you would not be startled. . . . Demonic obstructions . . . can only disturb your samādhi because your mind moves. As soon as your mind moves, the obstacles slip right in. If you don't move, no demon in existence will have any way to get at you. No spell that can be recited can influence you. It was because Ānanda didn't have sufficient power of mental concentration that the Mātaṅga woman was able to confuse him. If he had had the genuine Śūraṅgama Samādhi, there would have been no need for the Buddha to speak the Śūraṅgama Sūtra or the Śūraṅgama Mantra. And you and I would not be able to study them now. (II, 166–8)

11
Distortions in Visual Awareness
Based on Karma

Ānanda said to the Buddha, "The World-Honored One has elucidated the teaching concerning causes and conditions and concerning the existence of things in and of themselves, but we have not yet understood the teaching about inhering and conjoining and not inhering or conjoining. And now when we hear further that the essence of visual awareness of which the true awareness is aware is not the same as the true awareness, another layer has been added to our confusion and distress.

"It is my humble wish that, with his great kindness, the Buddha will open our Wisdom-eye and reveal the enlightened mind in all its purity." With these words, he wept sorrowfully, bowed, and waited to receive the Sage's instructions.

Then the World-Honored One took pity on Ānanda and on the others in the great assembly. He wished to make clear to them the wondrous path of practice that would lead them all to the samādhi of the Great Dhāraṇī.[43] He said to Ānanda, "You have a keen memory, but it serves only to increase your erudition. You have not yet understood the practice of calming the mind from which subtle insight arises. Listen carefully as I give instruction point by point for your sake, and also for the sake of all in the future who have outflows, so that they may attain full awakening.

"All beings are bound to the cycle of saṃsāra, Ānanda, due to the false distinctions made by two kinds of distorted awareness. Wherever these two kinds of awarenesses arise, beings undergo the karma of the cycle. What are these two kinds of distorted awareness? The first is the distorted awareness based on the karma of individual beings; the second is the distorted awareness based on the karma beings share.

As you read this section of text, you should experience terror. You should be shocked. The Buddha tells Ānanda that all beings of this world are bound to

---

[43] Skt. *dhāraṇī*, mantra. The Great Dhāraṇī is the Śūraṅgama Mantra.

the cycle of death and rebirth, passing through a succession of lives. They spin around like the wheel of an automobile, sometimes being born in the heavens, sometimes entering the hells. Sometimes they become asuras, sometimes they are people. Sometimes they become animals. Sometimes they are hungry ghosts.[44] . . . The cycle of death and rebirth keeps on turning under the power of two kinds of distorted awareness which result when the conscious mind makes false distinctions. These distortions in awareness stem from individual and shared karma. . . . For any karma you create, both individual and shared, there is an appropriate consequence which you must undergo. If you are virtuous and act for the good, you may be reborn in the heavens. If you commit offenses, you will fall into the hells. . . . The process is entirely impartial. (II, 175–6)

"What is the distorted awareness based on individual karma, Ānanda? Let us consider the example of a person with an eye disease.[45] At night, when he looks at a lamp, it seems to him that circular bands of light surround the lamp with the entire spectrum of colors. What do you think? Are the circles of colored light that appear around the lamp at night an aspect of the lamplight or an aspect of his own visual awareness? If the circles of colored light were an aspect of the lamplight, Ānanda, wouldn't they be seen by other people besides the person with the eye disease, instead of being visible only to him? On the other hand, if the circles of colored light were an aspect of the person's visual awareness, wouldn't his awareness itself be colored? If that were the case, what kind of thing would this colored awareness be?

Individual karma is what makes you different from other people. . . . It is created from deluded thoughts of great expectations for the self. . . . In the analogy, "other people" represents the Buddhas and the great Bodhisattvas; the "person with the eye disease" represents ordinary beings; the lamp represents true reality, since when the Buddhas and Bodhisattvas look, they see true reality, while ordinary beings see a distorted reflection. (II, 178–83)

---

[44] Skt. *preta*. Ch. 餓鬼. See part 9.7.
[45] The symptoms the Buddha describes suggest that glaucoma is probably meant.

"Further, Ānanda, if the circles of colored light were not an aspect of the lamplight, then when the person with the diseased eyes glanced around him at a screen, a curtain, a table, or a sleeping mat, he would see the colored circles surrounding them as well. And if the circles of colored light were not an aspect of his visual awareness, he would not see the circles at all. Why then does he in fact see them?

"Therefore, you should know that, although the colors are in fact intrinsic to the lamplight, the illusory circles of colored light arise from the disease in his eyes. However, although the circles of colored light and his awareness of them are due to the disease, his awareness of the disease is not itself diseased. In short, you cannot say that the illusory circles of color are an aspect of the lamplight or an aspect of his visual awareness. But you also cannot say that they are not an aspect of the lamplight or of his visual awareness. In the same way, in the analogy of the two moons, the second moon is neither the real moon nor a reflection of the real moon. When pressure is applied to the eyeball, one sees two moons. Those who understand this will not argue that the second moon, which results from the pressure on the eye, is the real moon or that it is not the real moon, or, further, that it is an aspect of visual awareness or is not an aspect of visual awareness.

"The same is true of the illusory circles of light around the lamp: they arise from the disease in the eyes. Can you say now that they are an aspect only of the lamplight or only of visual awareness? You cannot. Even less can you distinguish them as neither an aspect of the lamplight nor an aspect of visual awareness.

> In the analogy of the person with the eye disease, his awareness of the colors represents ordinary beings' distorted awareness . . . while his awareness of his disease represents the pure seeing of the Buddhas and Bodhisattvas. . . . The second moon is analogous to the circles of color seen by the person with the eye disease. (II, 184–5)

"What is meant by the distorted awareness that is based on shared karma? Ānanda, in Jambudvīpa's seas there are three thousand land masses. In their midst lies a great continent, and in that continent, from east to west, there are two thousand three hundred large countries. On the various islands in the ocean there may be two or three hundred countries, or in some cases only one or two countries, or as many as thirty, forty, or fifty.

"Suppose, Ānanda, that among them is an island where there are two countries only, and that the people of one of these countries share the experience of unfortunate circumstances. It may be that the people of that country see many inauspicious phenomena. They may see two suns or two moons, or rings or half-rings of white or colored light around the sun or the moon. They may see meteors or comets streaking down or across the sky, or else patterns of inauspicious energies in a bowed shape or in the shape of ears above or beside the sun, or bands of light reaching across the sky — many such inauspicious phenomena as these.[46] Only the people of that one country see these phenomena; the people in the other country do not see them at all or even hear of them.

"Ānanda, I will now compare these situations in order to clarify them. First let us consider the distorted visual awareness based on beings' individual karma. When the person with an eye disease sees the illusory circles of colored light around a lamp, the circles seem to him to be external objects, but in fact what the person sees is a consequence of the disease. The disease places a distorting strain on his visual awareness; it is not the colored light that places the strain. However, what is aware of the disease is not defective. In the same way, all that you can now see — the mountains, the rivers, the many lands, and the various forms of life — are the result of a disease that has existed in your visual awareness since time without beginning. The essence of visual awareness and what it is aware of[47] cause what seem to be external phenomena to appear. Once we add another layer of understanding to our enlightenment, our awareness and

---

[46] Of these meteorological phenomena, the "two suns" can be identified as parhelia, or mock suns, and the "rings," "half-rings," and the "energies in a bowed shape or in the shape of ears" may be identified as four different types of solar halo. All of these are rare occurrences due to reflections from clouds of ice crystals in the atmosphere.

[47] That is, the observing division and the observed division of the eighth consciousness.

what it is aware of become defective.[48] While the awareness that is added to enlightenment is defective, however, the awareness that is the fundamental, enlightened, understanding awareness is not defective. That is, the true awareness that is aware of the defective awareness is not itself defective. That true awareness, which is aware of the essence of awareness, is not to be confused with the ordinary visual awareness, or the awareness of sounds, or any of the other types of awareness.

"To restate: your visual awareness of me now, and of yourself and of the ten classes of beings that can be seen in the world, is a defective awareness. It is not the awareness that is aware of the defect. The true nature of the essence of visual awareness is not defective, and therefore it is not what is ordinarily referred to as visual awareness.[49]

"Ānanda, consider the distortion in visual awareness experienced by the people of that one country, in response to their shared karma. Compare it to the distorted visual awareness experienced by the person whose eyes are diseased, in response to his individual karma. The situations of the person with the eye disease and the people of that one country are similar, in that the illusory circles of colored light are a consequence of the eye disease, while the inauspicious phenomena seen by the people of that country are due to the miasmal energies that arise from their shared karma. Both the individual karma and the shared karma have come into being because of distortions in awareness that have existed since time without beginning.

"Nevertheless, all the beings with outflows and all the lands in the ten directions, including the Sahā world, with its four great seas and with the three thousand landmasses of Jambudvīpa, are fundamentally the enlightened, wondrous, luminous mind that understands and has no outflows. The conditions necessary for them all to arise are the illusory, diseased distortions in visual awareness, in awareness of sounds, and in all the other types of awareness. When these conditions are present in

---

[48] For a full explanation of this important point, see part 4.2 below.
[49] This "true nature" which is not defective is the Buddha-nature.

combination, the beings and lands come into being; when these conditions are not present, the beings and lands cease to be.

"When you remain entirely untouched by conditions, whether or not they are present in combination, you bring to an end all the causes of coming into being and ceasing to be. At that moment, you will awaken to perfect enlightenment, which is your true nature and which neither comes into being nor ceases to be. It is the pure, fundamental mind, the fundamental, everlasting enlightenment."

12
Visual Awareness Exists Neither
Through Inhering Nor in Conjoining

"Ānanda, you have already understood that the wondrous, luminous, enlightened nature of your visual awareness does not arise from causes and conditions and that it does not come into being on its own. But you do not understand yet that the original, enlightened nature of your visual awareness also does not exist because of inhering or because of conjoining, nor because of a lack of inhering or a lack of conjoining.[50]

"I will now ask you again, Ānanda, about the objects you perceive before you. Your deluded thinking about the world tells you that what causes these objects to exist is either inhering or conjoining. Therefore you wrongly suppose that what causes the enlightened mind[51] to exist is either inhering or conjoining.

"Suppose the wondrous, pure nature of your visual awareness[52] exists through inhering. Does it then exist through inhering in light? Does it exist through inhering in darkness? Does it exist through inhering in space? Does it exist through inhering in solid objects? If it exists through inhering in light, then when you see in the presence of light, precisely where in the light does it inhere? Visual awareness and light each have their own distinct qualities, so if visual awareness were inherent in light, what qualities would each of them have then? Either they would have the ability to see, in which case you would be seeing your own awareness, or they would not have the ability to see, in which case you would not

---

[50] "Inhering" (Skt. samavāya) translates Ch. he 和, and "conjoining" (Skt. saṁyoga) translates Ch. he 合. The allusion here is probably to the teachings of the Indian Vaiśeṣika school. "Inhering" refers to the inseparable inhering of essential qualities and karma in a substance, whereas "conjoining" refers to the coming together of two substances in ways that do not change their distinct, essential qualities.

[51] That is, the enlightened nature of visual awareness.

[52] Ch. jian jing 見精. In previous appearances in the text, this has meant the observing division of the eighth consciousness, but the context here makes plain that our enlightened awareness, expressed previously as Ch. jian xing 見性, is meant in this case.

be able to see light. In any case, how can light be inherent in your visual awareness, since the enlightened nature of your visual awareness is in fact already complete in itself? Likewise, since light is already complete in itself, how could your visual awareness have been inherent in light? Again, since your visual awareness is different from light, it would cease to be itself if it were to inhere in light, and light would likewise cease to be what we call light if it inhered in visual awareness; each would lose its nature. In short, it cannot be right to say your visual awareness exists through inhering in light. Nor can it be right to say your visual awareness exists through inhering in darkness, in space, or in objects.

"Once again, Ānanda, does the wondrous, pure nature of your visual awareness exist through conjoining with light? Does it exist through conjoining with darkness? Does it exist through conjoining with space? Does it exist through conjoining with objects?

"If your visual awareness existed in conjoining with light, then in total darkness, when no light is present, you would not be aware of the darkness since your awareness would be conjoined with light rather than with darkness. If, even so, you could see darkness without your awareness being conjoined to darkness, it follows that you would not see light when your awareness was conjoined to light.[53] And if you could not see light when your awareness had been conjoined to it, then since you could not see light, how would you know when it was light or dark? The same arguments could be made to show that your visual awareness does not exist through conjoining with darkness, with space, or with objects."

Ānanda said to the Buddha, "World-Honored One, I am now thinking that the wondrous, fundamental, enlightened nature of our visual awareness does not exist either through inhering in or through conjoining with the objects before us or with our processes of perceiving of them."

The Buddha said, "Now you are saying that your enlightened awareness does not exist either through inhering or through conjoining. I will

[53] Because if one could see darkness without visual awareness being conjoined to it, the corollary would be that to be conjoined to darkness would not allow one to see it. The same would apply in the case of light.

continue to question you, then. If the wondrous, essential nature of your visual awareness does not inhere in or conjoin with anything, then are you saying that it does not inhere in light? That it does not inhere in darkness? That it does not inhere in space? That it does not inhere in solid objects?

"If it did not inhere in light, then a boundary would necessarily exist between your visual awareness and the light. Look carefully now: where is your awareness? Where is the light? And where is the boundary between them? If, Ānanda, your visual awareness were nowhere within the confines of light, it would follow that your awareness and the light had not come into contact, and so you would not be able to see where the light is. Then how could a boundary exist between them? The same can be said of the notion that your visual awareness does not inhere in darkness, in space, or in solid objects.

"Moreover, if the wondrous, essential nature of your visual awareness did not become conjoined to anything, then does it not become conjoined to light? Does it not become conjoined to darkness? Does it not become conjoined to space? Does it not become conjoined to objects?"

"If your visual awareness did not become conjoined to light, then light and your awareness would be entirely incompatible, just as light and your awareness of sounds are incompatible. They would never come into contact. Further, since you would not be able to see where the light is, how could you know whether or not your awareness had become conjoined to it? The same would be true of your visual awareness not becoming conjoined to darkness, to space, or to solid objects."

III
The Matrix of the Thus-Come One

1
The Five Aggregates Are
the Matrix of the Thus-Come One

"Ananda, you have not yet understood that the objects we perceive are unreal and illusory. They are subject to change, appearing here and there and disappearing here and there. Yet these illusions, each with its conventional designation, are in fact within the essential, wondrous enlightenment. The same is true of the five aggregates,[1] the six faculties, the twelve sites,[2] and the eighteen constituent elements.[3] It is an illusion that they come into being when both their causes and their conditions are present, and it is an illusion that they cease to be when either their causes or their conditions are absent. You simply have not yet understood that, fundamentally, everything that comes and goes, that comes into being and ceases to be, is within the true nature of the Matrix of the Thus-Come One,[4] which is the wondrous, everlasting understanding — the unmoving, all-pervading, wondrous suchness of reality. But, though you may seek within the everlasting reality of the Matrix of the Thus-Come One for what comes and goes, for confusion and awakening, and for coming into being and ceasing to be, you will not find them there.

> Each and every perceived object looks to you like it actually exists, but in reality it is entirely illusory and transitory. . . . The coming into being of the objects we perceive is an illusion, and their ceasing to be is an illusion. . . . Nevertheless their nature is in truth the luminous essence of wondrous enlightenment. They come forth from our true mind. When delusion arises, there is a division into what observes and what is observed.[5] Both arise from the pure nature

---

[1] Skt. *skandha*, Ch. *yun* 蘊. See the introduction, p. xlvii.

[2] The twelve sites consist of the six faculties of perception together with the six categories of perceived objects.

[3] The eighteen constituent elements are the six faculties, the six categories of perceived objects, and the six consciousnesses.

[4] Skt. Tathāgata-garbha, Ch. *rulai zang* 如來藏. See the introduction, p. xxxi and note 33.

[5] Ch. *jian fen* 見分 and *xiang fen* 相分. The fundamental division of the eighth, or "storehouse," consciousness into observer and what is observed was basic to the teachings

and luminous essence of wondrous enlightenment, which is the everlasting true mind. They do not come from elsewhere. . . .

When you do not understand, there is coming and going, there is confusion and enlightenment, there is death and rebirth. But if you understand the everlasting true mind, if you recognize your own fundamental nature, the pure nature and luminous essence of the everlasting true mind, you put an end to all the illusory coming into being and ceasing to be. Then if you look for such characteristics as coming and going, confusion and enlightenment, and death and rebirth, you won't find them. (III, 1–3)

A. The Aggregate of Form

"Ānanda, how is it that the five aggregates are, fundamentally, the Matrix of the Thus-Come One, whose nature is the wondrous suchness of reality?[6] Consider this example, Ānanda: a clear-sighted person looks up at a clear sky, where nothing but empty space is to be seen. Suppose that, for no particular reason, this person happens to stare, without moving his eyes, until they are stressed to the point that he sees in the empty air a disordered display of flowers, along with various other images that are

---

of the Consciousness-Only school. This division is described at some length in this Sutra at part 4.1. See also the introduction, p. xxx.

[6] In this part of the Sutra, the Buddha corrects wrong understandings of the causes of the coming into being of the various fundamental categories of our experience. He makes several points. First, although objects that we experience are dependent on causes and conditions, which must all be present for these objects to temporarily exist, they do not come into being out of any of those causes and conditions. Second, they do not come into being on their own; that is, they cannot come into being independent of those causes and conditions. Third, since there is no process of something real actually coming into being, the objects that we experience have no real, independent existence of their own. Rather, they are distorted experiences that are based on our fundamental ignorance. When that fundamental ignorance is transcended, we experience ourselves and the world as they really are.

Throughout part 3, the Buddha presents his argument in a series of syllogisms according to the procedures of logical argumentation that were later codified as part of Buddhist logic. For each syllogism, the Buddha begins by briefly describing a situation drawn from common experience to serve as an instance of the truth of what he is proposing. Having applied the instance to the proposition, he next offers one or more negative examples to show the absurdity of negating the proposition. Lastly, he states the conclusion, in which the proposition is restated as proven. See p. xxxiii.

disordered and chaotic and lack any real attributes. You should know that the aggregate of form can be described in similar terms.

"Now, this disordered display of flowers, Ānanda, does not come into being from space, nor does it come into being from the person's eyes. Suppose, Ānanda, that the display of flowers did come from space. But what has come into being from space would have to be subject to disappearing back into space; and space would not be empty if things came into being out of it and disappeared back into it. But if space were not empty, there would not be room in it for those displays of flowers to appear out of it or to disappear back into it, any more than there is room in your body, Ānanda, for another Ānanda.

"On the other hand, if this disordered display of flowers came from the person's eyes, the display of flowers could disappear back into his eyes. Now, we may suppose that, if this display of flowers has come from the eyes, it must share in the visual awareness of the eye-faculty. If it were visually aware, then having come out from the eyes into the air, it would be able to see the eyes from the air. But if it does not share in the awareness of the eye-faculty, then having obscured a portion of the otherwise empty air, it will also obscure the vision of the eye-faculty as it returns to the eye-faculty. Besides, the person's vision cannot have been obscured, since he is seeing the display of flowers. And did we not say to begin with that this person was clear-sighted as he looked up at the clear sky?

"Therefore you should know that the aggregate of forms is an illusion. It does not come into being from causes and conditions, nor does it come into being on its own.

B. The Aggregate of Sense-Perception

"Ānanda, consider the example of someone whose hands and feet are at rest and whose entire body is at ease. At this moment, he has forgotten about his body, and he is feeling neither comfort nor discomfort. Then, for no particular reason, he rubs the palms of his hands together in the empty space in front of him, and he has the illusory experience of roughness or smoothness and of cold or heat. You should know that the aggregate of sense-perception can be described in similar terms.

"Now, these illusory sense-perceptions, Ānanda, do not emerge from space, nor do they emerge from the palms of the person's hands. That is to say, Ānanda, if space could cause tactile perceptions in the palms of his hands, would it not equally be able to cause tactile perceptions elsewhere on the body? But it makes no sense to say that space can cause tactile perceptions in one part of the body and not another.

"If the tactile perceptions had emerged from the palms of his hands, what need would there have been to rub the palms together in order to produce the perceptions? Further, if the tactile perceptions had emerged from the palms of his hands, then the person's palms would have been aware of the perceptions emerging. And when the person moved his hands apart, the perceptions would have to sink back into his wrists and arms, into the bones and marrow, which would have to be aware of the path those perceptions took. In such a case, what the mind perceived as emerging and returning would have to be something that was capable of coming and going in the body. If there were such a thing, what need would there have been for the person to rub the palms of his hands together in order to experience these tactile perceptions?[7]

"Therefore you should know that the aggregate of sense-perception is an illusion. It does not come into being from causes and conditions, nor does it come into being on its own.

C. The Aggregate of Cognition

"Ānanda, consider the example of someone whose mouth waters at the mention of sour plums, or who feels a sudden ache in the sole of his foot as he thinks of walking along the edge of a precipice. You should know that the aggregate of cognition can be described in similar terms.

"Now, the circumstance of the mouth watering at the mention of the plums, Ānanda, was not caused by the actual plums that were mentioned, nor was it caused by the person's mouth. Why? If the mouth watered because of the actual plums, Ānanda, that would mean that the plums were responsible for mentioning themselves. What need would there be

[7] The rubbing of the palms together represents fundamental ignorance; the sensations of smoothness, etc., represent the aggregate of sense-perception.

for some person to mention them? On the other hand, if the mouth were responsible for the watering, would that mean that the mouth heard the plums being mentioned? Were not ears needed for that? If the ears were the cause, then would that not mean that the ears could produce saliva?[8]

"The same points about the watering of the mouth at the mention of sour plums can be equally applied to the ache that is felt in the sole of one's foot when one thinks of walking along the edge of a precipice.

"Therefore you should know that the aggregate of cognition is an illusion. It does not come into being from causes and conditions, nor does it come into being on its own.

D. The Aggregate of Mental Formations

"Ānanda, consider the example of a stretch of rapids. The waves follow one upon another, and those that are behind never overtake those that are ahead. You should know that the aggregate of mental formations can be described in similar terms.

"Now, the rapids are not brought about by space, Ānanda, nor are they brought about by the water itself. They are not identical to the water, but though they are not themselves the water, they are at the same time not separate from the water. Nor are they separate from space.

"Understand it this way, Ānanda: if the rapids were brought about by space, then that would mean that space in its infinite reach throughout the ten directions would be a ceaseless deluge, and the entire universe would inevitably drown. If the rapids were brought about by the water, then the nature of the rapids would not be the same as the nature of water. The rapids and the water would be separate and distinct; but clearly, they are not. On the other hand, if the rapids and the water were identical, then when the water became still, it would cease to be water. However, the rapids and the water cannot be separate either, since there can be no rapids without water. Nor can the rapids be separate from space, since outside of space nothing exists.

---

[8] No actual plum is present. The person in the example merely thinks of plums. The thought of the plums represents fundamental ignorance, and the watering of the mouth represents the aggregate of cognition.

"In this way you should know that the aggregate of mental formations is an illusion. It does not come into being from causes and conditions, nor does it come into being on its own.

E. The Aggregate of Consciousness

"Ānanda, consider the example of a person who takes up an empty pitcher[9] and plugs up its two spouts so that it seems he has confined some space in the pitcher. Believing that he is carrying this pitcherful of space, he travels a thousand miles to another country with the intention of making a present of it. You should know that the aggregate of consciousness can be described in similar terms.

"The space that is in the pitcher, Ānanda, does not in fact come from the place where the person began his journey, nor is it transported to the country he travels to. It is like this, Ānanda: if the space had been transported from the first country by being confined in the pitcher, there must have been a loss of space at the place where the pitcher had come from. Moreover, if the space had been brought to the second country, then if the spouts were unplugged and the pitcher turned upside-down, the space within it would be seen to pour out.

"In this way you should know that the aggregate of consciousness is an illusion. It does not come into being from causes and conditions, nor does it come into being on its own."

---

[9] Ch. *pinqie* 頻伽, probably an abbreviated form of *jialing pinqie* 迦陵頻伽, a transliteration of the Skt. *kalaviṅka*. In its usual sense, *kalaviṅka* is the name of a bird. Here it probably refers to a pitcher with two spouts crafted in the shape of the bird.

2
The Six Faculties Are
the Matrix of the Thus-Come One

A. The Eye-Faculty

"Moreover, Ānanda, how is it that, fundamentally, the six faculties are the Matrix of the Thus-Come One, whose nature is the wondrous suchness of reality? Ānanda, you will recall the example of a person who stares into space to the point that his eyes become strained. What the eye-faculty perceives when it is under strain, and also the eye-faculty itself, come into being through the strain placed on the awakened mind. The strain causes the distortion in perception.[10]

"For seeing to take place, the illusory phenomena of light and darkness must first enter the eye-faculty; this is what we call seeing.[11] Apart from light and darkness, seeing has no ultimate basis. Understand it this way, Ānanda: what we call seeing does not take place because of light or darkness, nor because of the eye-faculty, nor because of space. Why? If what we call seeing took place because of light, it would cease in total darkness, and you would not see the darkness. If it took place because of darkness, it would cease once light were present, and so you would not see the light.[12]

"Further, seeing cannot take place because of the eye-faculty, because clearly there is a need for light or for darkness if seeing is to occur. It follows that the eye-faculty has no independent existence. Finally, if seeing took place because of space, then when we look straight ahead, we would see the objects before us as usual, but we would also be able to look back on our own eyes from space. If space were doing the seeing, what would seeing have to do with the eye-faculty?

[10] That is, the strain placed on the mind by fundamental ignorance.

[11] The text has *jian xing* 見性, literally the "nature of seeing," but here the reference is not to the enlightened nature of our visual awareness but to the ordinary process of seeing.

[12] The argument here is similar to that in parts 1.2d, and 2.1.

"In this way you should know that the eye-faculty is illusory. It does not come into being from causes and conditions, nor does it come into being on its own.

B. The Ear-Faculty

"Ānanda, consider the example of a person who forcefully stops up his ears with his fingers. The strain exerted on the ear-faculty may cause a sound to be heard inside his head. What the ear-faculty perceives when it is under strain, and also the ear-faculty itself, come about through the strain placed on the awakened mind. The strain causes the distortion in perception.

"For hearing to take place, the illusory phenomena of sound and silence must enter the ear-faculty; this is what we call hearing. Apart from sound and silence, hearing has no ultimate basis. Understand it this way, Ānanda: what we call hearing does not take place because of sound or silence, nor because of the ear-faculty, nor because of space. Why? If it took place because of silence, it would cease once sounds were present, and so we would not hear sounds. If what we call hearing took place because of sound, hearing would cease in total silence, and we would not be aware of the silence.

"Further, hearing cannot take place because of the ear-faculty alone, because clearly there is a need for sound or for silence if hearing is to occur. It follows that the ear-faculty has no independent existence. Finally, if hearing took place because of space, then space would not be what we call space, because it would have the ability to hear. And if space could hear, what would hearing have to do with the ear-faculty?

"In this way you should know that the ear-faculty is illusory. It does not come into being from causes and conditions, nor does it come into being on its own.

> Hearing occurs through dependence on the two illusory perceived objects of sound and silence. Hearing and seeing are like magnets. . . . The eyes look at things and become unclean; the ears attract sounds and become unclean. Our true nature is fundamentally pure, but because the eye and ear attract unclean external objects, our true nature becomes unclean also. It is like

inhaling cigarette smoke . . . which passes into the lungs, and although ordinary people cannot see into their own insides, the fact remains that the throat, windpipe, and lungs become coated with tar. . . . In the same way, sights and sounds are taken in and coat our true natures with a kind of tar that covers it over and obscures its light. As recorded in the Sixth Patriarch's Dharma-Jewel Platform Sūtra,[13] Shen Xiu said,

> The body is a bodhi tree,[14]
> The mind a mirror on its stand.
> It must be wiped clean day and night,
> So that no dust remains.

Actually, this verse is a fine expression of what needs to be done, but these are not the words of one who has become aware of his true nature. Great Master Shen Xiu's verse describes practice at a stage prior to the seeing of one's true nature. It likens practice to dusting a mirror over and over again to keep it clean. . . . After Shen Xiu composed this verse, the Sixth Patriarch, the Great Master Hui Neng, replied with the following verse:

> There is no tree in bodhi.
> The mirror needs no stand.
> For really there is nothing.
> Where could the dust alight?

Master Hui Neng was already enlightened, and so he no longer needed to do the work of dusting the mirror. (III, 31–2)

C. The Nose-Faculty

"Ānanda, consider the example of a person who, as he breathes in through his nose, continues to inhale sharply until at length the strain exerted on his nose-faculty gives rise to an illusory sensation of cold. As

---

[13] *The Sixth Patriarch's Dharma-Jewel Platform Sūtra, with the commentary of Tripitaka Master Hua,* Buddhist Text Translation Society, trans. (San Francisco: Sino-American Buddhist Association, 1977), 52–8.

[14] A reference to the tree under which the Buddha Śākyamuni was sitting when he attained full awakening (bodhi). The tree is a species of banyan (*ficus religiosa*).

he experiences this sensation, he becomes aware of whether his nostrils are clear or blocked, and whether odors are pleasant or unpleasant or neither pleasant nor unpleasant. What the nose-faculty perceives when it is under strain, as well as the nose-faculty itself, come about through the strain placed on the awakened mind. The strain causes the distortion in perception.

"For smelling to take place, the illusory phenomena of openness or blockage in the nasal passages must be present in the nose-faculty; then what we call smelling can occur. Apart from openness and blockage, smelling has no ultimate basis. Understand it this way, Ānanda; what we call smelling does not take place because of openness or blockage, nor because of the nose-faculty, nor because of space.

"Why? If what we call smelling took place because the nasal passages are open, it would cease when they are blocked, and you would not be aware of the blockage. If it took place because of the blockage, it would cease once the nasal passages were open, and so you would not be aware of odors, whether they are pleasant, unpleasant, or neither pleasant nor unpleasant. Further, smelling cannot take place because of the nose-faculty, because clearly there is a need for openness in the nasal passages if smelling is to occur. It follows that the nose-faculty has no independent existence.

"Finally, if smelling took place because of space, then space would be able to smell the nose. Besides, if space were doing the smelling, what would smelling have to do with the nose-faculty?

"In this way you should know that the nose-faculty is illusory. It does not come into being from causes and conditions, nor does it come into being on its own.

D. The Tongue-Faculty

"Ānanda, consider the example of a person who licks his lips repeatedly to the point that his tongue-faculty is subjected to strain. If he is sick, he will experience a bitter taste; otherwise the taste will seem slightly sweet. His experience of sweetness or bitterness demonstrates that the tongue-faculty is still active when no tastes are present. What the tongue-faculty perceives when it is under strain, as well as the tongue-faculty itself, come about through strain placed on the awakened mind. The strain causes the distortion in perception.

> The Matrix of the Thus-Come One is bigger than anything else and contains everything. There is nothing it does not contain. . . . Where are we now? We are all in the Matrix of the Thus-Come One. "We haven't seen what the Matrix of the Thus-Come One looks like," you may say. In fact, you see it every day, but you don't recognize it. In all your daily activities you are within the Matrix of the Thus-Come One. What your eyes see, what your ears hear — absolutely everything is within the Matrix of the Thus-Come One. . . . In China there is the saying, "I can't tell what Mount Lu really looks like, because I myself am standing on Mount Lu." (III, 41–2)

"For tasting to take place, the illusory attributes of sweetness or bitterness, or else an absence of flavor, must come into contact with the tongue-faculty; this is what we call tasting. Apart from sweetness and bitterness, and from the absence of flavor, tasting has no apparent basis. Understand it this way, Ānanda: what we call tasting does not take place because of sweetness or bitterness or the absence of flavor, nor does it take place because of the tongue-faculty, nor does it take place because of space.

"Why? If tasting took place because sweetness or bitterness is present, how would you become aware of an absence of flavor? If it took place because no flavor is present, it would vanish in the presence of a sweet or bitter taste. How then would you become aware of sweetness or bitterness? Further, tasting cannot take place because of the tongue-faculty, because there is clearly a need for a flavor such as sweetness or bitterness, or else the absence of flavor, if tasting is to occur. It follows that the tongue-faculty has no independent existence.

"Finally, if tasting took place because of space, then space would have the ability to taste, and space, not your tongue, would have awareness of flavors. If space were aware of flavors, what would tasting have to do with the tongue-faculty?

"In this way you should know that the tongue-faculty is illusory. It does not come into being from causes and conditions, nor does it come into being on its own.

E. The Body-Faculty

"Ānanda, consider the example of a person who joins his hands together when one hand is warm and the other cold. If the cold hand is colder than the warm hand is warm, it will make the warm hand become cold, and if the warm hand is warmer than the cold hand is cold, it will make the cold hand become warm. With the exchange of warmth and cold from the prolonged contact between the two hands, the person becomes aware of contact and, subsequently, separation. What the body-faculty perceives when it is under strain, as well as the body-faculty itself, come about through strain placed on the awakened mind. The strain causes the distortion in perception.

"What we call tactile awareness occurs when the illusory phenomena of contact and separation are felt by the body-faculty. This tactile awareness of contact and separation may be pleasant or unpleasant, but without them, tactile awareness has no ultimate basis. Understand it this way, Ānanda: what we call tactile awareness does not take place because of contact and separation, nor because of any pleasantness or unpleasantness of the sensation, nor because of the body-faculty, nor because of space.

"Why? If tactile awareness took place because of contact, how would you become aware of separation when contact ceased? By the same logic, it cannot take place because sensation is pleasant or because it is unpleasant. Further, tactile awareness cannot take place because of the body-faculty, because clearly there is a need for contact or separation and for pleasantness or unpleasantness if tactile awareness is to occur. It follows that tactile awareness has no independent existence.

"Finally, if tactile awareness took place because of space alone, then space would be aware of tactile sensations; then what would tactile awareness have to do with the body-faculty?

"In this way you should know that the body-faculty is illusory. It does not come into being from causes and conditions, nor does it come into being on its own.

F. The Cognitive Faculty

"Ānanda, consider the example of a person who is tired and falls asleep. Having slept enough, he awakens and tries to remember his dreams. He recalls some elements of his dreams but cannot remember others. This succession of sleeping, waking, remembering, and forgetting is an example of the distorted stages of coming into being, abiding, changing, and perishing within the cognitive faculty. What we call the cognitive faculty engages in a habitual process of bringing into our awareness an orderly succession of mental objects. What the cognitive faculty perceives when it is under strain, as well as the cognitive faculty itself, come forth from the strain placed on the awakened mind. The strain causes the distortion in perception.

"In their two aspects of coming into being and perishing, unreal perceived objects accumulate in our cognitive awareness. The cognitive faculty is attracted to these internal mental objects. What we call cognitive awareness is this internal flow of visible objects, sounds, and so forth before they enter the mind's ground.[15] Apart from the fluctuation between sleep and waking, cognitive awareness has no apparent basis. Understand it this way, Ānanda: what we call cognitive awareness does not take place because of waking and sleeping or because of the coming into being and perishing of mental objects; nor does it take place because of the cognitive faculty, nor does it take place because of space.

"Why? If cognitive awareness took place because of waking, you would have no cognitive awareness when you were asleep, and then how could you experience sleep? By the same logic, cognition cannot arise because cognitive objects arise, since when those cognitive objects perish, the cognitive faculty would perish also. Nor can cognitive awareness take place because of the perishing of cognitive objects, since when cognitive objects subsequently arose, cognitive awareness would perish. What then would be aware of the objects that arose? Further, cognitive awareness cannot be present because of the cognitive faculty. Why? Although sleeping and waking are dependent on the body's becoming active or

---

[15] That is, the eighth consciousness.

dormant, yet apart from a state of sleep or waking, cognitive awareness has no more existence than a mirage of flowers in space. Finally, if cognitive awareness took place because of space, then space would be aware of cognitive objects. What then would cognitive awareness have to do with the cognitive faculty?

"In this way you should know that the cognitive faculty is an illusion. It does not come into being from causes and conditions, nor does it come into being on its own."

3
The Twelve Sites Are
the Matrix of the Thus-Come One

A. The Eye-Faculty and Visible Objects

"Moreover, Ānanda, how is it that, fundamentally, the twelve sites[16] are the Matrix of the Thus-Come One, whose nature is the wondrous suchness of reality? Ānanda, look once again at the fountains, the pools, and the trees of the Prince Jetri's Grove. What do you think? Does the presence of visible objects cause your eye-faculty to see? Or to the contrary, does the eye-faculty cause the visible objects to be present?

"Ananda, if the eye-faculty caused the presence of visible objects, then when you looked at an empty sky, in which no visible objects are present, all the visible objects that you were not looking at would have to disappear. If everything were to disappear, such that nothing were present, then how could we know what space is?[17] The corollary supposition — that space is present because your eye-faculty is there to see it — can be similarly rejected.

"Suppose, on the other hand, that the presence of visible objects caused your eye-faculty to see. Then when you looked at empty space, in which no objects are present, your eye-faculty would no longer exist. If your eye-faculty no longer existed, nothing would be seen, and in that case, how could we know what visible objects are — or what space is?

"Therefore, you should know that the eye-faculty and visible objects, and space as well, have no real existence. These two sites — the eye-faculty and visible objects — are illusions. Fundamentally, they are not dependent on causes or conditions, and yet they do not come into being on their own.

---

[16] That is, the six faculties and the six kinds of perceived objects.

[17] The notion "space" only makes sense in contrast with the notion of what is not space — that is, visible objects.

B. The Ear-Faculty and Sounds

"Moreover, Ānanda, you have heard the beating of the drum in Prince Jetri's Grove when a meal is ready. The assembly gathers, and then the bell is struck. The drumbeats and the peals of the bell each follow one upon another in clear succession. What do you think? Do the sounds come to the ear-faculty? Or to the contrary, does the ear-faculty go out to the sounds?

"Ānanda, suppose the sounds come to the ear. Then the situation could be compared to my going on my almsround in Śrāvastī so that I am no longer in Prince Jetri's Grove. Now if sounds came to your ear in order for you to hear them, Ānanda, then neither Mahākāśyapa nor Mahāmaudgalyāyana — not to speak of the rest of the twelve-hundred-fifty elder monks — would hear the bell calling them to the meal. How would they know it was time to eat?

> The Buddha says that when he goes to the city of Śrāvastī on his alms-rounds, he is no longer present in Prince Jetri's Grove. One cannot be in two places at once. Thus, if the sound definitely goes to Ānanda's ear, then neither Maudgalyāyana nor Kāśyapa would hear it. The Buddha is really not making sense here. Sound spreads out; everyone would have heard the bell despite what the Buddha is saying. He is deliberately trying to befuddle Ānanda just to see how Ānanda will answer. (III, 64)

"Ānanda, suppose that the ear-faculty goes out to a sound in order for you to hear it. Then the situation can be compared to my returning to Prince Jetri's Grove so that I am no longer in Śrāvastī. If your ear-faculty went out to the drum in order to hear it, then you would not be able to hear the bell at the same time — nor would you be able to hear other sounds, such as the noise made by elephants, horses, oxen, and sheep. On the other hand, if no sounds reached the ear-faculty, you would not be able to hear either.

"Therefore, you should know that sounds and the ear-faculty have no real existence. These two sites — sounds and the ear-faculty — are illusions. Fundamentally, they are not dependent on causes or conditions, and yet they do not come into being on their own.

C. The Nose-Faculty and Odors

"Moreover, Ānanda, you can smell the sandalwood incense[18] burning in a censer. A small pinch of this incense, once lit, can be smelled everywhere around Śrāvastī for a distance of a dozen miles. What do you think? Does the fragrance come into being from the sandalwood incense? Does it come into being from your nose-faculty? Or does it come into being from space?

"Ānanda, suppose that the fragrance comes into being from your nose-faculty. If it comes into being because of the nose, then the nose must emit fragrance.[19] But the nose is not made of sandalwood; how then could it produce the fragrance of sandalwood? Clearly, the fragrance must enter the nose in order for you to smell it. It makes no sense to say that you smell it when the fragrance comes out of the nose.

"Suppose that the fragrance comes into being from space. Since space is by nature everlasting and unchanging, a fragrance that came into being from space would therefore be ever-present. What need would there be then to burn the sandalwood in the censer?

"Suppose that the fragrance comes from the wood. Now, the fragrant wood gives off smoke when it is burned. For the nose to smell the smoke, the smoke must come into contact with the nose-faculty. Yet the fragrance has already spread a dozen miles in every direction long before the smoke itself has risen very far into the air.

"Therefore, you should know that sandalwood incense and the nose-faculty have no real existence. These two sites — the nose-faculty and odors — are illusions. Fundamentally, they are not dependent on causes or conditions, and yet they do not come into being on their own.

D. The Tongue-Faculty and Flavors

"Ānanda, to obtain your two daily meals,[20] you and the others in the assembly take up your almsbowls. In them you may receive curds, cheese,

---

[18] Skt. *candana*, Ch. *zhan tan* 旃檀.

[19] Because what produces something must be like in nature to the thing produced.

[20] The reference is to breakfast and the midday meal. With some exceptions, Buddhist monastics take a vow not to eat after noon.

or ghee, which are considered to have excellent flavors. What do you think? Do these flavors come into being from space, from the tongue, or from the food?

"Suppose, Ānanda, that these flavors came into being from the tongue. Now, you have only one tongue. Suppose then that the flavor of the curds does come from the tongue. Then if a lump of sugar were placed on the tongue, the tongue would not be able to taste it unless it could change its nature. If the tongue cannot change its nature so that it can taste a variety of flavors, it cannot be capable of tasting. If it could change, that would mean you would have several tongues. How then does the one tongue you do have recognize a variety of flavors?

"Suppose the flavors come from the food. But the food has no consciousness; how could it be aware of flavors? If the food were aware of its own flavors, then it would be as if someone else were eating. How would you be able to taste it?

"Suppose that the flavors come from space. But suppose you were to take a mouthful of space: would it have a flavor? Let us say that it does — that it has a salty taste. If it could place a salty taste on your tongue, it would inevitably make your face salty as well. Everyone in the world would be like fish in the sea. Since you would perpetually be tasting salt, you would never be aware of a bland taste; and if you were never aware of a bland taste, you would not be able to distinguish a salty taste either. Indeed, you would not be able to taste at all. How then could you be said to have an awareness of flavors?

"Therefore, you should know that food and the tongue-faculty have no real existence. These two sites — the tongue-faculty and flavors — are illusions. Fundamentally, they are not dependent on causes or conditions, and yet they do not come into being on their own.

E. The Body-Faculty and Objects of Touch

"Ānanda, every morning at daybreak you touch your head with your hand. What do you think? Is the awareness of the contact present in your hand or in your head? If it is only your hand that is aware of the contact, then your head will not be aware of it; how can that amount to the sensation you experience? And if it is just your head that is aware of the contact, then your hand must not be aware of it; how could that be what we mean by the sensation you experience?

> The practice of passing the hands over the head was adopted when the Buddha Śākyamuni was in the world. Many people who had followed other paths later became his disciples. As a result, the Buddha taught the monks to touch their own heads, which they keep shaved, three times every day in order to help them remember that they were monks. The practice continues to this day. (III, 77–8)

"If both your head and your hand had a separate awareness of the contact, Ānanda, you must have two bodies.[21] Conversely, if your head and hand together experience a single awareness of contact, then your head and your hand must be a single object. If they were a single object, how could there be contact between them? Given that your head and your hand are two separate objects, which of them is aware of the contact? The one that is aware cannot be the perceived object, and the one that is the perceived object cannot be what is aware. Nor can the contact be between you and space.

"Therefore, you should know that, in fact, your body-faculty and objects of touch have no real existence. These two sites — the body-faculty and the objects of touch — are illusions. Fundamentally, they are not dependent on causes or conditions, and yet they do not come into being on their own.

F. The Cognitive Faculty and Objects of Cognition

"Ānanda, objects of cognition are always arising in your mind in three categories: pleasant, unpleasant, and neither pleasant nor unpleasant.[22]

---

[21] The translation here follows the commentary of the Ven. Yuanying (421).

[22] The mind is constantly experiencing the sensations presented to it by the first five consciousnesses (the consciousnesses of the eye, ear, nose, tongue, and body), and these sensations are divided by the mind into the categories of pleasant, unpleasant, and neither pleasant nor unpleasant. Thoughts and emotions may also be analyzed according to the same three categories.

Now, do these objects of cognition arise from your cognitive faculty, or do they arise from some source other than your cognitive faculty?

"Ānanda, if these objects of cognition arose from your cognitive faculty, they could not be objects of cognition,[23] and they would not then be what your cognitive faculty can interact with.[24] How then could they be a site for the arising of your mind-consciousness?

"Suppose they arose from some source other than your cognitive faculty. Would they be aware of themselves as objects of cognition, or would they not? If they were aware, they would have to be part of your cognitive faculty. If they were aware and yet arose from some place other than your cognitive faculty, but were not objects of cognition, they could only be located in someone else's cognitive faculty. But given that these objects of cognition are something you are aware of, they must be present in your cognitive faculty, and so they cannot after all be present in someone else's cognitive faculty.

"Finally, if these objects of cognition are not aware and arise from some other source than your mind, then at what site might they be located, given that they are neither visible objects, nor sounds, nor odors, nor flavors, nor such attributes as separation, contact, cold, and warmth? Nor are they space. Since there is nothing in the world humans perceive beyond visible objects, the other perceived objects, and space, and since objects of cognition are distinct from the cognitive faculty, what place is left for objects of cognition to be located?

"Therefore, you should know that, in fact, your cognitive faculty and objects of cognition have no real existence. These two sites of perception — the cognitive faculty and objects of cognition — are illusions. Fundamentally, they are not dependent on causes or conditions, and yet they do not come into being on their own."

---

[23] Were they to arise from the cognitive faculty, then they would share its capacity to be aware.

[24] They could not have the attributes of both the cognitive faculty and objects of cognition at the same time.

4

The Eighteen Constituents Are
the Matrix of the Thus-Come One

A. The Coming into Being of the Eye-Consciousness

"Moreover, Ānanda, how is it that, fundamentally, the eighteen constituents are the Matrix of the Thus-Come One, which is the wondrous suchness of reality? Ānanda, according to your understanding of it, the eye-faculty and visible objects are the conditions for the coming into being of the eye-consciousness. But does this consciousness come into being from the eyes, such that it is restricted by the boundaries of the eye-faculty? Or does it come into being from visible objects, such that it is restricted by the boundaries of visible objects?

> The eighteen constituents are the eyes, ears, nose, tongue, body, and mind; visible objects, sounds, odors, flavors, objects of touch, and objects of cognition; and eye-consciousness, ear-consciousness, nose-consciousness, tongue-consciousness, body-consciousness, and mind-consciousness. The six faculties are matched to the six sense-objects, and between them are produced the six consciousnesses. The consciousnesses are what make distinctions. . . . Thus the eyes see visible objects and distinguish them as being attractive or unattractive. With the ears it is the same: they hear sounds as pleasing or displeasing. . . . Visible objects, sounds, odors, flavors, and objects of touch all have physical attributes. Only objects of cognition lack physical attributes. Nonetheless, when the cognitive faculty is matched with objects of cognition, distinctions are made in the mind; thus the mind also has a consciousness. (III, 91–2)

"Suppose, Ānanda, that the eye-consciousness came into being from the eye-faculty. Now, without the presence of visible objects or of space, the eye-consciousness could not make distinctions, and even if it existed in this situation, what use would it be? Your eye-consciousness is neither blue, yellow, red, nor white. There is nothing to indicate where it is. On what then would the constituent that is the eye-consciousness be based?

"Suppose the eye-consciousness came into being from visible objects. Then in the presence of space, where there are no visible objects, your eye-consciousness would cease to be. How then could it be aware of space?

"Again, if your eye-consciousness came into being from visible objects, then when the objects changed, your eye-consciousness would change along with them. If it came into being from visible objects and yet did not change along with them, where would it exist? But if it did change, it would no longer have the characteristics of eye-consciousness. Also, it cannot come from visible objects because, if it did, given that it does not change, it could not become aware of space.

"Suppose then that the eye-consciousness came into being from both the eye-faculty and visible objects. But it cannot arise from a combination of the two, because then it would be internally divided. Nor can the eye-consciousness arise from the two as separate entities, because then it would be a chaotic mixture. How could the eye-consciousness be something so undefined?

"Therefore, you should know that the eye-faculty and visible objects cannot be the conditions for the coming into being of the eye-consciousness, because none of these three constituents — eye-faculty, visible objects, and eye-consciousness — has an independent existence. Fundamentally, they do not come into being from causes and conditions; nor do they come into being on their own.

B. The Coming into Being of the Ear-Consciousness

"Moreover, Ānanda, according to your understanding of it, the ear-faculty and sounds are the conditions for the coming into being of the ear-consciousness. But does this consciousness come into being from the ear-faculty such that it is restricted by the boundaries of the ear-faculty? Or does it come into being from sounds, such that it is restricted by the boundaries of sound?

"Suppose, Ānanda, that it came into being from the ear-faculty. But without the presence of either sound or silence, the ear-faculty would not be aware of anything. If the ear-faculty lacked awareness, because there would be no objects for it to be aware of, then what attributes could the consciousness have? You may insist that it is the ears that hear. But without the presence of sound or silence, no hearing can take place. Also, the ear is covered with skin, and the body-faculty is involved with objects of touch. Could the ear-consciousness come into being from that faculty? Since it cannot, what can the ear-consciousness be based on?

"Suppose the ear-consciousness came into being from sounds. If the ear-consciousness owed its existence to sounds, then it would have nothing to do with hearing. But if no hearing is taking place, how would you know where sounds are coming from? Suppose, nevertheless, that the ear-consciousness did arise from sound. Since a sound must be heard if it is to be what we know as a sound, the ear-consciousness would also be heard as a sound. And when it is not heard, it would not exist. Besides, if it is heard, then it would be the same thing as a sound; it would be something that is heard. But what would be able to hear it? And if you had no awareness, you would be as insentient as grass or wood.

"Do not say that sounds, which have no awareness, and the ear-faculty, which is aware, can intermingle to create the ear-consciousness. There can be no such place where these two can mix together, since one is internal and the other is external. Where else then could the ear-consciousness come into being?

"Therefore, you should know that the ear-faculty and sounds cannot be the conditions for the coming into being of the ear-consciousness, because none of these three constituents — ear-faculty, sounds, and ear-consciousness — has an independent existence. Fundamentally, they do not come into being from causes and conditions; nor do they come into being on their own.

C. The Coming into Being of the Nose-Consciousness

"Moreover, Ānanda, according to your understanding of it, the nose-faculty and odors are the conditions for the coming into being of the nose-consciousness. But does this consciousness come into being from the nose-faculty, such that it is restricted by the boundaries of the nose-faculty? Or does it come into being from odors, such that it is restricted by the boundaries of odors?

"Ānanda, suppose it came into being from the nose. Now, in your opinion, what should we consider the nose to be? Should we take it to be a part of the body that is shaped like a pair of talons? Or should we take it to be the faculty that is aware of the natures of various odors?

"Suppose we take the nose to be a part of the body shaped like a pair of talons. But then the nose belongs to the body-faculty, which is aware of objects of touch. What belongs to the body-faculty is not the nose-faculty, and the body-faculty perceives objects of touch. Nothing would remain to be called 'nose-faculty.' How could the nose-consciousness be based on it?

"Ānanda, suppose that we take the nose to be the faculty that is aware of odors, then once again, in your opinion, what is it that is aware? Is it the part of the body shaped like a pair of talons? If so, then it would be its nature to be aware of objects of touch. It could not be the nose-faculty that is aware of odors.

"Suppose it is space that is aware of odors. If space were itself aware, then it would not be a part of your body that would be aware. In that case, space, given that it is aware, would have to be you, and your body would have no awareness. Then you, Ānanda, would not be here now at all.

"Suppose it is odors that are aware. If awareness were really a function of odors, how would you expect to be involved? If your nose were what produced odors, both pleasant and unpleasant, then such odors would not come from sandalwood incense or from the foul-smelling airāvaṇa.[25]

> The airāvaṇa tree emits an extremely foul stench that can be smelled from a long way off. Its stench is like that of a corpse that for several weeks has been decaying under the blazing sun. The red flowers of the airāvaṇa tree are very beautiful but very poisonous and to eat them means immediate death. (III, 108)

"If those odors don't come from those two things, then clearly it must be your nose itself that has an odor. Would its odor be pleasant or unpleasant? If it were pleasant, it could not be unpleasant, and if unpleasant,

[25] Probably one of the jackfruits.

it could not be pleasant. Thus if it really were odors, both pleasant and unpleasant, that were aware, then you would have to have two noses, or else I would be questioning two people about the Path. Which one would be you? Since you after all have only one nose, which cannot both stink and be fragrant, then if odors were in fact aware, stench would have to be fragrant and fragrance would have to stink. Neither would have a nature of its own. On what then would the nose-consciousness be based?

"Suppose, again, that the nose-consciousness came into being from odors. If that were the case, then just as the eye-faculty can see everything but itself, so the nose-consciousness, if it came into being from odors, could not be aware of odors. Since it is aware of odors, it cannot come into being from them; and if after all it were not aware of odors, it would not be the nose-consciousness. Besides, since odors have no awareness, the constituent element of the nose-consciousness cannot come into being from them; and if it did, the consciousness could not become aware of odors. Therefore the nose-consciousness cannot come into being from odors.

"Finally, since there can be no place that is intermediate between a faculty, which is internal, and its object, which is external, the nose-consciousness must ultimately be a distortion and an illusion.

"Therefore, you should know that the nose-faculty and odors cannot be the conditions for the coming into being of the nose-consciousness, because none of these three constituents — nose-faculty, odors, and the nose-consciousness — has an independent existence. Fundamentally, they do not come into being from causes and conditions; nor do they come into being on their own.

D. The Coming into Being of the Tongue-Consciousness

"Moreover, Ānanda, according to your understanding of it, the tongue-faculty and flavors are the conditions for the coming into being of the tongue-consciousness. But does this consciousness come into being from the tongue-faculty, such that it is restricted by the boundaries of the tongue-faculty? Or does it come into being from flavors, such that it is restricted by the boundaries of flavors?

"Ānanda, suppose it came into being from the tongue-faculty. Then you would not be able to taste the flavors that we find in the world, such as sugar cane, sour plums, coptis rhizome, salt, wild ginger, ginger, and cinnamon.[26] You would only be able to taste your own tongue-faculty. Would it be sweet or bitter? Suppose it were bitter: what would be tasting it? Since the tongue-faculty cannot taste itself, what would the tongue-consciousness consist of? If your tongue-faculty were not bitter, bitter flavor could not come into being from it. On what then would the tongue-consciousness be based?

"Suppose the tongue-consciousness came into being from flavors. Then the tongue-consciousness would itself have flavor, and just as in the previous case of the nose-faculty, the tongue-consciousness would not be able to taste its own flavor. How then would it be aware of the presence or absence of any flavor? Further, flavors do not come into being from any one thing. Since flavors come from many different things, there would have to be many tongue-consciousnesses. But given that there is after all just one tongue-consciousness, then if that single tongue-consciousness indeed came into being from flavors, it would have to itself be a combination of such flavors as salty, bland, sweet, and hot. Their various characteristics would have to change into a single flavor, and you would not be able to distinguish one from another. Since your tongue-consciousness could not make distinctions among them, it could not be what we call a consciousness, and so could not be the constituent that is the tongue-consciousness. Nor could it come into being from space.

"Do not say that the tongue faculty and flavors come into contact and combine to create a constituent at their place of contact. If flavors, which are external, and the tongue-faculty, which is internal, did combine, then there would be no place of contact. They would cease to exist as separate constituents.

[26] This list of edibles exemplifies seven flavors in sequence: sweet, sour, bitter, salty, pungent, hot, and astringent. Coptis rhizome (Ch. *huang lian* 黃連), is a low-growing perennial of the family *ranunculaceae.* The root is bitter and astringent to the taste. It is still widely used to control infection and reduce fever. Wild ginger (Ch. *xi xin* 細辛) is a medicinal plant distinct from ginger; it represents pungency. However, the translation is uncertain.

"Therefore, you should know that the tongue-faculty and flavors cannot be the conditions for the coming into being of the tongue-consciousness, because none of these three constituents — tongue-faculty, flavors, and tongue-consciousness — has an independent existence. Fundamentally, they do not come into being from causes and conditions; nor do they come into being on their own.

E. The Coming into Being of the Body-Consciousness

"Moreover, Ānanda, according to your understanding of it, the body-faculty and objects of touch are the conditions for the coming into being of the body-consciousness. But does this consciousness come into being from the body-faculty, such that it is restricted by the boundaries of the body-faculty? Or does it come into being from objects of touch, such that it is restricted by the boundaries of objects of touch?

"Suppose it came into being from the body-faculty. Then there could be no contact with objects of touch or separation from them, and these are said to be two conditions for the body-consciousness's awareness. How then could the body-consciousness be limited to the body?

"Suppose it came into being from objects of touch. Then your body would not be involved. Yet who can be without a body and still be aware of contact with and separation from objects of touch? Insentient things cannot have tactile awareness; and it is the body-consciousness that is aware of objects of touch. Only with a body-faculty can there be awareness of contact with objects.

"Further, for you to be aware of your body as an object of touch in itself, there needs to be contact, but it is your body-faculty that comes into contact with objects. But an object cannot be identical with a faculty; the body-faculty cannot be an object. Fundamentally, neither the body-faculty nor objects of touch are sufficient as places of support for the body-consciousness. If the body-consciousness were joined to the body-faculty, it would have the essential nature of the body-faculty; yet if it were not joined to the body-faculty, it would have the same nature as space.

"Since the body-consciousness cannot come into being either from the faculty, which is internal, or its objects, which are external, how could it exist between them? Since it cannot exist between them, and since the internal faculty and the external objects are all empty of an inherent nature, what could the body-consciousness be based on?

"Therefore, you should know that the body-faculty and objects of touch cannot be the conditions for the coming into being of the body-consciousness, because none of these three constituents — body-faculty, objects of touch, and body-consciousness — has an independent existence. Fundamentally, they do not come into being from causes and conditions; nor do they come into being on their own.

> The various principles explained above demonstrate that the body-consciousness cannot be found. . . . In the provisional teachings, the body-faculty and contact with objects of touch are the conditions for the action of the body-consciousness. In the ultimate teaching, none of these three exist. They do not have their origin in causes and conditions, nor do their natures have an independent existence. They manifest from within the Matrix of the Thus-Come One. They have no fixed location. The provisional teachings cannot be compared to the truths of the ultimate teaching. What was spoken previously was an expedient teaching. . . . The Buddha's teachings about causes and conditions refuted the theory of independent existence of phenomena, as propounded by followers of wrong paths. That is why Ānanda became attached to the teaching of causes and conditions and couldn't give up on the idea. He thought the teachings that had been given previously could not be superseded. Why is the Buddha now negating the principles which he previously explained? For the Buddha himself not to accept the Dharma which he himself had spoken before was to contradict himself, wasn't it? It is at this point that Ānanda has many doubts and keeps coming up with questions. So now the Buddha tells Ānanda that he explained the laws of causes and conditions earlier in order to counteract the non-Buddhist sects; it was certainly not ultimate. It was certainly not the essential Dharma. Now that the ultimate truth of the Middle Way — the genuine Dharma — is being explained, the former teachings no longer apply; and you cannot continue to hold on to them. Ānanda has not yet understood that. (III, 125–6)

F. The Coming into Being of the Mind-Consciousness

"Moreover, Ānanda, according to your understanding of it, the cognitive faculty and its objects are the conditions for the coming into being of mind-consciousness. But does this consciousness come into being from the cognitive faculty, such that it is restricted by the boundaries of the cognitive faculty? Or does it come into being from its objects, such that it is restricted to the boundaries its objects?

"Ānanda, suppose the mind-consciousness came into being from the cognitive faculty. Now, your cognitive faculty has to be considering something in order for it to be functioning. If no objects of cognition are present, the cognitive faculty does not arise. If the cognitive faculty has not manifested, how would the mind-consciousness function?

"Further, the natures of both your mind-consciousness and your cognitive faculty are such that they make distinctions.[27] Do they differ from one another, or are they the same? If the mind-consciousness were the same as the cognitive faculty, it would be the cognitive faculty; then how could the mind-consciousness come into being from the cognitive faculty? If the mind-consciousness were different from the cognitive faculty, it would not be conscious of anything. If it were not conscious of anything, how could it come into being from the cognitive faculty? If it is conscious, how can you differentiate it from the cognitive faculty? Since neither a sameness nor a difference can be identified, on what can the mind-consciousness be based?

"Suppose, finally, that the mind-consciousness came into being from objects of cognition. Now, all your experiences of the external world are experiences of visible objects, of sounds, of odors, of flavors, or of objects of touch. Each of these categories of objects has the attribute of complementing one of five faculties. None of them complements the cognitive faculty. If you nevertheless insist that your mind-consciousness must come into being from objects of cognition, you should consider carefully

---

[27] "Cognitive faculty" here is the seventh or individuating consciousness. Both the sixth consciousness and the seventh make distinctions, but those made by the seventh are more subtle (Yuanying, 450).

what the essential attributes of objects of cognition and the other perceived objects might be. If you exclude the essential attributes of visible objects and if you exclude their absence — as well as excluding the essential attributes of sound and silence, openness and blockage, and separation and contact — beyond these, what would be left for objects of cognition to be? Visible objects, the absence of visible objects, and the other kinds of perceived objects and their absence are what arise, and they are what perish, while objects of cognition, which we are now supposing to be the cause of the mind-consciousness, cannot come into being independently without another perceived object being present. Therefore, if objects of cognition were what cause the mind-consciousness to come into being, what essential attributes would it have? Since objects of cognition have no independent attributes, how could the mind-consciousness arise from them?

"Therefore, you should know that the cognitive faculty and objects of cognition cannot be the conditions that are necessary for the coming into being of the mind-consciousness, because none of these three constituents — cognitive faculty, objects of cognition, and mind-consciousness — has an independent existence. Fundamentally, they do not come into being from causes and conditions, nor do they come into being on their own."

5

The Seven Primary Elements Are the Matrix of the Thus-Come One

Ānanda said to the Buddha, "World-Honored One, the Thus-Come One has often discussed causes and conditions and aggregating and merging. He has shown that the various phenomena that we see in the world are caused by the merging or aggregating of the four primary elements. Why has the Thus-Come One now rejected causes and conditions and self-generation as explanations? I cannot reconcile this idea with the Buddha's previous teachings. Only pity us and instruct us and all beings how to know the ultimate truth of the Middle Way. Teach us the Dharma that is not mere words devoid of meaning."

People's bodies are a combination of four primary elements, which are earth, water, fire, and wind. The places in our bodies which are hard and solid belong to the primary element earth. The warmth in our bodies belongs to the primary element fire. Saliva, tears, and mucus belong to the primary element water. Our breath belongs to the primary element wind. While we are alive our body is under our control, but after we die these four primary elements disperse. The warmth in our body returns to the primary element fire, the moisture returns to the primary element water, the solids return to the primary element earth, and our breath returns to the primary element wind. People who do not understand about the body want to help the body in all that it does. What they don't know is that in this way their true natures become slaves to an illusory form. Every day they are confused as they toil and rush about desperately. Ultimately, what is it all for? Ultimately, what meaning is there in it? If one asks people these questions, they act like Ānanda, mouth agape and speechless. They can't come up with a reason.

Because people do not understand about the body, they spend all their energy on a lifeless thing. They don't work on behalf of what is really alive. What dead thing am I referring to? Although we are still living, our bodies may be considered already dead. What living thing am I referring to? Although we are not aware that it is alive, our spirit is young and full of life. It is our inherent

119

Buddha-nature. But people don't know that they should investigate their own Buddha-nature, and they work instead on behalf of their bodies, such that their bodies control them. From morning till night they help the body get good things to eat and fine clothes to wear. Just what is this body, anyway? . . . It isn't anything to grasp onto. Don't look upon it as so important, because even though you can't give up your attachment to it, when you die and the four elemental qualities disperse, you will have let go. (III, 133–4)

The World-Honored One then said to Ānanda, "Since you have renounced the teachings of the Lesser Vehicle — of the Hearers of the Teaching and the Solitary Sages — and since you have resolved to strive diligently to realize the supreme awakening, I will now instruct you in the ultimate truth. You need no longer bind yourself up with words that are devoid of meaning and with distorted thinking about causes and conditions. You are very learned, but you are like someone who can discuss medicines yet cannot identify them when they are actually set before him. The Thus-Come One says that you are indeed to be pitied. Listen carefully now. For your sake and for the sake of all who in the future will undertake the Bodhisattva's journey, I will explain in detail how you can come to thoroughly understand the ultimate truth." Ānanda was silent and waited for the Buddha's enlightened instruction.

"Ānanda, according to what you have said, the merging or aggregating of four primary elements brings about the various phenomena that are found in the world and that are subject to change. Let us suppose, Ānanda, that the primary elements have separate essential natures that cannot aggregate or merge.[28] In that case, their external attributes, too, could not aggregate or merge any more than space can aggregate or merge with perceived objects. Suppose, on the other hand, that the essential natures of the primary elements can aggregate and merge. Then their aggregating and merging would not differ from the various changes that take place in the world and that cause things to arise and perish through an unending process of coming into being and ceasing to be. Be-

---

[28] The "essential nature" and the "real nature" (below) of the primary elements are the Matrix of the Thus-Come One; their attributes are solidity, heat, liquidity, and movement.

ings, too, are born and die, and having died they are born again, forever coming to life and perishing again, Ānanda, like a torch that is swung endlessly in a circle to form a wheel of flame, or like water that turns to ice and then becomes water again.

> Ānanda should know that the suchness of reality conforms to circumstances yet does not change; it does not change yet conforms to circumstances. How is that explained? The suchness of reality — which is also called the Matrix of the Thus-Come One, true reality, and our true mind — is like water that becomes ice: that is, it conforms to circumstances, just as water can turn into ice when it is cold. But the ice can also melt and become water again. . . . Enlightenment is like water; affliction is like ice. . . . If you were to pour a bowl of water over someone's head, he wouldn't feel any pain. But if you hit someone over the head with a piece of ice, you might even kill him. Ice and water are actually the same thing, but water in its solid form can kill people, while in its liquid form it supports life. Because of this, affliction is compared to ice; full awakening is compared to water. The Buddha's sutras say that affliction is actually full awakening, just as ice is actually water. You don't add anything to water to make ice, and you don't add anything to ice to produce water. The potential to become ice is already in the water, and the potential to become water is already in the ice. Thus, the Sutra here speaks of ice becoming water again. But in order to turn your ice into water, you have to develop a certain amount of skill. You have to use yang light to illumine it; then the ice can turn into water. This refers to our daily practice of meditation in stillness, which can illumine our afflictions so that they turn into water. (III, 141–2)

A. The Primary Element Earth

"Let us consider the nature of the primary element earth. It may take as large a form as a continent and as small a form as a mote of dust. In its most subtle aspect, the primary element earth appears as particles that are so fine that they can hardly be distinguished from space itself.[29] If

---

[29] According to the *Abhidharmakośa* 85d-88a (2: 474), the smallest particles of matter are called *paramāṇu* (Skt.), and seven paramāṇu make one *aṇu* (Skt.). A paramāṇu cannot be divided, because if it were, its earth-element nature would disappear and all that would

these minute particles were divided further into seven parts, they would then be as small as perceived objects can be. If they were divided yet further, nothing would be left but space.

"Now if these most minute particles could be divided until they became space, Ānanda, then space would be capable of bringing perceived objects into being. You asked just now whether the various phenomena that we see in the world are caused by the merging or aggregating of the four elemental qualities. You should see that space, in whatever amount, could never be accumulated in order to bring into being even a single one of these most minute particles. Nor can it be true that these most minute particles are created by the particles themselves. Further, if these most minute particles could be divided to assume the nature of space, then conversely, how many such particles must be aggregated to bring space into being?

"In fact, when perceived objects are aggregated or merged, they do not become space; and when space accumulates, it does not become a perceived object. Besides, although perceived objects can indeed be divided, how can space be accumulated?

"You simply do not know that, in the Matrix of the Thus-Come One, the real nature of the primary element earth is identical to the real nature of emptiness. The real nature of the primary element earth is fundamentally pure and extends throughout the Dharma-Realm. The extent to which beings are aware of that real nature depends on the capacity of their understanding. The primary element earth appears to them in accord with their karma. Ordinary beings, in their ignorance, mistakenly suppose that the primary element earth comes into being from causes and conditions or that it comes into being on its own. These are distinctions and constructs made by the conscious mind. They are mere words, devoid of meaning.

remain would be space (Vasabhandu, *Abidharmakośabhāsyam,* Leo M. Pruden, trans., from the earlier French translation by Louis de la Vallée Poussin [Berkeley: Asian Humanities Press, 1988–90], 4.23).

B. The Primary Element Fire

"Ānanda, the nature of fire is such that it has no independent existence but is dependent on conditions. Let us consider a family in the city. They have not yet eaten dinner. When they set about to cook their meal, someone holds up a reflecting surface to the sun in order to start a fire.

"Ānanda, an example of an aggregation is our community here, which includes you, the twelve hundred and fifty monks, and myself. Although there is but one community, we can discern that it consists of separate individuals, each of whom was born into a certain class, clan, and family. For example, there is Śāriputra, who is a Brahmin; Uruvilvā, who belongs to the Kāśyapa clan; and you, Ānanda, who are of the Gautama family.

"In the example of the family starting a fire to cook a meal, Ānanda, then suppose that the sun, the reflecting surface, and the tinder act together to create the fire. Then when the reflecting surface is held up to the sun so that a fire may be lit, does the fire emerge from the reflecting surface? Does it emerge from the tinder? Does it come from the sun?

"Suppose that the fire came from the sun, Ānanda, such that the sun by itself would be able to set fire to some tinder that you were holding. Then it should also be able to set fire to a grove of trees merely by shining on it. Suppose that the fire emerges from the reflecting surface, such that the fire as it emerges ignites the tinder. Why doesn't the reflecting surface melt as you hold it up? Far from melting, it doesn't even become very hot. If the fire came into being from the tinder, what need would there be for sunlight to be reflected by the mirror? Carefully consider this further. Someone is holding up the reflecting surface, the sunlight comes from the sky, the tinder comes from an herb that has been grown in soil, but where does the fire come from? The sun and the reflecting surface are far apart and cannot come into contact. Yet it cannot be that the fire comes into being on its own.

"You still do not know that, in the Matrix of the Thus-Come One, the real nature of the primary element fire is identical to the real nature of emptiness. The real nature of the primary element fire is fundamentally pure and extends throughout the Dharma-Realm. The extent to which beings are aware of this real nature depends on the capacity of their understanding. You should know, Ānanda, that anywhere in the entire world, throughout the Dharma-Realm, a reflecting surface can be held up to the sun to start a fire. Since a fire can be started anywhere in the world, how could it be limited to one particular place? In fact, the primary element fire becomes apparent to beings in accord with their karma. Ordinary beings, in their ignorance, mistakenly suppose that the primary element fire comes into being from causes and conditions or that it comes into being on its own. These are distinctions and constructs made by the conscious mind. They are mere words, devoid of any real meaning.

C. The Primary Element Water

"Ānanda, the nature of water is variable, neither always flowing nor always still. Consider the ascetic masters[30] Kapila, Cakra, Padma, and Hastā,[31] along with other great magicians in the city of Śrāvastī. On bright nights with the full moon shining, these magicians each hold up a bowl to the moon in order to collect water which contains the moon's essence, and this they mix with their hallucinatory herbs.

> Magicians deal with illusion, with what is not real. The magicians mentioned here wanted to use the essence of moonlight in their illusion-causing drugs, which muddled people's minds. These drugs were like the present-day LSD, which, although not mixed with essence of moonlight, is nonetheless close to the kind of drug being discussed. These drugs caused people to see everything as strange and to think of themselves as having already become ascetic masters. They caused nervous disorders and caused people to be confused and unreliable. (III, 159)

"Now, does the water come out of the bowl? Is it already present because it is inherent in space? Or does it come from the moon?

---

[30] Skt. ṛṣi. See part 9.10.

[31] The sage Kapila has already been mentioned; see the prologue, note 25. Cakra, Padma, and Hastā are probably abbreviations of longer names, but they are not clearly identified in the commentarial tradition.

"Suppose, Ānanda, that it came from the moon. If moonlight coming from such a distance could cause water to emerge from the bowl, then while crossing that distance it would cause water to emerge from the trees that it passed. Then what need would there be for the bowl? But since water does not emerge from the trees, it is clear that the water does not in fact come from the moon.

"Suppose the water came from the bowl. Then the water would be flowing out of the bowl all the time. What need would there be to wait for a bright full moon at midnight?

"Suppose the water came from space. Since space is boundless, the water too should be boundless. Then the heavens and the world of people would all be immersed in a deluge. What then will have happened to the beings that move on land, in water, and in the air?

"Carefully consider this further. The moon moves through the sky. The magician holds up the bowl to collect the water. Where in fact does the water come from? The moon and the bowl are far apart; they cannot come into contact and they cannot merge. Yet it cannot be that water comes into being on its own.

"You do not yet know that, in the Matrix of the Thus-Come One, the real nature of the primary element water is identical to the real nature of emptiness. The real nature of the primary element water is fundamentally pure and extends throughout the Dharma-Realm. The extent to which beings are aware of that real nature depends on the capacity of their understanding. One person holds up a bowl in one place and water comes forth there and anywhere throughout the Dharma-Realm, such a bowl can be held up so that water will come forth. Since water can be found anywhere in the world, how could it be limited to one particular place? In fact, the primary element water becomes apparent to beings in accord with their karma. Ordinary beings, in their ignorance, mistakenly suppose that the primary element water comes into being from causes and conditions or that it comes into being on its own. These are distinctions and constructs made by the conscious mind. They are mere words, devoid of meaning.

The primary elements are found in the true minds of all of us living beings. We are endowed not only with water but also with fire, wind, earth, space, awareness, and consciousness. These seven primary elements are all present in our minds. But though they all exist there, they are not mixed together chaotically. . . .

The text says that the nature of water is fundamentally pure and extends throughout the Dharma-Realm. Thus, within true emptiness there is wondrous existence. You can come to understand these principles if you contemplate them with your true mind. In other words, once you yourself have gained sufficient spiritual skill while sitting in meditation — once you have gained the power of samādhi and genuine wisdom — then you will understand the truth of the principles explained in this Sutra. But these principles will not be easy to understand now if you are trying to fathom their meaning with your conscious mind. (III, 163)

D. The Primary Element Wind

"Ānanda, the nature of wind is insubstantial. It is neither always in motion nor always still. When you take your place in the great assembly, you always adjust your precept robe. Suppose that as you do so, the corner of your robe moves toward the person next to you. As a result, that person will feel a slight puff of wind against his face. Does this puff of wind arise from the corner of your robe? Does it arise from the space around it? Or does it come into being from that person's face?

"Ānanda, suppose the puff of wind arises from the corner of your robe. Then you would be wearing wind, and your robe would billow out and fly off your body. Yet as I now expound upon the Dharma in the midst of the assembly, my robe hangs straight down. Look at my robe: where is the wind? In fact there is nowhere in the robe for the wind to be hidden.

"Suppose the wind comes into being from space. Then what need would there be for your robe to move in order for someone to feel that puff of wind? Further, space is always present; if the wind arose from it, then the wind would always have to be blowing. Conversely, if no wind were blowing, then space would cease to exist. But, while we can observe an absence of wind, what would the absence of space look like? In truth, if space came into being and ceased to be,[32] it would not be what we call space. Therefore, wind cannot come into being from what we do call space.

"Suppose then that the wind came into being from your neighbor's face. Then it would be you, rather than your neighbor, who would feel the puff of wind. Why is it your neighbor who in fact feels the puff of wind when you adjust your robe?

"Consider this matter with care. It is you who adjust your robe. It is your neighbor who feels the puff of wind on his face. Space itself is still; it is never observed to move. From where then does the wind come when it blows against your neighbor's face? Wind and space have different natures and cannot aggregate or merge with each other. And yet it cannot be that wind comes into being on its own, independent of anything else.

"You apparently do not know that, in the Matrix of the Thus-Come One, the real nature of the primary element wind is identical to the real nature of emptiness. The real nature of wind is fundamentally pure and extends throughout the Dharma-Realm. The extent to which beings are aware of that real nature depends on the capacity of their understanding. Ānanda, just as a puff of wind arises with a small movement of your robe, so a puff of wind will arise anywhere throughout the Dharma-Realm, in any land, when someone moves his robe. Since wind can arise anywhere in the world, how could it be limited to one particular place? In fact, the primary element wind becomes apparent to beings in accord with their karma. Ordinary beings, in their ignorance, mistakenly suppose that the primary element wind comes into being from causes and conditions or that it comes into being on its own. These are distinctions and constructs made by the conscious mind. They are mere words, devoid of any real meaning.

E. The Primary Element Space

"Ānanda, the nature of space is that it is invisible. It is discerned only in the presence of visible objects. Consider, for example, how the Brahmins — for example, the Bhāradvāja clan — and the Kṣatriyas, Vaiśyas, Śūdras,

---

[32] Space is unconditioned.

and Caṇḍālas[33] in the city of Śrāvastī dig wells to find water when they build a new dwelling, since the city is far from the river. When they dig out the soil to the depth of one foot, space will be discernable in the well to the depth of one foot. When they dig out the soil to the depth of ten feet, space will be discernable in the well to the depth of ten feet. How much space is discerned depends on how much soil has been removed. Now, does the space in the well come into being out of the soil? Does it come into being because of the digging? Or does it come into being on its own?

"Ānanda, suppose the space in the well came into being on its own, without a cause. Why then in the place where the well is to be dug, is there no space before the soil is removed? Why can one see only solid land, which one cannot pass through?

"Suppose the space in the well comes into existence from the soil. Then when the soil is removed, space should be seen to enter the well. If no space enters in as the soil comes out, how could the space in the well be said to come into being from the soil? But if space does not come out of the soil to enter the well, then the soil and the space must be bound together with no distinction between them. Why then, when the soil is removed, doesn't the space come out with it?

"Suppose the space in the well comes into existence because of the digging. Then the digging should bring space out of the well, along with the soil. But if the space does not come into existence from the digging, then only the soil would have been moved. Why then does the space appear?

"Carefully consider this further; consider it closely and carefully. The well-digger chooses the appropriate place to dig. The soil comes out as the well is dug. But what of the space? How does it come into existence? The soil that is removed is solid matter, while the space is insubstantial, so they cannot function together. They cannot be aggregated or combined with each other. And yet it cannot be that space comes into existence on its own, without any cause.

---

[33] These are, respectively, the priestly class of traditional Indian society, the warrior class, the merchant class, the peasant class, and a class of outcastes.

"Given that the fundamental nature of space is all-pervasive and does not move, you should know that the real natures of earth, water, fire, and wind — which, together with space, we may consider as five primary elements — are completely interfused with one another. In their fundamental natures, all are one with the Matrix of the Thus-Come One, neither coming into being nor ceasing to be. When we discussed the first four primary elements, Ānanda, you did not understand that fundamentally they are the Matrix of the Thus-Come One; therefore, you still need to ponder whether or not the primary element space can come out of a well that has been dug and whether or not space can enter into the well.

"You have altogether failed to realize that the primary element space is inherent in the Matrix of the Thus-Come One and is identical to the real nature of emptiness. The real nature of the primary element space is fundamentally pure and extends throughout the Dharma-Realm. The extent to which beings are aware of that real nature depends on the capacity of their understanding. Just as when one well is dug, space appears in it, Ānanda, so space will appear in any well that is dug anywhere in the ten directions. Since space is everywhere throughout the ten directions, how could it be limited to one particular place? In fact, the primary element space becomes apparent to beings in accord with their karma. In their ignorance, beings in this world mistakenly suppose that space comes into existence from causes and conditions or that it comes into being on its own. These are distinctions and constructs made by the conscious mind. They are mere words, devoid of meaning.

F. The Primary Element Awareness

"Ānanda, you do not become visually aware unless space and visible objects are present. For example, you are now in Prince Jetri's Grove, where it is light in the morning and dark in the evening. It is bright at midnight when a full moon has risen but dark when there is no moon. At these times, you can discern light and darkness because of your visual awareness. Now, is your visual awareness identical to light and darkness and to space? Is it separate from them? Is it both identical to them and separate from them? Is it neither identical to them nor separate from them?

"Suppose, Ānanda, that your visual awareness is fundamentally identical to light, darkness, and space. But consider light and darkness: each disappears in the presence of the other. When it is dark, it is not light, and when it is light, it is not dark. Therefore, if your visual awareness were identical to darkness, it would disappear when it is light. If instead it were identical to light, it would cease to exist when it is dark. Once it had ceased to exist, how could it see either darkness or light? And how could it be identical to light and darkness, given that they are not present at the same time, whereas visual awareness neither comes into being nor ceases to be?

"Suppose that your visual awareness is not identical to light or to darkness. Then, in the absence of light, darkness, and space, can you determine what attributes your visual awareness might have, in and of itself? In the absence of light, darkness, and space, a visual awareness such as this would be no more possible that a turtle with fur or a rabbit with horns. Therefore, without these three — light, darkness, and space — how could your visual awareness come to exist? Since light and darkness are opposites, how could your visual awareness be identical to them? On the other hand, since your visual awareness cannot exist in and of itself and apart from these three, how could it be different from them? Further, no division can be discerned between your visual awareness and space; there is no boundary between them. How is it that they are not identical? Yet when you see light and then darkness, the nature of your visual awareness does not change. How is it that they are not different?

"You should examine this question in even greater detail. Examine it minutely; consider it most carefully. Light comes from the sun, and it is dark on a moonless night. We see through space but not through earth. But what causes our visual awareness, as we have just described it, to come into being? Its nature is to perceive, while space is insentient, so they cannot merge or become aggregated with one another. And yet our visual awareness cannot come to exist on its own, without any cause.

"Given that the fundamental natures of visual awareness, awareness of sounds, and cognitive awareness are all-pervasive and do not change,[34] you should know that the real natures of what we may consider to be six primary elements — our visual awareness; infinite, motionless space; and earth, water, fire, and wind, which are in motion — are completely interfused with one another. In their fundamental natures, all are within the Matrix of the Thus-Come One, neither coming into being nor ceasing to be.

"Ānanda, your basic disposition has become so murky that you do not realize that, fundamentally, your visual awareness, your awareness of sounds, your tactile awareness, and your cognitive awareness are the Matrix of the Thus-Come One. You should contemplate your visual awareness, your awareness of sounds and odors, your tactile awareness, and your cognitive awareness: do they come into being and cease to be? Are they identical to each other, or are they different? Or else, do they neither come into being nor cease to be? Are they neither identical to each other nor different?

"You still do not know that the real nature of your visual awareness is inherent in the Matrix of the Thus-Come One and identical to your enlightened understanding, and that the essence of enlightenment is your illuminating awareness. Fundamentally pure, it extends throughout the Dharma-Realm. The extent to which beings are aware of its real nature depends on the capacity of their understanding. Just as the awareness of one sense-faculty, the eye, extends throughout the Dharma-Realm, so also do the wondrous, resplendent powers of hearing, smelling, tasting, tactile awareness, and cognitive awareness extend throughout the Dharma-Realm. They fill up the entirety of space throughout the ten directions. How could they be limited to one particular place? In fact, the primary element visual awareness becomes apparent to beings in accord with their karma. In their ignorance, ordinary beings mistakenly suppose that visual awareness comes into existence from causes and conditions or that it

[34] All six consciousnesses are understood to be included in this and similar passages throughout.

comes into being on its own. These are all distinctions and constructs made by the conscious mind. They are mere words, devoid of real meaning.

G. The Primary Element Consciousness

"Ānanda, the nature of consciousness is that it has no real basis.[35] Its coming into existence in response to the six faculties and their objects is an illusion. Look around now at the sages assembled here. As you glance from one to another, your eyes see them as if in a mirror, which does not make distinctions. But your consciousness will identify each of the sages in turn as Mañjuśrī, Pūrṇamaitrāyaṇīputra, Maudgalyāyana, Subhūti, and Śāriputra. Now, does this distinction-making faculty, this primary element consciousness, arise from your eye-faculty? Does it arise from perceived objects? Does it arise from space? Or does it arise abruptly, without a cause?

"Ānanda, suppose your primary element consciousness arose from your eye-faculty. Then in the absence of light, darkness, objects, and space — if none of these four were present — your eye-faculty would not function. If your eye-faculty were not functioning, what would cause your consciousness element to arise?

"Suppose your consciousness arose from perceived objects rather than from the eye-faculty. In that case, you would not be seeing either light or darkness, and if you were not aware of light or darkness, you would not be aware of objects and space either. If you could not see any of these, how could your consciousness element arise out of them?

"Suppose your consciousness element arose from space rather than from perceived objects or from the eye-faculty. But without the eye-faculty, nothing visible can be perceived, and so you would not be aware of light, darkness, perceived objects, or space. If no perceived objects were present before your eye-faculty, then the conditions for seeing would be absent, and there would be no place for seeing to occur. The same would apply to hearing, tactile awareness, and cognitive awareness.

---

[35] "Consciousness" here includes the first six consciousnesses: the consciousnesses of the eye, ear, nose, tongue, body, and mind.

But suppose it is based on space rather than on the perceiving faculties or on their perceived objects. However, space is identical to nothingness. And even if space were something, it is not the same as an actual perceived object. If space nevertheless caused your consciousness to arise, how would you be able to make distinctions about anything?

"Suppose your consciousness appears abruptly, without any cause. Why then doesn't the moon suddenly start shining in broad daylight?

"You should examine this question even more closely and in more detail. Seeing is a function of your eye-faculty. The perceived objects that appear in your environment have form, while space lacks form. Which of them could be the cause of consciousness? Consciousness is active, while the eye-faculty is still,[36] and so they cannot combine or be aggregated with each other. The same is true of consciousness and the ear-faculty, the nose-faculty, the body-faculty, and the cognitive faculty. Yet the primary element consciousness cannot come to exist on its own, without a cause.

"Given that the primary element consciousness is not caused by any of these factors, you should know that your distinction-making eye-consciousness, ear-consciousness, body-consciousness, and mind-consciousness do not come from anywhere; all are complete and pure and do not come into being from anything. The real natures of what we may call the seven primary elements — these last two,[37] together with space, earth, water, fire, and wind — are completely interfused with one another. In their fundamental natures, all are within the Matrix of the Thus-Come One and are one with the Matrix of the Thus-Come One, neither coming into being nor ceasing to be.

"Ānanda, your mind is coarse and shallow. You have not realized that, fundamentally, your eye-consciousness, ear-consciousness, and your discerning, distinction-making mind-consciousness are all inherent in the Matrix of the Thus-Come One. You should contemplate all of your six consciousnesses: are they identical to each other, or are they different?

---

[36] In that consciousness makes distinctions about perceived objects, while the perceiving faculties merely receive the sense-data.

[37] That is, consciousness and awareness.

Do they exist, or are they empty? Are they neither identical to each other nor different? Are they neither existent nor empty?

> The Buddha admonishes Ānanda again: "Your thoughts are too coarse, too superficial." Ānanda doesn't stop and think or look into things. He's too impulsive and reckless. The word "shallow" refers to his mind, the mind which is the opposite of his deep mind. In the verse he is about to speak, Ānanda says, "This deep resolve I offer in the myriad Buddha-lands. By this may I repay the kindness shown me by the Buddha." But now the mind that he is relying on is shallow; it's not his deep mind. He is not paying close attention to what is going on. (III, 198)

"You simply do not know that the primary element consciousness is inherent in the Matrix of the Thus-Come One and is the enlightened understanding, and that the illumination of enlightenment is the true consciousness. It is the wondrous and pure enlightenment that extends throughout the Dharma-Realm. It contains all space throughout the ten directions. How could it be limited to one particular place? In fact, it becomes apparent to beings in accord with their karma. In their ignorance, ordinary beings mistakenly suppose that consciousness comes into existence from causes and conditions or that it comes into being on its own. These are distinctions and constructs made by the conscious mind. They are mere words, devoid of real meaning."

6
Ānanda's Vow

At that time, Ānanda and the rest of the great assembly, having received
the subtle and wondrous instruction given by the Buddha, the Thus-Come
One, felt that their bodies and minds were emptied and hardly seemed
to exist. They were free of all concerns and impediments. All in the assembly became aware that their minds pervaded the ten directions and
that they could see everything throughout space in all ten directions as
clearly as one might see an object such as a leaf in the palm of one's hand.
They saw that all things in all worlds are the wondrous, fundamental,
enlightened, luminous mind that understands, and that this mind, pure,
all-pervading, and perfect, contains the entire universe. They looked
back upon their own bodies born of their parents and saw them to be like
minute particles of dust drifting about everywhere in the air, arising and
perishing, or like solitary bubbles floating on vast, calm seas, appearing
and then vanishing without a trace. They fully understood that the fundamental, wondrous mind is everlasting and does not perish.

"Their bodies and minds were emptied" means that, basically, there wasn't
anything at all. Everything was empty; the defilements had been washed
away, and all that was left now was the light of the Buddha-nature. This is
serenity. Everything is empty. Inside, there is no body or mind; outside, there
is no world. When one attains this state, there isn't anything at all. Why aren't
we serene? It is because we are still attached to our bodies. If someone says
one sentence about us, we become afflicted. Whenever anyone is the least
bit rude to us, we can't let it go. We are not at peace. The members of the
Buddha's Śūraṅgama assembly, however, were serene, and they were "free
of all concerns and impediments." Because they were serene, they were not
hindered by their bodies and minds. . . . If we look upon everything as being no problem, as being very ordinary, then there's nothing going on at all.
There's a saying: "If a mountain collapsed right in front of you, you wouldn't be
surprised." No matter what great calamity occurs, even if your house should
fall in, you pay no attention. If you pay no attention, then even if your house

does fall in on you, it won't harm you. Why do things harm you? It's because you can't let go of them. You are hindered by them. You get scared, and so you get hurt. If you aren't afraid, if you have your wits about you, then it doesn't matter where you are. . . .

The members of the great Śūraṅgama Dharma-assembly awakened at that time to the truth that the emptiness throughout the ten directions, and the entire experience described here, was in their own minds. It was not beyond a single thought of the mind. To the ends of space, throughout the Dharma-Realm, there is no place that the mind does not reach. Since the mind is that big, the great is compressed into the small. The members of the Śūraṅgama Dharma-assembly could see the emptiness of the ten directions as clearly as you can see something that you are holding in the palm of your hand. All had now opened the celestial eye and the wisdom-eye.[38] Therefore, they could perceive that the myriad phenomena are only the mind and that the mind contains the myriad phenomena. Our true mind contains the true and the false and is without a location. It reaches to the ends of space and pervades the Dharma-Realm. So where is it? It is neither there nor not there. Thus, the mind contains the myriad phenomena, and the myriad phenomena arise from the mind. All phenomena perish due to the mind as well.

When the mind arises, all phenomena arise;
When the mind ceases to be, all phenomena cease to be.

Thus, the true mind neither comes into being nor ceases to be, and phenomena, too, neither come into being nor cease to be. . . . (III, 202–4)

With the celestial eye open, you can see not only outside your body but inside it. When you look at your body, you see it as a crystal container. You look in this crystal container and can see what color your blood is. When you open your celestial eye, your wisdom-eye, and your Buddha-eye, you can see what is in every part of your body. You can see what sickness there is, the places where the blood and energy don't flow well. You can see inside and

---

[38] The five spiritual eyes are the physical eye; the celestial eye, which can see things at a distance and in the past and future; the wisdom eye, which discerns the emptiness of phenomena; the Dharma-eye, which illuminates the teachings: and the Buddha-eye, which allows one to see Buddhas and Bodhisattvas.

outside. Here the members of the great assembly looked upon everything in the ten directions as upon something held in the palms of their hands, and they also saw their own internal organs. They saw the insides of their own bodies. Their bodies were the same size as the empty space of the ten directions. (III, 205–6)

Then Ānanda, having understood what he had not understood before, bowed to the Buddha, and placing his palms together, spoke these verses in the Buddha's praise:

"The deep and wondrous honored one, all-knowing, pure, and still,
Śūraṅgama, the King of Mantras, rarest in the world,
Extinguishes distorted thoughts from countless eons past —
No need to wait forever to attain the Dharma-body.

"I vow to reach enlightenment, and as a Dharma-King,
Return to rescue beings countless as the Ganges' sands.
This deep resolve I offer in the myriad Buddha-lands.
By this may I repay the kindness shown me by the Buddha.

"I ask the Buddha to be witness as I take this vow
To enter first the murky realms of five turbidities,[39]
If even just one being still has not become a Buddha,
Then I will wait before I seek the leisure of nirvana.

"Greatest in valor and in power! Great Compassionate One!
I pray you'll now eradicate the subtlest of my doubts
And lead me quickly to attain supreme enlightenment,
And sit within the places for awakening everywhere.

"If emptiness should vanish, even that
Will never shake this vajra-solid vow."

---

[39] Of time, perception, afflictions, individual beings, and lifespans. See part 5.1.

IV
The Coming into Being of the World of Illusion

1
Adding Understanding to Understanding

Then Pūrṇamaitrāyaṇīputra stood up amidst the great assembly. He uncovered his right shoulder, knelt with his right knee on the ground, respectfully placed his palms together, and said to the Buddha, "World-Honored One, you who are foremost in virtue and in inspiring awe have just now eloquently proclaimed, for the sake of all beings, the ultimate truth taught by the Thus-Come Ones. The Thus-Come One has often praised me as the one most skilled in expounding the Dharma, but as I have been listening to the Thus-Come One's voice as he has been setting forth such subtle and wonderful Dharma, I might as well be a deaf man trying to hear a mosquito from a distance of more than a hundred paces. Such a man could not even see the mosquito, let alone hear it.

"Although the Buddha's clear explanations have largely dispelled my doubts, I have not yet reached the point at which I might thoroughly understand this truth and so be free of doubt entirely. World-Honored One, although Ānanda and those like him have become enlightened,[1] they have not yet put an end to their habits and outflows. But I am among those in the assembly who are free of outflows. And yet, having just now heard the Buddha explain this Dharma, I find that I am assailed by doubts.

"World-Honored One, if in fact the aggregates, the faculties, the various perceived objects, and the consciousnesses are all the Matrix of the Thus-Come One, which is itself fundamentally pure, then how is it that suddenly there came into being the mountains, the rivers, and all else on this earth that exists subject to conditions? And why are all these subject to a succession of changes, ending and then beginning again?

"The Thus-Come One also said that everywhere throughout the Dharma-Realm, the primary elements — earth, water, fire, and wind — are in their fundamental nature completely interfused with each other, tranquil and everlasting. World-Honored One, if the primary element

---

[1] At this point in the narrative, Ānanda is still a first-stage Arhat. Among the Arhats, only those at the fourth stage, like Pūrṇa, are free of outflows.

141

earth extended everywhere throughout the Dharma-Realm, how could it coexist with water? And if the primary element water extended everywhere throughout the Dharma-Realm, the primary element fire could not come into being. How may we understand that primary elements water and fire can both pervade empty space without overcoming each other in mutual annihilation?

"World-Honored One, the nature of the primary element earth is that it is solid, while the nature of the primary element space is that it is a transparent void. How could they both exist everywhere throughout the Dharma-Realm? I am not sure how I should understand the implications of this concept. I only hope that, out of great kindness, the Thus-Come One will explain this to all of us and so clear away the clouds of our confusion."

Having made his request, Pūrṇa bowed to the ground and then waited respectfully and earnestly to hear the Thus-Come One's sublime and compassionate instruction.

Then the World-Honored One said to Pūrṇa and to all the other Arhats in the assembly, who were all free of outflows and needed no further instruction, "Today, for the sake of everyone in the assembly, the Thus-Come One will explain the most supreme truth among all supreme truths, so that all the Hearers of the Teaching in this assembly who have no further aspirations, and all of you Arhats who have not yet experienced the two kinds of emptiness[2] but have turned toward the Great Vehicle, as well as others, may enter the true *araṇya*,[3] the still and quiet place, the state of genuine practice that will lead you to become Buddhas. Listen carefully as I explain."

Pūrṇa and all the others, out of reverence for the sound of the Buddha's words of Dharma, listened in silent respect.

In true araṇya, there is no chaos. No one talks. A lot of people may dwell together, but it's as if no one were there. Not even the sound of a mosquito can

---

[2] The emptiness of people and phenomena. People are empty of any real and permanent self or soul, and phenomena are empty of any real and permanent essential attributes.

[3] Skt. *araṇya*. A quiet place in a forest or other wilderness, and by extension, a place where spiritual practitioners dwell.

be heard. If you want to follow the correct path, you should learn not to talk so much. When there is too much talking, other people cannot enter samādhi. (IV, 13)

The Buddha continued, "Pūrṇa, you have asked me why the mountains, the rivers, and everything else on this great earth have come into being from the Matrix of the Thus-Come One, which is fundamentally pure. Now, have you not often heard the Thus-Come One speak of the wondrous understanding which is intrinsic to our inherent enlightenment, to our fundamental, wondrous, luminous understanding?"

Pūrṇa replied, "Yes, World-Honored One, I have often heard the Buddha expound upon this."

"Inherent enlightenment" refers to each person's truly enlightened nature. "Wondrous understanding" refers to stillness and constant illumination, . . . an everlasting quietness that nevertheless can illumine the entire Dharma-Realm. The word "wondrous" also represents purity. The inherent, enlightened nature is the one truth; it is the Buddha-nature inherent in us all, the primary nature that multiplies to become the myriad things. . . . It is the fundamental enlightenment, the natural and primary essence inherent within us. It neither increases or decreases, is neither produced nor destroyed, is neither defiled nor pure. (IV, 15)

The Buddha said, "When we talk about this understanding which characterizes enlightenment, do we mean an understanding that is intrinsic to our inherent enlightened nature? Or does our inherent enlightenment lack understanding until we gain it when enlightenment is realized?"

Pūrṇa said, "Our inherent enlightenment is characterized by understanding only when that understanding is added to it."

The Buddha said, "Suppose, as you say, that for our inherent enlightenment to be characterized by understanding, that understanding must be added to it when enlightenment is realized. But an enlightenment to which an understanding is added cannot be a true enlightenment. Such an enlightenment would indeed lack understanding if understanding were not added. But an enlightenment that lacks understanding cannot be the true intrinsic enlightenment that is inherently pure and endowed with understanding. Therefore, if you think that an understanding must be added to your inherent enlightenment, you are falsifying the true understanding, the true enlightenment.

"That is, nothing need be added to true enlightenment, but once an understanding is added nevertheless, that understanding must understand something.[4] Once the category of 'something understood' is mistakenly established in the mind, the category 'that which understands' is mistakenly established as well.[5] At first, there is neither sameness nor differentiation, but then that which is differentiated is clearly distinguished.[6] That which differs from what is differentiated is distinguished as being uniform.[7] Because the category of what is differentiated and the category of what is uniform have been established, the category of what is neither uniform nor differentiated is further established.[8]

> Enlightenment is not something that requires the addition of understanding . . . because understanding is already inherent in enlightenment. Once an understanding is added, an object is established. This is the first of the three subtle aspects of delusion. Once an object is falsely set up, you as a false subject come into being as a reaction to the false object. This is the source of your deluded thinking. . . . In this way, subjectivity is created. This ultimately unreal process is the second subtle aspect of delusion, the aspect of evolving.
>
> The general import of this section of text is that basically we are all Buddhas. Then if we originally were Buddhas, how did we become ordinary beings? And why haven't ordinary beings become Buddhas? Where does the problem lie? Originally we were no different from the Buddhas. But living beings can be created from within the Buddha-nature. . . . The Buddha-nature is radiant; it is our

[4] This is coming into being, the first of three subtle aspects of delusion, which is the self-verifying division of the eighth consciousness.

[5] This is evolving, the second subtle aspect of delusion, which is the observing division of the eighth consciousness.

[6] This is appearance, the third subtle aspect of delusion, which is the observed division of the eighth consciousness. It is comprised of perceived objects, space, and beings.

[7] That is, space.

[8] That is, beings, considered uniform yet differentiated because all share sentience while taking various forms.

fundamental enlightenment, and it is the wondrous light of the enlightenment inherent in us all. It is from within this light that the beings are created.

To illustrate this point, I will use an analogy which is not totally apt but which will suffice to make the principle clear. A manifested body of the Buddha is like a photograph of a person — except that the photograph has no awareness. A Buddha can create a manifested body whose nature comes from the Buddha and whose features have a likeness to the Buddha's. Another analogy would be a reflection in a mirror. When we pass by the mirror there is a reflection; once we have gone by, the reflection disappears. The same can be said of a manifested body of a Buddha.

Our fundamental, inherent enlightenment is also like a mirror. Suddenly in the mirror an image appears, and in the same way, the first ignorant thought arises when an understanding is added to our inherent understanding. . . . For another analogy, we can say that fundamental enlightenment is like a light which is already on. If you flip the switch, you have added something extra, and in the process you have turned the light off, (IV, 17–9)

"The turmoil of this mutual complementarity gives rise to mental strain, and as the mental strain is prolonged, grasping at objects of mind begins. Mental strain and grasping at objects together create a turbidity of mind, out of which the afflictions are generated. Motion becomes the world of perceived objects, and stillness is distinguished as space. In addition to space, which is undifferentiated, and the world, which is differentiated, are conditioned phenomena that are neither differentiated nor the same.

In this passage, the first five of the six coarse aspects of delusion are mentioned. . . . Previously to this, the text mentioned the coming into being of what is neither uniform nor differentiated, together with the coming into being of the world and space. Now in the midst of this, turmoil is created. This turmoil eventually brings about mental strain, which is the first coarse aspect of delusion, the delusion of mundane knowledge. Prolonged weariness produces defilement; this prolongation is the second coarse aspect, that of continuation. The third is the aspect of grasping. The combination of these in a murky turbidity is the fourth coarse aspect, the aspect of clinging to names. . . . From the various conditions just discussed, afflictions arise, and with afflictions come the mountains, the rivers, and everything else on earth. This is the fifth coarse aspect, the aspect of karma.[9] (IV, 20–2)

"Once a light of understanding is added to enlightenment, the darkness of the primary element space appears, and the interaction of these two complements generates a disturbance in the mind. That disturbance becomes the disk[10] of wind that is the essence of the primary element wind, and this disk then supports the world of perceived objects. In reaction to the mental disturbance generated by the interaction of the darkness of mental space and the understanding that has been added, there arises a firm attachment to that understanding, and this firm attachment is categorized as solidity. This solidity is the disk of vajra, which is the essence of the primary element earth. This is how, from the firm attachment to the light of the added understanding, the disk of vajra, which holds the world together, comes into being.

"Thus the disk of vajra is generated from the firm attachment to the added understanding, and the disk of wind is generated from the disturbance arising from the interaction of the two complements, the light of the added understanding and the darkness of mental space. From the friction between the disk of wind and the disk of vajra there arises the light of the disk of fire, which is characterized by changeability. Moisture arises from the shining of the disk of vajra and turns to vapor in the presence of fire. Thus the disk of water comes into being and encompasses the worlds in the ten directions.

"As fire flares up and water descends, their interaction brings about solidity. From the primary element water, the oceans come into being, while the continents and islands come into being from the primary element earth.[11] Thus fire sometimes emerges from the oceans, and rivers and streams flow across the lands. Mountains form where the primary

---

[9] The sixth and final coarse aspect of delusion is suffering due to karma.

[10] Skt. *maṇḍala*, Ch. *lun* 輪. Here the term is understood to mean the essence of the primary elements, and in this passage the two characters *lun* 輪 (wheel or circular object) and *jing* 精 (essence) are used interchangeably.

[11] The implication is that steps previous to this one have all been within the eighth consciousness.

element fire is stronger than the primary element water; thus rock gives off sparks when struck and melts when heated. Vegetation grows where the primary element water is stronger than the primary element earth; thus the trees and grasses are reduced to ash when burned and exude liquid when they are compressed. These distorted interactions together produce the seeds that become the causes for the perpetuation of the world of perceived objects.[12]

"Further, Pūrṇa, you should know that beings' deluded understanding is due simply to the error of adding an understanding to inherent enlightenment. The inevitable consequence is the establishment, through delusion, of the categories 'something understood' and 'that which understands.' So it is that the ear-faculty is aware only of sounds and the eye-faculty is confined to visible objects. All six objects, which are perceived through delusion — visible objects, sounds, odors, flavors, objects of touch, and objects of cognition — are each placed in a separate category, resulting in a division into seeing, hearing, smelling, tasting, tactile awareness, and cognition.

"Some beings are born due to being bound together by shared karma; other beings are born due to union or else due to separation.

"A point of light is seen to appear. When the light is seen clearly, deluded thoughts arise — both hatred in response to incompatible points of view and love in response to compatible ways of thinking. The thought of love flows out to the fertilized egg, which is then drawn into the womb. Thus the parents' intercourse leads to the attraction of a being with whom they share a common karma. Due to these causes and conditions, the fetus develops, passing through the *kalala* stage,[13] the *arbuda* stage,[14] and the stages that follow.

> When a person comes into being, it is the eighth consciousness which arrives first, and when a person dies, the eighth consciousness is the last to leave. The body remains warm until the eighth consciousness leaves it; then the eighth

---

[12] The first of the three perpetuations.
[13] The human fetus at the end of the first week after conception.
[14] The fetus at the end of the second week.

consciousness continues as the "body between existences," also called the "body between the five aggregates." This body has the appearance of a person or an animal or otherwise, depending on what kind of being it belonged to in the life just completed, as if it had been cast from a mold. No matter how far away from its potential father and mother it may be, it will find them if its karma is bound to theirs. It is surrounded by darkness, but when its future parents have intercourse, it will see a pinpoint of light at that place, and it will be drawn to it like steel to a powerful magnet. This in turn leads to conception. If the body between existences is male, it will love the mother and hate the father. It will want to strike its father and steal its mother and have intercourse with her. If the body between existences is female, it will love the father and be jealous of the mother. With that one thought of ignorance, it enters the womb. Thus people are born from love and desire and they die from love and desire. (IV, 29–30)

"Birth from a womb, birth from an egg, birth in the presence of moisture, and birth via metamorphosis come about in response to these circumstances: birth from an egg arises from mental activity; birth from a womb occurs because of emotion; birth in the presence of moisture occurs through union; and birth via metamorphosis is brought about through separation. Because of emotion, mental activity, union, and separation, beings may shift from one form of birth to another form. They ascend or fall entirely in accord with their karma. These are the causes and conditions for the perpetuation of beings.[15]

"Pūrṇa, beings bind themselves to each other with their thoughts of love, love so strong that they cannot bear to be apart, and thus there come into being all the world's fathers, mothers, children, and grandchildren in an uninterrupted succession of births. The root of all this is emotional desire.

"Because of excessive desire and emotional love, all crave nourishment,[16] a craving which will not cease. Thus all of the world's beings,

[15] Beings are the second of the perpetuations.

[16] The text is compressed. According to Ven. Yuanying, the meaning is more precisely: "Because of greed and love, they must have a body and life; once they have body and life, all have the desire to nourish them" (565).

whether born from eggs, via metamorphosis, in the presence of moisture, or from a womb, devour one another and are in turn devoured, each according to the measure of its strength or weakness. The root of all this is the desire to kill.

"Suppose then that a human being eats a sheep. The slaughtered sheep is reborn as a human. When the human who ate the sheep dies, he in turn becomes a sheep. This pattern holds among all ten kinds of beings as they devour one another in a continuing cycle of death and rebirth. The evil karma of this mutual devouring accompanies each of them from life to life to the farthest reaches of the future. The root of all this is the urge to steal.

> Stealing is taking what is not given. For instance, when you eat the flesh of a sheep, the sheep certainly did not give it to you. . . . If you kill a sheep for no reason but to eat its flesh, you have stolen its life. So it is reborn as a person and you are reborn as a sheep, and in this way you keep stealing from each other. (IV, 42)

"Suppose you are in debt to someone for having taken his life; he will want to take your life in repayment. Due to such causes and conditions, beings must pass through hundreds of thousands of eons in an everlasting succession of deaths and rebirths.

"Suppose someone loves someone else for his or her mind, or for his or her beauty. Due to such causes and conditions, beings must pass through hundreds of thousands of eons in an everlasting succession of entanglements.

"The roots of all this are killing, stealing, and emotional love. Those three and nothing else are the causes and conditions for the perpetuation of retribution in accord with karma.[17]

"Pūrṇa, these three distorted perpetuations ultimately derive from adding an understanding to inherent enlightenment. From this added understanding, a false understanding arises. From that, a deluded awareness brings into being the mountains, the rivers, and all the other

---

[17] The third of the perpetuations.

conditioned phenomena in this world. Due to that illusory awareness, we experience the world as constantly changing patterns, which are perpetually coming into our awareness and then disappearing."

2
The Buddhas' Enlightenment Is Irreversible

Pūrṇa then asked, "If our wondrous enlightenment is fundamentally wondrous, awake, and endowed with luminous understanding, and if the mind of the Thus-Come One neither increases nor diminishes, how is it then that all beings and all conditioned phenomena — the mountains, the rivers, and everything else on earth — suddenly arise without a reason? Also, now that the Thus-Come One has realized wondrous emptiness and understanding, will the mountains, the rivers, and all other conditioned phenomena on this earth, as well as the habits and outflows of beings, ever arise for him again?"

> This section of text voices Pūrṇa's doubt. He wonders whether the Buddha-nature has a beginning and whether there will be a time when the Buddha will no longer be a Buddha and will become an ordinary being again. (IV, 50)

The Buddha said to Pūrṇa, "Consider the analogy of someone who loses his way in a village and becomes confused about which way is north and which way is south. Has he mistaken his directions because of confusion, or because of understanding?"

> The village in this analogy represents the Matrix of the Thus-Come One. The person who has lost his way represents ordinary beings, who are afflicted with deluded thoughts. North and south represent the false and the true, confusion and enlightenment. (IV, 53)

Pūrṇa replied, "He is lost neither because of confusion nor because of understanding. Confusion has no basis in reality, and so how can it be a cause of his being lost? As for understanding, how could that be a cause of being lost?"

The Buddha said, "Suppose this confused person who has become lost in the village unexpectedly meets someone who knows which direction is which and who points out the way to him so that he understands. What do you think, Pūrṇa? He was lost in the village, but now will he become lost again?

"He will not, World-Honored One."

"The same is true, Pūrṇa, of the Thus-Come Ones throughout the ten directions. Confusion has no basis in reality. In its very nature it is ultimately empty. There never was anything real about the confusion; it only seems that there have been confusion and understanding. Once one has awakened from one's confusion, the confusion disappears, and from that awakening, no confusion can arise again."

"Or again, a person with an eye-disease may see a mirage of flowers in the air, but once the disease is cured, the flowers he saw in the air will disappear. Suppose that person is foolish enough to look up at the place where the flowers disappeared and expect to see them reappear. Would you consider such a person to be foolish or wise?"

Pūrṇa replied, "There never were any flowers in the air. They appeared because his visual awareness was distorted. Seeing the flowers disappear into the air was also a distortion. To expect them to reappear would be foolish to the point of madness. How could one possibly call such a crazed person merely foolish, much less call him wise?"

The Buddha replied, "Since you understand that, why have you asked whether mountains, the rivers, and everything else in this world will arise again for the Buddhas, who are the Thus-Come Ones and who have realized wondrous emptiness and luminous understanding?

"Again, consider the example of a gold mine. The ore contains gold mixed with impurities. Once the gold has been refined, it will not revert to ore. Nor will wood that has burned to ash ever become wood again.

"The same is true of the nirvana that is the full awakening realized by all Buddhas, the Thus-Come Ones."

3
The Interfusing of the Primary Elements

"Pūrṇa, you have also asked how it is that the primary elements — earth, water, fire, and wind — are in their fundamental natures completely interfused with each other everywhere throughout the Dharma-Realm. You wonder how it is that the primary elements water and fire do not overcome each other in mutual annihilation. You also asked why it is that the primary elements space and earth can both exist everywhere throughout the Dharma-Realm while being incompatible with each other.

"Consider, Pūrṇa, that the essential attribute of space is the absence of anything else; still, that does not prevent everything else from appearing within it. How can that be, Pūrṇa? The sky is bright when the sun shines. It darkens when clouds gather. There is movement through it when the wind blows. After a rain, the sun reappears and the air is clear. A turbid mist arises when water condenses out of the air. In a dust storm, the air is obscured. And reflections appear in water that is clear and still. Do these various conditioned phenomena appearing in different circumstances come into being because of these conditions, or do they come into being from space?

"Suppose, Pūrṇa, that these phenomena arise because of the circumstances just mentioned. Then, for example, when the sun is shining, does the brightness in the air come into being because the sun is shining? If so, then the sun should be everywhere in the ten directions. Why do we see it as a distinct round object in the sky? If, on the other hand, the brightness of the sky comes into being because of space, then all of space would be shining of its own accord. Why is it not resplendent with light at midnight, or when there are clouds or fog? It should be clear to you that the brightness in the sky is not due to the sun or to space, although the brightness cannot be present without both the sun and space.

"The same can be said of the true, wondrous understanding which is enlightenment. If one develops the category 'space' in one's mind, then space will appear within enlightenment. Earth, water, fire, and wind each appear within enlightenment if one establishes each of them as categories. All of them appear interfused together in enlightenment if one establishes the category 'all.'

"How can they all appear together? Pūrṇa, it is like the sun's reflection in a body of water. When two people who are observing the reflection move apart, one to the east and one to the west, they will each see the sun's reflection moving along with them. The reflection moves east with the person moving east and west with the person moving west; in itself the reflection has no fixed location. Do not quibble by asking how a single reflection can move in two separate directions. And do not ask how the two reflections appeared previously as one. Such questions concern mere illusions, and nothing about reality can be established from them.

"You should realize that all these phenomena are fundamentally unreal, and so one cannot specify anything about them. To assert anything about them would be as absurd as to expect illusory flowers in the sky to bear fruit. How then can you ask whether the primary elements will overcome each other in mutual annihilation? You should realize that, in their fundamental natures, the primary elements are a single reality, which is simply the wondrous, awakened enlightenment — the wondrous, awakened, enlightened mind. Fundamentally, the primary elements — water, fire, and the rest — do not exist at all. Why then do you keep asking how they can exist together?

"Pūrṇa, you mistakenly suppose that within the Matrix of the Thus-Come One, space and the primary element earth are mutually incompatible and cannot coexist. But within the Matrix of the Thus-Come One, space and the world of perceived objects are everywhere throughout the Dharma-Realm. Movement associated with wind, the stillness associated with space, the brightness associated with the sun, and the darkness associated with clouds are all present within the Matrix of the Thus-Come One. Beings, however, suffocated by their confusion, turn their backs on enlightenment and embrace this world of perceived objects. Amidst the stress of beings' entanglement with perceived objects, the world of conditioned phenomena appears.

"With my wondrous, luminous understanding that neither comes into being nor ceases to be, I am identical to the Matrix of the Thus-Come One. The Matrix of the Thus-Come One is itself the wondrous, enlightened, luminous understanding, which illuminates the entire Dharma-Realm. Within it, therefore, the one is infinitely many and the infinitely many are one. The great appears within the small, just as the small appears within the great. I sit unmoving in this still place for awakening, and my Dharma-body extends everywhere and encompasses the infinity of space in all ten directions. On the tip of a fine hair, magnificent Buddha-lands appear. Seated within each mote of dust, I turn the great Wheel of the Dharma. Because I have freed myself from the world of perceived objects, I have become one with enlightenment. Therefore the suchness of reality manifests — the inherent nature that is wondrous, luminous, and awake.

"Thus the Matrix of the Thus-Come One — the fundamental, wondrous, perfect mind — is not the distinction-making mind, nor is it space, nor is it earth, nor water, nor wind, nor fire. It is not the eye-faculty, nor the ear-faculty, nor the nose-faculty, nor the tongue-faculty, nor the body-faculty, nor the cognitive faculty. Neither is it visible objects, nor sounds, nor odors, nor flavors, nor objects of touch, nor objects of cognition. It is not the eye-consciousness, nor the mind-consciousness, nor any of the other consciousnesses. It is neither the fundamental ignorance that is the adding of an understanding to our inherent enlightenment, nor the ending of that ignorance, nor is it old age and death nor the ending of old age and death.[18] Neither is it the fundamentally unsatisfying nature of

---

[18] These are the first and the last two of the twelve links in the chain of dependent co-arising (Skt. *pratītyasamutpāda*, Ch. *yin yuan* 因緣), which is also translated as "dependent origination" and "interdependent arising." Here all twelve links are understood to be included. They are:

1) Because there is ignorance; there are formations.
2) Because there are formations, there is consciousness.
3) Because there is consciousness, there are name and form.
4) Because there are name and form, there are the six faculties.
5) Because there are the six faculties, there is contact.
6) Because there is contact, there is perception.
7) Because there is perception, there is craving.

existence, nor is it the accumulation of the causes of dissatisfaction, nor the ending of dissatisfaction, nor the path to the ending of dissatisfaction.[19] It is neither wisdom nor the attaining of wisdom. It is none of the six perfections — neither giving, nor following precepts, nor vigor, nor patience, nor mindfulness, nor wisdom.[20] Nor is it anything else — not the realization of the enlightenment of the Buddha, who is the Thus-Come One, the Arhat, the One of Right and Universal Wisdom.[21] It is not the permanence, the bliss, the true self, or the purity of the great nirvana. It is not any of these things, be they mundane or world-transcending. To be none of these is what the Matrix of the Thus-Come One is. That is the wondrousness of the inherently luminous mind that understands.

> If you can understand that within the Buddha's Dharma there is no "is" and no "is not," you can become enlightened. In the Sixth Patriarch's Dharma-Jewel Platform Sūtra, the Patriarch Hui Neng asks Hui Ming, "When there is no thought of good and no thought of evil, what is the Venerable Ming's original countenance?"[22] . . . The absence of affirmation and negation, or rightness and wrongness, is itself the inherent Buddha-nature, the fundamental, wondrous, perfect mind. If you can truly understand that, you will have everything, and at the same time you will have nothing. . . . You will have all the Dharma-treasures in the Matrix of the Thus-Come One, and you will have no afflictions. . . .

    8) Because there is craving, there is grasping;.
    9) Because there is grasping, there is becoming.
    10) Because there is becoming, there is birth.
    11) and 12) Because there is birth, there is old age and there is death.

[19] The Four Noble Truths. "Unsatisfying nature" and "dissatisfaction" render the Skt. duḥkha, Ch. ku 苦. "Suffering" is a widely used but somewhat misleading alternate translation.

[20] These are the six pāramitās, or perfecting practices, of the Bodhisattva. The text here gives transliterations of the Skt. dāna, śīla, vīrya, kṣānti, dhyāna, and prajñā. The word "pāramitā" has the sense of "that which brings one across the sea of suffering to the shores of nirvana."

[21] "Arhat" is here a titular name for the Buddha, as is "One of Right and Universal Wisdom" (Skt. samyaksaṁbuddha, Ch. zheng bian zhi 正編知).

[22] Op. cit., 80.

> The paragraph of text just above spoke of the emptiness of the Matrix of the Thus-Come One. Next the Buddha will show how this emptiness is not empty. (IV, 75–6) . . . Words of negation are used, but that does not signify total negation; what still exists is the fundamental, wondrous, perfect mind. (IV, 87) . . . The Sutra has said that all things are not the Matrix of the Thus-Come One; now it will say that all things are the Matrix of the Thus-Come One. (IV, 89) . . . If the Matrix of the Thus-Come One were empty and if that were all there is to it, it would not be wondrous. But true emptiness is what gives rise to wondrous existence, and wondrous existence produces true emptiness. . . . The Matrix of the Thus-Come One is apart from emptiness and existence and yet not apart from emptiness and existence. (IV, 90–1)

"Yet it is the distinction-making mind, it is space, it is earth, it is water, it is wind, it is fire. It is the eye-faculty, the ear-faculty, the nose-faculty, the tongue-faculty, the body-faculty, and the cognitive faculty. It is visible objects, it is sounds, it is odors, it is flavors, it is objects of touch, and it is objects of cognition. It is the eye-consciousness, the ear-consciousness, and all the other consciousnesses. It is that fundamental ignorance which is the adding of an understanding to our inherent enlightenment, and it is the ending of that ignorance; it is old age and death and the ending of old age and death. It is also the fundamentally unsatisfying nature of existence, the accumulation of the causes of dissatisfaction, the ending of dissatisfaction, and the path to the ending of dissatisfaction. It is all of the six perfections — giving, following precepts, vigor, patience, mindfulness, and wisdom. It is everything, including the Thus-Come One, who is the Arhat and the One of Right and Universal Wisdom. It is the permanence, bliss, true self, and purity of the great nirvana. It is every one of these, be they mundane or world-transcending. To be all of these is what the Matrix of the Thus-Come One is. That is the wondrousness of the inherent luminous mind that understands.

"It is apart from 'is' and 'is not' and yet both is and is not.[23]

---

[23] This tetralemma might be restated: "The Matrix of the Thus-Come One is identical with worldly and world-transcending phenomena and yet is not identical to them. It both is and is not identical to them and neither is nor is not identical to them.

"How then, with their conscious minds,[24] could beings who are bound to worlds in the three realms of existence — or even world-transcending Hearers of the Teaching and the Solitary Sages — possibly fathom the supreme awakening of the Thus-Come Ones? How could they gain the Buddha's ability to know and to see merely by using the world's words?

"Marvelous sounds can be brought forth from lutes, harps, and mandolins only when there are skilled fingers to play them. In the same way, all beings, including you, are fully endowed with the resplendent, enlightened, true mind. When I arrange my fingers to form the ocean-mudra, the light of the ocean-mudra samādhi shines forth. But the moment a thought arises in your mind, you must endure the stress of involvement with perceived objects. It is simply because you have not diligently pursued the path to supreme enlightenment. Instead, you are fond of the Lesser Vehicle and are content with a lesser goal."

[24] That is, the distinction-making mind of the sixth consciousness.

4
Delusion Has No Basis:
The Parable of Yajñadatta

Pūrṇa said, "The Thus-Come One and I are alike in that we are both fully endowed with the precious, awakened, perfect, luminous, true, wondrous, pure mind that understands. Nevertheless, for a time without beginning I was plagued with the deluded acts of my mind, and for a long time I was bound to the cycle of death and rebirth. Although I have since become a sage,[25] my enlightenment is not fully perfected, whereas the World-Honored One has put an end to all delusion so that only what is wondrous, true, and everlasting remains. I venture to ask the Thus-Come One why all beings suffer from delusion. Why do they keep covered their wondrous, luminous understanding so that they continue to be submerged in saṁsāra?"

The Buddha said to Pūrṇa, "You have put your coarser doubts to rest, but your more subtle doubts have not yet been ended. I will now question you about this matter by referring to a mundane event. Have you not heard about Yajñadatta, the man from Śrāvastī who saw a face with perfectly clear features in the mirror one morning and became enraptured with it? Then he became upset because he supposed he had lost his own face. It struck him that he must have turned into a headless ghost.[26] For no good reason he ran madly out of his house. What do you think? What caused this man to run madly about for no good reason?"

Pūrṇa replied, "He was clearly insane. That and nothing else was the cause."

---

[25] That is, he became an Arhat at the fourth stage, at which one is no longer subject to rebirth.

[26] Ch. *limei* 魑魅. The translation is uncertain. The limei ghost is described in indigenous Chinese works as a kind of animal spirit or ghost that usually lives in the mountains. The corresponding Sanskrit is not clear. Given the context here, it is possibly the headless ghost known as *blemya*. See J. Duncan and M. Derret, "A *Blemya* in India," in *Numen,* 49: 4 (2002), 460–74.

The Buddha said, "The luminous understanding of wondrous enlightenment is perfect; that fundamental, perfect luminous understanding is wondrous. How could there be in it any basis for what is clearly a delusion? And if there were a basis for this delusion, how could it be what we call deluded?

"Thus your deluded thoughts have followed one upon another, each one leading to the next. Confusion is added to confusion, eon after countless eon, numberless as motes of dust. Although the Buddha can reveal this process to you, he cannot reverse it for you.

> Most people put their energy into the physical body, which has no life of its own and which keeps you hopping on its behalf. But in the future, your body will certainly die. Those who practice in accord with the Dharma should apply their skill to what does have life, which is our true nature that does not die. (IV, 105)

"Therefore beings are not aware of the cause of their confusion. Because they do not realize that confusion is based only on confusion, their confusion persists. They need merely to realize that confusion has no ultimate basis, and the basis of their deluded thoughts will disappear. There is no need for them to wish that the cause of their confusion would disappear, because no cause existed in the first place. Thus someone who has become fully enlightened is like one who relates the events of a dream from which he has just awakened. His mind is now sharp and clear; what reason could he have then to wish to try to return to his dream to obtain some object that he had dreamt of?

> You encounter confusion and it seems to really exist, but actually it is an illusion. Confusion lacks any real existence. . . . The person who said he didn't have a head thought he didn't have one, but it was really there on his shoulders all along. Confusion is a temporary lack of clarity. It can't obliterate your enlightened nature. . . .(IV, 105)
>
> The person whose mind is sharp and clear represents the Buddha, who can speak of the Dharma . . . to destroy confusion and delusion, but he cannot physically get hold of deluded and confused mental states and show them to you. All he can do is use analogies to instruct you. Don't expect him to pull out

the states of mind for exhibit. In this way he's like a person who awakens from a dream and can talk about all the things that took place in the dream, but he can't pull out the things that he dreamt of and show them to you. (IV, 106)

"Even less could delusion have any basis; fundamentally, delusion has no existence. In the same way, there was no reason for Yajñadatta's experience that day in the city. Were his madness to suddenly cease, it would not be because he had recovered his head from anywhere outside of himself. How could his head have actually been missing, even while he was still in his madness?

"Pūrṇa, the same is true of the essential nature of delusion. Where could its basis lie? All that is needed is for you not to follow after the distinctions you make concerning the perpetuations — the world, beings, and retribution in accord with karma. Once you have eliminated the three conditions[27] that are necessary for the coming into being of these three perpetuations, their three causes will not become active again. Thus the madness in your mind that is like Yajñadatta's madness will cease of its own accord, and just that ceasing is enlightenment. That supreme, pure, luminous mind that understands has always extended everywhere throughout the Dharma-Realm. It cannot be bestowed upon you by someone else. What need is there to work yourself to the bone in pursuit of awakening?

"Consider, for example, a person who does not know that a wish-fulfilling pearl is sewn into his coat.[28] Destitute and homeless, wandering from place to place as he begs for his food, he is indeed poor, but his wish-fulfilling pearl is still with him. Then it so happens that someone wise points out his pearl to him, and now it can fulfill his every wish. He becomes very rich, and he realizes that his magical pearl can only have come from within himself."

---

[27] When Ānanda speaks next, he restates what he takes to be the Buddha's position here, and he identifies these "three conditions" as killing, stealing, and sexual desire. The three causes are not defined in the text; anger, desire, and delusion, the three poisons of the mind, are probably meant.

[28] The parable is told in full in chapter eight of the Lotus Sūtra.

If the Yajñadatta within you, your mad mind, ceases — if your distorted thinking, your perpetual state of confusion, your lack of enlightenment disappears — then full awakening appears. But awakening does not come from outside yourself. Nor do you need to nourish it within yourself. You have had it all along. (IV, 110)

People who desire riches and honor and entertainment and pleasure, don't realize that these mundane attainments are not the genuine riches or the genuine honor. The poorest people are those who do not recognize truth and do not understand that their true nature is like the hidden wish-fulfilling pearl in the parable. They don't understand about their true nature, but it is still the nature of the Matrix of the Thus-Come One, the supreme, pure, luminous mind. It is not lost; it is still inherently yours. If you practice according to the Buddha's Dharma and have faith in it, you will understand that your true nature is inherent within you, and you will come to discover your innate wealth. This is the true riches and honor.

The wise person in the parable is the Buddha. Showing the poor person the pearl in his clothing represents his pointing out to us our true inherent nature. . . . The person's becoming wealthy represents someone's awakening as he comes to understand his inherent enlightened nature. . . . When we study the Śūraṅgama Sūtra, we should each discover the wish-fulfilling pearl in our clothing. If you discover the pearl, you will be the world's wealthiest person, in this sense:

Stopping the thoughts of the mind
Is true wealth and honor.
Ending selfish desires forever
Is the true field of blessings.

If your deluded mind comes to a stop and your disorderly thoughts disappear, then you have obtained genuine wealth and honor. (IV, 111–2)

Then Ānanda came forward from his place in the great assembly to bow at the Buddha's feet. He stood and said to the Buddha, "World-Honored One, you have just now been saying that once we put to rest the karmas of killing, stealing, and sexual desire so that these three conditions no longer arise, their three causes will not become active again.

Then the madness in our minds that is like Yajñadatta's madness will cease of its own accord, and that ceasing itself is full awakening, which no one else can bestow upon us. Isn't all this clearly an example of the working of causes and conditions? Why then does the Thus-Come One now reject the doctrine of causes and conditions? World-Honored One, it was through hearing about causes and conditions that I became enlightened, as did others of us younger Hearers of the Teaching, who still need instruction. Here also in this assembly now are Mahā-Maudgalyāyana, Śāriputra, Subhūti, and others who once followed Brahmin elders. They too heard the teaching about causes and conditions, and as a result, they made the resolve to enter the monastic life. They put an end to their outflows and became enlightened. Now you say that one does not after all realize enlightenment through causes and conditions. If that is so, the ultimate truth must be what Maskari Gośālīputra[29] and those others in Rājagṛha[30] teach — that enlightenment happens on its own. I only hope that now the Buddha will compassionately clear up the confusion which has been suffocating us."

The Buddha said to Ānanda, "Let us compare what you have said to the case of Yajñadatta in Śrāvastī. If the causes and conditions for his madness were to disappear, his sanity would naturally reappear on its own. Your argument concerning causes and conditions and things coming into being on their own amounts to nothing more than that. Ānanda, his head was just as it always was. It was already fundamentally part of him. Otherwise he would not have been who he was. How then could causes and conditions be involved in his running madly about out of fear that his face had disappeared?

"His head was intact from the beginning. But if his madness were indeed due to causes and conditions, wouldn't causes and conditions have also led to his head actually disappearing? Yet his head has always been present. His madness and terror arose from delusion. No actual change

[29] See part 2, note 10.
[30] A city in the kingdom of Magadha on the northeast Ganges Plain in what is now Bihar.

had taken place. How then could his madness have arisen from causes and conditions? And if his madness were fundamentally part of him — if madness and terror were the way he was in the first place — then why would his madness not have been already evident? But if his madness was not fundamentally part of him — if he was not deluded about his head all along — why did he run madly about?

"Had Yajñadatta awakened and realized that his head was fundamentally part of him, he would have understood that his running about was madness. From this it should be clear to you that your objections about causes and conditions and about things coming into being on their own cannot be taken seriously. That is why I said that once the three causes and three conditions are eliminated, the enlightened mind is revealed. If you were to say that the enlightened mind comes into being with the cessation of the mind that arises and perishes, then you would be saying that the enlightened mind, too, is subject to arising and perishing. In truth, the effortless path to enlightenment is the ending of both arising and perishing.

"Suppose, further, that it is possible that the enlightened mind could come into being on its own. Then it should be clear that it would come into being only with the perishing of the mind that comes into being and ceases to be. But that is still a coming into being and ceasing to be. Do not think that something which does not arise and perish must therefore be said to have come into being on its own.[31] For example, a mixture is said to be created when components with different attributes are combined. What cannot be mixed together is said to be something that is fundamental. In fact, what is fundamental is not fundamental; what is mixed is not in fact a mixture. Neither what is mixed nor what is fundamental exists. Yet the nonexistence of the mixed and the fundamental must also be negated. Only then do we have a teaching that may be called Dharma that is more than mere speculation. This is a teaching that must be left behind, and the leaving behind, too, must be left behind. That may be called the Dharma that transcends idle speculation.

[31] This is the substance of Ānanda's objection above.

"For you, awakening and nirvana are still so distant that you will have to spend eons in difficult practice before you will reach them. Your ability to memorize all twelve types of discourse spoken by the Buddha[32] and proclaimed by the Thus-Come Ones in all ten directions — with their pure and wondrous truths innumerable as the River Ganges' sands — has merely helped you to indulge in idle speculation. Certainly you have the ability to speak about causes and conditions and about things coming into being on their own with such understanding that people call you foremost in erudition; yet despite your many eons of accumulated learning, you were not able escape your difficulty with the young Mātaṅga woman. Why did you need me to recite the Śūraṅgama Mantra for you? In the young Mātaṅga woman's heart the fires of lust were extinguished, and instantly she became a sage who must return only once.[33] Now she has joined a group of vigorous practitioners of my Dharma. In her, the river of love has gone dry, and so now you are free of her.

"Therefore, Ānanda, the many eons you have spent committing to memory the Thus-Come One's esoteric, inconceivable, wondrous, and majestic Dharma are not equal to a single day spent cultivating karma that is free of outflows and is far removed from the two worldly torments of hate and love. The young Mātaṅga woman was a courtesan, and yet her love and desire were dispelled by the spiritual power of the mantra; now she is a nun named Prakṛti.[34] She and Rāhula's mother, Yaśodharā,[35] have both become aware of their previous lives, and they know that, among the causes of their actions during many lifetimes, their craving for emotional love was the cause of their suffering. Now they have escaped their

---

[32] The twelve are prose passages, reiterative verses, instructional verses, teachings concerning causation, narratives, accounts of the Buddha's previous lives, accounts of manifestations of spiritual power, analogies, questions and answers concerning doctrine, teachings spoken without request, broadenings of the teaching, and predictions of enlightenment.

[33] Skt. anāgāmin, a third-stage Arhat.

[34] The name means "Nature," that is, one who understands her own nature.

[35] Yaśodharā was the wife of the Buddha Śākyamuni while he was still Prince Siddhartha. Rāhula was their son.

bonds and have received predictions.[36] Why do you then continue to cheat yourself by standing still, merely watching and listening?"

When Ānanda and the others in the great assembly had heard the Buddha's instructions, their doubts and delusions were dispelled. Their minds awakened to the truth, and in body and mind they felt a serenity that they had never known before.

[36] That is, that at such and such a time and place they would become Buddhas with such and such names.

V
Instructions for Practice

1
Five Layers of Turbidity

Once again Ānanda wept as he bowed at the Buddha's feet. Then he knelt, and with his palms joined he said respectfully to the Buddha, "The Supreme, Compassionate, Pure, and Noble King has skillfully opened our minds. In response to our various situations and circumstances, he has been able to urge us on and to pull us benighted ones out of the sea of suffering in which we have been drowning.

"World-Honored One, now that I have heard the Buddha explain this Dharma, I know that the Matrix of the Thus-Come One, which is the wondrous, enlightened mind that understands, extends throughout all ten directions. I know that it encompasses and supports the lands of the Thus-Come Ones in all ten directions — those pure and splendid lands of the Wondrous, Enlightened Kings. However, the Thus-Come One has also admonished me for merely listening to the Dharma without applying it to my practice. Now, therefore, I am like a wanderer who unexpectedly meets a celestial king. The king bestows upon the wanderer a magnificent house. The house is now his, yet in order to go in he will still need to find a door. I only hope that the Thus-Come One will not withhold his compassion from all of us in this assembly who are covered in darkness, so that we may renounce the Lesser Vehicle. May he show us the road that leads from our original resolve to the Thus-Come Ones' bodiless nirvana.[1] May he enable those of us who still need instruction to subdue our age-old habit of dependence on the objects of the senses, to master the dhāraṇī,[2] and to gain the wisdom and vision of the Buddhas." Having made this request, Ānanda bowed to the ground, and all in the assembly single-mindedly awaited the Buddha's compassionate instruction.

Then the World-Honored One took pity on all the Hearers of the Teaching and on the Solitary Sages in the assembly who did not yet abide

---

[1] Skt. *anupadhi-śeṣa nirvāṇa*, Ch. *wu yu niepan* 無餘涅槃, literally "nirvana without remainder." The phrase refers to the nirvana of a Buddha that follows the death of his physical body; it is the body that does not remain.

[2] The Śūraṅgama Mantra.

effortlessly in the fully awakened mind. He took pity also on the beings who would be born after the Buddha's bodiless nirvana, during the time of the Dharma's ending. He revealed the wondrous path of practice in accord with the Supreme Vehicle, so that all would resolve their minds upon becoming fully awake.

> The period when the Buddha Śākyamuni was in the world is called the time of the right Dharma. During this period, which continued for a thousand years, people devoted themselves to meditation and samādhi. After the Buddha had entered nirvana and the thousand years of the time of the right Dharma had passed, the time of the semblance of Dharma began. It, too, lasted for a thousand years. During this period, people devoted themselves to building temples and stupas. They didn't enter samādhi but instead sought to earn blessings from their work. When the Buddha was in the world, people sought wisdom, but during the time of the semblance of Dharma, they "ignored the roots and held on to the branches." After the time of the semblance of Dharma came the time of the Dharma's ending, which we are in now. In this time, people devote themselves neither to meditation and samādhi nor to the building of temples and stupas. They devote themselves to fighting. Wherever you go in the present age, people quarrel with people, families fight with families, and countries war against countries. In every space and corner of the globe there is contention and unrest. When we sit in meditation and study the Sutras, we make the time of right Dharma appear within the time of the Dharma's ending. (IV, 140)

He instructed Ānanda and the others in the assembly as follows: "You have all made a firm resolve to become enlightened, and you have not wearied of your practice of the samādhi of the Buddhas, the Thus-Come Ones. Therefore, you should now understand two definitive principles concerning your resolve to become enlightened. What are these two definitive principles? The first of the two, Ānanda, is that all of you who wish to renounce the Lesser Vehicle of the Hearers of the Teaching and to practice in accord with the Vehicle of the Bodhisattvas so that you can gain the wisdom and vision of the Buddhas, must examine the resolve that is the basis of your practice that leads to enlightenment.[3] Is this resolve identical to the awakening that will be the result of your practice,[4] or is it not?

"If the mind that comes into being and ceases is the basis of your practice, Ānanda, then you will not be able to ride the Buddha's Vehicle to where there is nothing that comes into being or ceases to be. For this reason, you should shine the light of your understanding on the phenomena of the material world. Since all phenomena are subject to change and decay, how could any of them serve as a basis for the practice of Dharma? Contemplate the phenomena of the world, Ānanda: which one of them does not decay? But you will never hear of space decaying. Why? Space is unconditioned, and so it has never been and can never be subject to dissolution.

"In your own body, what appears as solid is composed of the primary element earth, what is moist contains the primary element water, what has warmth belongs to the primary element fire, and movement constitutes the primary element wind. Because these four primary elements are bound together, your pure, perfect, wondrous enlightened mind that understands is divided into the functions of seeing, listening, touching, and cognition.[5] Turbidity, in five layers, comes about as a result.

"What is turbidity, Ānanda? Let us consider an example. Water in its original state is pure and clear, while soil, ashes, and sand in their original states are solid and opaque. These defining attributes of water and of soil, ashes, and sand are such that they are mutually incompatible. Suppose that someone werc to pick up some soil and throw it into clear water. The soil now loses its solidity, and the water loses its purity. Together they appear clouded or, we may say, turbid. The five layers of turbidity occur in the same way.

"As you look into space throughout all ten directions, Ānanda, no separation can be made between space and your visual awareness of it. If only space existed, then there would be nothing to be aware of it. If only

[3] Ch. *yin di* 因地.
[4] Ch. *guo di* 果地.
[5] The text here mentions the eye-consciousness, ear-consciousness, etc., using informal language. Smelling and tasting are understood to be included.

awareness existed, then there would not be anything for it to be aware of. Therefore space and visual awareness become entangled with each other. With this entanglement, based on delusion, the turbidity of time comes into being. This is the first layer of turbidity.

"Your body is composed of the four primary elements. Your visual awareness, your hearing, your tactile awareness, and your mental awareness[6] become strictly defined, while water, fire, wind, and earth participate in bringing about the attributes of the faculties that have awareness. Thus awareness and the primary elements become entangled with each other. With this entanglement, based on delusion, the turbidity of perception comes into being. This is the second layer of turbidity.

> There are external turbidities, which can be explained in terms of the world, but here the text discusses the internal turbidities, which can be explained in terms of the body. In fact the external turbidities exist because of the internal turbidities. If you can get rid of your internal turbidities, the external turbidities will subside as well.[7] (IV, 148)

"Further, your mind is habituated to recollecting the past, to being aware of the present, and to anticipating the future. Because of these habits, the six consciousnesses arise and embrace the six kinds of perceived objects. Without these objects, your mind-consciousness has no attributes, and without your perception of them, these objects have no

[6] All six consciousnesses are implied.

[7] The external turbidities are aspects of the world and beings during the period of decline of an eon. The five are the turbidity of the eon; the turbidity of mistaken views among the beings of that time; the turbidity of afflictions among the beings; the turbidity of beings, who become defiled at that time; and the turbidity of lifespans, in that the average lifespan declines drastically at that time. The internal turbidities, on the other hand, correspond to the three subtle and six coarse attributes of delusion. The first turbidity corresponds to the first of the three subtle attributes (the coming into being of the self-verifying division of the eighth consciousness); the second turbidity corresponds to the second and third of the subtle attributes (the coming into being of the observing and the observed divisions of the eighth consciousness); the third turbidity corresponds to the first four of the coarse attributes of delusion; the fourth turbidity corresponds to the fifth coarse attribute; and the fifth turbidity corresponds to the sixth coarse attribute. For discussion of the six coarse attributes of delusion, see part 4.1 above.

identity. Objects you perceive and your mind-consciousness become entangled with each other. With this entanglement, based on delusion, the mind becomes turbid with afflictions. These afflictions are the third layer of turbidity.

"Further, by night and by day, beings ceaselessly come into being and perish. They always desire to continue to experience the world indefinitely through their faculties of perception. Their karma leads them to continually move from one land to another. Their thoughts and their karma become entangled with each other, and with this entanglement, based on delusion, there is the fourth layer, the turbidity of individual beings.

"The fundamental natures of your seeing, your hearing, and your other awarenesses do not differ from one another, but the six objects of perception separate them so that your awareness is forced to become differentiated. Although the six sense-consciousnesses share a single fundamental awareness, their functioning has become distinct. The consciousnesses and their objects are no longer in their correct relationship. They become entangled with each other, and with this entanglement, based on delusion, there is the fifth layer, the turbidity of lifespans.

"Ānanda, now you wish to transform your visual, aural, tactile, and mental awareness, together with the other kinds of awareness, into the permanence, bliss, true self, and purity of the Thus-Come One. To accomplish this, you must pull out the root of death and rebirth and rely on that pure and perfect nature that neither comes into being nor ceases to be. Use the purity of your true nature to make disappear the distinction between your original state of enlightenment and the illusory state of what comes into being and ceases to be. The original enlightened understanding, which neither comes into being nor ceases to be, must be the basis of your practice.[8] Then you will attain the awakening that will be the result of your practice.

"The process may be compared to the settling of turbid water. If you keep it undisturbed in a container so that it is completely still and quiet,

---

[8] This is the first of the two definitive principles mentioned just above.

the sand and silt in it will settle naturally, and the water will become clear. This may be compared to the initial stage of subduing the afflictions that arise from transitory perceptions of objects. When the sand and silt have been removed so that only clear water remains, then fundamental ignorance has been eliminated forever. When the water is quite pure and clear, nothing that may happen will be a cause of affliction. All will be in accord with the pure and wondrous attributes of nirvana."

When someone throws dirt into clean water, the water turns muddy. The dirt loses its solidity, and the water loses its clarity. This is an analogy for beings, who are within the Matrix of the Thus-Come One, but who get mixed up with the four primary elements and the five layers of turbidity and give rise to ignorance and affliction. From the one truth arises the false. . . . An analogy could compare the true to our body and the false to our shadow. Our shadow exists only when there is a light shining on the body. The shadow represents ignorance, because ignorance is also unreal; it is something false which arises from the true. But, because this one falseness arises, every kind of falseness arises.

As for the analogy of dirt thrown into water, when you practice meditation in order to return to purity, your body is like the undisturbed container. . . . But you must be completely unmoving. It's not the case that you can move your legs at the first sign of pain, or that you can lean back and relax when your back hurts. . . . One who is still and unmoving is not afraid of anything, much less a little leg pain. With the settling of the sand and silt, which represent your ignorance and affliction, your true nature, represented by the pure water, appears. . . . But if you simply let the mud stay in the bottom of the container, then as soon as the vessel is moved, the mud will be stirred up again. That represents a resurgence of ignorance and affliction in your mind. . . . If the mud is completely removed from the water, then you will have rid yourself of your fundamental ignorance forever. At that point, you have become a Buddha. (IV, 154–6)

2
Choosing One Faculty
in Order to Liberate All Six

"The second principle is that, if you are resolved to become fully awakened, you must courageously dedicate yourself to practice in accord with the Bodhisattva Vehicle. You must decisively let go of everything that has conditioned attributes. Carefully examine the source of your afflictions, which since time without beginning have created your karma and nurtured its growth. Who is it that creates this karma and undergoes retribution? If, during your quest for full awakening, Ānanda, you do not examine and contemplate the sources of affliction, you will not be able to understand the illusory and distorted nature of the perceiving faculties and their objects. At what point did you become so disoriented? If you do not know that, how can you expect to subdue your afflictions and aspire to becoming a Buddha?

"Ānanda, consider some worldly person who wishes to untie a knot. If he cannot see the knot, how will he know how to untie it? You have never heard of space being broken into parts. Why? Space has no shape or form. Therefore, it can neither be divided nor put together again.

> Untying the knot refers to the instruction that you must know the source of delusion if you are to get rid of it. . . . The fact that there are no knots in space represents the nature of the Matrix of the Thus-Come One, which is inherent in you and is free of delusion. (IV, 161)

"But now your eyes, ears, nose, tongue, body, and mind are like conspirators who have introduced thieves into your house to plunder your valuables. In this way, since time without beginning, beings and the world of time and space have been tied to each other because of illusion, and that is why beings cannot transcend this world.

> People think that the six faculties are helpful, but actually it is just these six destructive things that steal the Dharma-jewels of our true nature. People consider their eyes, ears, nose, tongue, body, and mind to be their best friends.

But these so-called friends are the ones who invite thieves into your house to plunder your valuables. It is said,

> What the eyes don't see
> The mouth won't crave.
> What the ears don't hear
> Won't lead the mind to error.

You see someone eating something, and it's as if a hand reaches out of your throat to grab it. The mouth is gluttonous because the eyes have seen something good to eat. Or you see something or someone beautiful and you want that person or thing, but once you get your wish, it becomes a source of affliction. And if you don't get your wish, you're also afflicted. . . . The six consciousnesses that are produced by the interaction of the eyes, ears, nose, tongue, body, and mind with their objects are what is meant by "outflows." But the thieves will not be able to rob you if you can reach the level at which —

> The eyes see visible forms,
> But inside there is nothing;
> The ears hear sounds,
> But the mind is unaware.

If you don't have the skill — if you lack samādhi — and if you run out through your eyes, ears, nose, tongue, body, and mind instead of turning your light around to illumine within, then you have outflows, and you are being robbed of your inherent wealth, . . . which is nothing less than your everlasting true mind within the Matrix of the Thus-Come One. (IV, 162–5)

"What do I mean, Ānanda, by 'beings and the world of time and space'? 'Time' denotes flux and change; 'space' denotes location and direction. You already know that the directions are north, south, east, west, northeast, southeast, northwest, southwest, above, and below, while time is divided into past, present, and future. Thus locations are tenfold and the flow of time is threefold, making ten directions and three periods of time. Because beings are entangled in illusion, they constantly move about in time and space, which become interconnected.

"Although space can be defined as extending in ten directions and can be clearly understood as such, people in general only take account of north, south, east, and west. They do not consider above and below to be specific directions, and they see the four intermediate directions as merely relative to the others, while the four cardinal points are understood to be fixed. Therefore, we can say that space is fourfold and time threefold, and that the three times and four directions multiplied together make a total of twelve.

"Again, if we multiply these numbers in three stages; first, by each other, to make twelve, next by ten and then again by ten, we reach a total of twelve hundred. Applying this to the six faculties of perception, we may measure the efficacy of each, with a total of twelve hundred signifying the greatest possible efficacy.

"Ānanda, you can now determine the degree of efficacy of each of the faculties of perception. Consider the efficacy of the eye-faculty. You can see in front of you but not behind you. In front of you there is light, but behind you there is darkness. Adding in your partial vision at your left and right, your capacity to see is effective by only two thirds. The overall efficacy of the eye-faculty, then, is incomplete, in that it functions in three directions but not in the fourth. Know then that the efficacy of the eye-faculty may be expressed as eight hundred.[9]

"Consider the ability of the ear-faculty to hear in all ten directions without exception. The sounds we hear may be distant or nearby. When there is silence, our hearing is unbounded. Know then that the efficacy of the ear-faculty may be expressed as twelve hundred.

"Consider the ability of the nose-faculty to smell. The breath moves through the nose in and out. But in the space between inhaling and exhaling, the breath is lacking. Upon examination, we can say that the nose-faculty is lacking one of three aspects. Know then that the efficacy of the nose-faculty may be expressed as eight hundred.

---

[9] That is, 800 of 1200, or two thirds. We see in three of four directions, but to our right and to our left we see only half as well as we see in front of us; forward vision counts as one, plus a half for each area of peripheral vision, for a total of two out of three (the third being the area behind us).

"Consider the ability of the tongue-faculty to proclaim wisely both worldly and world-transcending wisdom. Languages differ from place to place, but meanings know no boundary. Know then that the efficacy of the tongue-faculty may be expressed as twelve hundred.

"Consider the ability of the body-faculty to be aware of contact. It is conscious of pleasure and discomfort. It has awareness upon contact and lacks awareness once there is separation. Separation is a single quality, while contact is twofold. Upon examination, then, we may say that the body-faculty is lacking in one of three aspects. Know then that the efficacy of the body-faculty may be expressed as eight hundred.

"Consider the ability of the cognitive faculty to silently include within its scope all worldly and world-transcending phenomena in all ten directions and all three periods of time. It excludes neither the thoughts of sages nor the distorted thoughts of ordinary beings; it knows no boundary. Know then that the efficacy of the cognitive faculty may be expressed as twelve hundred.

"Ānanda, you now wish to go upstream against the current of the river of desire, which leads to death and rebirth. You wish to go against the current that flows through the faculties until you reach the source, where there is neither coming into being nor ceasing to be. You should investigate how the six faculties function: which ones function upon contact with their objects and which ones function while apart from their objects; which are the more easily employed in the practice of reversing your attention and which ones are less easily employed;[10] which ones are best suited for breaking through to enlightenment and which ones are not fully efficacious. If you can discern which of your faculties can lead you to break through to enlightenment, then you will be able to go upstream against the current that carries the karma in which, due to your delusion, you have been immersed since time without beginning. One day of practice that relies on a fully effective faculty is equivalent to an eon of practice that relies on a faculty that is not fully effective. I have already

---

[10] Nose, body, and tongue function upon contact with their objects; eyes, ears, and mind function while apart from their objects. Eye and ear are more easily employed than the others (Yuanying, 681).

given you a full explanation of the fundamental purity and perfect clarity of the six faculties, and I have now given numerical equivalents for the efficacy of each one. It is up to you to choose carefully which one to concentrate on. I will clarify this to help you move forward vigorously.

"The Thus-Come Ones in all ten directions chose one of the eighteen constituent elements of perception for their practice that led to their gaining the perfect, supreme, complete awakening. For them, none of the eighteen constituents was superior or inferior. But because you are at a lower level and have not yet fully developed that wisdom which is independent of conditions, I have explained all this to you in detail so that you will be able to choose one faculty as a gateway to deep practice. If you take that path until you have left behind all distortion within that one faculty, then all the other faculties will be purified as well."

Ānanda said respectfully to the Buddha, "World-Honored One, how can I choose one gateway that will allow me to reverse my outflows and purify all six of my faculties of perception at the same time?"

The Buddha said to Ānanda, "You have already reached the level of one who has entered the stream of the sages,[11] and you have abandoned the deluded views held by beings in the three realms of existence.[12] But you still do not understand the illusory habits which you have accumulated in life after life since time without beginning. You will need to practice even more to get rid of the subtle aspects of your habits as they come into being, abide, decay, and perish.

"Now you should consider whether the six faculties are one or six. If they are one, Ānanda, why can't the ears see, and why can't the eyes hear? Why can't the head walk? Why can't the feet speak? If the six faculties are indeed six, which one of them is now receiving my instruction in this subtle, wondrous gateway to the Dharma as I explain it to this assembly?"

Ānanda replied, "I am hearing it with my ears."

The Buddha said, "If it is just your ears that hear it, do they then have

---

[11] Skt. *srota-āpanna*, "stream-enterer," the first of the four Arhat stages, in which one "enters the stream" of sagehood.

[12] That is, in the realms of desire, form, and formlessness.

no connection to your body or your mouth? And yet you ask about the teaching with your mouth, and as you receive it, you show your respect with your body. Therefore — as to the idea that the faculties must be one if they are not six, and that they must be six if they are not one — we cannot say that fundamentally they are both one and six, nor can we say that they are neither one nor six. In your disoriented state, in which you have been sinking and undergoing change[13] since time without beginning, you have conceived the idea that there is "one" and "six" within the fundamental perfect clarity. As a sage at the first level, you have purified the six, but you have not done away with the one.

"By analogy, suppose one were to try to fit some space into a variety of containers. Because containers differ in shape, we could say the spaces within them also differ in shape. If you take away the containers and look at the space that was within them, you will say that the space has become one again. But how could space become unified or separated because of what you have done? Indeed, how could the space be said to be either one or not one? You should understand that the same is true of the six faculties of perception.

"The essence of seeing[14] is generated out of the wondrous perfection of the pure mind because it adheres to the appearance of the two attributes of light and darkness. That essence of seeing then reveals the essence of visible objects,[15] and the two then become entangled with one another, thus creating the essence of the eye-faculty. The essence of the eye-faculty is composed of the four primary elements in their pure state, and that is why it may be called the faculty's 'essence.' The physical eye takes the shape of a grape and is composed of the four primary elements in their coarse state. The eye-faculty recklessly races outward in pursuit of visible objects.

"The essence of hearing is generated out of the wondrous perfection

---

[13] That is, sinking in the sea of affliction and moving from one body to another through the process of death and rebirth.

[14] The observing division of the eighth consciousness.

[15] The observed division of the eighth consciousness. The same pattern is applied to the other faculties and their objects.

of the pure mind because it adheres to the two opposing attributes of sound and silence. That essence of hearing then gathers into itself the essence of sound, and the two then become entangled with one another, thus creating the essence of the ear-faculty. The essence of the ear-faculty is composed of the four primary elements in their pure state, and that is why it may be called the faculty's 'essence.' The physical ear takes the shape of a curled new leaf and is composed of the four primary elements in their coarse state. The ear-faculty recklessly races outward in pursuit of sounds.

"The essence of smelling is generated out of the wondrous perfection of the pure mind because it adheres to the two contrasting attributes of openness and blockage. The essence of smelling takes in the essence of odor, and the two then become entangled with one another, thus creating the essence of the nose-faculty. The essence of the nose-faculty is composed of the four primary elements in their pure state, and that is why it may be called the faculty's 'essence.' The physical nose takes the shape of a pair of talons and is composed of the four primary elements in their coarse state. The nose-faculty recklessly races outward in pursuit of odors.

"The essence of tasting is generated out of the wondrous perfection of the pure mind because it adheres to the two interacting attributes of flavor and lack of flavor. The essence of tasting mixes itself with the essence of flavor, thus creating the essence of the tongue-faculty. The essence of the tongue-faculty is composed of the four primary elements in their pure state, and that is why it may be called the faculty's 'essence.' The physical tongue takes the shape of a crescent moon and is composed of the four primary elements in their coarse state. The tongue-faculty recklessly races outward in pursuit of flavors.

"The essence of the sense of touch is generated out of the wondrous perfection of the pure mind because it adheres to the two interacting attributes of contact and separation. The essence of tactile awareness seizes upon the essence of what is touched, thus creating the essence of the body-faculty. The essence of the body-faculty is composed of the four primary elements in their pure state, and that is why it may be called the faculty's 'essence.' The physical body, with its torso which takes the shape of a skin-covered drum, is composed of the four primary elements in their coarse form. The body-faculty recklessly races outward in pursuit of tangible objects.

"The essence of cognition is generated out of the wondrous perfection of the pure mind because it adheres to the two mutually perpetuating attributes of coming into being and perishing. The essence of mental awareness grasps the essence of objects of cognition, thus creating the essence of the cognitive faculty. The essence of the cognitive faculty is composed of the four primary elements in their pure state, and that is why it may be called the faculty's 'essence.' The cognitive faculty, which is, as it were, seen in a dark room, responds to the four primary elements in their coarse form. The mind-faculty recklessly flows outward in pursuit of mental objects.

"So it is, Ānanda, that the six faculties come into being out of the awakened mind when another understanding is added to that awakened mind. As a result, the essential understanding is lost and the faculties adhere to what is distorted, and each one assumes a different function. Therefore, if you were now to be deprived of both light and darkness, would your seeing continue to exist or would it not? If you were deprived of both sound and silence, would your hearing lose its fundamental characteristics or would it not? If you were deprived of both openness and blockage, would your capacity to smell continue to exist or would it not? If you were deprived of both the presence and the absence of flavors, would your capacity to taste continue to exist or would it not? If you were deprived of both contact and separation, would your sense of touch still exist or would it not? If you were deprived of both the coming into being and perishing of the objects of cognition, would your capacity for cognition still exist or would it not?

"All that you need to do is not allow your attention to be diverted by the twelve conditioned attributes of sound and silence, contact and separation, flavor and the absence of flavor, openness and blockage, coming into being and perishing, and light and darkness. Next, extricate one faculty by detaching it from its objects, and redirect that faculty inward so that it can return to what is original and true. Then it will radiate the light of the original understanding. This brilliant light will shine forth and extricate the other five faculties until they are completely free.

> The text says literally: "All you need is not to follow." This section of the Sutra is very important. Why don't people become enlightened? . . . It is because they let themselves be distracted by illusory objects of perception. They are under the influence of their perceptions of objects and cannot gain control over them. But you don't have to comply; you don't have to be under their influence. You can go against the current and decline to follow the twelve conditioned attributes of light and darkness, sound and silence, openness and blockage, flavors and blandness, contact and separation, and coming into being and ceasing to be. (IV, 195)

"If your six faculties are freed from the objects that they perceive so that the light of your understanding is not diverted into one or another of the faculties, then the light of your understanding will manifest through all the faculties so that all six of them will function interchangeably.

"Ānanda, you know, do you not, that here in this assembly, Aniruddha is blind and yet can see; that the dragon Upananda is deaf and yet can hear; that the goddess of the River Ganges has no sense of smell and yet can discern fragrances; that Gavāmpati's malformed tongue cannot taste, and yet he is aware of flavors; and that the spirit Śūnyatā is incorporeal but just now has a sense of touch — you can see him here temporarily as he is illumined by the light of the Thus-Come One. By nature, however, he is as bodiless as the wind. And like all who abide in the samādhi of cessation[16] and who have attained the stillness of the Hearers of the Teaching, Mahākāśyapa, here in this assembly, long ago caused his cognitive faculty to cease, and yet without relying on the thinking mind, his understanding is clear and perfect.

"Once all your faculties are completely disengaged, Ānanda, a pure

---

[16] Skt. *nirodha-samāpatti,* Ch. *mie jin ding* 滅盡定, that is, cessation of the sixth consciousness (the mind-consciousness) and of the seventh consciousness (the individuating consciousness). Practitioners at this ninth level of samādhi have put an end to the aggregates of sense-perception and cognition.

brilliance will shine forth from within them. Then all coarse perceived objects — indeed all phenomena subject to change in the material world — will be transformed, just as ice is transformed when it melts in hot water. Then, responding in the time it takes for a single thought to arise, all phenomena will merge into your supreme awareness.

"Ānanda, consider someone who, seeing only with his eyes, quickly closes his eyes so that total darkness surrounds him. His six faculties will be enveloped in the darkness such that his eyes will not be able to distinguish the head from the feet on someone else's body. But he will be able to tell the head and the foot apart if he traces their shape with his hands. He will be able to identify them as accurately as he would have done by using his eyes.

"Now, if his visual awareness were dependent on the presence of light, he would have no visual awareness when he was immersed in darkness. But without light, he can still perceive. Total darkness need not prevent him from being aware of distinctions among objects. In the same way, once your faculties and their objects have melted away, how could your awareness and understanding not become perfect and wondrous?"

3
The Example of the Bell's Sound

Ānanda said respectfully to the Buddha, "World-Honored One, as the Buddha has said, when one's practice is based on the resolve to seek what is everlasting, one's mind should be correlated to the mental state of the enlightenment that will be the result of one's practice. This result, World-Honored One, may be called Full Awakening, Nirvana, the Suchness of Reality, the Buddha-nature, the Pure[17] Consciousness, the Emptiness of the Matrix of the Thus-Come One, and the Wisdom of the Great Perfect Mirror. Those are seven different names for what is pure and perfect, everlasting and indestructible, that essential nature which is like the most durable vajra.

"If, ultimately, seeing, hearing, and the other sense-consciousnesses do not exist on their own apart from light and darkness, sound and silence, openness and blockage, and so forth, then in the same way the mind-consciousness must cease to exist when it is apart from its own objects. How then can these consciousnesses, which will ultimately perish, be the basis for practice as one strives for the Thus-Come Ones' everlasting realization as it is characterized by those seven names?

"World-Honored One, suppose that in the final analysis no seeing can take place when neither light nor darkness are present. In the same way, no thought-processes can take place if no objects are being presented to the faculty of cognition. Then no matter how much I look here and look there, going about in circles in an exhaustive search, I can find nothing that fundamentally is my mind or my mind's objects. On what then can I base my quest for supreme enlightenment?

"What the Thus-Come One has just said contradicts his previous words about what is clear, pure, perfect, and everlasting.[18] It seems to be mere speculation. How can these words spoken by the Thus-Come One be true?

---

[17] Skt. *amala-vijñāna,* the eighth consciousness transformed into a pure consciousness.
[18] Ānanda here alludes to the discussion of visual awareness in part 2.

185

I only hope the Buddha, out of his great kindness, will set me free from the doubts that I am clinging to."

The Buddha said to Ānanda, "You are very learned, but you have not yet put an end to your outflows. You know the reasons for delusion, but when you encounter delusion you fail to recognize it. It is to be feared that, though you are sincere, you still do not quite trust the teaching. I will have to make use of another everyday situation to dispel your doubts."

The Buddha then instructed Rāhula to strike the bell once, and he asked Ānanda, "Do you hear?"

Ānanda and the others in the assembly answered, "We hear."

When the bell had ceased ringing, the Buddha asked again, "Now do you hear?"

Ānanda and the others in the assembly answered, "We do not."

Then Rāhula struck the bell once more, and the Buddha asked once again, "Now do you hear?"

Ānanda and the others again replied, "We hear."

The Buddha asked Ānanda, "How is it that you heard and then did not hear?"

Ānanda and the others said respectfully to the Buddha, "We heard the bell when it was struck, but when at length the sounding of the bell had died away and its reverberations had faded, we no longer were hearing."

The Buddha then instructed Rāhula to strike the bell yet again, and he asked Ānanda, "Is there a sound now?"

Ānanda and the others in the assembly answered, "Yes, there is a sound."

In a little while the sound faded, and the Buddha asked, "And now is there a sound?"

Ānanda and the others replied, "There is no sound."

After a moment Rāhula again struck the bell, and the Buddha asked again, "And is there a sound now?"

Ānanda and the others said, "There is."

The Buddha asked Ānanda, "How is it that there was a sound and then no sound?"

Ānanda and the others in the assembly answered respectfully, "When the bell was struck, there was a sound, but when at length the sounding of the bell had died away and the reverberations had faded, there was no longer any sound."

The Buddha said to Ānanda and the others in the assembly. "Why have you given such muddled answers?"

Ānanda and the others thereupon asked the Buddha, "Why do you say that our answers were muddled?"

The Buddha replied, "When I asked you whether you heard, you said that you had heard. When I asked if there was a sound, you said that there was a sound. Since you did not clearly distinguish between hearing and sound in your answer, how could I not say that your answer was muddled?

"Ānanda, once the sounding of the bell and its reverberations had faded, you said that you no longer heard. If it were true that you had stopped hearing, your essential capacity for hearing[19] would have ceased to exist. It would be like a dead tree that is unable to grow again, in that you would have been unable to hear the bell if it were struck again. You knew when the bell's sound, which is a perceived object, was present and when it was absent. But how could it be that your essential capacity for hearing was present and then absent? If your essential capacity for hearing were in truth no longer present, what then would be aware that the sound had ceased? Therefore, Ānanda, although the sounds you hear come into being and cease to be, neither the presence nor the subsequent absence of sound can cause your essential capacity for hearing to come into being and then cease to be.

> Ānanda and the members of the great assembly all said that they did not hear once the bell's sound died away. That's where their problem lay. . . . They thought that when there is no sound, there is no hearing. But actually, when there is no sound, what is it that perceives that there is nothing to be heard?

[19] This is another way of expressing the meaning of Ch. *wen xing* 聞性, earlier rendered as "the enlightened nature of hearing."

. . . If you were really without hearing, then you would not know whether there was sound or not. (IV, 215)

Although the sound ceases, the enlightened nature of hearing has not ceased to function. It is still in operation, because the enlightened nature of hearing neither comes into being nor ceases to be. It is sound that comes into being and ceases to be. Thus when the sound ceased and Ānanda said that he did not hear, he was mistaken. (IV, 218)

"You are still deluded. In your confusion you take hearing and the presence of sound to be the same thing. You consider something everlasting to be something that will come to an end. In the final analysis, it cannot be said that hearing in its essential nature is dependent on the presence of sound or silence, or dependent on whether the ears are obstructed or unobstructed.

"Consider someone who has fallen deeply asleep on his bed. While he is sleeping, someone in his household starts beating clothes or pounding rice. The dreamer hears the sounds of the beating or the pounding and mistakes them for something else, perhaps the striking of a drum or the ringing of a bell. In his dream he wonders why the striking of the bell or drum sounds like clothes being beaten or like rice being pounded. He wakes up suddenly, and he immediately recognizes the sound of the pounding. He tells the people in his household, 'I just had a dream in which I mistook your pounding rice for the beating of a drum.'

He is so sound asleep that he does not wake up when someone calls him. But even though he does not awaken, the enlightened nature of his hearing is still present. He perceives sounds, albeit mistakenly, even though he is asleep. The mistake is not made by the enlightened nature of hearing but by the sixth consciousness, the mind-consciousness. (IV, 221)

"Ānanda, how was it that this dreamer could have been conscious of sound or silence? How was it that his ears were unobstructed and functioning? Although his body was asleep, the enlightened nature of his hearing did not sleep. Even when the body wastes away, its energy dissipates, and its life force moves on, how could that essential capacity to hear dissipate along with them?

"Nevertheless, since beings have allowed their attention to be drawn to sights and sounds and have allowed themselves to be carried along in their streams of thought, as it has been since time without beginning, they have not yet awakened and do not yet understand the purity, the wondrousness, and the permanence of their own essential nature. Instead of attending to what is everlasting, they attend to what comes into being and perishes, and as a result, in life after life, they are mired in impurity and are bound to the cycle of death and rebirth. But if they turn away from what comes into being and perishes and hold fast to what is true and everlasting, then the light of the everlasting will appear, and as a result the faculties, their objects, and the sense-consciousnesses will fade away and disappear.

"By entirely disengaging yourself from two impurities — defiled mental processes and defiled emotional attachment to those processes — your Dharma-eye will become clear and bright. How then could you fail to go on to realize a supreme understanding and awakening?"

"Defiled mental processes" refers to the observed division of the eighth consciousness, while "defiled emotional attachment" refers to the observing division. . . . Attachment to these processes leads to emotion, and with emotion comes defilement. . . . Emotion causes people to be born in a stupor and die in a dream. If you can separate yourself from emotional attachment to both aspects of the eighth consciousness, your "Dharma-eye will become clear and bright." The Dharma-eye referred to here is not necessarily the Dharma-eye that is one of the five spiritual eyes. It can be interpreted figuratively to mean that you have gained access to your inherent wisdom. It is even more wonderful if you actually open your Dharma-eye so that, throughout the ten directions and the three periods of time to the ends of empty space and the Dharma-Realm, everything is seen as a Dharma-treasury. . . .

Everyone should pay particular attention to this short passage of Sutra text. Don't get attached to emotional love and become involved in making distinctions and indulging in deluded thinking. Separate yourself from them. This teaching is very important; don't take it lightly. (IV, 230–1)

Ānanda said respectfully to the Buddha, "World-Honored One, the Thus-Come One has now explained the second of the unalterable principles.[20] But let us consider an example from ordinary life. Someone trying to untie a knot must understand how the knot was tied in the first place. I believe that otherwise he will not be able to untie it. World-Honored One, we Arhats in the assembly who still need instruction may be compared to the person who is trying to untie a knot. Since time without beginning we have been born into ignorance and have perished in ignorance. Although we are learned and have strong roots in the Dharma, and although we have entered the monastic life and call ourselves monks, it is as if we were subject to a fever that recurs every other day. I only hope that the greatly compassionate one will be moved to deeply pity us who are drowning in the sea of afflictions. How are the knots of our bodies and minds tied, and where do we begin to untie them, so that we and the suffering beings of the future may be freed from the cycle of death and rebirth and fall no longer into the three realms of conditioned existence?"

Having spoken these words, he bowed to the ground, as did all the others in the assembly. He shed tears as he eagerly awaited the sublime instructions given by the Buddha, the World-Honored One.

Then the World-Honored One took pity on Ānanda and on all the others in the assembly who still needed instruction, wishing that, for the sake of the future, they might transcend the conditioned world and become guides for the time yet to come. As he circled his hand over the crown of Ānanda's head, his hand shone with light that was the color of the purple-tinted gold of the River Jambu. Then throughout all ten directions, every world in which Buddhas were dwelling quaked in six ways. Each one of the numberless Thus-Come Ones of those worlds emitted resplendent light from the crown of his head. Those beams of light shone down upon the crown of the Thus-Come One's head as he was seated in Jetri's Grove. No one in the assembly had witnessed such an event before.

[20] Ānanda here refers to the Buddha's statement at the beginning of part 5.2 above: "The second principle is that, if you are resolved to become fully awakened, you must courageously dedicate yourself to practice in accord with the Bodhisattva Vehicle. You must decisively let go of everything that has conditioned attributes."

The earth trembled and moved in six ways at this point because the Buddha was about to proclaim a very important teaching. All the Buddhas of the ten directions came to praise him in a single voice. The quaking also represents the liberation of the six faculties — in the analogy, the release of the six knots. Ānanda has just asked about the source of the six knots and how to untie them, and the Buddha is about to explain the teaching on this point. . . . Further, Thus-Come Ones as numerous as fine motes of dust emitted lights of various colors to represent the supremacy of the Dharma that the Buddha was about to speak. (IV, 239–40)

Note that it was the light, not the Buddhas themselves, that came to the Jetri Grove. The light from as many Thus-Come Ones as there are sand-grains in the River Ganges and as numerous as fine motes of dust came to shine upon the crown of the Buddha Śākyamuni's head. This demonstrates that the Path taught by all Buddhas is the same path. . . . The Buddhas' lights are mutually interfused, and so are the Buddhas' minds. The same is true of people's minds. If you are upset with someone, that person will realize it even if you haven't said a word. The person may not know it consciously, on the level of his sixth mind-consciousness which makes distinctions, but there is a reaction that occurs in his eighth consciousness. . . . Therefore, if you want to influence someone to change by means of positive reinforcement, you can think all kinds of good thoughts to influence them, but the process will be gradual. Bit by bit you can cause them to awaken. (IV, 241)

Then Ānanda and all the others in the great assembly heard the numberless Thus-Come Ones from throughout the ten directions speak in one voice, though with different tongues, saying: "Well done, Ānanda! You want to understand the ignorance that you were born with. The source of the knot — what causes you to be bound to the cycle of death and rebirth — is your six faculties of perception, nothing more. Also, since you wish to understand the supreme enlightenment, you should understand that it is through those same six faculties that you can quickly gain bliss, liberation, and stillness, wondrous and everlasting."

At the same time they all heard the Thus Come Ones speak to Ānanda in unison. Although there were many speakers, the voice was the same. What these Thus-Come Ones had to say here was meant not only for Ānanda but also for you and me and everyone else who is studying the Śūraṅgama Sūtra. This instruction is a very important section of the text. It concerns a crucial point: the matter of death and rebirth. If you understand this section, you can quickly put an end to death and rebirth. If you don't understand it, you'll have to redouble your effort to make progress in your study and practice. (IV, 243)

It is because of their six faculties that people keep being deluded in life after life and death after death. Why? The eyes see visible objects and fall under their influence. The ears hear sounds and chase after them. The nose smells fragrances and goes out after them. The tongue tastes flavors and seeks for them. The body is touched and pursues the objects it touches. The mind entertains thoughts and races after them. . . . That is what causes the problem of death and rebirth. The Buddha said a little earlier in the Sutra, "All you need is not to follow." Don't follow the distinction-making mind. Don't pursue the activities of the six faculties, their six objects, and the six sense-consciousnesses.

The sea of suffering is boundless,
But turn your head and you'll find the shore.

Turn your head and you'll find the shore of enlightenment. . . . Now that you recognize the role of the six faculties, you should not mistake a burglar for your own child. You should not keep spinning around at the portals of the six faculties. (IV, 244–5)

But the Thus-Come Ones also tell Ānanda that the six faculties are the road to enlightenment as well and the permanence, bliss, true self, and purity of nirvana. (IV, 246)

Though Ānanda heard these words of Dharma, he did not understand them. He bowed his head and said respectfully to the Buddha, "How can it be that nothing more than the six faculties binds us to the cycle of death and rebirth while at the same time they cause us to gain wondrous and everlasting bliss?"

The Buddha said to Ānanda, "The faculties and their objects come from the same source. What binds and what unbinds are one and the same. The consciousnesses are by nature illusory, like flowers seen in the sky. In response to objects, Ānanda, there is perception, and in response to the faculties there are objects. Neither the objects nor perceptions of them have an essential nature; they are dependent on each other, like intertwining reeds. Know, therefore, that the establishment of perceived objects such that they exist separately within your awareness is the foundation of ignorance. When objects are not perceived as separate from awareness, that itself is nirvana, which is the true purity, free of outflows. Why would you allow anything else to be added to it?"

Then the World-Honored One, wishing to restate these principles, spoke these verses:

"In our true nature, all conditioned things are seen as empty;
That which arises from conditions is illusory.
That which is unconditioned is not born, nor does it perish;
It too has no reality, like flowers in the sky.

"Though we use words to try to speak the truth, all words are false,
Not only words that aim at truth, but false words — all are false.
Both that which is called 'true' and that which is called 'false' are false,
How can there be, therefore, observer and what is observed?

"In the perceiver and perceived, there's nothing that is real;
They are like vines that only stand by twisting round each other.
Entanglement and liberation share a common basis;
The Path of Sages and of common folk is one path only.

"You should consider now these vines that twist around each other.
The vines have no existence, yet they do not lack existence.
The darkness of confusion is our basic ignorance;
The light of understanding brings about our liberation.

"A knot must be untied according to a certain sequence,
And when the six have been untied, the one will vanish too.
Choose one perceiving faculty and realize your breakthrough.
Enter the current. Realize the true enlightenment.

"From subtle *ādāna*, the storehouse-consciousness,[21]
The energy of habits can burst forth into a torrent.
Lest you confuse the true with what's untrue,
I rarely speak of this.

"But when your mind grasps hold of your own mind, what's not illusion
Then becomes illusory. And if you don't grasp hold,
Then what is called "illusion" and "what's not illusion" too
Will not arise. How could what is illusion be established?

"This Dharma may be called the wondrous lotus-flower,
The royal, indestructible, magnificent awakening.
This practice of samāpatti,[22] though likened to illusion,
Can quickly bring you past the ones who need no further training.[23]

"This peerless Dharma is the road that all World-Honored Ones[24]
Have walked to reach the gateway to nirvana."

In the third stanza, the Buddha points out that sages and ordinary people do not walk on separate paths. . . . The difference is that ordinary people turn their backs on enlightenment and cleave to their experience of perceived objects, while the sages turn their backs on perceived objects and become one with enlightenment. Ordinary people are confused, sages have awakened, but the source of both confusion and awakening is the same. (IV, 254)

The Buddha Śākyamuni tells Ānanda to choose one of his faculties and break through to enlightenment. The method for spiritual practice is to work at the entrance to the six faculties. That is, the eyes are not influenced by visible

---

[21] Skt. *ādāna-vijñāna*, is another name for *ālāya-vijñāna*, the storehouse-consciousness, (the eighth consciousness). It stores the seeds of past intentional actions until conditions have matured for their "sprouting" into awareness. *Ādāna* has the sense of "maintaining," in that it is essential for the maintenance of embodied seeds and life.

[22] Ch. *san mo ti* 三摩提 is probably a transliteration of *samāpatti* (contemplative insight), but possibly of *samādhi*.

[23] That is, past the level of the Arhat.

[24] The text has the Skt. *Bhagavān*.

194

objects, the ears are not influenced by sounds, the nose is not influenced by odors, the tongue is not influenced by flavors, the body is not influenced by objects of touch, and the mind is not influenced by objects of cognition. You transform what takes place at the entrance to the six faculties. You reverse the light of your attention to illuminate the mind within. You do not seek outside. You guard and gather in your body and mind. You seek within yourself.

You have to select one of the faculties that will lead you to break through to enlightenment. The Buddha has already laid the groundwork for this. He has discussed the efficacy of each of the faculties and has told Ananda to judge which ones are more complete. . . . The Buddha has implied that the ear will be the best choice, but he has not yet said it plainly. (IV, 260)

When they had heard this supreme, compassionate instruction which the Buddha, the Thus-Come One, had spoken in this combination of instructional and reiterative verses,[25] with their luminous and wondrous truths, lucid and incisive, Ānanda and the others in the great assembly all rejoiced, and their mind's eye opened to an understanding that was entirely new to them.

---

[25] The reference is to two forms of Buddhist Sanskrit verse. The *gāthā*, here rendered as "instructional verse," was "a metrical narrative or hymn, with moral purport . . . a detached stanza, distinguished from *geya* [here rendered as 'reiterative verse'], which repeated the ideas of preceding prose passages." William Edward Soothill and Lewis Hodus, *A Dictionary of Buddhist Terms* (London: Kegan Paul, 1934), 225a. The verse spoken here by the Buddha contains elements of both forms — a "combination," as the text says.

4
The Analogy of the Six Knots

Ānanda put his palms together, bowed to the ground, and said respect-fully to the Buddha, "I have heard the Buddha, out of his unbounded compassion, speak these true words of Dharma concerning the purity, wondrousness, and everlastingness of our real nature. But I still do not fully understand the sequence for releasing the knots such that 'when the six are untied, the one will vanish.' I only hope that the Buddha will show us great kindness and that, taking pity once again on this assembly and on beings of the future, he will bestow upon us words of Dharma that will cleanse us of impurities."

The Thus-Come One straightened his inner garment[26] and arranged his robe.[27] Still sitting in the Lion's Seat, he reached out onto the table in front of him, which was inlaid with seven kinds of precious things.[28] He picked up an elegant presentation scarf[29] which had been given to him by a god from the Heaven of Self-Restraint.[30] Before the assembly he tied a knot in the scarf, and showing it to Ānanda, he said, "What is this?"

Ānanda and the others respectfully answered, "It is a knot."

The Thus Come One thereupon tied another knot in his elegantly pat-terned scarf and again asked Ānanda, "And what is this?"

Ānanda and the others in the assembly again respectfully answered, "It is another knot."

The Buddha tied a sequence of similar knots in his elegantly patterned scarf until six knots had been tied on top of one other. Each time, as he held up the knot he had just tied, he asked Ānanda, "And what is this?"

---

[26] Skt. nivāsana.

[27] Skt. saṁghāṭi, a garment that winds around the body, leaving the right shoulder bare.

[28] The seven precious things are gold, silver, lapis lazuli, crystal, mother-of-pearl, roseate pearls, and carnelian. The pearls found off the coasts of India and Sri Lanka were prized for their faint roseate hue. Carnelian is a reddish form of agate.

[29] The practice of presenting a scarf to a teacher when seeking the teacher's advice is still observed in some Buddhist traditions.

[30] Skt. suyāma. The third in the hierarchy of six heavens in the realm of desire. See part 9.13a.

Each time Ānanda and the others in the great assembly replied in the same manner: "It is another knot."

> The scarf represents the nature of the Matrix of the Thus-Come One; the six knots represent the six faculties of perception. (V, 4)

The Buddha then said to Ānanda, "The first time that I tied a knot in this elegantly patterned scarf, you said that it was a knot. To begin with, this precious scarf was in fact merely a scarf. Why did you answer a second and a third time, 'It is another knot'?"

Ānanda said respectfully to the Buddha, "Basically, World-Honored One, this precious, elegantly patterned, and beautifully woven scarf is a single thing, but it seems to me that when the Thus-Come One tied it once, he made what we would call a knot. If he had tied it a hundred times, we would say there were a hundred knots. In fact, there are six knots in the scarf; the Buddha did not tie as many as seven, nor did he stop at five. Why then does the Thus-Come One acknowledge the first knot, but not the second or the third?"

The Buddha said to Ānanda, "You understand that this precious scarf is a single strip of cloth. My tying it six times might be said to have made six knots, but examine the question more carefully. The implication of your answers is that, although the essential nature of the scarf is unchanged, the knots have nevertheless changed it. What do you think? When I first tied a knot in the scarf, you said it was the first knot. I ask you: would you call the sixth knot I tied the first knot?"

> The Buddha demonstrates that the nature of the Matrix of the Thus-Come One is fundamentally one. . . . Though six knots have been made, the fundamental essence of the Matrix is still one. (V, 6)

"No indeed, World-Honored One. Since there are six knots, we certainly cannot say that the sixth knot is the first knot. With all my lives devoted entirely to learning and debate, what would lead me to confuse the sixth knot with the first?"

The Buddha said, "You are right. The six knots are not identical. Let us examine how they were made. They were all created out of the one scarf;

still, it would not do to confuse their order. The same may be said of the six faculties of perception. Within what is ultimately one, differentiation eventually arises."

Originally they were identical, but the eyes function as eyes, the ears function as ears, the nose functions as a nose, the tongue functions as a tongue, the body functions as the body, and the mind functions as the mind. Originally they were one and the same, but now they are divided. Even then, if they worked together, it would be all right. They could all reverse their direction and shine within. The eyes could turn their light inward, the ears could listen within and hear the true nature, the nose would not be influenced by odors, the tongue would not be influenced by flavors, the body would not be influenced by tactile sensations, and the mind would not be influenced by objects of cognition. If they could all work together to shine their light inward, they would still be one. But they can't work together. The eyes see visible objects and are influenced by them, the ears listen to sounds and are influenced by them, the nose smells odors and is influenced by them, the tongue tastes flavors and is influenced by them, the body enjoys objects of touch and is influenced by them, and the mind grasps objects of cognition and is influenced by them. What is important is to not follow after them, but ordinary people are unable to avoid following after them. (V, 7–8)

The Buddha said to Ānanda, "Suppose you were displeased by the six knots in your scarf and would prefer it to be a single length of cloth. How would you go about untying the knots?"

Ānanda said, "As long as these knots are in the scarf, there will naturally be disagreement about which one of them is which. But if the Thus-Come One were now to untie them all and no further knots were tied, then there would be no question as to which was which, since there would be no first knot left, much less a sixth."

The Buddha said, "'When the six are untied, the one will vanish' is the same idea.[31] Since time without beginning, due to your deranged confusion about the nature of your mind, your awareness has become distort-

---

[31] What follows here is a summary of teachings presented in part 4.1.

ed, and these distortions have not ceased. The strain on the awareness generates perceived objects. It is as in the example of your eyes staring until they become so stressed that they see flowers in the sky.[32] Amidst the clarity of enlightened understanding, deranged confusion arises for no good reason. The mountains, the rivers, and everything else in this world — as well as the processes of dying and being reborn and of entering into nirvana — are mere derangements caused by stress, mere distortions, mere flowers in the sky."

"Deranged confusion" refers to the three subtle aspects of delusion: coming into being, evolving, and appearance.[33] These are produced by one unenlightened thought; at this point the first knot is tied. "Your awareness becoming distorted" refers to mundane knowledge, which is the first of the coarse aspects of delusion. That "the distortions have not ceased" refers to continuation, the second of the coarse aspects of delusion. The third through sixth knots represent the rest of the coarse aspects of delusion, which are the aspect of grasping, the aspect of clinging to names, the aspect of karma, and the aspect of suffering due to karma. (V, 10–1)

Ānanda asked, "How is untying the knots like releasing the stress?"

The Thus-Come One thereupon picked up the knotted scarf, and having tugged the scarf to its left end, he asked Ānanda, "Is this the way to untie it?"

Ānanda replied, "No, World-Honored One."

Then, having tugged at the other end of the scarf, the Buddha again asked Ānanda, "Is that the way to untie it?"

Ānanda again replied, "No, World-Honored One."

The Buddha said to Ānanda, "I have now tugged on both ends of the scarf, but I was not able to untie the knots that way. How would you untie them?"

Ānanda said respectfully to the Buddha, "World-Honored One, you must pull on the scarf from within each knot. Then they will come undone."

[32] See part 3.2a.

[33] The three subtle and six coarse aspects of delusion are explained in part 4.1 above.

The Buddha said to Ānanda, "Yes, you are right. If you wish to untie the knot, you pull on the scarf from within each of the knots.

"Ānanda, I have explained that the Dharmas for becoming a Buddha arise through causes and conditions, but these Dharmas are not the coarse attributes that arise from inhering in perceived objects or conjoining to them. The Thus-Come One explains worldly and world-transcending phenomena, and he knows the fundamental causes and the conditions by which these phenomena arise — to the point that he knows how many drops of rain are falling in a world that lies beyond as many other worlds as there are sand-grains in the River Ganges, and near at hand, he understands the fundamental reasons for every sort of phenomenon: why pines are straight, why brambles bend, why geese are white, why crows are black.

"Therefore, Ānanda, carefully choose one faculty of perception from among the six. If you untie the knot of that faculty, its objects will disappear by themselves. All delusion will melt away. How can what remains not be what is real?

> The Buddha instructs Ānanda to choose one of the faculties of perception, based on the previous discussion about their relative merits, and then to apply his practice to that faculty until he is free of it and of its objects, as if a knot has been untied. Then all deluded mental activity based on coming into being and perishing will cease to be. What is it like when all our deluded mental activity is gone? When the false is gone, all that is left is the true. The true will be all that is. Stop the mind that is dependent of perceived objects, and the nature of the wondrous suchness of reality will appear. . . .
>
> At this point in the Sutra, you should be particularly attentive. You should develop your skill by working on one of the six faculties. Any one of them will do: eyes, ears, nose, tongue, body, or mind. The entrance to any of the six faculties is the Path. All are a part of the Matrix of the Thus-Come One. All you have to do is choose one faculty and put your mind to it in your practice, and you can return to the fundamental essence which is the Matrix of the Thus-Come One. (V, 16)

"Ānanda, I now ask you: can we untie the six knots in this cotton scarf[34] all at the same time?"

"No, World-Honored One. These knots were tied in sequence in the first place, so now they must be untied in sequence. Though the six knots are all in the same scarf, they were not tied all at the same time. Therefore, in freeing them, they cannot be untied all at the same time."

The Buddha said, "The same may be said of freeing the knots of the six faculties. In the first stage of freeing a faculty, one understands that the self is empty. Once that emptiness is fully understood, one can become free of attachment to phenomena. Once one is free from attachment to phenomena, then both self and phenomena have been emptied and will no longer arise. This is the patience that the Bodhisattva develops by means of samādhi — the patience with the state in which no mental objects come into being."

[34] Skt. *kārpāsa*.

VI
Twenty-Five Sages

1
Twenty-Five Sages Speak of Enlightenment

Having received this instruction from the Buddha, Ānanda and the others in the great assembly gained such wisdom and such a thorough and complete understanding that they now had no doubts about what the Buddha had said. Ānanda placed his palms together and bowed to the ground before the Buddha, and then said, "Today our bodies and minds have been filled with light, and we are delighted that our understanding is unimpeded. However, although we have now understood the meaning of 'when the six are untied, the one will vanish,' we do not yet know which one of the sense-faculties can lead us to break through to enlightenment.[1]

"World-Honored One, I have drifted from age to age, homeless and alone. How could I have known — how could I have imagined — that I would meet the Buddha as a member of his family? I am like an infant who has suddenly been reunited with its beloved mother. I have met the Buddha and have had the opportunity to become fully enlightened, and I have been given a hidden teaching. But if my basic mode of understanding nevertheless remains the same, then I might as well never have heard the Buddha's teaching at all. I only hope that he will be greatly compassionate towards us and will out of kindness bestow upon us a secret and awe-inspiring Dharma that will be the Thus-Come One's ultimate instruction." Having spoken these words, he bowed to the ground and then returned to his place in the assembly. He withdrew into the hidden recesses of his mind, hoping that he would receive from the Buddha a secret and private transmission.

Ānanda is asking the Buddha to bestow upon him the secret teaching, that is, the Śūraṅgama Samādhi. He wants the Buddha to transmit this teaching to him secretly, without anyone else present being aware of it. . . . The Buddha knows what is on Ānanda's mind, but he does not respond directly to

---

[1] Ch. *yuan tong* 圓通, which more literally might be translated "penetrate all the way through" or "connect without obstruction."

Ānanda's request. Instead he asks the assembled sages to speak about how they broke through all obstructions and became enlightened. (V, 22)

Then the World-Honored One said to the assembly of great Bodhisattvas and great Arhats, who were free of outflows, "I now ask all of you Bodhisattvas and Arhats: having made a resolve to become enlightened, which one of the eighteen constituent elements did you make use of in order to break through to enlightenment? By what expedient did you enter samādhi?"[2]

[1][3] Ājñātakauṇḍinya and the other four monks then stood up and bowed at the Buddha's feet.[4] Ājñātakauṇḍnya said respectfully to the Buddha: "When we were in the Deer Park and the Pheasant Garden, we saw the Thus-Come One soon after he had become a Buddha, and upon hearing him speak, we understood the Four Noble Truths. The Buddha questioned us monks, and I was the first to truly understand. The Buddha thereupon verified my understanding and gave me the name Ājñāta.[5] The wondrousness of sound, which had been hidden, was everywhere revealed to me. So it was that I became an Arhat by contemplating sound. The Buddha has asked us how we broke through to enlightenment. I believe that the contemplation of sound is the best method."

[2] Twenty-five sages now testify to the efficacy of twenty-five practices involving or related to the eighteen constituents or to the seven primary elements. The constituents and the elements are presented largely in the order in which they are discussed in part 3 above. The exceptions are that the six kinds of perceived object are given first, with sounds preceding visible objects, and that the ear-faculty is presented last.

[3] The numbering of the sages has been added for the present translation.

[4] Each of the first six sages focused his practice on understanding the unreality of one of the kinds of perceived objects and then on understanding these objects' true nature, which is the Matrix of the Thus-Come One, as shown in part 3 above. Ājñātakauṇḍinya and the four monks were the ascetics whom the Buddha taught first after his enlightenment. Accordingly, Ājñātakauṇḍinya is the first to answer the Buddha's question here. His testimony, which is that his enlightenment came through hearing the Buddha's instructions, praises the efficacy of sound as a focus of contemplation.

[5] His name was Kauṇḍinya. "Ājñāta" is an epithet interpreted as meaning "the first to know."

It is said that the Pheasant Garden was a grove of trees where a flock of pheasants lived. The grove once caught fire, and the pheasants wetted down their wings with water and beat out the fire, so this spot was a very auspicious one. There was an unusually magical atmosphere about the place. The geomantic properties were excellent. People who undertake a spiritual practice should find places to live that are endowed with such an efficacious atmosphere, because it is easier to get enlightened there. (V, 24–5)

[2] Upaniṣad[6] stood up, bowed at the Buddha's feet, and said to him respectfully: "I also saw the Thus-Come One soon after he had become a Buddha. I learned to contemplate the attribute of impurity, and I developed a strong aversion to it. I came to understand that the nature of visible objects is that they arise from impurity. Whitened bones turn to dust, disperse into space, and vanish. I understood that neither space nor visible objects truly exist,[7] and thus I needed no further instruction. The Thus-Come One verified my understanding and gave me the name Upaniṣad. Visible objects as I had perceived them no longer existed, but their wondrousness, which had been hidden, was everywhere revealed to me. So it was that I became an Arhat by contemplating visible objects. The Buddha has asked us how we broke through to enlightenment. I believe that the contemplation of visible objects is the best method."

[3] The virgin youth Sublimity of Fragrance[8] then stood up, bowed at the Buddha's feet, and said to him respectfully: "I heard the Thus-Come One teach how to contemplate attentively all attributes subject to conditions. I then took my leave of the Buddha and retreated to a pure and peaceful dwelling. I observed that when monks lit sandalwood incense, its fragrance silently entered my nostrils. In my contemplation I realized that the source of the fragrance was neither wood, nor space, nor smoke, nor fire; it came from no place and went to no place. As a result of this contemplation, my distinction-making consciousness disappeared, and I gained freedom from outflows. The Thus-Come One verified my

---

[6] Upaniṣad testifies to the efficacy of contemplating visible objects.

[7] That is, they have no permanent, independent attributes and so are empty.

[8] This sage testifies to the efficacy of odors as the objects of contemplation.

understanding and gave me the name Sublimity of Fragrance. Fragrance as I had perceived it vanished, but its wondrousness, which had been hidden, was everywhere revealed to me. So it was that I became an Arhat through contemplating the sublimity within fragrance. The Buddha has asked us how we broke through to enlightenment. I believe that rectifying the mind by means of fragrance is the best method."

[4] King of Healing and Master of Healing,[9] two princes in the Dharma, then stood up in the assembly together with five hundred gods from the Heavens of Brahma.[10] King of Healing and Master of Healing said respectfully to the Buddha: "For countless eons, we have served the world as skillful physicians. We have tasted one hundred and eight thousand kinds of medicinal substances — herbs, woods, metals, and minerals — that are to be found in the Sāha world. We know how each of them tastes — whether bitter, sour, salty, bland, sweet, or hot — and we know their inherent characteristics, the various ways they may be combined, and the changes that they effect — whether they are cooling or warming, toxic or benign. We understand them all.

"While reverently serving the Buddha, we came to understand that the nature of flavors is that they are neither empty nor existent. We understood that flavors do not arise from the body nor from the mind,[11] nor are they independent of the body and mind. Thus by discerning the differences among flavors, we became enlightened. The Buddha, the Thus-Come One, verified our understanding, and he named us two brothers the Bodhisattva King of Healing and the Bodhisattva Master of Healing. Now in this assembly we are princes in the Dharma. So it was that through flavors we realized enlightenment and understood, and we ascended to the Bodhisattva level. The Buddha has asked us how we broke through to enlightenment. We believe the contemplation of flavors to be the best method."

[9] These two sages, who count as one in the enumeration of twenty-five, testify to the efficacy of flavors.

[10] That is, the first three heavens of the realm of form; see part 9.11 below.

[11] That is, flavor arises neither from the tongue-faculty (the "body") nor from the tongue-consciousness (the "mind"). (Yuanying, 777)

[5] Bhadrapāla[12] and his sixteen Bodhisattva companions stood up in the assembly and bowed at the Buddha's feet. Bhadrapāla said respectfully to the Buddha: "In the past, when we heard the Buddha's Awe-Inspiring Royal Voice speak about the Dharma, we followed him into the monastic life. When it was time to bathe, I followed the custom and entered the bathhouse. Suddenly, upon contact with the water, I understood that the water was neither washing away the dirt nor washing my body. In the midst of this I became tranquil as I understood that there was nothing there.

"I have never forgotten that event from that lifetime until this one, and now I have followed the Buddha Śākymuni into the monastic life and need no further instruction. The Buddha has named me Bhadrapāla. The wondrousness of tangible objects has been revealed to me, and I am now a child of the Buddha.[13] The Buddha has asked us how we broke through to enlightenment. Having considered what I have attained, I believe that the contemplation of tangible objects is the best method."

[6] Mahākāśyapa[14] stood up with Bhikṣunī Purple-Golden Radiance and others, and they bowed at the Buddha's feet. Mahākāśyapa said respectfully to the Buddha: "When the Buddha Sun, Moon, and Lamplight appeared in this world during a previous eon, I had the opportunity to follow him, to hear the Dharma, and to study and practice it. After that Buddha entered nirvana, I made offerings to his relics,[15] and I lit lamps in order to perpetuate his radiance. I gilded an image of that Buddha so that it shone with a purple-golden radiance. From that time onwards, in life after life, my body has always been perfect and flawless and has shone with a purple-golden light. Bhikṣunī Purple-Golden Radiance and these others with me were my followers, and together we made a commitment to become enlightened.

---

[12] This sage testifies to the efficacy of tangible objects — in this case, bathwater. His name means "Virtuous Protector."

[13] That is, a Bodhisattva.

[14] Mahākāśyapa testifies to the efficacy of objects of cognition.

[15] Skt. śarīra, Ch. she li 舍利, a sage's relics that remain after cremation.

"What I contemplated was the diminishing and perishing of the sixth kind of object — the objects of cognition. Simply by the practice of contemplating the emptiness and stillness of these mental objects, and thereby entering a samādhi of cessation, I am able, with both body and mind, to pass through a hundred thousand eons as if they lasted no longer than a snap of the fingers.[16] So it was that I became an Arhat by contemplating the emptiness of objects of cognition. The World-Honored One has declared me foremost in the practice of beneficial asceticism.[17] The wondrousness of objects of cognition was revealed to me, and I put an end to all outflows. The Buddha has asked us how we broke through to enlightenment. Considering what I have attained, I believe that the contemplation of the objects of cognition is the best method."

> We should remember an important point: the relationship between Mahākāśyapa and Purple-Golden Radiance, his wife in life after life, has not been based on emotional desire. Rather they married in every life in order to practice together and do the Buddha's work. (V, 40)

[7] Aniruddha[18] then stood up, bowed at the Buddha's feet, and said to him respectfully: "When I first entered the monastic life, I was too fond of sleep. The Thus-Come One admonished me, saying that I was no better than an animal. After the Buddha scolded me, I rebuked myself and wept. For seven days I did not sleep, and as a result I went blind in both eyes.

---

[16] Mahākāśyapa is said to be sitting in that samādhi of cessation inside Mount Jizu in southwestern China, where he is waiting for the Bodhisattva Maitreya to appear in the world as the next Buddha so that he can present Maitreya with the Buddha Śākyamuni's robe and bowl.

[17] Skt. dhūta. The twelve ascetic practices approved by the Buddha as beneficial are wearing ragged robes, possessing only three robes, making the almsround for one's food, making the almsround sequentially, eating only one meal a day, eating a fixed and moderate amount of food, not drinking juices after noon, dwelling in a quiet place, dwelling beneath a tree, dwelling out in the open, dwelling in a graveyard, and never lying down.

[18] The next five sages relate how they used one of their faculties of perception to turn their attention inward. Aniruddha begins the sequence by testifying to the efficacy of the eye-faculty.

"The World-Honored One taught me a vajra samādhi of taking delight in illuminative vision. As a result, without using my eyes I could see everything in all ten directions with penetrating accuracy and clarity, just as one might see a piece of fruit in the palm of one's hand. The Thus-Come One verified my understanding. So it was that I became an Arhat. The Buddha has asked us how we broke through to enlightenment. I believe that to turn the faculty of seeing around and trace it back to its source is the best method."

[8] Kṣudrapanthaka[19] stood up, bowed at the Buddha's feet, and said to him respectfully: "I have a poor memory and have little learning. When I first encountered the Buddha, heard the Dharma, and entered the monastic life, I tried for a hundred days to memorize a single line of one of the Thus-Come One's verses. But when I had learned the second part of the line, I could no longer remember the first part, and when I had learned the first part of the line again, I could no longer remember the second part.

When one enters the monastic life, the first thing one is given to learn is a short verse to be recited every morning, as follows:

Do no evil deed with body, speech, or mind;
Give no trouble to any being in the world.
With right thought, see the emptiness of the realm of desire;
And keep your distance from unhelpful asceticism.

Although five hundred Arhats were there to help him, Kṣudrapanthaka had failed to learn a single line of this verse after a hundred days of study. He was that slow. He'd remember "with body, speech, and mind," but then he'd forget "do no evil." By the time he'd learned "do no evil" again, he'd forgotten "body, speech, and mind." His brother, Kṣudra, saw what was happening and ordered him to go back to being a layman. "Go find a wife and be done with it," he said, and he sent Kṣudrapanthaka on his way. Kṣudrapanthaka thought,

[19] Consideration of the ear-faculty, instead of being next in the sequence, is postponed for consideration by the Bodhisattva Who Hears the Cries of the World, the twenty-fifth sage. Kṣudrapanthaka here testifies to the efficacy of the nose-faculty.

"I want to be a monk like all these other people. What meaning is there in my being a layman again?" So he took a rope, went into the back gardens, and prepared to hang himself. Just as he was ready to do it, the Buddha appeared in the form of a tree spirit and asked him, "What are you up to?"

"I'm not going to go on living."

"Not go on living? After you die, what then?"

"I don't know."

"Don't die," the tree spirit said. "Don't take your own life. There's a reason why you are stupid. You should strive to change your faults of the past. Once you change, everything will work out fine."

"What are the reasons from the past that make me so stupid now?" Kṣudrapanthaka asked.

When Kṣudrapanthaka asked that question, Śākyamuni Buddha appeared in his own form and said, "In a past life you were a Master of the Canon with five hundred disciples. Every day they wanted to study with you, but you did not teach them. You didn't lecture on the Sutras or explain the Dharma, even if people requested it. They might kneel before you for three days and nights, and still you would not speak to them about the Dharma. Because you would not explain the Dharma, you became stupid to the point that you don't understand a single sentence of the Canon."

Upon hearing that, Kṣudrapanthaka was greatly ashamed. . . .

The Buddha then picked up a broom and asked, "Do you know what this is?"

"It's a broom."

"Can you remember that?"

"Yes."

Then the Buddha instructed him, "Just recite 'Sweep, sweep, sweep' all day long."

Kṣudrapanthaka recited that for a few weeks.

Then the Buddha stopped by to ask, "How are you doing? Can you remember what I told you?"

"Yes, I remember it," Kṣudrapanthaka replied.

"Fine," said the Buddha. "I'll just change the words a little to 'Sweep clean.' Try reciting that now."

So Kṣudrapanthaka recited "Sweep clean, sweep clean, sweep clean."
And he used that invisible broom to sweep his own defilement clean, the
defilement of his stinginess with the Dharma. Remember this. Take the principles that I am explaining to you in the Śūraṅgama Sūtra and explain them
to others. If you do that, in future lives you will have exceptional wisdom and
intelligence. If you practice the giving of Dharma, you will never be stupid.
(V, 45–7)

"The Buddha took pity on me for being so slow, and he instructed me
to find a quiet place where I could regulate my breathing. I contemplated
my breath in the most minute detail until I could discern in every instant
its arising, continuing, diminishing, and ceasing. All of a sudden my mind
was freed from every impediment such that my outflows were ended. So
it was that I became an Arhat. I took my place at the Buddha's feet, and
he verified that I needed no further instruction. The Buddha has asked
us how we broke through to enlightenment. I believe that contemplating
the emptiness of the breath is the best method."

Kṣudrapanthaka recounts how the Buddha taught him to regulate the breath.
This practice involves holding the in-breath for ten counts and then extending
the out-breath for ten counts. One inhalation and one exhalation is counted
as one breath. One observes the arising, continuing, diminishing, and perishing of each breath. . . . When Kṣudrapanthaka says, "All of a sudden my mind
was freed from every impediment," he is referring to enlightenment. It is like
a door suddenly being thrown open to the outside. All the air in the room is
immediately purified. (V, 50–1)

[9] Gavāṁpatī[20] stood up, bowed at the Buddha's feet, and said to him
respectfully: "I committed an offense in the karma of speech. Once, during an eon in the past, I insulted an elder monk, and as a result, in life
after life I have suffered from an illness which causes me to chew like a
cow. The Thus-Come One showed me how, by practicing a Dharma of the
mind-ground, I could make all flavors become one and so be purified. By
this practice my distinction-making mind ceased, and I entered samādhi.

[20] This sage testifies to the efficacy of the tongue-faculty.

Then my contemplation was that the knowledge of flavors does not come from the tongue-faculty and does not come from any object of taste. By means of this contemplation, I transcended all worldly outflows. Within, I let go of my mind and body, and without, I took my leave of this world. I left the three realms of existence far behind; I was like a bird escaping from its cage. I departed from all impurity and put an end to my defilements, and my Dharma-eye became clear. So it was that I became an Arhat. The Thus-Come One himself verified that I need no further instruction. The Buddha has asked us how we broke through to enlightenment. I believe that redirecting the awareness of flavor away from the flavors and back to itself is the best method."

[10] Pilindavatsa[21] stood up, bowed at the Buddha's feet, and said to him respectfully: "After I had first committed myself to following the Buddha on the Path, I heard the Thus-Come One say many times that nothing in this world can bring true joy. One day, as I was reflecting upon this teaching during my almsround in the city, I failed to notice a poisonous thorn lying in the road. I stepped on it, and pain suffused my entire body. I reflected on the sensation: I was aware of a deep pain, but I was also aware of my awareness of the pain, and I realized that in the pure mind there is neither pain nor awareness of pain. I had this further thought: how can it be that one body has two awarenesses? I held fast to this thought, and before long my body and mind became suddenly empty. During the next twenty-one days my outflows gradually ceased. So it was that I became an Arhat. The Buddha himself verified that I need no further instruction. The Buddha has asked us how we broke through to enlightenment. I believe that to purify one's tactile awareness until the body is forgotten is the best method."

[11] Subhūti[22] stood up, bowed at the Buddha's feet, and said to him respectfully: "Ever since a time during the eons of the remote past, my mind has been without impediment, and I have been able to remember as many of my past lives as there are sand-grains in the River Ganges. Even

---

[21] This sage testifies to the efficacy of the body-faculty.

[22] This sage testifies to the efficacy of the cognitive faculty.

in my mother's womb, I have been aware of the stillness of emptiness. I have understood that everything throughout the ten directions is empty, and I have also led other beings to understand that all is empty. The Thus-Come One revealed to me that the essential nature of our awareness is true emptiness and that the essential nature of emptiness is perfect understanding. So it was that I became an Arhat, and I immediately entered the sea of the magnificent, luminous emptiness of the Thus-Come Ones. My wisdom and my vision were then the same as the Buddha's. He verified that I needed no further instruction and that I had no equal in my achievement of liberation through understanding that all is empty. The Buddha has asked us how we broke through to enlightenment. I understood that all is empty and also that what understands emptiness and the emptiness that is understood are empty as well. To return the cognitive faculty to purity so that all phenomena are understood to be empty: that is the best method."

[12] Śāriputra[23] stood up, bowed at the Buddha's feet, and said to him respectfully: "Ever since a time during the eons of the remote past, my eye-consciousness has been pure. Thus for as many lifetimes as there are sand-grains in the River Ganges, I have been able in a single glance to understand without impediment the various changing phenomena, both worldly and world-transcending. I once met the Kāśyapa brothers walking together along a road. I joined them, and they explained to me the doctrine of causes and conditions. I thereupon woke up to the boundlessness of the mind. I followed the Buddha into the monastic life. The clarity of my visual awareness was perfected, and I became utterly fearless. So it was that I became an Arhat and the Buddha's senior disciple. I was reborn from the Buddha's mouth — reborn by being transformed by the Dharma. The Buddha has asked us how we broke through to enlightenment. I myself was able to verify that my eye-consciousness had become radiant with light, and when that light reached its ultimate intensity, it illuminated the wisdom and vision of the Buddhas. I believe that this is the best method."

---

[23] This sage and the five that follow testify to the efficacy of each of the six consciousnesses in turn.

Before Śāriputra became a monk, according to one account, he met Aśvajit while he was out walking along a road. Aśvajit was one of the five monks whom the Buddha taught first, in the Deer Park. Śāriputra saw Aśvajit walking in a most awe-inspiring and correct manner, with magnificent deportment.

His eyes did not look,
His ears did not listen.

That is, he didn't look at people out of the corner of his eye, and he didn't listen to what was going on around him. . . .

Śāriputra had studied with a non-Buddhist teacher, a Brahmin, and after the teacher died, Śāriputra had no teacher. It was then that he met Aśvajit while he was walking along a road. Because he admired Aśvajit's deportment, he asked Aśvajit who his teacher was. Aśvajit replied with a verse:

All phenomena arise from conditions,
All phenomena cease because of conditions:
The Buddha, the great elder monk,
Often speaks of this.

When Śāriputra heard that verse, he immediately became enlightened as a first-stage Arhat. Upon his return to his living quarters, he repeated the verse to Maudgalyāyana. When Maudgalyāyana heard it, he too became enlightened. Then, together with their two hundred followers, they became disciples of the Buddha. They all entered the monastic life and became part of the assembly that always accompanied the Buddha.

That's one account. Here the Sutra says that Śāriputra met the Kāśyapa brothers. Since some say that Śāriputra met the Kāśyapas and others say that he met Aśvajit, I think they were probably all out walking together. Note that the text uses the word "brothers," which could include Aśvajit as well as the Kāśyapa brothers, since monks are brothers in the Dharma. While they were walking, they were discussing causation, and one said: "I say that phenomena arising from causes and conditions are empty. Their names are false, and yet they are also the truth of the Middle Way." Probably when Śāriputra heard that, he approached them and asked, "What are you talking about? And who is your teacher?" It was then that Aśvajit spoke the verse quoted above. (V, 63–4)

[13] The Bodhisattva Universal Goodness[24] stood up, bowed at the Buddha's feet, and said to him respectfully: "I have been a prince in the Dharma in the assemblies of as many Thus-Come Ones as there are sand-grains in the River Ganges. Throughout all ten directions, the Thus-Come Ones teach their disciples who have an innate propensity for the path of the Bodhisattva to undertake the practice of universal goodness — the practice for which I am named.

"World-Honored One, with my ear-consciousness I am aware of the thoughts and viewpoints of every individual being, including the beings in worlds that are beyond still other worlds as many as the sand-grains in the River Ganges. Whenever any of these beings even considers undertaking the practices of Universal Goodness, I generate hundreds of thousands of distinct bodies, and mounted on my six-tusked elephant, I go separately to the places where these beings are. Even if a being is heavily impeded[25] and is not able to see me, I circle my hand on the crown of that being's head to lend support and give comfort in order to help him succeed in his practice. The Buddha has asked us how we broke through to enlightenment. I have described the basis of my practice: my mind listens with the complete understanding that results from free and unattached discernment. That is the best method."

The Bodhisattva Universal Goodness is distinguished by the greatness of his practice. He is noted for his Ten Great and Royal Vows, which are:

1) to revere and respect all Buddhas;

2) to praise the Thus-Come Ones;

3) to practice the giving of offerings;

4) to repent of one's faults and to reform;

5) to rejoice in the merit of others;

6) to request that the Wheel of Dharma be turned;

---

[24] Skt. Samantabhadra, Ch. Puxian 普賢. This Bodhisattva, who is an important focus of reverence in the Mahāyāna tradition, here testifies to the efficacy of the ear-consciousness.

[25] That is, by karma.

7) to ask the Buddhas to remain in the world;

8) to always practice as the Buddhas instructed;

9) to always remain in harmony with other beings;

10) to dedicate one's merit to the benefit of all.

These are the Ten Great and Royal Vows of the Bodhisattva Universal Goodness. The fortieth chapter of the Avataṁsaka Sūtra is devoted to this Bodhisattva and his vows. His practices and the power of his vows are especially great, and so he has a great deal of affinity with beings. He rides a six-tusked white elephant. The color white symbolizes the Buddhas' Vehicle, and the six tusks represent the six perfections.[26] (V, 66)

Here he tells the World-Honored One that he listens with the true mind, not with the ear-faculty. . . . Whenever he discerns someone practicing in accord with his Ten Vows, he circles his hand on the crown of that person's head to convey comfort and support. So people who practice in accord with Dharma will sometimes feel as if there were a bug crawling on the top of their head or as if someone were patting them on the head. Sometimes you might feel as though an insect were crawling on your face. When this happens you should not try to brush away the sensation with your hand, since it could be a Buddha or a Bodhisattva blessing you. If you are sincere, you can experience this feeling. (V, 67)

[14] Sundarananda stood up, bowed at the Buddha's feet, and said to him respectfully: "When I first entered the monastic life to follow the Buddha on the Path, I kept the precepts perfectly, but in trying to enter samādhi, my mind was always too scattered and too easily distracted so that I could not put an end to my outflows. The World-Honored One taught Mahā-Kauṣṭhila and me to focus our attention on the whiteness visible at the tip of the nose. After three weeks of focusing my attention in this way, my breath looked like smoke as it entered and left my nostrils. My body and mind shone with an inner light that illuminated the entire world. Everything became as clear and as pure as crystal. The smokiness of the breath in my nostrils was gradually refined until it be-

---

[26] Skt. pāramitā. See part 4.3, p. 156, and note 20.

came white. My true mind was revealed and my outflows were ended. My in-breath and out-breath were transformed into light that shone upon worlds throughout all ten directions. So it was that I became an Arhat. The World-Honored One predicted that in the future I would realize perfect enlightenment. The Buddha has asked us how we broke through to enlightenment. I refined my breath until at length it shone with light, and when the light shone everywhere, my outflows were ended. This is the best method."

[15] Then Pūrṇamaitrāyaṇīputra stood up, bowed at the Buddha's feet, and said to him respectfully: "Ever since a time during the eons of the remote past, I have been able to speak with unimpeded eloquence. When I have explained suffering and emptiness, I have penetrated deeply into ultimate reality. Indeed I have been able to give subtle and wondrous instruction to the assembly in the hidden gateways to the Dharma taught by as many Thus-Come Ones as there are sand-grains in the River Ganges. In doing so, I have become completely fearless.

"Knowing that I was endowed with great eloquence, the World-Honored One instructed me to use the sound of my voice to propagate the Dharma. I followed the Buddha as his assistant in turning the Wheel, and so it was that by means of the Lion's Roar, I became an Arhat. The World-Honored One verified that my skill in speaking the Dharma was without peer. The Buddha has asked us how we broke through to enlightenment. With the sound of Dharma I overcame adversaries and subdued demons,[27] and I put an end to my outflows. This then is the best method."[28]

[16] Upāli then stood up, bowed at the Buddha's feet, and said to him respectfully: "I was the one who accompanied the Buddha when he escaped the city and left his household. I was there to watch the Thus-Come One as he diligently practiced austerities for six years. I myself saw the Thus-Come One subdue demons, bring under his influence the followers of wrong paths, and free himself from the outflows of worldly greed and

---

[27] That is, the five aggregates.

[28] Here the Sutra considers the tongue as the organ of speech rather than its usual role in the Sutra as the organ of taste.

desire. The Buddha instructed me in the precepts that I had received, and I gradually mastered the three thousand kinds of awe-inspiring deportment with their eighty thousand subtle aspects of demeanor. I purified my conduct by following the fundamental precepts and the precautionary regulations.[29] My body became still and my mind vanished. So it was that I became an Arhat. Now I am the precept-master in the Thus-Come One's assembly. He himself verified that I follow the precepts with my mind and with my conduct. Everyone in the assembly sees me as a leader. The Buddha has asked us how we broke through to enlightenment. I learned to govern my conduct until my body was at ease in being governed, and next I gradually learned to govern my mind until my thoughts accorded naturally with what is right. Only then did both my body and my mind gain unobstructed understanding. This is the best method."[30]

The three thousand kinds of awe-inspiring deportment are calculated as follows: the two hundred and fifty precepts that monks follow are counted four times with regard to walking, sitting, standing, and lying down, making one thousand, and then counted three more times as they apply to the karma made by body, speech, and mind, for a total of three thousand.

Each of the four attitudes of the body — walking, standing, sitting, and lying down — inspires awe with its particular manner. One should walk like a gentle wind, that is, in a slow and stately manner, without impulsiveness or haste. Second, one should stand like a pine, straight up, without slouching. Third, one should sit like a bell, that is, like one of those huge, heavy bells of old that hung solid and unmoving. Fourth, one should recline in the auspicious bow-like position, on the right side, with the right hand under the cheek and the left hand resting on the left thigh.

As for the eighty thousand subtle aspects of demeanor, the Sutra is giving an approximate number. This number is derived by multiplying the three thousand kinds of awe-inspiring deportment of body, speech, and mind by

[29] Ch. *xing ye* 性業 and *zhe ye* 遮業.

[30] The Sutra here conflates two personages in the Buddhist tradition: Upāli, the precept-master, and Channa, who was the Buddha's charioteer before the Buddha left his royal household to seek enlightenment.

their seven expressions — that is, freedom from greed, hatred, and delusion, and avoidance of killing, stealing, lying, hurtful words, coarse language, and duplicity. To the resulting twenty-one thousand, one applies the four causes of affliction: greed, hatred, delusion, and the four of them combined.

The "fundamental precepts" are the ones that forbid killing, stealing, sexual misconduct, and lying. It is sometimes said that violations of these prohibitions cannot be removed, but actually, if you firmly resolve to change your behavior, you still have a chance. As for the "precautionary regulations," these forbid acts which lead you to commit offenses which otherwise you would not have committed. (V, 84–5)

[17] Great Maudgalyāyana then stood up, bowed at the Buddha's feet, and said to him respectfully: "Once when I was on the road seeking alms, I met the three Kāśyapa brothers — Uruvilvā, Gayā, and Nadī — and they proclaimed the Thus-Come One's explanation of the profound principles of causation. Immediately I resolved to become enlightened, and my mind was entirely free of impediment. The Thus-Come One kindly accepted me, and then the precept robe suddenly appeared on my body while my hair and beard all at once fell from me. Now I travel throughout all ten directions with nothing to impede me. My spiritual powers were revealed and are now esteemed as unsurpassed. So it was that I became an Arhat. Not only the World-Honored One, but Thus-Come Ones throughout the ten directions praise me for the perfect clarity, purity, ease, and fearlessness with which I exercise my spiritual powers. The Buddha has asked how we broke through to enlightenment. I used the method of returning the mind-consciousness[31] to its pure source[32] so that the light of my mind shone forth and revealed the turbid flux within.[33] That flux gradually subsided until it became brilliantly clear. That is the best method."

[18] Then Fire-Head[34] approached the Buddha, put his palms together, bowed at the Buddha's feet, and said to him respectfully: "I often recall

---

[31] That is, the sixth consciousness.

[32] That is, the true mind.

[33] That is, the flux of the mind-consciousness.

[34] Skt. Ucchuṣma, Ch. Huatou 火頭.

that many long eons ago, I was afflicted with an excess of sexual desire. At that time there was in the world a Buddha named King of Emptiness, who said that a blazing fire grows in people with too much sexual desire. He taught me to observe the flow of hot and cold energies along the bones all through my body. A spiritual light became focused within me and transformed my excessive desire into the fire of wisdom. Since then, all the Buddhas I have served have given me the name 'Fire-Head.' So it was that I became an Arhat on the strength of the Blazing Fire Samādhi. I made a great vow: that whenever someone is about to become a Buddha, I will serve as a spiritual warrior and will come to subdue that person's demons and adversaries. The Buddha has asked us how we broke through to enlightenment. I closely observed the places of warmth in my body until they became unobstructed and there could be free movement through them. A magnificent light blazed forth in my mind and lit the way to supreme enlightenment. This then is the best method."[35]

> Fire-Head is a powerful vajra-lord, one of those guardians of the Dharma whom this Sutra refers to as vajra-warriors.[36] . . . Why does the text say that he "approached the Buddha," instead of saying that he "stood up"? The reason is that Fire-Head would have already been standing. Vajra-warriors are spirits, and spirits cannot sit in the presence of the Buddha. They must stand. As for ghosts, they are not only forbidden to sit; they are not even allowed to stand. They must kneel. (V, 91–2)

[19] Then the Bodhisattva Ground-Leveler stood up, bowed at the Buddha's feet, and said to him respectfully: "I can recall being a monk during the time that the Thus-Come One Universal Illumination was present

---

[35] This is the first of seven testimonies concerning the seven primary elements, presented in a slightly different order than in part 3.5 above, in that here fire is considered first and awareness is considered last. These sages describe how they understood the essential identity of mind, body, and world through the contemplation of one or another of the primary elements, which are present everywhere. Fire-Head begins the series with testimony describing the contemplation of the fire in his body and eventually of the fire in his mind.

[36] See part 8.2 below.

in the world. It was my constant labor then to carry in sand or dirt to level roadways or to build bridges wherever highways or fords were so narrow or so dangerous as to obstruct cart traffic or to cause injury to horses. Moreover, during the time that countless Buddhas appeared in the world, I applied myself with diligence to the laborious task of carrying goods for people. I would go to the gates of towns, take up the goods, set them down at their destination, and then walk away without seeking any payment. And when there was a widespread famine during the time that the Buddha Viśvabhū[37] was in the world, I would carry both goods and people on my back, and whether I carried them for a short or long distance, I would accept only a small coin. If an ox-cart was mired in mud, I would free it by applying my spiritual powers to push the cart until its wheels could turn freely.

"At one time, the king of that country invited the Buddha Viśvabhū to partake of a vegetarian feast. I leveled the road that the Buddha Viśvabhū was to take and then waited there for him by the roadside. That Thus-Come One circled his hand on the crown of my head and told me, 'You should level the ground of your mind. Then the ground throughout the entire world will become level as well.' Immediately my mind opened, and I saw that my body was in part composed of particles of the primary element earth and that these particles were not different from the particles of which the world is made. I saw that the inherent nature of these particles was such that they could never actually come into contact with each other. Even the particles of which clashing swords are composed do not collide. In this way I learned how to be patient when no mental objects arise. So it was that I became an Arhat. I then resolved to advance through the Bodhisattva's stages. I listened to the Thus-Come Ones proclaim this wondrous lotus-flower[38] which was the basis for my attaining the Buddha's wisdom and vision. My understanding was verified, and I now serve as a leader in this assembly.

---

[37] The thousandth and last of the Buddhas of the previous eon.
[38] That is, the Śūraṅgama Samādhi.

"The Buddha has asked how we broke through to enlightenment. By attentive contemplation I realized that the particles of the primary element earth of which my body is composed are no different from the particles of the primary element earth of which the world is partly composed. Fundamentally, they are all the Matrix of the Thus-Come One; their manifestation as particles is an illusion. When they disappeared, my understanding was complete, and I entered upon the path to enlightenment. This then is the best method."

[20] The Pure Youth Moonlight stood up, bowed at the Buddha's feet, and said to him respectfully: "I can remember when a Buddha named Water and Sky was in the world, as many eons ago as there are sandgrains in the River Ganges. He taught Bodhisattvas to enter samādhi through the contemplative practice of insight into the fundamental nature of water. My contemplation was that all the fluids in my body share the same fundamental nature. I began by contemplating saliva and mucus, and then phlegm, stomach acid, marrow, blood, urine, excrement, and so forth. In all the fluids that circulate through my body, my contemplation was that the fundamental nature of water is the same. I saw too that the water inside my body is not different from the water outside my body. Even as far away as the Fragrant Seas of the Royal Floating-Banner Lands,[39] the fundamental nature of water is one and the same.

> Moonlight entered the monastic life as a virgin youth, but he is no longer a youth when he speaks here. By this time he had become an elder among the Bodhisattvas. People referred to him as a pure youth in honor of his having become a monk when he was still young and undefiled. (V, 99)

"At this stage, when I was first striving to perfect this contemplation, I was aware of only the water in my body, although I still understood that I had a body. I was a monk at the time, and once when I was sitting quietly in my room, a young disciple of mine peeked in to the room through a

---

[39] According to Buddhist cosmology, the Fragrant Seas are bodies of water that lie in concentric circles around Mount Sumeru; they are separated from each other by circular mountain ranges.

window. Seeing nothing but water in the room, the boy in his ignorance took up a small piece of tile and tossed it into the water. It hit the water with a splash. He skipped away, looking back over his shoulder. As I emerged from samādhi, I felt a sharp pain in my heart. It was like the pain Śāriputra felt upon encountering a hostile ghost. I thought to myself, 'I am already an Arhat, and for a long time I have not created any conditions that would lead to illness. How is it then that this pain has arisen in my heart? Does this mean that I have retreated?'

"At that moment the boy ran up to me and told me what he had done. I instructed him: 'When you see the water again, open the door immediately, wade into the water, pick up the piece of tile, and go out again.'

"The boy listened respectfully to my instructions, and after I had again entered samādhi, he saw the piece of tile in the water exactly as before. He opened the door, removed the tile, and went out. I emerged from samādhi, and my body was again free of pain.

"During the time that I was making my contemplations, I met countless Buddhas. At length, when the Thus-Come One Royal Self-Mastery and Spiritual Powers Vast as Mountains and Seas was in the world, my body vanished. Then the fundamental nature of the water in my body and of all the waters of the Fragrant Seas in worlds throughout the ten directions merged into true emptiness so that they were one and the same, without the slightest difference. Now the Thus-Come One has given me the title 'Pure Youth,' and I have joined the assembly of Bodhisattvas.

"The Buddha asked how we broke through to enlightenment. I understood that water, as it flows and circulates, in its fundamental nature is everywhere the same, and so I understood how to be patient when no mental objects arise. My enlightenment was perfected. This is the best method."

The incident that the Pure Youth Moonlight mentions occurred when Śāriputra was sitting in meditation. It happened that two ghosts flew past him. One of them was named Excessively Cruel and the other was named Relentlessly Cruel. Relentlessly said to Excessively, "Do you see that elder monk meditating over there? How about if I go smack him on the head?"

Excessively said to Relentlessly, "Don't do it. You don't want to hit a monk. Better not mess with someone practicing in accord with Dharma."

Excessively left the scene, but Relentlessly did not heed his advice. He whacked Śāriputra over the head with a bludgeon. As a result, Śāriputra had a headache when he came out of samādhi. He thought, "I've already been verified as an Arhat, and I haven't any illness, so why does my head ache?" He went to ask the Buddha about it.

The Buddha explained, "You were struck by a ghost called Relentlessly Cruel, and as a result of what he did to you, he has already fallen into the Unrelenting Hell. The blow he dealt you was so powerful that it could have split Mount Sumeru in half had it been aimed in that direction. Fortunately, the power of your samādhi is great; otherwise you would have been smashed to smithereens." (V, 101–2)

[21] The Dharma-Prince Brilliance of Lapis Lazuli stood up, bowed at the Buddha's feet, and said to him respectfully: "I can remember when a Buddha named Infinite Voice was in the world, as many eons ago as there are sand-grains in the River Ganges. He taught Bodhisattvas that the wondrous understanding which is our original enlightenment may be attained by making this contemplation: the world and beings' bodies are unreal phenomena that are made to move by the power of the primary element wind.

"Accordingly, I contemplated how the world is established; I contemplated how time moves through it; I contemplated how my body moves and then is still, and how thoughts move in my mind. I understood that all these movements are fundamentally identical. None of them is different from the others. I came to understand that it is the nature of all movement to arise from nowhere and to go nowhere. The countless numbers of deluded beings throughout the ten directions are equally unreal. In the billion worlds that make up this great system of worlds, beings are indeed like a swarm of mosquitoes trapped in a jar, droning in their confusion, buzzing madly in their confinement. After meeting the Buddha Infinite Voice, I was able to be patient when no mental objects arose. My mind opened, and in the east I saw the Land of the Unmoving Buddha.

There I became a Dharma-Prince in the service of Buddhas throughout the ten directions. My body and mind gave forth light that shone through all things without obstruction.

"The Buddha has asked us how we broke through to enlightenment. I awakened to my enlightened mind through the contemplative insight that the primary element wind has no essential attributes of its own. I entered samādhi, and together with Buddhas throughout the ten directions, I transmitted the teaching of the wondrous One Mind. This is the best method."[40]

> As soon as we allow thoughts to arise in our minds, we have created wind within our minds. Once there is wind in our minds, the many kinds of external winds arise. (V, 105)

[22] The Bodhisattva Matrix of Space[41] stood up, bowed at the Buddha's feet, and said to him respectfully: "When the Thus-Come One and I were with the Buddha Light of Samādhi, my body became infinite. Then four great and precious pearls that I held in my hands illuminated countless Buddha-lands throughout the ten directions, and I saw that all these lands were as empty as space. Then my mind was like a great flawless mirror in which there shone ten kinds of subtle, wondrous, magnificent lights that illuminated all ten directions to the ends of space. All the Royal Banner Lands were reflected in this mirror and thereupon were drawn into my body without conflicting with it, since my body was the same as space. I became skilled in entering an infinite number of lands, in which I did the great work of the Buddhas and developed a great power to respond to beings in accord with what they require.

---

[40] The Bodhisattva Brilliance of Lapis Lazuli contemplates the identity not only of body and world but of mind, body, and world, in that all are impelled by the primary element wind — that is, they all move.

[41] The Bodhisattva Matrix of Space contemplates the identity of mind, body, and world (here, the Buddha-lands). All are pervaded by the primary element space. First, he understands the identity of lands and space and, second, the identity of mind and space, in that his mind becomes a flawless mirror. Third, he sees that his body is also identical with space, and fourth, since body and world are identical, lands can enter his body.

"This great spiritual power arose through my attentive contemplation that the first four primary elements have no essential attributes of their own; that they come into being and cease to be as a result of deluded acts of mind; and that space and the lands of the Buddhas are one and the same — no different at all. It was through this contemplation that I understood, and I learned to be patient when no mental objects arise. The Buddha has asked us how we broke through to enlightenment. I contemplated the boundlessness of space and entered samādhi. In this way my wondrous powers reached a luminous perfection. This is the best method."

[23] The Bodhisattva Maitreya stood up, bowed at the Buddha's feet, and said to him respectfully: "I can recall the time when a Buddha named Brilliance of Sun, Moon, and Lamp was in the world; it was as many eons ago as there are motes of dust. I entered the monastic life as a disciple of that Buddha. At that time I was deeply preoccupied with a wish to be well known. I enjoyed cultivating friendships with eminent families of the nobility. That World-Honored One then taught me to enter samādhi by focusing on a contemplation that all things exist only in consciousness.[42] While in this samādhi, I have throughout many eons served as many Buddhas as there are sand-grains in the River Ganges. My yearning for fame vanished without a trace. Eventually, during the time when the Buddha Blazing Lamp was in the world, I brought to an unsurpassed wondrous perfection this samādhi of consciousness-only. I then understood that all the lands of the Buddhas throughout all space — both lands which are partly pure and partly impure and lands which are entirely pure — exist only within consciousness. World-Honored One, because I understood in this way that all things exist only in consciousness, I understood that it is from the true nature of consciousness that all Buddhas come forth. Thus, in accordance with predictions, I have taken my place as the one who will be the next Buddha.

"The Buddha has asked us how we broke through to enlightenment. I focused on a practice of contemplating that everything in the ten direc-

---

[42] According to Buddhist tradition, the Bodhisattva Maitreya is the founder of the Consciousness-Only school. See page xxx.

tions exists only in consciousness. My mind gained perfect understanding, and I understood the true nature of reality. I left far behind any dependence on what is external and freed myself forever from incessant categorizing. I learned to be patient with the state of mind in which no mental objects arise. This then is the best method."

[24] Then the Dharma-Prince Great Strength[43] stood up with fifty-two Bodhisattva companions. They bowed at the Buddha's feet, and the Bodhisattva Great in Strength said respectfully to the Buddha: "I can recall the time when a Buddha named Infinite Light was in the world, as many eons ago as there are sand-grains in the River Ganges. During that eon, twelve Thus-Come Ones appeared in succession, and the last of these, the Buddha Light Surpassing the Sun and Moon, taught me the samādhi of mindfulness of the Buddha.

The Dharma-Prince Great Strength and the Dharma-Prince Who Hears the Cries of the World[44] were sons of the Buddha Amitābha when he was a Universal Monarch[45] in a previous life. When Amitābha became a Buddha, these two Bodhisattvas served him. They are his daily companions, one on his left, one on his right. When the Buddha Amitābha retires as teacher and host of the Western Land of Ultimate Bliss, the Dharma will disappear during the first half of the night, and in the second half of the same night, the Bodhisattva Who Hears the Cries of the World will become a Buddha there in the Land of Ultimate Bliss. When the Bodhisattva Who Hears the Cries of the World retires as the resident Buddha of the Western Land, the Bodhisattva Great Strength will become a Buddha in the same way.

The Bodhisattva Great Strength is so powerful that if he raises his hand, moves his foot, or moves his head, the earth quakes and trembles. When he walks about, the earth shakes.

The fifty-two Bodhisattva companions who stand up and bow to the Buddha along with Great Strength represent fifty-two stages of a Bodhisattva's

[43] Skt. Mahāsthāmaprāpta, Ch. Dashizhi 大勢至.

[44] Skt. Avalokiteśvara, Ch. Guanshiyin 觀世音, the twenty-fifth of these sages. See note 49 below.

[45] Skt. *cakravarti-rāja*, in Indian tradition, a wise, benevolent, and capable world-ruler.

progress: the Ten Stages of Stabilizing the Mind, the Ten Abodes, the Ten Practices, the Ten Dedications, the Ten Grounds, Equivalent Enlightenment, and Wondrous Awakening. (V, 119)[46]

"Consider someone who is always thinking of another person. This second person, though, has completely forgotten about the first person. Even if these two people were to meet, they might as well not have met, and even if they were to catch sight of one another, they might as well not have seen each other. But consider two other people who always have each other in mind so much so that they will be, in lifetime after lifetime, as inseparable as a man and his shadow. Similarly, the Thus-Come Ones in all ten directions think of all beings with compassion, just as a mother always thinks of her child. If the child were to run away from home, the mother's thinking of him will be of no use. But if the child is mindful of the mother, just as she is of him, the two will be inseparable in lifetime after lifetime. In the same way, beings who are always mindful of the Buddha, always thinking of the Buddha, are certain to see the Buddha now or in the future. They will never be far from Buddhas, and their minds will awaken by themselves without any special effort. Such people may be said to be adorned with fragrance and light, just as people who have been in the presence of incense will naturally smell sweet.

The Buddhas are always thinking about us; they are mindful of us, but we living beings aren't mindful of the Buddhas. We may happen to study a little of the Buddhas' Dharma, but we're not very clear about what's being said. "The Dharma is really wonderful!" we say, but we don't realize how wonderful it actually is. Why are the Buddhas mindful of us? It is because they see that all beings share the same essence. The Buddhas regard all beings as their fathers and mothers of the past and as the Buddhas of the future. The Buddha Śākyamuni said that all beings are endowed with the Buddha-nature, and all of them can become Buddhas. There's not a single being who cannot become a Buddha. It is this very point that makes the Buddhist teachings the

[46] See part 9.4 below, where fifty-seven stages are described: the fifty-two mentioned here, plus the stage of arid wisdom and the four additional stages.

most lofty and all-encompassing. It is why the Buddha Śākyamuni taught that we should abstain from killing, stealing, sexual misconduct, false speech, and intoxicants. These are the five fundamental Buddhist precepts, and to keep these precepts is a way of showing one's regard for all beings. Since the Buddha sees all beings as identical in essence to himself, he wishes to teach them how to change so that they can become Buddhas themselves. We come into this world and ignore what is fundamental while craving what is superficial. We turn our backs on enlightenment and cleave to the mundane objects of the senses. That is why we forget the Buddhas and never remember to be mindful of them. . . .

There are several ways to practice mindfulness of the Buddha:

1) You can be mindful of the Buddha by reciting his name. You can recite the name of whichever Buddha you choose. You can recite "Namo[47] Buddha Amitābha"; or you can recite "Namo Buddha Śākyamuni, our First Teacher": or maybe you'll want to recite "Namo Master Healer, the Buddha Who Dispels Disaster and Lengthens Life." No matter which Buddha it is whose name you choose to recite, the practice is the same. Your goal is to dispense with all extraneous thoughts and to consolidate your thoughts into the one mindful thought of the Buddha. If you don't have extraneous thoughts, you won't have any evil thoughts, and when nothing evil is arising in your mind, you're on the road to goodness.

2) You can practice mindfulness of the Buddha Amitābha by visualizing him. You consider the ray of white light that shines from between the Buddha's eyebrows. A hymn in his praise includes the lines: "The light of his brow shines five times as high as Mount Sumeru. His clear and pure eyes are as wide as the sea." Are you able to visualize that? If the scope of your mind is small, your concept of the Buddha will be fairly limited as you contemplate him. If the scope of your mind is vast, your conception of him can be monumental.

3) You can practice mindfulness of the Buddha by contemplating an image. In this practice you gaze upon an image of the Buddha Amitābha while you recite his name. As you are mindful of him, you reflect upon his magnificent appearance adorned with hallmarks. . . .

---

[47] Skt. *namas* or *namaste,* Ch. *namo* 南無, a respectful and reverent greeting.

4) You can practice mindfulness of the Buddha in terms of his true attributes; this is the practice of meditation in stillness. You pursue the question, "Who is this who is mindful of the Buddha?" . . .

In this passage of the text, the Bodhisattva Great Strength tells of his practice of mindfulness of the Buddha, a practice which is a very appropriate method for people in the present age. It is quite effective. Why? The sutras tell us that in this time of the Dharma's ending, not one person in a million will reach the goal of his or her practice, unless that practice involves mindfulness of the Buddha. Only then will people be able to reach enlightenment.

This practice of reciting the Buddha's name is very easy. It allows us to escape the three realms as by a side door. We are like a beetle that chews its way out of a stick of bamboo by gnawing sideways instead of by gnawing the length of the stick. People who are mindful of the Buddha can escape the three realms on a horizontal plane at their current level. They carry their karma with them into rebirth in the Buddha Amitābha's Pure Land. The karma they take with them is old karma; when they reborn in the Pure Land, they will not commit any new karma. However, once you know about reciting the Buddha's name, don't commit any more karmic offenses . . . because that will prevent your rebirth in the Pure Land. Once you know about mindfulness of the Buddha, you should change your ways. . . .

This section of text concerning the Bodhisattva Great Strength breaking through to enlightenment through mindfulness of the Buddha is extremely important. We should be mindful of the Buddha Amitābha because he has affinities with us. Ten eons ago, before he became a Buddha, when he was a monk called Dharma-Treasury, he made forty-eight great vows, and one of them was this: "If beings throughout the ten directions say my name and do *not* become Buddhas, I will not attain right enlightenment." But he did attain right enlightenment; and because of the power of Amitābha's vows, everyone who recites his name can be reborn in the Land of Ultimate Bliss. (V, 121–9)

"The basis of my practice was mindfulness of the Buddha. I became patient with the state of mind in which no mental objects arise. Now when people of this world are mindful of the Buddha, I act as their guide to lead them to the Pure Land. The Buddha has asked us how we broke through to enlightenment. In order to enter samādhi, I chose no other method than to gather in the six faculties while continuously maintaining a pure mindfulness of the Buddha. This is the best method."

2

The Bodhisattva Who Hears
the Cries of the World

[25] Then the Bodhisattva Who Hears the Cries of the World[48] stood up, bowed at the Buddha's feet, and said to him respectfully: "World-Honored One, I can recall the time when a Buddha named He Who Hears the Cries of the World was in this world, as many eons ago as there are sand-grains in the River Ganges. Before this Buddha I made the resolution to become fully awakened, and he instructed me to enter samādhi through a practice of hearing and contemplating.

> In a past eon, the Buddha Who Hears the Cries of the World taught the pres-
> ent Bodhisattva Who Hears the Cries of the World the practice of hearing and
> contemplating. Based on the wisdom of hearing, the wisdom of contemplating,
> and the wisdom of practice, he was able to enter samādhi. Here "contemplat-
> ing" does not mean the thinking of the mind-consciousness. Rather, it has the
> meaning of quiet consideration — the skill of meditation in stillness. (V, 131)

"I began with a practice based on the enlightened nature of hearing. First I redirected my hearing inward in order to enter the current of the sages. Then external sounds disappeared. With the direction of my hearing reversed and with sounds stilled, both sounds and silence cease to arise. So it was that, as I gradually progressed, what I heard and my awareness of what I heard came to an end. Even when that state of mind in which everything had come to an end disappeared, I did not rest. My awareness and the objects of my awareness were emptied, and when that process of emptying my awareness was wholly complete, then even that emptying and what had been emptied vanished. Coming into being and

---

[48] Skt. Avalokiteśvara, Ch. Guanshiyin 觀世音. The name can be interpreted as Avalokita-īśvara (The Sovereign Who Contemplates the World) or as Avalokita-svara (the One Who Hears the Cries of the World). Both alternatives, in their Chinese translations, are present in the Chinese Buddhist tradition; Guanzizai 觀自在 renders Avalokita-īśvara, and Guanshiyin 觀世音, often shortened to Guanyin 觀音, renders Avalokita-svara. The Chinese text of the Śūraṅgama Sūtra uses the name Guanshiyin.

ceasing to be themselves ceased to be. Then the ultimate stillness was revealed.[49]

> To listen wisely is to listen inside, not outside. You do not allow your mind to chase after sounds. Earlier in the Sutra,[50] the Buddha spoke of not following the six faculties and not being influenced by them. You reverse your hearing to listen to your own true nature.[51] Instead of listening to external sounds, you focus inwardly on your body and mind, you cease to seek outside yourself, and you turn around the light of your attention so that it will shine within yourself. (V, 133)

"All of a sudden I transcended the worlds of ordinary beings, and I also transcended the worlds of beings who have transcended the ordinary worlds. Everything in the ten directions was fully illuminated, and I gained two remarkable powers. First, my mind ascended to unite with the fundamental, wondrous, enlightened mind of all Buddhas in all ten directions, and my power of compassion became the same as theirs. Second, my mind descended to unite with all beings of the six destinies in all ten directions such that I felt their sorrows and their prayerful yearnings as my own. World-Honored One, because I had made offerings to the Thus-Come One Who Hears the Cries of the World, I received from that Thus-Come One a hidden transmission of a vajra-like samādhi such that my power of compassion became the same as the Buddhas'. I was then able to go to all lands and appear in thirty-two forms that respond to what beings require.

[1][52] "World Honored One, suppose there are Bodhisattvas who have entered samādhi and have advanced in their practice such that they are free from outflows. If these Bodhisattvas wish to reach a more sublime

---

[49] The testimony of this twenty-fifth and last sage focuses on the efficacy of the ear-faculty. The Bodhisattva first reversed the direction of his aural attention, thus emptying sounds; next he emptied his awareness. To this pattern of emptying subject and object, described by previous sages as well, he adds the further step of emptying the emptying.

[50] Part 5.

[51] See p. 182.

[52] The numbering was added for the present translation.

understanding, I will appear to them as a Buddha, and I will instruct them in the Dharma that will lead them to liberation.

[2] "Suppose there are sages who still need instruction but who have quieted their minds and have gained wondrous insight. If they wish to attain a more sublime and wondrous understanding, I will appear to them as a Solitary Sage who has reached enlightenment on his own,[53] and I will instruct them in the Dharma that will lead them to liberation.

[3] "Suppose there are sages who still need instruction but who have broken free of the links in the chain of dependent co-arising.[54] Because they have broken free, their transcendent nature appears. If they wish to attain a more sublime and wondrous understanding, I will appear to them as a Solitary Sage who has become enlightened through the contemplation of the conditioned world,[55] and I will instruct them in the Dharma that will lead them to liberation.

[4] "Suppose there are sages who still need instruction but whose minds dwell in emptiness, in accordance with the teaching of the Four Noble Truths, as they practice on the Path that leads to nirvana. If they wish to attain a more sublime understanding, I will appear to them as a Hearer of the Teaching, and l will instruct them in the Dharma that will lead them to liberation.

> The Bodhisattva appears in the body of an Arhat because in that way he can communicate with Arhats easily. He and they can become trusted friends. If you have no affinities with people, then no matter how well you may speak, you won't be believed. The Bodhisattva appears as various kinds of being in order to teach the beings of each kind to change so that they will awaken. (V, 141)

[5] "Suppose, further, that there are beings who clearly understand the desires of the mind, do not engage in the activities of desire, and wish to have bodies that are pure.[56] I will appear to them as a Brahma

---

[53] One of the two kinds of pratyekabuddha.

[54] See part 4, note 18.

[55] The other of the two kinds of pratyekabuddha.

[56] These are beings who wish for rebirth in the heavens of form, where beings are beyond the influence of coarse desires. See part 9.11

King, and I will instruct them in the Dharma that will lead them to liberation.

The ultimate aim of the Bodhisattva Who Hears the Cries of the World is to lead these beings to believe in the Buddha. But since at present their wish is to be born in the heavens, he teaches them how to do that. When they return from there, they will eventually come to believe in the Buddha. Ordinary people feel that the time involved in such a process is quite long, but actually from a Buddha's or a Bodhisattva's point of view, it is a mere moment, a mere blinking of the eye. In using this expedient, the Bodhisattvas are like parents who want their child to master an excellent profession which the child does not wish to enter. The parents comply and allow the child to study what he wishes, but after several false starts, he eventually decides to prepare for the very profession his parents had suggested. The Bodhisattva's method of teaching beings how to change is to first fulfill their wishes. But the ultimate aim is always to bring beings to enlightenment. (V, 142–3)

[6] "To beings who desire to be celestial lords and to govern the heavens, I will appear as Lord Śakra,[57] and I will instruct them in the Dharma that will lead them to fulfillment of their wish.

[7] "To beings who wish for a body that has the freedom and ease to roam throughout the ten directions, I will appear as the lord of the Heaven of Delight in Creating,[58] and I will instruct them in the Dharma that will lead them to fulfillment of their wish.

[8] "To beings who wish for a body that has the freedom and ease to fly through space, I will appear as the lord of the Heaven of Pleasure Derived from What Others Create.[59] I will instruct these gods in the Dharma that will lead them to fulfillment of their wish.

[9] "To beings who would like to govern ghosts and spirits in order to protect their countries, I will appear as a great celestial general. I will

---

[57] The ruler of the Heaven of the Thirty-Three, the third of the heavens of desire. See part 9.11.

[58] The fifth of the heavens of desire.

[59] The sixth of the heavens of desire,

instruct them in the Dharma that will lead them to fulfillment of their wish.

[10] "To beings who would like to rule a world in order to protect its inhabitants, I will appear as one of the Four Celestial Kings. I will instruct them in the Dharma that will lead them to fulfillment of their wish.

[11] "To beings who would like to be born into a celestial palace and to command ghosts and spirits, I will appear as a prince of one of the Four Celestial Kingdoms. I will instruct them in the Dharma that will lead them to fulfillment of their wish.

[12] "To beings who would like to be kings among people, I will appear as a human king. I will instruct them in the Dharma that will lead them to fulfillment of their wish.

[13] "To beings who would like to be heads of clans and would like to command everyone's respect and deference, I will appear as an elder, and I will instruct them in the Dharma that will lead them to fulfillment of their wish.

[14] "To beings who would like to be able to discuss celebrated writings and to live a pure life, I will appear as a layperson and will instruct them in the Dharma that will lead them to fulfillment of their wish.

[15] "To beings who would like to govern a country or to decide the affairs of a province or a district, I will appear as a minister of state, and I will instruct them in the Dharma that will lead them to fulfillment of their wish.

[16] "To beings who would like to employ numerology and other esoteric disciplines out of a wish to protect and nurture themselves, I will appear as a Brahmin, and I will instruct them in the Dharma that will lead them to fulfillment of their wish.

[17] "To men who would like to learn about becoming a monk and about observing the monastic precepts and regulations, I will appear as a monk, and I will instruct them in the Dharma that will lead them to fulfillment of their wish.

[18] "To women who would like to learn about becoming a nun and about observing the monastic precepts and regulations, I will appear as

a nun, and I will instruct them in Dharmas that will lead them to fulfillment of their wish.

[19] "To men who would like to observe the five precepts of the laity,[60] I will appear as a precepted layman, and I will instruct them in the Dharma that will lead them to fulfillment of their wish.

[20] "To women who would like to ground themselves on the five precepts of the laity, I will appear as a precepted laywoman, and I will instruct them in the Dharma that will lead them to fulfillment of their wish.

[21] "To virtuous women of high standing who would like to manage the affairs of a household or of a country, I will appear as a queen, or as the wife of a lord, or else as some other noblewoman, and I will instruct them in the Dharma that will lead them to fulfillment of their wish.

[22] "To young men who wish to remain celibate, I will appear as a pure young man, and I will instruct them in the Dharma that will lead them to fulfillment of their wish.

[23] "To young women who wish to remain celibate, never to be violated, I will appear as a pure young woman, and I will instruct them in the Dharma that will lead them to fulfillment of their wish.

[24] "To celestial beings who no longer wish to be celestial beings, I will appear in celestial form and will instruct them in the Dharma that will lead them to fulfillment of their wish.

[25] "To dragons who no longer wish to be dragons, I will appear as a dragon and will instruct them in the Dharma that will lead them to fulfillment of their wish.

[26] "To *yakṣas*[61] who wish to be free of being yakṣas, I will appear as a yakṣa and will instruct them in the Dharma that will lead them to fulfillment of their wish.

[27] "To *gandharvas*[62] who wish to be free of being gandharvas, I will appear as a gandharva and will instruct them in the Dharma that will lead them to fulfillment of their wish.

---

[60] Prohibiting killing, theft, sexual misconduct, lying, and intoxicants.

[61] See p. 241.

[62] Celestial musicians who are nourished by fragrances.

[28] "To asuras[63] who wish to be free of being asuras, I will appear as an asura and will instruct them in the Dharma that will lead them to fulfillment of their wish.

[29] "To kinnaras[64] who wish to be free of being kinnaras, I will appear as a kinnara and will instruct them in the Dharma that will lead them to fulfillment of their wish.

[30] "To mahoragas[65] who wish to be free of being mahoragas, I will appear as a mahoraga and will instruct them in the Dharma that will lead them to fulfillment of their wish.

[31] "To beings who enjoy being human and who wish to continue as humans, I will appear in human form and will instruct them in the Dharma that will lead them to fulfillment of their wish.

[32] "To nonhuman beings who wish to be free of being nonhuman — whether they have bodies or are bodiless, whether they are capable of cognition or are not capable of cognition — I will appear to them as they are and will instruct them in the Dharma that will lead them to fulfillment of their wish.

"These are the thirty-two pure and wondrous forms in which I appear in all lands in order to respond to what beings require. I accomplish this in samādhi, which I enter by redirecting my faculty of hearing inward to merge with the enlightened nature of hearing within, until the wondrous power of my self-mastery becomes effortless.

"World-Honored One, through the effortless, wondrous power of my vajra-solid samādhi, which I enter by redirecting my faculty of hearing inward to merge with the enlightened nature of hearing, I feel, as if they were my own, the sorrows and yearnings of all beings in the six destinies in all ten directions and in the three periods of time.[66] Therefore, by using both body and mind, I can cause all beings to develop such perfect merit that they will have nothing to fear in fourteen kinds of dangerous situations.

---

[63] Celestial fighters. See part 9.12.

[64] Celestial musicians. They have a human appearance, but with a single horn on their heads.

[65] Spirits who have the appearance of large pythons.

[66] That is, the past, present, and future.

"First, because I did not listen to sounds and instead contemplated the listener within, I can now hear the cries of suffering beings throughout the ten directions, and I can bring about their liberation.

"Second, I was able to turn my awareness around and restore it,[67] and therefore, should beings be caught in a conflagration, I can make sure that they are not burned.

"Third, since I was able to turn my awareness around and restore it, I can make sure that beings who are adrift in a flood will not be drowned.

"Fourth, because I have put an end to deluded acts of mind, and so have no thoughts of harming or killing, I can make sure that any being who enters the realms of ghosts will not be harmed by them.

"Fifth, when I had succeeded in merging my faculty of hearing with the enlightened nature of hearing, my six faculties dissolved into each other to become one with my faculty of hearing. Therefore, if beings are about to be attacked, I can cause the attackers' blades to shatter so that these beings will suffer no hurt, any more than water will be hurt by a knife that is plunged into it, or any more than light will be affected by a puff of wind.

"Sixth, my hearing was infused with an essential brilliance that illuminated the entire Dharma-Realm and dispelled the darkness of all hidden places. Therefore, I can ensure that beings will be invisible to any yakṣas, *rākṣasas, kumbhāṇḍas, piśācas, pūtanas,* or other such ghosts that might approach them.

Line 247 in the Śūraṅgama Mantra, *"yao cha jie la he,"* refers to the yakṣas. In the mantra, the names of the kings of various kinds of ghosts are called out. In general, ghosts may travel by land or in the air, and they may be male or female. (V, 154–5) Yakṣas, for example, are male; rākṣasas are female. Both are extremely fierce; their diet consists of human corpses. They recite mantras to remove the stench of a corpse so they can stand to eat the flesh.

A kumbhāṇḍa is a ghost shaped like a barrel. This ghost gives people nightmares. People may dream of some weird apparition, and though in

---

[67] That is, restore it to its original nature, which is the enlightened mind.

their dream they are mentally alert, they can't move physically. They become paralyzed. Sometimes, if a person's yang energies are weak and his yin energies prevail, the person can be paralyzed for a long time, and the ghost can eventually cause the person's death. There are many of these kumbhāṇḍas in this world.[68]

Piśācas are ghosts that eat human essence and energy and also the essence of grains. Pūtanas can cause people to get sick and have a fever. But if you cultivate the skill of redirecting your faculty of hearing inward to hear your true nature, or if you recite the name of the Bodhisattva Who Hears the Cries of the World, these ghosts will not be able to see you, though they may come right up beside you because you emit light which they fear. Since the ghosts belong to yin, they cannot see you if you have yang light. They can only find you if you give off yin energy. (V, 163–4)

"Seventh, sound itself completely dissolved as I reversed the direction of my hearing and became free of distorted perceptions of sense-objects. Therefore, if a being is confined by a cangue, I can make that cangue disappear.

"Eighth, when sound was extinguished once and for all and my hearing was perfected, my kindness gained an all-pervading power. Therefore, should beings be traveling on dangerous roads, I can make sure that they will not be robbed by highwaymen.

"Ninth, once my faculty of hearing had become merged with the enlightened nature of hearing and so had gained independence from perceived objects, then no object, no matter how enticing, could affect me. Therefore, I can cause beings who have a great deal of desire to break free of their desire.

In the Lotus Sūtra in the chapter on the universal gateway of the Bodhisattva Who Hears the Cries of the World, it is said that people who have a great deal

---

[68] The Ven. Hsüan Hua added later in his commentary, at part 8.3, "This paralysis [inflicted by the kumbhāṇḍa ghost] is only effective on people who have an excess of yin energy, such as people who are always worried and depressed, afflicted, upset, and distressed. People who follow the Buddha's Path can have pure yang energy — a kind of light" (VI, 129–30).

of desire can get rid of their desire through being constantly mindful and re-spectful of this Bodhisattva. That is the meaning of the present lines of text as well. "A great deal of desire" specifically refers to sexual desire. The biggest problem in human life, the one that is nearly impossible to resolve, is sexual desire. To see through the involvements of men and women and let these involvements go is to gain genuine liberation. If you can't see through your desire and let it go, you cannot get free, and you cannot become enlightened. If you have real spiritual skill, then when you eat you won't know that you're eating, and though you are fully dressed, you won't be aware of wearing what you are wearing. If you can forget about eating and wearing clothes, you will be even more able to renounce external things. . . . You can't decide that you want to become enlightened and at the same time be unwilling to part with the experiences of this world. If you can't separate yourself from the affairs of this world, you cannot become a Buddha. (V, 166–7)

"Tenth, once sounds were so purified that they ceased being objects of perception, then the ear-faculty and its objects became completely interfused so that there was nothing that perceived and nothing that was perceived. Therefore, I can cause beings burdened by anger and hatred to be free of their enmity.[69]

Earlier in the Sutra, the Buddhas of the ten directions told Ānanda that the six faculties of perception, which are the six thieves, are what cause people to fall, and that the six faculties are also what enable people to become Buddhas. If you use them well, they can help you. If you are unable to use them correctly, they can destroy you. It's like money: when you have it, if you understand that you should perform good and meritorious deeds with it to benefit other beings, then you won't have spent your money in vain. But if you gamble it away or buy drugs and other unwholesome things, then you have used your money to com-mit offenses. The principle is the same with the six faculties. (V, 168)

"Eleventh, once perceived objects had disappeared from my mind as I turned the light of my understanding inward, my body and mind and the

[69] Ven. Zhen Jiao notes that these people can be freed of their anger because they understand that there is no subject and no object (Zhen Jiao, 1615).

entire Dharma-Realm were as bright and translucent as crystal. There-fore I can bring freedom from stupidity to beings whose natures have been so darkened by their dullness that they have had no intention of ever becoming enlightened.[70]

"Twelfth, once perceived objects became interfused and returned to the enlightened nature of hearing, I could travel to distant lands without leaving the place for awakening, and all at the same time, without any disruption, I could travel among the worlds. There I can make offerings to an infinite number of Buddhas throughout all ten directions and serve each of these Buddhas as a Dharma-Prince. For that reason, should child-less beings anywhere in the ten directions wish for sons, I can cause them to have sons who will be virtuous, blessed, and wise.

Thirteenth, once my six faculties perfected an interconnected func-tioning and became united in their capacity to clearly perceive every-thing in all the worlds throughout the ten directions, my mind became like a great flawless mirror that reflected the emptiness of the Matrix of the Thus-Come One. I reverently served an infinite number of Thus-Come Ones and thoroughly mastered esoteric aspects of the Dharma. Therefore, should childless beings anywhere in the ten directions wish for daughters, I can cause them to have daughters who are upright, blessed, virtuous, compliant, wholesome in appearance, and liked and respected by all.

"Fourteenth, sixty-two times as many Dharma-Princes as there are sand-grains in the River Ganges appear in each of the worlds of this sys-tem of a billion worlds, with its hundreds of billions of suns and moons, to practice the Dharma and to act as exemplars in order to teach beings how to transform themselves. With skill and wisdom, these Dharma-Princes respond in various ways to what various beings require. I have broken through to the fundamental source of my ear-faculty, thus revealing the ear as a gateway to the wondrous. My body and mind, in a subtle and won-

[70] For these beings the text gives the Chinese characters *e dian jia,* 阿顛迦, presumably a shortening of *e dian di jia* 阿顛底迦, Skt. *ātyantika,* those devoid of intent to seek enlightenment.

drous way, have encompassed and pervaded the Dharma-Realm. Therefore, I can cause someone who recites my name to gain as many blessings and as much merit as someone else would gain from reciting the names of all those multitudes of Dharma-Princes — sixty-two times as many of them as there are sand-grains in the River Ganges. The blessings and merit that those two reciters will gain will be the same. World-Honored One, because, by means of my spiritual practice, I have completely broken through to enlightenment, the power of my name alone is equal to the power of all those many other names.

"In this way I cause beings to develop such merit that they will have nothing to fear in fourteen kinds of dangerous situations.

"Further, World-Honored One, because I have broken through to enlightenment and have reached the final destination of the Supreme Path, I have also mastered four immeasurably efficacious and wondrous powers.

"First, once I had realized the wondrousness within the wonder at the heart of my hearing, and once my hearing had disappeared into the essence of my mind, my hearing became indistinguishable from seeing, smelling, tasting, tactile awareness, and cognition. All six were completely interfused into a single pure and magnificent awareness. Therefore, I can assume many different and wondrous forms and can proclaim numberless esoteric and efficacious mantras. I may appear with one head, three heads, five heads, seven heads, nine heads, eleven heads, as many as one hundred and eight heads, or a thousand heads or ten thousand heads and more, even as many as eighty-four thousand indestructible heads. I may appear with two arms, four arms, six arms, eight arms, ten arms, twelve arms, or with fourteen, sixteen, eighteen, twenty, or twenty-four arms, or with as many as one hundred and eight arms, or with a thousand arms, or ten thousand arms and more, even as many as eighty-four thousand arms, with each hand forming a mudra. My hands may have two eyes, three eyes, four eyes, nine eyes, as many as one hundred and eight eyes, or a thousand eyes or ten thousand eyes and more, even as many as eighty-four thousand pure and magnificent eyes. In these forms, by displaying kindness, by inspiring awe, and by manifesting samādhi and wisdom, I can rescue and shelter beings, allowing them to attain great mastery and ease.

"Second, due to my practice of listening and contemplating, I broke free of the six kinds of sense-object such that I was no more obstructed by them than a sound is obstructed by a low wall. Therefore I have the wondrous power to appear in various forms, each of them reciting various mantras. Because these forms and these mantras have the power to deliver beings from danger, I am known in countless lands throughout the ten directions as one who causes beings to have nothing to fear.

"Third, by means of the fundamental, wondrous practice that led me to break through to enlightenment, I reached the pure source of the ear-faculty, and therefore, in whatever worlds I travel to, I can cause beings to disregard their bodies and their valuable possessions in their quest for my compassionate aid.

"Fourth, I have realized the ultimate, which is the Buddha-mind. Therefore, in all lands I can make offerings of precious valuables not only to the Thus-Come Ones throughout all ten directions but also to beings in the six destinies throughout the Dharma-Realm. As a result, those who seek a spouse shall obtain a spouse, those who seek a child shall have a child, those who wish for samādhi shall gain samādhi, those who wish for a long life shall live long, and those who seek the Great Nirvana shall attain it.

"The Buddha has asked us how we broke through to enlightenment. By the means that I have described, I entered through the gateway of the ear-faculty and perfected the inner illumination of samādhi. My mind that had once been dependent on perceived objects developed self-mastery and ease. By entering the current of the awakened ones and entering samādhi, I became fully awake. This then is the best method.

"World-Honored One, that other Buddha — that Thus-Come One who is called 'He Who Hears the Cries of the World' — praised my mastery of this method for breaking through to enlightenment. Before his great assembly, he bestowed on me his own name, He Who Hears the Cries of the World. Because I hear throughout all ten directions with perfect clarity, my name 'He Who Hears the Cries of the World' is known in all the worlds throughout the ten directions."

Then the World-Honored One, seated on his Lion's Seat, sent forth a magnificent light from his hands, his feet, and his forehead. The light traveled far to pour down upon the crowns of the heads of as many Thus-Come Ones and Dharma-Prince Bodhisattvas as there are motes of dust throughout the ten directions. And all those Thus-Come Ones, from as many places as there are motes of dust, sent forth from their hands, their feet, and their foreheads magnificent beams of light that poured down upon the crown of the Buddha Śākyamuni's head and poured down as well upon the great Bodhisattvas and Arhats in the assembly. As the sound of Dharma reverberated from groves and ponds, those beams of light interlaced with each other like the strands of a magnificent net — something no one in the assembly had ever seen before. All gained the ability to enter the vajra-solid samādhi. Then lotus-flowers — some blue, some yellow, some red, some white, each adorned with a hundred gems — floated down together from the heavens, and space throughout the ten directions took on the colors of the seven precious things. The mountains, the rivers, and everything else in this Sāha world all vanished at the same time. Throughout the ten directions, Buddha-lands as many as motes of dust were seen to merge into a single world, while there rang forth everywhere the sounds of chant and song.

3
The Bodhisattva Mañjuśrī's Recommendation

Then the Thus-Come One said to the Dharma-Prince Mañjuśrī, "Consider now what has been said by these twenty-five sages — these great Bodhisattvas and these Arhats who need no further instruction — about the methods they used in order to take their first step toward awakening. They all said that theirs was the best method for breaking through to enlightenment. In fact, none of the methods employed by these sages can be ranked as superior or inferior to the others. But now it is Ānanda whom I wish to teach how to become enlightened. Which then of these twenty-five methods of practice is most suitable for beings at Ānanda's level? And which one, after my nirvana, will lead beings of this world to practice in accord with the Vehicle of the Bodhisattvas and to follow the path to supreme enlightenment? Which of these methods will lead them most easily to success?"

Having respectfully received the Buddha's instruction, Mañjuśrī stood up, bowed at the Buddha's feet, and infused with the Buddha's majestic spirit, responded to his request by speaking these verses:[71]

"Clear is the oceanic nature of enlightenment;
Flawlessly clear it is, and wondrous at its origin.
But from within that fundamental mind that understands,
Objects appear, and with creation of these objects then
The fundamental understanding vanishes.

"Then from confusion and delusion, empty space appears;
And all the worlds come into being clinging to that space;
Due to delusion, clarity will turn to solid land;
Due to false awareness, beings then come forth as well.

"And thus does space arise within the great enlightenment,
Appearing like a solitary bubble on the sea,

[71] In the Chinese, there are 250 five-character unrhymed lines without stanza divisions.

And thus do beings with outflows and the worlds uncountable
Arise within that empty space, and when space disappears —
And when that bubble bursts — could the three realms not vanish also?

"Single is the fundamental nature we return to;
Many are the Dharma-gateways that will bring us there.
Not one among these sages failed in gaining perfect insight.
Their methods — some of them directed outward and some inward —
All will succeed, some rapidly, and some more slowly,
Once they've made their resolution to attain samādhi.

"Objects of sight,[72] entangled with cognition, will become
Defiled. Essentially, such objects lack transparency,
And how could objects that one cannot see through clearly
Guide beings toward a breakthrough to enlightenment?[73]

"Language and speech require a mix of various sounds[74]
In order to form words and sentences expressing meanings.
But words and phrases can't express all meanings; how could sounds
Guide beings toward a breakthrough to enlightenment?

"Odors must be in contact with the nose for us to smell them;
If nose and odors aren't in touch, no smelling can occur.
And since the act of smelling is inconstant, how could odors
Guide beings toward a breakthrough to enlightenment?

"Experience of flavors is not part of our true nature;
For tasting to occur, there must be contact with a flavor.

---

[72] At this point, Mañjuśrī begins a consideration of the methods used by the twenty-five sages, starting with Upaṇṣad's contemplation of the impurity of visible objects.

[73] All the methods are effective, as the twenty-five sages have attested, as the Buddha has just confirmed, and as Mañjuśrī has just noted; however, what is being determined here is the most effective method for Ānanda and for future beings.

[74] Ājñātakauṇḍinya and sounds are the referent here; Mañjuśrī now proceeds to consider each of the other objects of perception and each of the faculties of perception, largely in the order they were presented by the sages.

Tasting is discontinuous; how then could flavors
Guide beings toward a breakthrough to enlightenment?

"Objects of touch are sensed upon their contact with the body;
Without that contract, no perception of them can take place.
But contact will be intermittent; how could tangibles
Guide beings toward a breakthrough to enlightenment?

"Those inner objects of the mind are what we call defilements;
Since these are objects, each of them must have precise location.
Observer and observed cannot be everywhere; then how
Could mental objects guide all beings to enlightenment?

"Although the faculty of seeing does indeed see clearly,
Still it perceives what lies before it, not what lies behind.
Of four directions it can see but two at once;[75] how could it
Guide beings toward a breakthrough to enlightenment?

"Breath enters in the nostrils, then goes out again; however
Between each in-breath and each out-breath, there must be a pause.
The breath is discontinuous; how could the nose
Guide beings toward a breakthrough to enlightenment?

"The tongue, with nothing placed on it, can have no tasting function;
It senses flavors only when they're present. When dispersed,
Awareness of them ceases; how then could the tongue
Guide beings toward a breakthrough to enlightenment?

"What's true of taste is true of tactile objects and the body:
They're not the best for contemplation toward awakening.
Body and objects, being finite, do not always meet;
How could the body guide all beings to enlightenment?

---

[75] Above, in part 5.2, the eye-faculty is rated at two-thirds efficacy rather than half, as here. In the earlier passage, peripheral vision was included. But here the point is that the eye-faculty sees *clearly* only halfway around.

"The borders of cognition with the faculty of mind
Aren't clear enough for beings to tell which one of them is which.
Beginners cannot free themselves from thinking, nor from thoughts;
How could this faculty guide beings toward enlightenment?

"Observe that the eye-consciousness involves a threefold joining;[76]
It is dependent; basically it has no attributes.
No independent essence of its own; how could it then
Guide beings toward a breakthrough to enlightenment?

"Ear-consciousness, if it's aware throughout the ten directions,
Is drawing power from great practice in past lives.
Beginners' minds cannot advance into this practice; how then
Could it guide beings to a breakthrough to enlightenment?

"The contemplation of the nose is an expedient
That merely focuses the mind upon a single spot.
But such a focus is confined to just one place; how could it
Guide all beings toward a breakthrough to enlightenment?

"Wielding the sounds of words to speak about the Dharma
Wakens the speaker, based on past accomplishment.
But words and sentences do not lack outflows; thus could speech
Guide beings toward a breakthrough to enlightenment?

"Avoiding violation of the precepts regulates
The body only; such restraints do not apply to beings
Who have no body.[77] How could what does not apply to all
Guide beings toward a breakthrough to enlightenment?

"Spiritual powers are based on practice in past lives; such powers
Are not related to cognition's making of distinctions.

---

[76] The six sense-consciousnesses are now considered, followed by the seven primary elements. The "threefold joining" refers to the combining of a perceiving faculty and a perceived object to activate the corresponding consciousness.

[77] That is, gods on the planes of formlessness.

251

There has to be an object for cognition to occur;
How could cognition then guide beings to enlightenment?

"Consider contemplating earth: it's solid and opaque;
One can't move through it. What's conditional must lack
The nature of a sage. How could this contemplation, then,
Guide beings toward a breakthrough to enlightenment?

"Consider contemplating water: contemplating thus
Involves cognition, which is neither true nor real.
Contemplation by itself won't reach the state that's *thus;*
Then how could water guide all beings toward enlightenment?

"Consider contemplating fire: disdaining one's desire,
Is not the same as ending it. This contemplation, then,
Is not a method suited to beginners.[78] How could fire
Guide beings toward a breakthrough to enlightenment?

"Consider contemplating wind: movement and stillness
Must be opposites, and opposition cannot be
A basis for awakening. Thus how could wind
Guide beings toward a breakthrough to enlightenment?

"Consider contemplating space: space lacks awareness,
Beginning from primordial darkness. Being unaware
Is not the same as full awakening. How then could space
Guide beings toward a breakthrough to enlightenment?

"Consider contemplating consciousness: this consciousness[79]
Is intermittent. Its existence in the mind, as well,
Is only an illusion. How then could this consciousness
Guide beings toward a breakthrough to enlightenment?

---

[78] Fire-Head (Ucchuṣma) was able to subdue his desire by contemplating fire; but he was not a beginner.

[79] The primary element consciousness, which includes the first six consciousnesses (of eye, ear, nose, tongue, body, and cognition). See also part 3.5g.

"No practice is entirely continuous,
So even mindfulness[80] perforce arises and must halt.
An intermittent practice's results are intermittent.
How could awareness guide all beings to enlightenment?

"I now respectfully say this to the World-Honored One —
The One who came to be a Buddha in this Sahā world
In order to transmit to us the true, essential teaching
Meant for this place — I say that purity is found through hearing.
All those who wish to gain samādhi's mastery
Will surely find that hearing is the way to enter.

"For leaving suffering behind and gaining liberation,
How excellent the method that the One
Who Hears the Cries of the World has just proclaimed!
Throughout the ages many as the River Ganges' sands,
He enters countless Buddha-lands. He has the ease of mastery
And he bestows his fearlessness on beings in danger.

"Most wondrous is the voice of the One Who Hears the Cries!
Its sound is pure and like the ocean-tide! Throughout the worlds
He rescues worldly beings, brings them peace, and if they wish,
He helps them leave the world and reach nirvana everlasting!

"I now can recommend respectfully the practice
Taught by the One Who Hears the Cries of the World.
A being whose mind is tranquil hears the sound
Of drumbeats coming from all ten directions,
And yet he'll hear each of the drums distinctly.
And so our hearing faculty must be the perfect one,
The one that's genuine and true.

"The eyes can't see through objects that are solid;
The tongue and nose are likewise limited.

---

[80] This last consideration is of the primary element awareness as related to the practice of mindfulness of the Buddha Amitābha.

For bodily awareness, contact's needed,
And, too, the mind's chaotic, lacking order.

"But sounds are heard close by and from afar;
And even walls may fail in blocking them.
No other faculty's the equal of our hearing;
Both true and genuine, it is the one for breaking through.

"We're capable of hearing sounds and silence both;
They may be present to the ear or not.
Though people say that when no sound is present,
Our hearing must be absent too, in fact
Our hearing does not lapse. It does not cease
With silence; neither is it born of sound.
Our hearing, then, is genuine and true.
It is the everlasting one.

"And when cognition ceases in a dream,
That does not mean that hearing is suspended.
The ear's awareness goes beyond mere thought.
No other faculty, of mind or body,
Can ever be the equal of our hearing.

"And now, for beings of this Sahā world,
I have explained the method based on hearing.

"Confused about the nature of our hearing,
Beings, by permitting their attention
To go out pursuing sounds, have bound themselves
To birth and death's unending cycle.

"Ānanda's erudition just could not prevent
His falling prey to an improper scheme.
By heeding sounds, how could he not have fallen?
But had his striving been against the current,[81]
Would he not have then avoided error?

[81] That is, if he had been practicing directing his hearing inward.

"Ānanda, listen closely! Aided by the awe-inspiring
Power of the Buddha, I have now explained to you
This regal, genuine, and marvelous samādhi.
Indestructible, beyond the reach of mundane thought,
It is the mother of all Buddhas.

"Though you may hear of all the secret Dharma-gateways
That Buddhas numberless as motes of dust may teach,
Just learning them is useless if you first do not
Get rid of all your outflows, which are based upon desire.
You've heard and practiced all these Buddhas' Buddha-Dharmas;
Why haven't you been hearing your own hearing?

"People say that hearing comes about because of sounds,
Not on its own. If that's what you call 'hearing,' though,
Then when you turn your hearing round and set it free from sounds,
What name are you to give to that which is set free?

"Return just one of the perceiving faculties
Back to its source, and all six faculties will then be free.
For what we hear is mere illusion, like the objects of our vision —
Like what is seen by one whose eyes are covered by a film.
The Threefold Realm is like those flowers in an empty sky,[82]
But turn the hearing inward, and the faculties are cured.
Their objects vanish, and awareness is completely pure.

"In perfect purity, the brilliance of awareness shines
Unhindered and in still illumination of all space,
In contemplating worldly things as the events of dreams.
The young Mātaṅga woman was a figure in a dream.
Just who was really there with power to entice you?

"Consider this analogy from ordinary life:
A puppet-master can present illusions — men and women

---

[82] The eye-disease is given as an example in part 2.11.

Made to move by pulling on a string; but if he chooses
Not to pull upon the string, the scene returns to stillness
And all is shown to be illusion.

"Just so are our six faculties. Originally
A pure and single understanding, they divide;
And once divided, each of them makes contact with its objects.
But then if one of them is redirected inward,
All six as a result will cease to function separately,
And their defiling objects vanish instantly.
Thus our understanding is perfected
In a wondrous purity.

"Those who still have remnants of their basic ignorance
Need more instruction. Those whose understanding is perfected,
Their illumination ultimate — these are the Thus-Come Ones.

"Great Assembly! Ānanda! Halt the puppet show
Of your distorted hearing! Merely turn your hearing round
To listen to your genuine true nature,
Which is the destination of the Path that is supreme.
This is the genuine way to break through to enlightenment.

"It is the way that the innumerable Buddhas followed
Straight to nirvana's gate. All Thus-Come Ones of eons past
Succeeded by this method. Through this method, Bodhisattvas,
Too, right now are gaining perfect understanding.

"Among the people of the future, those who undertake
A spiritual practice should rely upon this teaching.
I myself became enlightened by this very method.
He Who Hears the Cries is not the only one.

"The Buddha, the World-Honored One, made a request
That I consider methods that will rescue beings
Who in the Dharma's ending-time resolve their minds
Upon attainment of transcendence and nirvana.

The best of all the methods is the practice
Taught by the One Who Hears the Cries of the World.

"The sages who attained enlightenment by other means
Were aided by the Buddha's awe-inspiring spiritual power,
And each was specially taught how to abandon all affliction.
Some of these paths are shallow, some go deep; these teachings vary.

"I bow now in respect to all the Buddhas, and I bow
To all their Dharma-treasuries and to the marvelous ones
Who've put an end to outflows.[83] And may beings of the future
Be empowered so that they will have no doubts
That this one method is the most accessible.

"It is the easiest way to reach enlightenment.
It is the teaching most appropriate
For Ānanda and for the beings drowning
In the Dharma's ending-time. They only need
This practice of the faculty of hearing
For them to break through to enlightenment,
For it surpasses all the other methods.
It is the genuine path to the true mind.

We say that the faculty of hearing functions when there is sound, but does it still function when there is no sound? It does, because the nature of hearing is not subject to coming into being and ceasing to be. Therefore, turn the attention of your hearing-faculty inward. From now on, don't go out after the six sense-objects with your six faculties. Bring your faculties back. Reverse the direction of your hearing-faculty and listen to your true nature until your nature merges with the unsurpassed path to enlightenment. What is your true nature? When you hear it, you will recognize it. Now, before you have heard it, you wouldn't understand even if I told you. For instance, when I myself drink a cup of tea, I know whether my tea is hot or cool, but you don't know. If you

---

[83] The text is terse here. The translation follows the interpretation of the Ven. Yuanying (979). "The marvelous ones" are the fourth-stage Arhats.

want to know, you will have to pour some for yourself. If you want to arrive at your true nature, you first have to reverse the attention of your hearing-faculty to listen within.

When you reverse the direction of your hearing, how do you listen? Use your ears. But don't listen to the sounds outside. Don't try to figure out what is happening in the street or who is saying what nearby. Turn the hearing inward and listen inside yourself. In this way your own nature will be revealed. When you have turned your hearing around, you will be set free from external sounds. What name are you to give to that which is set free? If you can divorce yourself from sounds, you will hear and yet not hear. Is this then really what we call "hearing"? It is and it isn't. It isn't, yet it is. Hear and yet do not hear. That's what is meant by getting free of sounds. You do hear, but it's not the same as the way you heard before. Even though it is said that ordinary hearing can reach far and near, it still has a limit. If you genuinely reach a state of mind in which you are hearing your true nature, you can hear throughout the Dharma-Realm, provided that you choose to do so. But you can also choose not to listen to any of the sounds throughout the Dharma-Realm. You have control. What do we call what is free of sound then? It does not have a name. That which is beyond even the name "hearing" is true hearing. (V, 215–6) . . .

Why does Mañjuśrī choose the ear-faculty? It is the easiest practice for success in spiritual cultivation. The skill used in reversing the hearing to hear the true nature is the skill used when you meditate in stillness.[84] When you sit in meditation, don't spend all your energy on seeking what is outside yourself. Turn your light around to shine within. Then ask yourself, "Who is this who is mindful of the Buddha?" "Who?" Put the "who" into your mind and then listen with your ears. Don't pause in your pursuit of "who?" Don't let your skill disperse. Inquire into this topic in everything you do. It's said:

Walking, standing, sitting, reclining,
Don't be apart from *this*.
If you depart from *this*,
You've made a mistake.

---

[84] Skt. *dhyāna,* Ch. *chan* 禪.

What is *this*? It is the question, "Who is mindful of the Buddha?" You don't have to ask this question out loud; ask it in your mind and listen to it with your ears. Listen within, not outside. After you have listened within, your mind and the enlightened nature of hearing will eventually merge. And then in some unexpected way, at some unexpected moment, you will suddenly become enlightened. But you definitely must bring your mind and nature together. Don't let them scatter in all directions. Don't let them get dissipated outside yourself. Gather them in. As you reverse your hearing to listen to your true nature, eventually, naturally, your skill will develop. (V, 221)

Then Ānanda and all the others in the great assembly, having received such profound instruction, gained a clear understanding of their faculties and the corresponding consciousnesses. As they contemplated the Buddha's full awakening and great nirvana, Ānanda and the others were like someone who has traveled far from home on matters of business: although the traveler has not yet been able to return, he knows the road that will lead him home. The entire assembly of beings, ten times as many as the sand-grains of the River Ganges — gods, dragons, and other celestial beings; sages of the Lesser Vehicle who still needed instruction; and others who only recently had made the resolve to become Bodhisattvas — all now discovered their inherent true mind so that they would forever be free of affliction. All opened their pure Dharma-eye. The nun named Nature, upon hearing these verses, became an Arhat.[85] These numberless beings all made the resolution to seek the unsurpassed, correct, and perfect enlightenment.[86]

---

[85] This is the young woman of the Mātaṅga clan whose mantra set in motion the events of the Sutra, as related in the prologue.

[86] Skt. *anuttara-samyak-sambodhi,* the enlightenment of the Buddha.

VII

Four Clear
and Definitive
Instructions on Purity

1
On Sexual Desire

Ānanda straightened his robes and in the midst of the assembly placed his palms together and bowed. At once joyful and sorrowful, he now understood perfectly the path his mind had taken. Wishing to benefit the beings of the future, he bowed his head and said respectfully, "Greatly Compassionate World-Honored One, now I understand this Dharma for becoming a Buddha. I can practice this method unhindered by the slightest doubt. I have often heard the Thus-Come One say that Bodhisattvas resolve to help others make the crossing[1] before completing the crossing themselves, while the Buddhas, having already completed the crossing, act in the world by guiding others to enlightenment. I myself have not completed the crossing, but I vow to bring across all beings who live in the future in the time of the Dharma's ending.

"World-Honored One, the beings of that time will have become more and more distant from the Buddha. As many false teachers as there are sand-grains in the River Ganges will pretend to teach the Dharma. Should any beings of that time wish to guard and focus their minds so that they can enter samādhi, how may I guide them towards establishing a place for awakening where their practice will be secured against demonic disturbances and where they will not retreat from their resolve to become enlightened?"

Then the World-Honored One praised Ānanda before the great assembly, saying, "Excellent! Excellent! You have asked how a place for awakening may be established in order to rescue and protect beings who are sinking and drowning during the time of the Dharma's ending. Listen carefully, and I will tell you." Ānanda and all the others in the assembly replied that they would respectfully accept and follow the instructions.

The Buddha said to Ānanda, "When I have explained the vinaya, you have often heard me speak of the three essential elements of spiritual practice: precepts, which require us to guard and focus the mind;

[1] That is, across the sea of afflictions to the shore of nirvana.

263

samādhi, which arises from following precepts; and wisdom, which appears out of samādhi. These are the three practices that end outflows.

"Ānanda, why do I say that to follow the precepts is to guard and focus the mind? In all worlds, beings in the six destinies[2] whose minds are free of sexual desire will not be bound to an unending cycle of deaths and rebirths. No matter how much you may practice in order to transcend the stress of entanglement with perceived objects, you will never transcend that stress until you have freed yourself from sexual desire. Even very intelligent people who can enter samādhi while practicing meditation in stillness will be certain to fall into the realm of demons upon their rebirth if they have not renounced sexual activity. The best among them will become kings among demons; those at intermediate levels will be members of demon hordes; female demons will be at the lowest levels. These demons will attract groups of disciples and will tell them that they have realized unsurpassed enlightenment. After my nirvana, in the time of the Dharma's ending, many such demonic hordes will sweep like wildfire across the world and will openly parade their lustfulness while pretending to be good and wise teachers. These demons will cause beings to fall into the pit of sexual desire and wrong views concerning desire, and they will stray off the road to perfect enlightenment. Therefore, when you teach people to practice samādhi, first teach them to rid their minds of sexual desire. That is the first of four clear and definitive[3] instructions on purity that have been given by the Thus-Come One and by all the Buddhas of the past, World-Honored Ones.

When deviant teachers explain their methods, their primary topic is sexual desire. The things they say are unprincipled. This should be distinguished

---

[2] The six destinies are gods, humans, animals, ghosts, denizens of the hells, and asuras. See part 9.

[3] "Definitive" here renders Ch. *jueding* 決定. The meaning seems to be the same as Ch. *liao yi* 了義, which in turn renders the Skt. *nitartha*, teachings that are definitive in that they require no further elaboration. The opposite of nitartha is Skt. *neyartha*, Ch. *bu liao yi* 不了義, teachings that are not definitive, in that they need further explanation to elucidate, among other things, the particular circumstances in which the teaching was given. The text uses *bu liao yi* 不了義 below (see note 8).

clearly from the teachings of Bodhisattvas, who out of their compassion use kind words and a protective heart in their teaching, knowing that all living beings are steeped in desire. Every living being has thoughts of sexual desire. So a Bodhisattva does not expect them to put an end to emotional love and desire immediately, but he uses all kinds of expedient means to get them to see through and renounce sexual desire. Then they can put a stop to it themselves. This is the state of a Bodhisattva, totally different from the state of the deviant teachers who encourage beings in their desires. (VI, 6)

In fact, if you do not put an end to your sexual desire, it will be impossible for you to escape the mundane defilements of the world, because thoughts of sexual desire are themselves defiling. . . . Not to speak of engaging in lustful practices, even the presence of such thoughts is unclean. If you don't renounce sexual desire, it's entirely unreasonable to hope to become enlightened and become a Buddha. (VI, 11)

"Therefore, Ānanda, one who practices entering samādhi while practicing meditation in stillness without renouncing sexual activity is like one who cooks sand in the hope that it will turn into rice. A hundred thousand eons might pass and it would still be nothing but hot sand, since it wasn't rice to begin with. It was merely sand.

"In seeking the wondrous enlightenment of the Buddha while you still have sexual desire, you may gain some understanding of that wondrous enlightenment, but that understanding will be rooted in sexual desire. If the basis of your understanding is sexual desire, you will continually be reborn among the three lowly destinies, bound to the cycle of death and rebirth with no hope of escape. Then how will you find your way to practice and realization of the Thus-Come Ones' nirvana?

If you do not put an end to your sexual desire and yet keep up your spiritual practice and sit in meditation every day, you will be practicing on the one hand and will have outflows on the other. Everything you gain will be dissipated. Whatever you gain in your practice will be lost tenfold in outflows. . . . Unable to renounce sexual desire, you still sit in meditation with the hope of getting enlightened, with the aim of gaining a little bit of confused bliss. This is just like cooking sand in the hope of getting rice. It's useless. . . .

There's something else to be said here. If you can put an end to sexual desire, then even if you are together with the opposite sex all day long, no problem will arise. . . . If one really has no sexual desire, then:

The eyes see things,
But inside there is nothing.
The ears hear sounds,
But the mind doesn't know.

No matter how pleasing a sound comes to the ear, your mind is unaware of it. Then you've gotten someplace. And if you can reach the point that you can walk, sit, and even lie down together with someone of the opposite sex without there being any incident, without any sexual desire arising, then you have something that will count. It's not that your mind still races, but you grit your teeth and tell yourself firmly that you can guard your mind against sexual desires. That doesn't count. It has to be that not one thought arises, that your mind does not move, that there is no trace of lust in your heart. If even just occasionally you are aware of what the opposite sex is all about, then you've failed the test. (VI, 15–7)

"You must purge yourself of the most subtle promptings of sexual desire, both physical and mental, to the point that you have purged even the act of purging. Then there will be hope that you may realize the full awakening of the Buddhas.

"What I have said is what Buddhas teach. Māra, the Evil One,[4] teaches otherwise."

---

[4] Skt. Pāpāyān, Ch. boxun 波旬, "evil one," an epithet of Māra, king of the demonic legions who inhabit the sixth heaven of the realm of desire.

2
On Killing

"Also, Ānanda, in all worlds, beings in the six destinies whose minds are free of all desire to kill will not be bound to an unending cycle of deaths and rebirths. No matter how much you may practice samādhi in order to transcend the stress of entanglement with perceived objects, you will never transcend that stress until you have freed yourself from thoughts of killing. Even very intelligent people who can enter samādhi while practicing meditation in stillness are certain to fall into the realm of ghosts and spirits upon their rebirth if they have not renounced all killing. The best among them will become ghosts of great power; those at intermediate levels will become flying yakṣas or leaders of ghostly hordes; those at the lowest levels will be rākṣasas that travel along the ground. These ghosts and spirits will attract groups of disciples and will tell them that they have realized the supreme enlightenment. After my nirvana, in the time of the Dharma's ending, these ghosts and spirits will spread like wildfire across the worlds as they make the claim that eating meat will not obstruct the path to enlightenment. I have instructed the monks that there are five situations in which eating meat will not compromise purity. Ānanda, but even then I have used spiritual power to change the meat so that all traces of sentience have been removed.

> The five circumstances in which eating meat will not compromise purity are eating the flesh of an animal that one did not see killed; eating the flesh of an animal whose killing one did not hear; eating the flesh of an animal that one knows was not killed for one's own sake; eating the flesh of an animal that died a natural death; and eating the flesh of an animal whose corpse has been scavenged by birds. (VI, 22)

"I have compassion also for those who wish to live purely but who live among humid marshlands or in hot deserts where grains and vegetables cannot be grown. Out of great kindness and by means of my spiritual power, I change the meat they eat so that it is without sentience. It is merely called meat and merely tastes like meat. But, after my nirvana, how will people who eat the flesh of beings deserve to be called disciples of Śākyamuni?

"You should understand that these people who eat flesh may gain some modicum of mental awakening while practicing samādhi, but they are all great rākṣasas who in the end must fall into the sea of death and rebirth. They are not disciples of the Buddha. Such people kill and devour each other, feeding on each other in an endless cycle. How could they possibly get out of the three realms?

"When you teach people in the world to practice samādhi, teach them to renounce all killing. That is the second of the clear and definitive instructions on purity that have been given by the Thus-Come One and by all the Buddhas of the past, World-Honored Ones.

"Therefore, Ānanda, one who enters samādhi while practicing meditation in stillness without renouncing all killing is like one who hopes that nobody will hear him shout if he stops up his own ears. He is trying to conceal what is perfectly evident. Bodhisattvas and pure monks walking on country paths will not even tread on living grasses,[5] much less uproot them. How then can it be compassionate to gorge on other beings' blood and flesh? Monks who will not wear silks from the East,[6] whether coarse or fine; who will not wear shoes or boots of leather, nor furs, nor birds' down from our own country; and who will not consume milk, curds, or ghee, have truly freed themselves from the world. When they have paid

---

[5] Lest they harm or kill sentient beings hidden in the grasses.

[6] That is, China. The prohibition applies to all silk, whatever its source. The prohibition appears in the *Eleventh Naihsarghika-Payantika of Bhikshu Precepts, Fascicle 7, Four Division Vinaya*. It reads as follows: "At that time, the Buddha was in the country called 曠野 (Wilderness). The group of six Bhikshus wanted to use silk together with other materials to make new sleeping mats. They looked for silk either already made or not, either dyed or not, either new or used. They went to the family that raised silkworms and said that they needed silk. The householder told them to wait for a little while until silkworms matured. The group of six Bhikshus waited there and watched. Pupas made noises when cocoons were exposed. When laypeople saw this, they criticized the Bhikshus and said: 'Śākyamuni's disciples kill living beings and have no remorse. How can they beg for silk to make new sleeping mats and yet claim that they practice proper Dharma?'"

their debts from previous lives, they will roam no longer through the three realms.

"Why? To wear parts of a being's body is to involve one's karma with that being, just as people have become bound to this earth by eating vegetables and grains. I can affirm that a person who neither eats the flesh of other beings nor wears any part of the bodies of other beings, nor even thinks of eating or wearing these things, is a person who will gain liberation.

Milk and milk products are not actually prohibited by the vinaya or by the Bodhisattva precepts. This passage of the Sutra text is describing those who hold the precept against killing with a maximum of purity. . . . There is room for flexibility here, but to avoid using anything that has any connection with living creatures is an extremely good thing. (VI, 26)

"What I have said is what Buddhas teach. Māra, the Evil One, teaches otherwise."

3
On Stealing

"Also, Ānanda, in all worlds, beings in the six destinies whose minds are free of all desire to steal will not be bound to an unending cycle of deaths and rebirths. No matter how much you may practice samādhi in order to transcend the stress of experiencing perceived objects, you will never transcend that stress until you have freed yourself from thoughts of stealing. Even very intelligent people who can enter samādhi while practicing meditation in stillness will be certain to fall into an evil realm upon their rebirth if they have not renounced stealing. The best among them will become energy-devouring nature-spirits; those at intermediate levels will be succubae or incubi; and those at the lowest levels will be unwholesome people possessed by such spirits. These unwholesome beings will attract groups of disciples and will tell them that they have realized the supreme enlightenment. After my nirvana, in the time of the Dharma's ending, many such strange and unwholesome spirits will sweep like wildfire across the world. By cunning and deceit they will establish their claim to be good and wise teachers who have reached the level of a sage. Their boasting will delude the ignorant and will instill fear that will rob people of their good judgment. Wherever they go, these unwholesome spirits will destroy families and reduce households to penury.

When I was in China I knew about some spectacular examples of these people. They could plunge a knife into the crown of their heads and yet not die. The spirit possessing them would remove the blade by the use of a mantra in such a way that the person didn't even bleed. Some would pound nails into their shoulders, and from the nails they would hang as many as four scythes weighing more than ten pounds each and then spin them. It was awesome to watch. The people who watched them were terrified. Sometimes these demons and followers of wrong paths were really talented. When you look into the Śūraṅgama Sūtra, you realize that long ago the Buddha described all the different kinds of beings in the world very clearly. Therefore, having read the Śūraṅgama Sūtra or heard it being read, you should be able to recognize whatever you come up against in the future. (VI, 32–3)

"I teach the monks to make their almsrounds in whatever place they find themselves so that they may let go of craving and become enlightened. The monks do not cook for themselves; and leading the rest of their lives this way, they wander from place to place in the three realms so that, at the end of their lives, they will not have to return. How then can thieves wear a monk's robe for the sake of personal gain, meanwhile engaging in all manner of acts which they falsely claim are in accord with the Buddha's Dharma? They slander those who have entered the monastic life, saying that fully ordained monks are merely following the path of the Lesser Vehicle. In this way they confuse countless beings and lead them astray, and they will all fall into the Unrelenting Hell.

> Why did the Buddha teach his monastic disciples to receive almsfood? First, when laypeople give food to members of the Sangha, they can be sure of blessings in the future and can put an end to their suffering and distress. Second, when monks go out for alms, they eat whatever they are given. If the food is good, they eat it; if it's bad, they eat it just the same. In this way, they get rid of their craving. If you cook for yourself, you'll think, "What I made today wasn't so good; tomorrow, though, I'll make something delicious. The day after that, I'll make something even better, and the day after that I'll make something simply spectacular." There's no end to it. . . . But when a monk goes out on his almsround, there is no opportunity to pick and choose. He simply eats his fill and then forgets about it. (VI, 38–9)

"I affirm that, after my nirvana, a monk whose resolve in the practice of samādhi is unshakable can, in a single moment, repay his debts from all his previous lives since time without beginning by burning lamp-oil on his body before an image of the Buddha, or else by burning off a part of one of his fingers, or else by burning a piece of incense on his body.[7] Then

---

[7] It is worth noting here that the Buddha recommends these asceticisms only for "monks whose resolve in the practice of samādhi is unshakable" — in other words, only for fully ordained monastics who are well advanced in their spiritual practice. The Ven. Master Hsüan Hua commented elsewhere that without real mastery of samādhi, such sacrificial

he will be able to bid a final farewell to this world and be forever free of outflows. He may not immediately understand how to advance towards supreme enlightenment, but he will have firmly committed himself to the Dharma. Without such small acts of physical renunciation, he will have to be reborn as a person again, even if he has attained freedom from all influences. He will still have to repay his debts from previous lives, just as, to repay my debts, I had to eat horse-feed.

> In a former life, the Buddha Śākyamuni was a Brahmin engaged in teaching spiritual practice to five hundred pure youths. At that time, there was another Buddha in the world. One day, when that Buddha went on his almsrounds with the monks, he instructed them to have the donors put a little extra in their bowls to accommodate a monk who was sick and could not go out. As they returned from their rounds, they passed by the mountain where the Brahmin who was to be the Budddha Śākyamuni dwelt. When this Brahmin got a whiff of the food from their especially full bowls, he became jealous. He said to his disciples, "Why do those bald monks get to eat so well? They should only be allowed horse-feed." His five-hundred disciples all agreed with him, of course, chiming in, "Right! They are only fit to eat horse-feed." After he became a Buddha, Śākyamuni took five hundred disciples to a certain country to spend the rainy-season retreat. The king of that country gave them a cordial welcome but then would not make any offerings of food to them. Eventually a horse-trainer in the country became aware that the Buddha and his monks were not being given any offerings of food, so he shared with the monks the grain that he fed his horses. Even though the Brahmin was eventually to become the Buddha Śākyamuni, and though his five hundred pure youths were to become five hundred Arhats, they still had to repay the debt from that slander they indulged in during a former life, and for ninety days they had to eat horse-feed. (VI, 42–3)

practices will likely backfire because, unless the practitioner has gained complete and unshakable detachment, the practice will be intensely painful and will engender regret, remorse, and anger against the Buddha and his teachings, resulting in a loss in merit and samādhi rather than a gain. To one monk who asked for permission to burn off a finger, Master Hsüan Hua, in refusing permission, replied, "Why don't you burn off your deluded thoughts instead?" The more moderate practice of searing the skin with incense-charcoal, however, is not an uncommon practice among both monastics and laity.

"Therefore, when you teach people in the world to practice samādhi, teach them to renounce stealing. That is the third of the clear and definitive instructions on purity that have been given by the Thus-Come One and by all the Buddhas of the past, World-Honored Ones. Ānanda, one who enters samādhi while practicing meditation in stillness but who does not renounce stealing is like one who tries to fill a leaking cup with water. He may keep on trying for countless eons, but he will never fill it up.

"Let a monk own nothing except his robes and his almsbowl; let him give to hungry beings the alms he does not need; let him greet the assembly by bowing with joined palms; let him take scoldings and beatings as praise; let him truly renounce his mind and body by sharing his flesh, bones, and blood with other beings; and let him never confuse beginners by misconstruing the Thus-Come One's teachings which are not definitive:[8] I can affirm that such a monk truly practices samādhi.

> When someone scolds you, you should act as if he is speaking some language you don't understand. . . . If someone hits you, just pretend you bumped into a wall. Suppose you were careless and walked into a wall and were left with a big lump on your head. If you then turned around and socked the wall with your fist, saying, "Why did you bump into me?" you'd only end up with an injured hand as well. If someone strikes you and you view it as if you'd bumped into a wall, the whole matter will end right there. (VI, 45)

"What I have said is what Buddhas teach. Māra, the Evil One, teaches otherwise."

[8] Ch. *bu liao yi* 不了義. See note 3 above.

4
On Making False Claims

"Ānanda, beings in the worlds' six destinies may be entirely free, in body and in mind of killing, stealing, and sexual desire, but their samādhi will not be pure if they make false claims.[9] If they do, they will be possessed by demons of craving or by demons of delusion, and they will lose sight of their potential for becoming a Buddha. They will say that they have achieved what they have not achieved and that they have become what they have not become. Wishing that worldly people might hold them in the highest honor, they will say that they have reached the stage of entering the stream,[10] or that they must be reborn once only, or that they need not be reborn, or that they are Arhats[11] or Solitary Sages, or that they are Bodhisattvas at one of the Ten Grounds or at one of the stages previous to the Ten Grounds.[12] In this way, in their craving for offerings, they encourage people to bow to them and to repent before them.

> Even if you are a Bodhisattva or a Buddha, you cannot say that you are. You must keep silent about it down to your last breath. You can only arrange for it to become known publicly after your death. While you are alive, the only reason to claim that you are a Bodhisattva or Buddha would be to induce people to believe in you so that they will give you money. As soon as people believe, then the offerings start to pour in. To make such claims is merely to practice deceit. (VI, 49)

"These people who have no trust in the Dharma[13] have ruined their potential for becoming a Buddha just as a tāla tree will die if it is cut down. The Buddha predicts that such people will destroy their founda-

---

[9] In condemning lying in general, the Buddha here focuses on a specific and particularly egregious instance.

[10] The Buddha now mentions the four stages of the Arhat.

[11] The term "Arhat" may refer only to the fourth stage, as here, or to all four stages.

[12] See part 9.4 on the fifty-seven stages of the Bodhisattva's enlightenment.

[13] Skt. *icchantika*.

tion in the Dharma and that they will never regain right knowledge and right viewpoints. They will sink into the sea of three kinds of suffering and will be unable to enter samādhi.

> The tāla tree, found in India, grows to great heights, but if it is chopped down, it will not grow again. These people destroy their seeds for future enlightenment, and so the seeds cannot come to fruition, just as a tāla tree that has been cut down cannot grow again. Such people are bereft of sense and insight. Immersed in the sea of three kinds of suffering, they cannot attain samādhi. The three kinds of sufferings referred to here are the suffering caused by knives, which refers to the hell of the mountain of knives; the suffering of blood, which refers to the hell of bleeding, in which one's entire body bleeds without cease; and the suffering of fire, which refers to the hell of burning. These people fall into these three terrible hells. (VI, 50–1)

"It is my command that after my nirvana, in the time of the Dharma's ending, the Bodhisattvas and the Arhats will appear before beings in whatever bodily form may be appropriate for rescuing them from the cycle of death and rebirth. The Bodhisattvas and Arhats may appear as elder monks or nuns, or as white-robed laity, or as kings, as high officials, as pure youths or maidens, or even as courtesans, widows,[14] libertines, thieves, slaughterers, or traffickers in stolen goods. Working side by side with these people, in order to lead them to enter samādhi, the Bodhisattvas and Arhats praise the Buddha's Vehicle. but they should never speak casually to people who have not yet studied the Dharma, saying, 'I am actually a Bodhisattva,' or 'I am actually an Arhat,' thus carelessly revealing the Buddha's hidden intent. They can only reveal themselves at the end of their lives, and then only in private.[15] Anyone who in any other way claims to be a Bodhisattva or an Arhat is deluding people with an egregious lie.

---

[14] The inclusion of widows in this last group testifies to the particularly demeaned and dependent state of widowed women in traditional Indian society.

[15] That is, to their close disciples whom they have named as their successors.

Bodhisattvas appear as different sorts of people because they want to convert those sorts of people. They employ four methods of attraction: giving, speaking kind words, benefiting others, and working alongside others. They may give wealth, Dharma, or courage — three kinds of giving. . . . But in giving in these various ways, they do not crave or expect repayment. . . . They make their gift and forget it. Then the three aspects of giving — the giver, the gift, and the recipient — are empty. (VI, 52–3)

"Therefore, when you teach people in the world to practice samādhi, teach them to refrain from making false claims. This is the fourth of the clear and definitive instructions on purity that have been given by the Thus-Come One and by all the Buddhas of the past, World-Honored Ones.

"Ānanda, one who does not refrain from making false claims is like someone who molds a piece of excrement into the shape of a piece of sandalwood incense in the hope that it will then be fragrant. That cannot be. I have taught the bhikṣus that the straightforward mind is the place for awakening and that there must be nothing whatever false in their cultivation of a stern and proper manner in all four comportments.[16] Why then would they make a public claim about their attainment, saying they had reached the level of a sage? One who makes such false claims is like a pauper who claims to be king. Such a one is deliberately seeking his death. Even less should one claim the title of Dharma-King![17] If your direction is not true at the start, you will veer away from the goal. One who seeks the enlightenment of the Buddhas in this way is like one who tries to bite his own navel. Who could expect to succeed? Monks whose minds are as straight as lute-strings and who are entirely genuine and truthful will never encounter demons when they enter samādhi. I can affirm that such people are certain to realize the unsurpassed wisdom and enlightenment of the Bodhisattvas.

"What I have said is what Buddhas teach. Māra, the Evil One, teaches otherwise."

---

[16] Walking, standing, sitting, and lying down.
[17] That is, a Buddha.

VIII
The Śūraṅgama Mantra

1
Establishing a Place for Awakening

"Ananda, you have asked about guarding and focusing the mind, and I have now told you about the wondrous method that will lead practitioners to enter samādhi. If you seek to become a Bodhisattva, you must first follow the four instructions on purity so that your comportment may be as pure as the glistening frost. Then very naturally you will no more be able to commit the three errors of the mind and the four errors of speech than a tree is able to leaf out in freezing weather. How could anything demonic happen to someone who faithfully follows the four instructions on purity, Ānanda? How much the more will that person be protected if his mind is not paying attention to sights, sounds, odors, flavors, tangible objects, or objects of cognition!

> The "wondrous method that will lead practitioners to enter samādhi" refers to gaining completely unobstructed understanding through the ear-faculty by turning the hearing around to listen to one's true nature so that one can realize supreme enlightenment.
>
> The Buddha has just said that anyone who seeks to become a Bodhisattva must follow these four rules of purity: not taking life, not stealing, not committing acts of sexual misconduct, and not making false claims. The prohibition against sexual misconduct refers not only to physical acts of lust but also to lust in the mind. You must get rid of both in order to transcend the stress of entanglement with perceived objects. You should become as pure as the glistening frost. Then, quite naturally, you will become enlightened. Then the three evils of the mind — greed, anger, and delusion — will have no cause to come forth, and the four errors of speech — coarse language, hurtful speech, lies, and duplicity — will not occur. (VI, 64–5)

"As for people who cannot get rid of their stubborn habits, teach them to recite single-mindedly the mantra of supreme efficacy, which is called 'Mahā-Sitātapatra' — the 'Great White Canopy.'[1] This is the mantra spo-

[1] That is, the Śūraṅgama Mantra.

ken by the Buddha whom I make appear from my unconditioned mind
— the Buddha who is seated invisible to ordinary sight, amidst a blaze of
light on a precious lotus-flower at the crown of my head.

What is most important is to recite the mantra single-mindedly. Don't have two
minds about it; don't recite the mantra and doubt its usefulness at the same
time. That is to be caught between belief and doubt. You are one person, but
you end up with two minds. One mind thinks that perhaps there is some usefulness to the recitation, while the other mind says, "What am I doing reciting
things that I don't even understand?" Watch out for that kind of dividedness.
Recite single-mindedly.

The Sanskrit word "mahā" means "great," and "sitātapatra"[2] refers to the
white canopy that appears in space above you when you recite. The size of
the canopy depends on the level of your skill. If your skill is great and lofty,
there will be no disasters for thousands of miles around you while you recite
this phrase of the mantra. If you have only a small amount of skill, the canopy
will only cover your own head and will protect you alone. When a greatly virtuous and highly accomplished member of the Sangha recites this line of the
mantra, his or her entire country can benefit from it. The entire area will be free
from calamities, great disasters will turn into small ones, and small disasters
won't happen at all. Now at this Dharma-assembly we are holding to explain
the Śūraṅgama Sūtra,[3] a lot of people are practicing this esoteric Dharma of
the Buddha, so I believe that all of America is benefiting from it. Americans
may not be aware of it, but our practice is saving many of their lives. It is all
done invisibly, and they never have any idea of who has saved them or even
that they have been saved. Nor do we wish them to know. This is a case of
there being no giver and no recipient. The three aspects of giving — giver, gift,
and recipient — are empty. When we rescue people, it is not necessary to get
them to thank us. This is just what is wonderful about it. (VI, 66–7)

[2] For recitation of the mantra, *sitātapatra* is represented by the Chinese transliterations
sa-dan-duo buo-da-la and *xi-dan-duo buo-da-la*. The phrase appears as lines 95, 365, and 531
in the mantra.

[3] At the Buddhist Lecture Hall, San Francisco, 1968. See the introduction, p. li.

"Consider, moreover, that in previous lifetimes during many eons, you and the young Mātaṅga woman developed affinities with each other, which led to habits of love and devotion. It has not been for one lifetime only, nor even for one eon only. Yet hearing me proclaim the Dharma freed her mind forever from the entanglements of love. Now she is an Arhat,[4] though she had been a mere courtesan, someone who had never intended to undertake spiritual cultivation. But by the hidden aid of the mantra's power, she quickly became one who needs no further instruction. You Hearers of the Teaching in this assembly who seek to board the greatest of vehicles in your resolute quest to become Buddhas should reach your goal with no more effort than the wind needs to scatter a handful of dust into the air. Is there any danger that you will meet with difficulty?

"Those who wish to establish a place for awakening in the time of the Dharma's ending should begin by undertaking to follow the monks' prohibitory precepts. They should seek a teacher, an elder monk who himself observes the precepts with purity. Further, they must receive precepts[5] from a member of the Sangha who is truly pure; otherwise they will not succeed in following those precepts. After the practitioners have received precepts, they should put on new clothes or newly washed clothes, and then in a quiet place burn incense and recite one hundred and eight times the efficacious mantra spoken by the Buddha who is made to appear from the mind of the Thus-Come One. Then they may establish the place for awakening and safeguard its boundaries.

"These spiritual practitioners should ask the peerless Thus-Come Ones throughout the ten directions — each without departing from his own land — to pour down a light of great compassion on the head of each practitioner. Then, Ānanda, in the time of the Dharma's ending, pure monks, nuns, and white-robed laity and other almsgivers, in whose minds all sexual desire and all craving have been extinguished and who

---

[4] At the third stage.

[5] That is, make formal vows to follow moral precepts in a ceremony of transmission presided over by a senior monk.

follow the Buddha's pure precepts, should enter a place for awakening and there make the vows of a Bodhisattva. If they can bathe before re-entering their place of awakening and if they can continue their practice throughout the six periods of the day and the six periods of the night without sleep for twenty-one days, I myself will appear before them to bless each one of them by circling my hand over the crown of his head, and I will help each one become enlightened.

The four great vows of a Bodhisattva are:

1) Beings can't be counted, but I vow to save them all.
2) Afflictions have no limit, but I vow to end them all.
3) Dharmas can't be numbered, but I vow to learn them all.
4) The Buddhas' bodhi is supreme; but I have vowed to realize it. (VI, 72)

Ānanda said respectfully to the Buddha, "World-Honored One, I have received the Thus-Come One's supremely compassionate instruction, and my mind has already awakened. I myself know how to practice so that I can realize the enlightenment of one who needs no further instruction. But suppose spiritual practitioners should wish to establish a place for awakening in the time of the Dharma's ending. How may they safeguard its boundaries in accord with the Buddha's rules concerning purity?"

The Buddha said to Ānanda, "People in the time of the Dharma's ending who wish to establish a place for awakening should begin by finding a strong white ox living in the Himalayas. It should be an ox that feeds upon rich and fragrant grasses and drinks only the pure waters of the mountain snows. The dung of such an ox will be of an exceptional purity.[6] Those who wish to establish a place for awakening may mix this pure ox-dung with sandalwood incense and spread the mixture upon the ground.

"The dung of an ox that does not live in the Himalayas will be foul-smelling and too unclean to be applied to the ground of a place for awakening. If that is all the spiritual practitioners can obtain, then instead

[6] In India to this day, farmers use the dry droppings of oxen for fuel and to plaster the walls of their houses.

they should look for a spot on the plain where yellow loam[7] can be found. They should dig up the loam from a depth of about five and a half feet[8] and then mix it with sandalwood incense, aloeswood incense, storax,[9] frankincense, saffron, teak resin, birthwort,[10] basil, spikenard,[11] and cloves. They should grind these ten fragrant substances into a powder, sift them together with the loam, and spread the mixture as a paste on the ground of the place for awakening. The place should be octagonal and sixty-five feet across.[12]

"A lotus made of gold, silver, copper, or wood should be placed in the center of the place for awakening, and a bowl filled with dew collected during the eighth lunar month should be placed in the center of the flower. An abundance of flower petals should be made to float upon the water in the bowl. Eight round mirrors should be arranged around the flower and bowl so that the mirrors face outward in each of the eight directions. Next, sixteen lotus flowers and sixteen elegant censers should be placed in front of the mirrors; the censers should alternate with the flowers. Only aloeswood incense should be burned in these censers, and they should be burned in such a way as to produce no flames.

"The practitioners should make fried cakes with sixteen jars of the milk of a white cow and then set the cakes out onto sixteen dishes. They should place raw sugar upon sixteen other dishes. Upon sixteen other dishes they should place gruel made from milk and rice; and in the same

---

[7] Probably loess, an unstratified deposit of yellow-brown loam, common in both India and China, as well as in North America and Europe.

[8] 1.65 meters, Ch. *wu chi* 五尺, five chi; one chi is equivalent to 33 centimeters in modern measure and the same in the Tang period, when the Sutra was translated into Chinese.

[9] A balsam secreted by the liquidambar tree in response to injuries in the bark, common in ancient commerce for its value as a fragrance.

[10] A widespread family (*aristolochiaceae*) of evergreen and deciduous woody vines and herbaceous perennials used in the treatment of wounds.

[11] A flowering plant of the valerian family. Its rhizomes can be crushed and distilled into an intensely aromatic amber-colored essential oil, used since ancient times as a perfume and in the Āryuvedic tradition as a sedative.

[12] 19.8 meters, Ch. *zhang liu* 丈六, six zhang; one zhang equals ten chi 尺 (see note 8 above).

manner, storax, honeyed ginger, clarified butter, and filtered honey should be distributed so that there are sixteen dishes of each of these eight kinds of offerings. These should be distributed by setting dishes containing each of the eight offerings behind each of the sixteen flowers as offerings to the Buddhas and great Bodhisattvas.

"At mealtime and at midnight, the practitioners should prepare a pint[13] of honey and mix it three times with clarified butter. They should place a small burner in front of the place for awakening, prepare a decoction of storax, bathe charcoal with the decoction, and then ignite the charcoal, letting it blaze forth. The butter and honey should be tossed upon the flames. As long as it lasts, the fragrant smoke will be an offering to the Buddhas and Bodhisattvas.

> There are many practices like this in the Esoteric school. Monks of this school often burn combinations of honey and butter and offer them to the Buddhas. They burn not only that but anything else of value, such as gold, jewels, and other valuable materials. They burn them first, then offer them to the Buddhas. (VI, 78)

"Outside the four walls of the room in which the place for awakening is located, the practitioners should hang banners and arrangements of flowers. Further, they should adorn the walls inside the room with images of the Thus-Come Ones and the Bodhisattvas of the ten directions. Centered on the wall facing south, images of the Buddha Vairocana, the Buddha Śākyamuni, the Bodhisattva Maitreya, the Buddha Akṣobhya, and the Buddha Amitābha should be displayed. On one side of those images, an image of one of the imposing manifestations of the Bodhisattva Who Hears the Cries of the World should be shown;[14] and on the other side, an image of the Bodhisattva-King Vajra-Treasury.[15] On either side

---

[13] Half a liter, Ch. *ban sheng* 半升, half of a sheng; the sheng is equivalent to slightly more than a liter.

[14] See part 6.2, p. 245.

[15] Ch. *jin gang zang wang pusa* 金剛藏王菩薩. This may be Vajrapāṇi. His followers are the *vajradhara,* who brandish the vajra-implement (sometimes translated as "thunderbolt").

of the door, images should be placed of Lord Śakra, King Brahma, Fire-Head,[16] the Blue Durgā,[17] Kuṇḍalī-rāja, Bhṛkuṭi, and the Four Celestial Kings, together with Vināyaka. Also, eight mirrors should be suspended from the ceiling in such a way that they directly face the other mirrors which have already been set up in the place for awakening. The mirrors will then reflect each other in infinite repetitions.

> The Buddha Akṣobhya is in the east; he is also known as the Buddha Master Healer. The name "Akṣobhya" means "unmoving." The east is usually associated with movement, but the Buddha of the east does not move. Amitābha is the Buddha of the West; his name means "infinite light." The alternative form of his name is "Amitāyus," which means "infinite life." . . . The Bodhisattva-King Vajra-Treasury is a Dharma-protector; his stern countenance can be terrifying to behold. Beside them, images of the Lords Śakra and Brahma are to be displayed. Śakra is the lord of the Heaven of the Thirty-Three; Brahma is lord of the Great Brahma Heaven. "Ucchuṣma" means "Fire-Head." Blue Durgā has a blue face and is a Dharma-protector. Kuṇḍalī-rāja is a vajra-spirit; his name means "releasing the knots of resentment." Bhṛkuṭi is also a Dharma-protector. Vināyaka is one of the names of the god Gaṇeśa, who has an elephant's head and a man's body. He too is a Dharma-protector. . . . The bizarre appearances of these Dharma-protectors are intended to instill awe in people so that they will behave themselves. At the door of the place for awakening, then, these images are placed on both sides for protection. (VI, 78–9)

"During the first seven days, the practitioners should bow with the utmost sincerity to the Thus-Come Ones, the great Bodhisattvas, and the Arhats of the ten directions. During the six periods of the day and the six periods of the night, the practitioners should recite the mantra continuously while circumambulating the place for awakening, single-mindedly repeating the mantra one hundred and eight times. During the next seven days, the practitioners should focus their minds on the Bodhisattva's vows,

---

[16] Fire-Head (Skt. Ucchuṣma) is the eighteenth of the twenty-five sages who speak in part 6.1 above.

[17] The Goddess Beyond Reach, an eight-armed form of Pārvatī, is often depicted riding a tiger or a lion. She is the mother of Gaṇeśa, who here is called Vināyaka.

not letting their minds turn aside from them. My instructions to you in the monastic code have included teachings about the making of vows.

"During the last seven days, the practitioners should single-mindedly recite the Buddha's Mantra of the White Canopy continuously throughout the twelve periods of the day and night. On the final day, the Thus-Come Ones from all ten directions will appear at the same time. They and their light will be reflected in the mirrors as each of them circles his right hand on the crown of the head of each of the practitioners. If people can practice samādhi in an excellent place for awakening like this in the age of the Dharma's ending, their bodies and minds will become as pure and bright as crystal. But, Ānanda, if the precept-master from whom a monk received precepts was not pure, or if any of the other monks in his group is not pure, then the practice in the place of awakening is unlikely to be successful.

> Throughout the six periods of the day and the six periods of the night, you should continually recite the mantra — the entire Śūraṅgama Mantra — while circumambulating the place for awakening. . . . You're not thinking of anything else; you're reciting single-mindedly. . . . Each time you recite, go through the mantra one hundred and eight times without stopping. (VI, 80–1)
>
> The mantra won't work if any one of the people involved is impure, that is, if they haven't followed the precepts strictly. One is not supposed to kill, but they have killed; or one is not supposed to steal, but they have stolen; one is not supposed to commit acts of sexual misconduct, but they have done so; one is not supposed to lie, but they have lied. The Buddha taught us not to lie, but they dispense with the "not" and just hold to the lie. If that is how it is, then all their work of spiritual cultivation, all the mantras they recited, will come to nothing. (VI, 83)

"After the three weeks, the practitioners should remain sitting upright and peacefully for a hundred days. If their roots in the Dharma are deep and strong, they will not rise from their seats during that time, and they will become Arhats at the first stage. Even if they do not reach the level of a sage in body and mind, they will be certain that in the future they will become Buddhas.

One sits in meditation, but not like some people who sit still for two hours and consider it a superb feat. They consider themselves to be outstanding people, but actually, if we compare that to what is described here, they are like kittens compared to a lion. "Sitting upright" means that one does not lean to the left or right, or lean forward or back, or get up or stretch out one's legs. "Sitting peacefully" means that one is not troubled by anything. Sitting for a hundred days means one does not sleep and does not get up to eat or even to relieve oneself. One simply sits for one hundred days. (VI, 84)

"You asked how to establish a place for awakening. This is how it should be done."

2
The Śūraṅgama Mantra

Ānanda bowed at the Buddha's feet and said to him respectfully, "Ever since I entered the monastic life, I have presumed upon the Buddha's affection. I have sought merely to be learned, and as a result, I have not yet gained freedom from conditioned phenomena.[18] I was ensnared by the evil Brahma-Heaven spell and could not escape, though my mind remained aware. Fortunately, Mañjuśrī arrived to rescue me with the efficacious mantra spoken by the Buddha at the crown of the Thus-Come One's head. But I benefited from its hidden power without actually hearing it myself. I sincerely hope that the Buddha will proclaim the mantra again out of his great kindness and out of his compassion for all the practitioners in this great assembly, as well as for beings of the future who will be bound to the cycle of death and rebirth, so that the esoteric sounds of the mantra may set their bodies and minds free."

Everyone in the great assembly thereupon bowed to the Buddha. They waited to hear the sections and sub-sections of the esoteric mantra.

> The sections of the esoteric mantra mentioned here are the five main divisions of the Śūraṅgama Mantra. The sub-sections are smaller parts consisting of several lines each, such as the opening lines, *"Na mo sa dan tuo, su qie duo ye, e la he di, san miao san pu tuo xie."* (VI, 89)
>
> The five sections of the mantra correspond to five regions: north, south, east, west, and center. . . . There are five sections because there are five great demonic armies in this world. Buddhas occupy the five regions to suppress the demons. If there were no Buddhas, the demons could appear openly in the world.
>
> Within the five sections of the mantra there are some thirty Dharmas, and within these are more than a hundred further Dharmas that can be discussed in detail. Five of the major kinds of these Dharmas are as follows:
>
> 1) Dharmas for accomplishment: These cause people who recite the mantra to have success in their endeavors and to fulfill their vows and wishes.

---

[18] That is, he is not yet an Arhat at the fourth stage.

2) Dharmas that bring benefit: Reciters of this mantra bring benefit to themselves and to other people as well.

3) Dharmas of hooking and summoning: These Dharmas allow the reciter to summon weird beings, demons, and ghosts and to capture them no matter how far away from the reciter they may be.

4) Dharmas of subduing: Demons also make use of spiritual powers and mantras. When you recite your mantras, they recite their mantras. But the Śūraṅgama Mantra can defeat all their mantras. The Mātaṅga woman's spell that got Ānanda into trouble lost its power as soon as the Śūraṅgama Mantra was recited, particularly because of the great five-line heart of the mantra:

chi tuo ni

e jia la

mi li zhu

bo li dan la ye

ning jie li.

This is the mantra for destroying the mantras and spells of celestial demons and followers of wrong paths.

5) Dharmas that prevent disasters: Any calamity that is to occur can be prevented by this mantra. For instance, someone who is about to fall into the ocean and drown can avoid catastrophe by reciting the Śūraṅgama Mantra. He might fall into the ocean, but he won't drown. Perhaps you are in a boat that by any measure ought to sink, but you recite this mantra and the boat does not go down. Maybe you're in an airplane that is destined to crash, but you recite the Śūraṅgama Mantra and the plane lands without incident. . . . Usually what happens is that there is alarm but no danger.

In general, the mantra contains Dharmas of auspiciousness. This means that when you recite the mantra, everything goes just as you would like. There are so many advantages to the mantra that in several years one could not even get close to expressing them all. (VI, 92–4)[19]

---

[19] The Venerable Master Hua Hsüan gave a detailed series of lectures explaining the meaning and use of each of the 554 lines of the mantra. See Tripitaka Master Hua, *Shurangama Mantra Verses and Commentary,* in five vols., trans. Buddhist Text Translation Society (Talmage, California: Dharma-Realm Buddhist University, 1981).

Then from the prominence at the crown of the World-Honored One's head[20] there welled forth a magnificent light, radiant as hundreds of precious gems, and a magnificent thousand-petal lotus welled forth from within that light. The Thus-Come One made appear a Buddha who was seated at the center of the magnificent flower, and from the crown of that Buddha's head, ten beams of light shone forth as if from hundreds of precious gems. Everywhere throughout space there appeare, from within those beams of ligh, ten times as many vajra-warriors as there are sand-grains in the River Ganges. Some of them held aloft a mountain, while others brandished a vajra-implement. All in the great assembly gazed upward, overwhelmed by awe and wonder. Hoping to receive the Buddha's compassionate blessing, they listened intently as the Buddha who sat invisible to ordinary sight amidst a blaze of light at the crown of the Thus-Come One's head proclaimed this spiritual mantra:[21]

I.

1) na mo sa dan tuo

2) su qie duo ye

3) e la he di

4) san miao san pu tuo xie

5) na mo sa dan tuo

6) fo tuo ju zhi shai ni shan

7) na mo sa po

8) bo tuo bo di

9) sa duo pi bi

10) na mo sa duo nan

11) san miao san pu tuo

12) ju zhi nan

13) suo she la po jia

14) seng qie nan

15) na mo lu ji e luo han duo nan

16) na mo su lu duo bo nuo nan

17) na mo suo jie li tuo qie mi nan

18) na mo lu ji san miao qie duo nan

19) san miao qie bo la

20) di bo duo nuo nan

21) na mo ti po li shai nan

22) na mo xi tuo ye

[20] The uṣṇīṣa.

[21] The numbering of the five groups and the individual lines are added for reference and are not recited as part of the mantra. In the Chinese text, the mantra is given in transliterated syllables, which convey approximate equivalents to the sound of the original syllables of the Sanskrit-related language that was used in India for the recitation of Buddhist mantras. The present translation gives a transliteration of the Chinese syllables according to the standard pinyin transliteration system. Readers who wish to recite the mantra from these pages should be familiar with the pinyin system.

23) pi di ye

24) tuo la li shai nan

25) she po nu

26) jie la he

27) suo he suo la mo tuo nan

28) na mo ba la he mo ni

29) na mo yin tuo la ye

30) na mo po qie po di

31) lu tuo la ye

32) wu mo bo di

33) suo xi ye ye

34) na mo po qie po di

35) nuo la ye

36) na ye

37) pan zhe mo he san mu tuo la

38) na mo xi jie li duo ye

39) na mo po qie po di

40) mo he jia la ye

41) di li bo la na

42) qie la pi tuo la

43) bo na jia la ye

44) e di mu di

45) shi mo she nuo ni

46) po xi ni

47) mo dan li qie na

48) na mo xi jie li duo ye

49) na mo po qie po di

50) duo tuo qie duo ju la ye

51) na mo bo tou mo ju la ye

52) na mo ba she la ju la ye

53) na mo mo ni ju la ye

54) na mo qie she ju la ye

55) na mo po qie po di

56) di li cha

57) shu la xi na

58) bo la he la na la she ye

59) duo tuo qie duo ye

60) na mo po qie po di

61) na mo e mi duo po ye

62) duo tuo qie duo ye

63) e la he di

64) san miao san pu tuo ye

65) na mo po qie po di

66) e chu pi ye

67) duo tuo qie duo ye

68) e la he di

69) san miao san pu tuo ye

70) na mo po qie po di

71) bi sha she ye

72) ju lu fei zhu li ye

73) bo la po la she ye

74) duo tuo qie duo ye

75) na mo po qie po di

76) san bu shi bi duo

77) sa lian nai la la she ye

78) duo tuo qie duo ye

79) e la he di

80) san miao san pu tuo ye

81) na mo po qie po di

82) she ji ye mu nuo ye

83) duo tuo qie duo ye

84) e la he di

85) san miao san pu tuo ye

86) na mo po qie po di

87) la dan na ji du la she ye

88) duo tuo qie duo ye

89) e la he di

90) san miao san pu tuo ye

91) di piao
92) na mo sa jie li duo
93) yi tan po qie po duo
94) sa dan tuo qie du shai ni shan
95) sa dan duo bo da lan
96) na mo e po la shi dan
97) bo la di
98) yang qi la
99) sa la po
100) bo duo jie la he
101) ni jie la he
102) jie jia la he ni
103) ba la bi di ye
104) chi tuo ni
105) e jia la
106) mi li zhu
107) bo li dan la ye
108) ning jie li
109) sa la po
110) pan tuo nuo
111) mu cha ni
112) sa la po
113) tu shai jia
114) tu xi fa
115) bo na ni
116) fa la ni
117) zhe du la
118) shi di nan
119) jie la he
120) suo he sa la ruo she
121) pi duo beng suo na jie li
122) e shai zha bing she di nan
123) na cha cha dan la ruo she
124) bo la sa tuo na jie li

125) e shai zha nan
126) mo he jie la he ruo she
127) pi duo beng sa na jie li
128) sa po she du lu
129) ni po la ruo she
130) hu lan tu xi fa
131) nan zhe na she ni
132) bi sha she
133) xi dan la
134) e ji ni
135) wu tuo jia la ruo she
136) e bo la shi duo ju la
137) mo he bo la zhan chi
138) mo he die duo
139) mo he di she
140) mo he shui duo she po la
141) mo he ba la pan tuo la
142) po xi ni
143) e li ye duo la
144) pi li ju zhi
145) shi po pi she ye
146) ba she la mo li di
147) pi she lu duo
148) bo teng wang jia
149) ba she la zhi he nuo e zhe
150) mo la zhi po
151) bo la zhi duo
152) ba she la shan chi
153) pi she la zhe
154) shan duo she
155) pi ti po
156) bu shi duo
157) su mo lu bo
158) mo he shui duo

159) e li ye duo la
160) mo he po la e bo la
161) ba she la shang jie la zhi po
162) ba she la ju mo li
163) ju lan tuo li
164) ba she la he sa duo zhe
165) pi di ye
166) qian zhe nuo
167) mo li jia
168) ku su mu
169) po jie la duo nuo
170) pi lu zhe na
171) ju li ye
172) ye la tu
173) shai ni shan
174) pi zhe lan po mo ni zhe
175) ba she la jia na jia bo la po
176) lu she na
177) ba she la dun zhi zhe
178) shui duo zhe
179) jia mo la
180) cha che shi
181) bo la po
182) yi di yi di
183) mu tuo la
184) jie na
185) suo pi la chan
186) jue fan du
187) yin tu na mo mo xie

II.

188) wu xin
189) li shai jie na
190) bo la she xi duo

191) sa dan tuo
192) qie du shai ni shan
193) hu xin du lu yong
194) zhan po na
195) hu xin du lu yong
196) xi dan po na
197) hu xin du lu yong
198) bo la shai di ye
199) san bo cha
200) na jie la
201) hu xin du lu yong
202) sa po yao cha
203) he la cha suo
204) jie la he ruo she
205) pi teng beng sa na jie la
206) hu xin du lu yong
207) zhe du la
208) shi di nan
209) jie la he
210) suo he sa la nan
211) pi teng beng sa na la
212) hu xin du lu yong
213) la cha
214) po qie fan
215) sa dan tuo
216) qie du shai ni shan
217) bo la dian
218) she ji li
219) mo he suo he sa la
220) bo shu suo he sa la
221) shi li sha
222) ju zhi suo he sa ni
223) di li e bi ti shi po li duo
224) zha zha ying jia

225) mo he ba she lu tuo la
226) di li pu po na
227) man cha la
228) wu xin
229) suo xi di
230) bo po du
231) mo mo
232) yin tu na mo mo xie

III.
233) la she po ye
234) zhu la ba ye
235) e qi ni po ye
236) wu tuo jia po ye
237) pi sha po ye
238) she sa duo la po ye
239) po la zhao jie la po ye
240) tu shai cha po ye
241) e she ni po ye
242) e jia la
243) mi li zhu po ye
244) tuo la ni bu mi jian
245) bo qie bo tuo po ye
246) wu la jia po duo po ye
247) la she tan cha po ye
248) nuo qie po ye
249) pi tiao dan po ye
250) su bo la na po ye
251) yao cha jie la he
252) la cha si jie la he
253) bi li duo jie la he
254) pi she zhe jie la he
255) bu duo jie la he
256) jiu pan cha jie la he

257) bu dan na jie la he
258) jia zha bu dan na jie la he
259) xi qian du jie la he
260) e bo xi mo la jie la he
261) wu tan mo tuo jie la he
262) che ye jie la he
263) xi li po di jie la he
264) she duo he li nan
265) jie po he li nan
266) lu di la he li nan
267) mang suo he li nan
268) mi tuo he li nan
269) mo she he li nan
270) she duo he li nu
271) shi bi duo he li nan
272) pi duo he li nan
273) po duo he li nan
274) e shu zhe he li nu
275) zhi duo he li nu
276) di shan sa pi shan
277) sa po jie la he nan
278) pi tuo ye she
279) chen tuo ye mi
280) ji la ye mi
281) bo li ba la zhe jia
282) qi li dan
283) pi tuo ye she
284) chen tuo ye mi
285) ji la ye mi
286) cha yan ni
287) qi li dan
288) pi tuo ye she
289) chen tuo ye mi
290) ji la ye mi

291) mo he bo shu bo dan ye
292) lu tuo la
293) qi li dan
294) pi tuo ye she
295) chen tuo ye mi
296) ji la ye mi
297) nuo la ye na
298) qi li dan
299) pi tuo ye she
300) chen tuo ye mi
301) ji la ye mi
302) dan tuo qie lu cha xi
303) qi li dan
304) pi tuo ye she
305) chen tuo ye mi
306) ji la ye mi
307) mo he jia la
308) mo dan li qie na
309) qi li dan
310) pi tuo ye she
311) chen tuo ye mi
312) ji la ye mi
313) jia bo li jia
314) qi li dan
315) pi tuo ye she
316) chen tuo ye mi
317) ji la ye mi
318) she ye jie la
319) mo du jie la
320) sa po la tuo suo da na
321) qi li dan
322) pi tuo ye she
323) chen tuo ye mi
324) ji la ye mi

325) zhe du la
326) po qi ni
327) qi li dan
328) pi tuo ye she
329) chen tuo ye mi
330) ji la ye mi
331) pi li yang qi li zhi
332) nan tuo ji sha la
333) qie na bo di
334) suo xi ye
335) qi li dan
336) pi tuo ye she
337) chen tuo ye mi
338) ji la ye mi
339) na jie na she la po na
340) qi li dan
341) pi tuo ye she
342) chen tuo ye mi
343) ji la ye mi
344) e luo han
345) qi li dan
346) pi tuo ye she
347) chen tuo ye mi
348) ji la ye mi
349) pi duo la qie
350) qi li dan
351) pi tuo ye she
352) chen tuo ye mi
353) ji la ye mi
354) ba she la bo ni
355) ju xi ye ju xi ye
356) jia di bo di
357) qi li dan
358) pi tuo ye she

359) chen tuo ye mi

360) ji la ye mi

361) la cha wang

362) po qie fan

363) yin tu na mo mo xie

IV.

364) po qie fan

365) sa dan duo bo da la

366) na mo cui du di

367) e xi duo na la la jia

368) bo la po

369) xi pu zha

370) pi jia sa dan duo bo de li

371) shi fo la shi fo la

372) tuo la tuo la

373) pin tuo la pin tuo la

374) chen tuo chen tuo

375) hu xin hu xin

376) pan zha pan zha pan zha
     pan zha pan zha

377) suo he

378) xi xi pan

379) e mu jia ye pan

380) e bo la ti he duo pan

381) po la bo la tuo pan

382) e su la

383) pi tuo la

384) bo jia pan

385) sa po ti pi bi pan

386) sa po na qie bi pan

387) sa po yao cha bi pan

388) sa po qian ta po bi pan

389) sa po bu dan na bi pan

390) jia zha bu dan na bi pan

391) sa po tu lang zhi di bi pan

392) sa po tu si bi li

393) qi shai di bi pan

394) sa po shi po li bi pan

395) sa po e bo xi mo li bi pan

396) sa po she la po na bi pan

397) sa po di di ji bi pan

398) sa po dan mo tuo ji bi pan

399) sa po pi tuo ye

400) la shi zhe li bi pan

401) she ye jie la

402) mo du jie la

403) sa po la tuo suo tuo ji bi pan

404) pi di ye

405) zhe li bi pan

406) zhe du la

407) fu qi ni bi pan

408) ba she la

409) ju mo li

410) pi tuo ye

411) la shi bi pan

412) mo he bo la ding yang

413) yi qi li bi pan

414) ba she la shang jie la ye

415) bo la zhang qi la she ye pan

416) mo he jia la ye

417) mo he mo dan li jia na

418) na mo suo jie li duo ye pan

419) bi shai na bei ye pan

420) bo la he mo ni ye pan

421) e qi ni ye pan

422) mo he jie li ye pan

423) jie la tan chi ye pan

424) mie dan li ye pan
425) lao dan li ye pan
426) zhe wen cha ye pan
427) jie luo la dan li ye pan
428) jia bo li ye pan
429) e di mu zhi duo
430) jia shi mo she nuo
431) po si ni ye pan
432) yan ji zhi
433) sa tuo po xie
434) mo mo yin tu na mo mo xie

V.

435) tu shai zha zhi duo
436) e mo dan li zhi duo
437) wu she he la
438) qie po he la
439) lu di la he la
440) po suo he la
441) mo she he la
442) she duo he la
443) shi bi duo he la
444) ba liao ye he la
445) qian tuo he la
446) bu shi bo he la
447) po la he la
448) po xie he la
449) bo bo zhi duo
450) tu shai zha zhi duo
451) lao tuo la zhi duo
452) yao cha jie la he
453) la cha suo jie la he
454) bi li duo jie la he
455) pi she zhe jie la he

456) bu duo jie la he
457) jiu pan cha jie la he
458) xi qian tuo jie la he
459) wu dan mo tuo jie la he
460) che ye jie la he
461) e bo sa mo la jie la he
462) zhai que ge
463) cha qi ni jie la he
464) li fo di jie la he
465) she mi jia jie la he
466) she ju ni jie la he
467) mu tuo la
468) nan di jia jie la he
469) e lan po jie la he
470) qian du bo ni jie la he
471) shi fa la
472) yin jia xi jia
473) zhui di yao jia
474) dan li di yao jia
475) zhe tu tuo jia
476) ni ti shi fa la
477) bi shan mo shi fa la
478) bo di jia
479) bi di jia
480) shi li shai mi jia
481) suo ni bo di jia
482) sa po shi fa la
483) shi lu ji di
484) mo tuo pi da lu zhi qian
485) e qi lu qian
486) mu que lu qian
487) jie li tu lu qian
488) jie la he
489) jie lan jie na shu lan

490) dan duo shu lan
491) qi li ye shu lan
492) mo mo shu lan
493) ba li shi po shu lan
494) bi li shai zha shu lan
495) wu tuo la shu lan
496) jie zhi shu lan
497) ba xi di shu lan
498) wu lu shu lan
499) chang qie shu lan
500) he xi duo shu lan
501) ba tuo shu lan
502) suo fang ang qie
503) bo la zhang qie shu lan
504) bu duo bi duo cha
505) cha qi ni
506) shi po la
507) tuo tu lu jia
508) jian du lu ji zhi
509) po lu duo pi
510) sa bo lu
511) he ling qie
512) shu sha dan la
513) suo na jie la
514) pi sha yu jia
515) e qi ni
516) wu tuo jia
517) mo la pi la
518) jian duo la
519) e jia la
520) mi li du
521) da lian bu jia
522) di li la zha
523) bi li shai zhi jia

524) sa po na ju la
525) si yin qie bi
526) jie la li yao cha
527) dan la chu
528) mo la shi
529) fei di shan
530) suo pi shan
531) xi dan duo bo da la
532) mo he ba she lu
533) shai ni shan
534) mo he bo lai zhang qi lan
535) ye bo tu tuo
536) she yu she nuo
537) bian da li na
538) pi tuo ye
539) pan tan jia lu mi
540) di shu
541) pan tan jia lu mi
542) bo la pi tuo
543) pan tan jia lu mi
544) da zhi tuo
545) nan
546) e na li
547) pi she ti
548) pi la
549) ba she la
550) tuo li
551) pan tuo pan tuo ni
552) ba she la bang ni pan
553) hu xin du lu yong pan
554) suo po he

3
The Powers of the Mantra

"Ānanda, all Buddhas throughout the ten directions are born from the esoteric lines of this Mantra of the White Canopy, with its subtle and wonderful phrases and sections spoken by the Buddha seated within the light at the crown of Thus-Come One's head.

"By means of this mantra of the mind, the Thus-Come Ones of the ten directions have gained supreme, right, and universal wisdom.

"Wielding this mantra of the mind, the Thus-Come Ones of the ten directions subdue all demons and show the right way to all who are on a wrong path.

"Conveyed by the power of this mantra of the mind, the Thus-Come Ones of the ten directions, each seated upon a magnificent lotus-flower, appear in response to the needs of beings in numberless lands.

"Holding fast to this mantra of the mind, the Thus-Come Ones of the ten directions appear in numberless lands to turn the great Wheel of the Dharma.

"Employing this mantra of the mind, the Thus-Come Ones of the ten directions bestow predictions upon beings everywhere, each one circling his right hand over the crown of the head of each of these beings. They bestow predictions[22] even upon beings who have not yet become enlightened.

"Relying on this mantra of the mind, the Thus-Come Ones of the ten directions also rescue beings everywhere from suffering in its various forms: the sufferings endured in the hells; the sufferings endured by hungry ghosts; the sufferings endured by animals; the sufferings endured by the blind, the deaf, and the mute; the sufferings caused by the presence of people one detests; the sufferings caused by the absence of people one loves; the sufferings caused by the failure to get what one wants; and the sufferings caused by the fire of the five aggregates. The Thus-Come Ones of the ten directions can rescue beings from sudden misfortunes, whether

---

[22] That is, predictions that at such and such a time and place, these beings will become Buddhas.

great or small, whether caused by thieves, armies, kings, imprisonment, wind, fire, flood, hunger, thirst, or penury. The Thus-Come Ones can dispel all these misfortunes by reciting this mantra.

"In harmony with this mantra of the mind, the Thus-Come Ones of the ten directions, in the four aspects of their comportment, have previously served good and wise teachers and have made appropriate offerings to them. They have been chosen as great Dharma-Princes among the disciples of as many Thus-Come Ones as there are sand-grains in the River Ganges.

"By putting into practice this mantra of the mind, the Thus-Come Ones of the ten directions gather together the beings with whom they have strong affinities and ensure that any of these beings who are adherents of the Lesser Vehicle will not be alarmed upon hearing the esoteric teachings concerning the Matrix of the Thus-Come One.

"Through reciting this mantra of the mind, the Thus-Come Ones of the ten directions realize supreme enlightenment and enter the perfect nirvana as they sit beneath a bodhi tree.

"By transmitting this mantra of the mind, the Thus-Come Ones of the ten directions pass on the work of the Buddha's Dharma to others so that after their nirvana the Dharma can endure and so that all can remain pure by following the precepts strictly and flawlessly.

"Were I to continue speaking of the virtues of this Mantra of the White Canopy, which is proclaimed from within the blaze of light at the crown of the Buddha's head, I could continue to explain it from morning to night without interruption and without repeating myself and yet still not finish, even if I were to keep on speaking for as many eons as there are sand-grains in the River Ganges.

"This mantra may also be called 'The Mantra that is Spoken from above the Crown of the Thus-Come One's Head.'

"All of you who still need instruction and have not yet escaped from the cycle of death and rebirth, but have vowed with great sincerity to become Arhats, must be certain to practice this mantra if you wish to remain free of demonic influences while you are seated in your place of awakening.

"Ānanda, the people of any country in any world can write out this mantra on birch-bark, palm-leaves,[23] papyrus,[24] or white cotton cloth — whatever material is native to their region — and each of them can keep the written mantra in a fragrant pouch. You should know that even if these people are dull-witted and cannot recite or memorize the mantra, they can still wear the pouch or keep it in their dwellings. If they do this, then throughout their lives, no poison will ever be able to harm them.

"Ānanda, I will now tell you more about how this mantra can protect beings of the world and rescue them from danger, how it can deliver them from every fear and help them attain transcendent wisdom.

"You should know that, after my nirvana, in the time of the Dharma's ending, people who can recite this mantra or teach others to recite it will be in no danger of being burned, or of being drowned, or of being harmed by mild or strong poisons. Further, when they are absorbed in samādhi, no evil spell will have the power to ensnare them, whether the spell be cast by gods, dragons, ghosts, or spirits, including terrestrial or celestial spirits, demonic ghosts, and nightmare ghosts. Any substance made venomous by spell, curse, or sorcerer's hex, any poisonous herb, any potion made toxic by the admixture of metals such as gold or silver, any noxious vapor derived from plants, trees, insects, or snakes, indeed any of the countless kinds of poisonous substances — all these will turn into ambrosia upon entering the mouths of people who recite this mantra. No evil spirit dwelling in a celestial body, nor any other ghost or spirit that harbors malice toward people, will have the power to work its evil on them. They will always be guarded and protected by Vināyaka and by other once-hostile ghost-kings who have been tamed by deep kindness.

There is a lot of sorcery in southern China, and also in Southeast Asia, based on mantras and spells. If you eat something poisoned by these sorcerers, you

---

[23] In India, sutras were often recorded on the leaves of the fan palm (*borassus flabelliformus*).

[24] Of this list of four writing surfaces, the third one, *zhi* 紙, paper, did not exist in ancient India. It was invented in China around 100 C.E. The Chinese translators evidently chose zhi as a recognizable substitute for the writing surface which was mentioned in the original Sanskrit but which did not exist in China. The present choice of "papyrus" is a guess at the original.

will be forever under their control and will have to do as they command. If you don't, you will die. In a world as large as this, many strange things exist. Don't suppose that if you haven't seen something, it cannot be. You may not believe that the strange things being discussed here exist, but they exist nonetheless (VI, 125).

"Ānanda, this mantra is always attended, day and night, by Bodhisat-vas in the lineage of the Bodhisattva-King Vajra-Treasury. Their numbers are eighty-four thousand ten billion trillion times the number of sand-grains in the River Ganges. Each of them is accompanied by a vast retinue of vajra-brandishing followers. These Bodhisattvas in the lineage of the Bodhisattva-King Vajra-Treasury will always be present to protect be-ings who recite this mantra and who are resolved to become enlightened. Indeed they will even protect beings whose minds are scattered and dis-orderly and lack samādhi, but who can nevertheless recite the mantra from memory.

"In ways that are hidden, all these Bodhisattvas in the lineage of the Bodhisattva-King Vajra-Treasury will focus their minds upon hasten-ing these beings toward developing spiritual awareness. These beings will then suddenly recall everything that happened to them during eighty-four thousand times as many eons as there are sand-grains in the River Ganges. They will understand these past events thoroughly and with complete certainty. From that time onward until their last rebirth they will never be born in inauspicious places where there are yakṣas, rākṣasas, pūtanas, kaṭapūtanas, kumbhāndas, piśācas, pretas, and other ghosts,[25] some of whom are visible and some of whom are not, and some of whom are intelligent and some of whom are not.

"Good people who, in eon after eon, read this mantra, recite it from memory, write it out, wear it on their bodies, or keep it in a safe place, making various offerings to it, will not be reborn into poverty or into lowly circumstances or in an unpleasant place. If they themselves have

---

[25] For more on ghosts, see the commentary at part 6.2, p. 241, and the Sutra text part 9.7. Pretas (Ch. *e gui* 餓鬼) are the "hungry ghosts." They cannot eat; whatever they take into their mouths to eat turns to fire.

not earned any karmic rewards, the Thus-Come Ones of the ten directions will transfer their own merit to them. Therefore, for an inexpressibly great number of uncountable eons as many as the sand-grains in the River Ganges, they will be born in the same generation in which a Buddha has been born. Their merit will be immeasurably great, and they will be as close to the Buddhas as the seeds of the akṣa are to each other. They will become permeated with the fragrance of spiritual practice. They will never be separated from the Buddhas.

"Further, the mantra can enable people who have broken their precepts to regain their purity. It can enable people who have not received precepts to become precepted. It can enable people who have not been vigorous to become vigorous. It can enable people who are lacking in wisdom to become wise. It can enable people who are impure to quickly become pure. It can enable people who do not follow the precepts concerning a pure diet[26] to succeed in following those precepts.

"Ānanda, suppose good people who recite this mantra violated precepts before the mantra has been given to then. Then, when they begin to recite the mantra, that karma from their precept-breaking offenses, whether grave or slight, will be immediately erased.

Someone who has violated the precepts can return to purity by reciting the Śūraṅgama Mantra, but this does not mean a mere casual recitation. Such a person must enter the mantra-recitation samādhi, in which the mantra wells up from the heart and the mantra and the person reciting it become one. The person cannot forget the mantra; it recites itself. . . . All other thoughts are wiped away, and all that remains in the mind is the recitation of the Śūraṅgama Mantra. It's like flowing water that goes on and on, rolling in from afar in wave after wave. It's like the wind that comes up invisibly but makes its presence known. When recitation reaches that state, it can enable people who have broken the precepts to regain the purity of the precepts. It can cause those who have not received the precepts to obtain them. It can cause

---

[26] A "pure diet" is one free of animal products and free of the plants of the onion family, as was made clear in part 7.2.

those who are not vigorous to become vigorous. People who aren't inclined to progress, who don't investigate the Buddha's Dharma, can spontaneously become vigorous from reciting the Śūraṅgama Mantra over a long period of time. It can enable those who lack wisdom to gain wisdom. . . . It can lead people who eat meat to become vegetarian, because they will no longer desire the flavor of meat. (VI, 133–5)

"These people may have taken intoxicants, or they may have eaten plants of the onion family or other impure foods, but the Buddhas, Bodhisattvas, vajra-brandishing warriors, gods, immortals, ghosts, and spirits will not consider that a transgression. These people may wear old and tattered clothes or clothes that have not been washed, but they will still be pure, whatever they do and wherever they are. Even if they do not set up a place for awakening, or do not enter a place for awakening, or do not follow the practice regimen, still, if they recite this mantra, their merit will be the same as if they had entered the place for awakening and had followed the practice regimen.[27] They may even have committed the five unnatural crimes,[28] which are deserving of the Unrelenting Hell; or they may be monks who have committed the four major offenses deserving of expulsion or nuns who have committed the eight major offenses deserving of expulsion;[29] yet their grave karma will be wiped away without a trace remaining, like a sand dune that has been scattered in a gale.

"Ānanda, there may be beings who, either in their present life or in their previous lives, have never repented of the serious and minor offenses they have committed during countless, innumerable eons in the past. But if they can read, recite from memory, or write out the mantra, or wear it on their person, or keep it where they are dwelling, either in their homes or where they are staying temporarily, then their accumulated karma will melt away as snow is melted by boiling liquid. Before

[27] That is, the procedure for reciting the mantra over a period of twenty-one days, as set forth above.

[28] The five unnatural crimes are matricide, patricide, killing an Arhat, disrupting monastic harmony, and shedding the blood of a Buddha.

[29] Skt. *pārājika.* The four that apply to all monastics were discussed in part 7: sexual misconduct, killing, theft, and making false claims.

long they will gain patience with the state of mind in which no mental objects arise.

"Moreover, if women who do not have children, and who wish to conceive, can recite the mantra sincerely and from memory, or if they wear this Mantra of the White Canopy, they will bear sons and daughters who are blessed with virtue and wisdom.

> The mantra should be worn above the heart, not below it, as a matter of respect. If you are not respectful toward the mantra, its efficacy will be depleted with regard to you. (VI, 141)

"If people who recite the mantra from memory wish for a long life, they will live a long life. What they wish to accomplish they will quickly accomplish. In the same way, they will also have health, good fortune, beauty, and strength. At the end of their lives, they will be reborn into whatever country in the ten directions they wish. They will certainly not be reborn among uncivilized people or at a lower level of society. By no means will they be born into any form that is less than human.

"Ānanda, suppose that in a village, a district, a province, or in an entire country, there is famine or plague, or perhaps in that place there is war, or the marauding of bandits, or the strife of rebellion, or other calamities. Then the spiritual mantra should be written out and placed on the four city gates, or in *caityas*[30] or on banners. The citizens of the country should be instructed to come to welcome the mantra with honor, to venerate it respectfully, and to sincerely make offerings to it. The citizens should also be instructed to wear the mantra on their bodies and place it in their homes. Then all the disasters will disappear.

> No matter what Dharma you practice, you must find the Middle Way. True enough, mantras are efficacious, but you must also develop your samādhi-power. Here the Sutra stresses the efficacy of the mantra, but the essential point of the Sutra is its instructions in the Dharma of reversing the hearing to

[30] *Caityas* are sacred buildings, either free-standing or carved into rock, containing stūpas surrounded by columns and adjacent areas for devotees to gather. The earliest extant caityas date from the Aśoka period (third century B.C.E.).

hear the true nature within. . . . Recite the mantra, but even while reciting you should be turning your light around to illumine within. (VI, 145)

"Ānanda, in any country and in any place where this mantra exists among the people, the celestial dragons are pleased, the weather is clement, the harvests are abundant, and all the people are happy and at peace. Further, the mantra can prevent disasters indicated by the positions of inauspicious celestial bodies. People will not suffer untimely deaths, nor will they be bound, fettered, or shackled. Day or night they will sleep peacefully, free from evil dreams.

"Ānanda, among the eighty-four thousand inauspicious heavenly bodies that indicate the coming of disasters in the Sāha world, twenty-eight major heavenly bodies are the more inauspicious among them, and among these, eight are the most influential. These heavenly bodies appear in a variety of forms. Their appearance can indicate the visitation of calamities upon living beings and the occurrence of uncanny events. But in any place where this mantra exists, all such calamities are prevented. An area of eighty-four miles[31] around such a place will be safeguarded so that no calamitous influence will ever be able to enter.

"These are the reasons why the Thus-Come One has proclaimed this mantra. In the future it will protect all who have just begun their spiritual practice so that they can enter samādhi and have peace and great tranquility in body and mind. Furthermore, they will not be harmed or vexed by any demon, ghost, or spirit, nor by any enmity, vulnerability to disaster, or karmic debt incurred in previous lives since time without beginning.

"Supposing that, besides you and others in the assembly who still need instruction, spiritual practitioners in the future establish a place of awakening and keep the precepts in accord with the instructions; supposing that they have received precepts from precept-masters who have maintained purity as members of the Sangha; and supposing that they harbor

---

[31] Skt. twelve *yojanas*, Ch. *shi er you xun* 十二由旬. A yojana was the distance a bullock could be driven before it had to be relieved of its yoke — about seven miles (eleven kilometers).

no doubts as they uphold this essential mantra; then if these good people do not gain a spiritual awakening while in this present body given them by their parents, the Thus-Come Ones of the ten directions have not told the truth."

4
Vows of Protection

When these words had been spoken, countless hundreds of thousands of vajra-brandishing warriors placed their palms together and bowed before the Buddha all at the same time, and they said to him respectfully, "In accord with what the Buddha has said, we will devote ourselves to protecting all those who undertake this practice on their path to enlightenment."

Then the King of the Brahma Heaven, the Lord Śakra, and the Four Celestial Kings bowed together before the Buddha, and they said to him respectfully, "If indeed there be good people who undertake a spiritual practice in accord with this Dharma, we will devote all our effort to protect these people so that their wishes will be fulfilled during their present lives."

Then Vināyaka and countless ghost-kings and ghost-generals, including great yakṣa-generals and kings of rākṣasas, pūtanas, kumbhāṇḍas, and piśācas, also placed their palms together, bowed before the Buddha, and said to him respectfully, "We too vow to protect these people and to lead them to quickly fulfill their resolve to become enlightened."

Further, innumerable sun-lords, moon-lords, rain-lords, cloud-lords, thunder-lords, lightning-lords, and other such lords, together with monitoring gods of the year,[32] and the retinues of the lords of the heavenly bodies, all bowed to the Buddha from their places in the midst of the assembly. They said to him respectfully, "We too will protect all these people in their spiritual practice so that they will be free of fear and will be secure and at peace in the places for awakening that they have established."

Moreover, countless mountain-spirits and sea-spirits, and myriads of other spirits that move on land, through water, and in the air, together with the wind-kings of the air and the gods on the four planes of form-

[32] These are gods whose duty it is to monitor beings' behavior (Yuanying, 1100).

lessness[33] paid obeisance to the Thus-Come One at the same time. They said to him respectfully, "We too will protect these people in their spiritual practice so that they can become enlightened without ever being troubled by demonic influences."

Then Bodhisattvas in the lineage of the Bodhisattva-King Vajra-Treasury, numbering eight-four thousand million billion[34] times the number of sand-grains in the River Ganges, stood up in the midst of the great assembly, bowed before the Buddha, and said to him respectfully, "World-Honored One, like these others, we all became enlightened long ago, but we have chosen not to enter nirvana. Instead, we continue in our meritorious work of constant attendance upon those whose practice is centered on this mantra, and during the time of the Dharma's ending, we will protect all who correctly practice this samādhi.[35]

"World-Honored One, these beings who cultivate their minds by correctly practicing this samādhi may be seated in their place of awakening, or they may be walking upon the roads, or their minds may not be focused while they are relaxing in their villages, but in any case we and our followers will constantly attend upon them and stand guard over them. Even if the demon-king who presides over the Heaven of Pleasure Derived from What Others Create[36] should seek to have his way with these beings, he will be utterly unable to do so. Lesser ghosts and spirits will be able to approach no closer than seventy miles from these good people — unless these ghosts and spirits are also resolved to become enlightened and are joyfully practicing meditation in stillness. World-Honored One, with our gem-encrusted vajra-implements we will smash to bits the skulls of evil demons if ever they or members of their retinues should seek to intrude upon these good people in order to disrupt their practice. We will always help these good people fulfill their wishes."

---

[33] See part 9.11g.

[34] The text has a transliteration of the large Sanskrit numbers *nayuta* and *koṭī*.

[35] "Correct practice" here refers to keeping the precepts and properly reciting the mantra (Yuanying, 1102).

[36] The highest of the six heavens in the realm of desire. See part 9.11g.

These demons can develop tremendous psychic powers, and they abound throughout the world, causing unrest and instigating trouble. If you recite the Śūraṅgama Mantra, then all the demons throughout the world are forced to behave to some extent. If no one can recite the Śūraṅgama Mantra, they will run rampant and will recklessly devastate this world. (VI, 158)

IX
Levels of Being

1

The Coming into Being
of the World of Illusion

Ānanda stood up, bowed at the Buddha's feet, and said to him respectfully, "I and those like me have been so unwise and dull-witted as to prefer the mere pursuit of learning to the attempt to put an end to our outflows. But now that the Buddha has kindly given us this instruction, our practice has been corrected. We are thoroughly delighted with the great benefit we have gained.

"World-Honored One, suppose someone has cultivated the Buddha's samādhi in this way but has not yet reached nirvana. What is meant by the stage of 'arid wisdom'?[1] What are the forty-four stages through which the mind must pass in order to reach the goal of spiritual practice? At what stage of mastery does one reach the Ten Grounds?[2] What does it mean to be a Bodhisattva at the stage of 'Equivalent Enlightenment'?"[3]

Having spoken these words, Ānanda bowed to the ground, and everyone in the great assembly gazed up unblinking with respectful admiration as they waited to hear the sound of the Buddha's compassionate voice.

The World-Honored One then praised Ānanda, saying, "Excellent! Excellent! On behalf of all in this great assembly and on behalf of all beings who practice samādhi in the time of the Dharma's ending as they seek to advance in accord with the Great Vehicle, you and others have asked me to point out the supreme right path of self-cultivation that will lead them from their mundane state to the great nirvana. You should listen carefully to what I say to you."

---

[1] "Arid" because one's desires have dried up and one has not yet experienced the moisture of Dharma. This is the first of the fifty-seven stages of the Bodhisattva's enlightenment, as outlined in part 9.4.

[2] Skt. daśabhūmi, Ch. shi di. 十地. See part 9.4.

[3] That is, equivalent to the enlightenment of a Buddha.

Ānanda and the others in the great assembly placed their palms together and let their minds become empty as they waited in silence to receive the teaching.[4]

> They cast out their extraneous thoughts, the deluded thinking of their conscious minds, their mad minds and wild natures. . . . Just as one might hollow out a log to make a boat, they hollowed out their minds so that they could receive the teaching. (VI, 162)

The Buddha said,[5] "You should know, Ānanda, that the wondrous enlightened nature is endowed with perfect understanding. It is apart from all names and attributes, and in it, at the fundamental level, there are no worlds and no beings. It is because of delusion that there is coming into being, and because there is coming into being, there is ceasing to be. Coming into being and ceasing to be are delusions. When delusion ceases, reality appears. This turning back from duality to reality is called the supreme awakening. It is also called the great nirvana of the Thus-Come Ones.

"Ānanda, you now wish to practice the true samādhi and to realize the great nirvana of the Thus-Come Ones. You should begin by understanding the causes for two distorted phenomena, that is, beings and the worlds in which beings exist. When these two phenomena do not come into being, the true samādhi of the Thus-Come One appears.

"What is the distorted phenomenon that we call beings, Ānanda? The enlightened nature of the true mind that understands is such that its understanding is perfect and complete. But, Ānanda, from this understanding, another understanding may be created as another entity, and from that other entity, a deluded awareness will come into being. Thus from within the original state which has no attributes whatever, that which has definite attributes comes into being.

---

[4] The Buddha does not answer Ānanda's question immediately. His answers are given in part 9.4.

5 The Buddha here gives a brief summary of the coming into being of self and world, which was the subject of a much longer exegesis in part 4. The Chinese text here is particularly terse.

Thus from the true the false arises. Based in the nature of the Matrix of the Thus-Come One, beings give rise to ignorance. Another way of putting it is that one tries to add an understanding to enlightenment when all along the nature of enlightenment is that it understands. In that one movement of delusion, coming into being — the first of the three subtle aspects of delusion — is created. And from that false nature, an observing subject is created; this is evolving, the second subtle aspect of delusion. . . . Next, death and rebirth come into being. . . . One creates karma, and after that one must undergo a retribution. This is appearance, the third of the subtle aspects of delusion. (VI, 165–6)

"Neither what comes into being nor what it comes into being from are based on anything, nor are they a basis for anything. Beings and the worlds they dwell in have no foundation, and yet, despite their having no foundation, beings and the worlds come into being.

The three subtle aspects of delusion are said to arise from ignorance, but ignorance has no independent existence. It cannot actually be the basis for anything. Ignorance itself is a false creation, an empty appearance. Therefore, although it seems to be that the three subtle aspects arise from ignorance, it does not really happen that way, because ignorance itself doesn't actually exist. (VI, 167)

"Confusion about the original perfect understanding results in delusion, but this delusion has no essential nature of its own; it is based on nothing. One may wish to return to what is real, but to wish for the real is already a falsification. The true nature of the suchness of reality is not a reality that one can seek to return to. If one were to try to return to it, one would merely experience something that does not have the attributes of reality.

It is a mistake to decide that you want to return to the truth, to go back to the source in order to seek for the truth. You will have just created more falseness. If you want to return to the truth, you should merely refrain from adding an understanding to your enlightened understanding. Don't place another head on top of your head. Don't go looking for your donkey while you're riding your donkey. The real nature of true suchness is not a truth that you can try to return to. It's not that you decide to return to inherent truth. Rather, you simply dispense with ignorance; that dispensing is itself the truth. There is no need to seek further. (VI, 168)

"Through their mutual interaction, there comes into being what does not really come into being, as well as what does not really abide, what is not really the mind, and what are not really phenomena. From the force of their coming into being, an understanding is created, and its influence leads to activity subject to karma. Similar karma mutually attracts, and because of the karma of this mutual attraction, there is a coming into being and then a ceasing to be. This is the reason for the distorted phenomenon of beings.

"What does not really come into being" refers to fundamental ignorance. "What does not really abide" refers to the eighth consciousness. "What is not really the mind" refers to the observing division of the eighth consciousness, and "what are not really phenomena" refers to the observed division of the eighth consciousness. Ignorance, karmic consciousness, and the observing and observed divisions have no real source and no independent existence of their own. Their very existence is illusory. Nonetheless, this sickness is contagious; that is what is meant by "through their mutual interaction." It is the same as with the interconnection of the eyes, ears, nose, tongue, body, and mind. As the faculties continue to gain strength, so does the karma they create. . . . and because of the karma they have created, there is death and rebirth. That is the reason for the deluded state that beings are in. The one unenlightened thought which is ignorance has the effect of a disorienting drug or the effect of too much wine. They no longer know what they should be doing. These beings simply go along with their karma. Whatever deeds of karma they create, they undergo retribution for those deeds. This is how the world comes into being. (VI, 169–71)

"Ānanda, what is the distorted phenomenon of worlds? Because of the existence of the mind and of what the mind observes, there arises the unreal phenomenon of beings divided into individual bodies, and from this, boundaries are established. Yet these bodies and their boundaries

316

are neither based on anything nor a basis for anything. There is no abiding nor any place of abiding; there is only a constant and unending flux. The three periods of time and the four directions of the worlds intersect and combine, and in this way, beings are transformed into any one of twelve classes.

"Thus in this world, because there is movement, there are sounds, and because there are sounds, there are visible objects. Because there are visible objects, there are odors. Because there are odors, there are objects of touch. Because there are objects of touch, there are flavors. Because there are flavors, there are objects of cognition. Because of the karma created by these six kinds of disordered mental activity, the twelve classes of beings are bound to the cycle of death and rebirth.

"Therefore, because of the visible objects, sounds, odors, flavors, objects of touch, and objects of cognition in this world, beings may be born in succession through the twelve classes, thus making a complete sequence. Beings are bound to the cycle of death and rebirth, and according to their various distorted attributes, they may be born into this world from an egg, or from a womb, or in the presence of moisture, or via metamorphosis. Some beings are born with bodies that they may or may not make visible, while others may be born without physical form. Some beings are born capable of cognition but lacking a physical body; others are born with their cognitive function inactive. Some beings have physical forms that are not self-sufficient, and others sometimes lack and sometimes do not lack physical form. Still other beings have a deficient understanding, and others sometimes lack and sometimes do not lack a cognitive capacity.

There are four conditions necessary for birth from an egg: there must be a father, a mother, individual karma, and warmth. Birth from a womb requires three conditions: a father, a mother, and individual karma. Birth in the presence of moisture requires only individual karma and the presence of moisture; and birth via metamorphosis requires only individual karma. (VI, 175)

2
Twelve Classes of Beings

[1][6] "Thus, Ānanda, beings are bound to the cycle of death and rebirth in this world as a result of illusion, which arises from distorted mental activity. That mental activity[7] combines with vital energies to create eighty-four thousand kinds of disordered predilections for flying or for being submerged. The result is the fetal stage[8] of beings who are born from eggs. These become the fish, birds, turtles, and snakes. In their multitudes, they have spread throughout the world.

[2] "Further, beings are bound to the cycle of death and rebirth in this world as a result of impure mingling, which arises from distorted desires. Those desires combine with procreative substances to create eighty-four thousand kinds of disordered predilections for standing upright or on four legs. The result is the fetal stage[9] of beings who are born from wombs. These become the humans, beasts, dragons, and ascetic masters. In their multitudes, they have spread throughout the world.

[3] "Further, beings are bound to the cycle of death and rebirth in this world as a result of attachments that arise from distorted inclinations. Those inclinations combine with warmth to create eighty-four thousand kinds of distorted predilections for fluttering motion. The result is the fetal stage of beings[10] who will be born in the presence of moisture. These are the dull-witted beings who creep or swim. In their multitudes, they have spread throughout the world.

---

[6] The numbering in this chapter has been added by the translators.

[7] The "mental activity" is that of the being who has experienced death and seeks rebirth. Its mental activity combines with the "vital energies" of its future parents at the moment of conception. The rhetorical pattern of this paragraph is repeated in the next three paragraphs for beings born from wombs, in the presence of moisture, and via metamorphosis.

[8] Skt. *kalala*.

[9] Skt. *arbuda*.

[10] Skt. *peśī*.

[4] "Further, beings are bound to the cycle of death and rebirth in this world as a result of transformations, which arise from the distorted desire to assume another form. This desire to assume another form, upon contact with another being's physical nature, combines to create eighty-four thousand kinds of distorted predilections for exchanging the old for the new. The result is the fetal stages[11] of beings that are born by metamorphosis. These are the creatures that fly or crawl. In their multitudes, they have spread throughout the world.

[5] "Further, beings are bound to the cycle of death and rebirth in this world as a result of stagnation, which arises from distortions due to hindrance. This hindrance, combining with an attachment to display, produces eighty-four thousand kinds of distorted predilections for glittering and shining. The result is the development of beings who may or may not make their bodies visible. These are the bioluminescent beings of either an auspicious or an inauspicious nature. In their multitudes, they have spread throughout the world.

[6] "Further, beings are bound to the cycle of death and rebirth in this world as a result of dispersion, which arises from distortions due to doubt. That doubt combines with darkness to create eighty-four thousand kinds of distorted predilections to avoid visible form. The result is the development of beings who have no physical form. These are the beings who abide in boundless space, or in boundless consciousness, or in infinite nothingness, or at the highest point where cognition is and yet is not absent.[12] In their multitudes, they have spread throughout the world.

> This group consists of beings without form; these are the beings in the four heavens on the formless planes. . . . Although their circumstances imply total negation, they still have consciousness and karma, and therefore they are subject to rebirth. (VI, 181)

---

[11] Skt. *ghana*. The ghana is mentioned in the text in each of the next eight paragraphs, but this seems to be a literary embellishment in the Chinese translation, since some of the beings do not seem to be among those that develop from a fetus. In these cases the present translation renders "ghana" simply as "development."

[12] For more on the gods on the planes of formlessness, see part 9.11g.

[7] "Further, beings are bound to the cycle of death and rebirth in this world as a result of deceptive imaginings, which arise from distortions due to shadowy images. Those shadowy images combine with memories to produce eighty-four thousand kinds of predilections for attachment to seclusion and obscurity. The result is the development of beings who are capable of cognition but lack a physical body. These are spirits, ghosts, and phantoms. In their multitudes, they have spread throughout the world.

> These are such beings as spirits, ghosts, and uncanny essences. In the beginning these beings come about because of shadowy images that unite with memory to become eighty-four thousand kinds of deluded thoughts that are hidden away, and no one is aware of them. Their random thoughts mass together, and from this comes the development of the beings that are capable of cognition but have no physical form. They multiply throughout the lands in the form of spirits, ghosts, and uncanny essences until their kinds abound. Some ghosts and spirits are devious, and some behave properly. Some ghost-kings are even manifestations of Bodhisattvas, while others are unreliable beings. Uncanny essences, however, are totally disorderly and devious. (VI, 182)

[8] "Further, beings are bound to the cycle of death and rebirth in this world as a result of dullness, which arises from distortions due to mental insufficiency. That insufficiency combines with obtuseness to produce eighty-four thousand kinds of predilections for the drying up of vitality. The result is the development of beings whose cognitive function is inactive. Their vital spirits come to inhabit earth, wood, metal, or stone. In their multitudes, they have spread throughout the world.

[9] "Further, beings are bound to the cycle of death and rebirth in this world as a result of mutual dependency, which arises from distortions due to the assumption of false identities. These false identities combine with impure influences to produce eighty-four thousand kinds of predilection for symbiosis. The result is the development of beings whose physical forms are not self-sufficient. These include various kinds of beings, such as sea anemones which rely on shrimp in order to see.[13] In their multitudes, they have spread throughout the world.

[13] One instance of the example given by the text could be the association of the shrimp

320

[10] "Further, beings are bound to the cycle of death and rebirth in this world as a result of an interaction, which arises with the invoking of beings whose fundamental natures are distorted. These invocations combine with the utterance of mantras or spells to produce eighty-four thousand kinds of predilections for being summoned. The result is the development of beings who sometimes lack and sometimes do not lack a physical form. These are the beings who are commanded by mantras, spells, and curses. In their multitudes, they have spread throughout the world.

> "Hooking and summoning," which has already been explained,[14] applies to these mantra spirits. One summons them by calling them by name. Usually one does not see such beings, but when someone recites a mantra, the beings may reveal their bodies, and often one can see them. . . . They are the hidden beings of mantras and incantations. In the Esoteric school there exist mantras which summon these kinds of beings. (VI, 185–6)

[11] "Further, revolving in a cycle of death and rebirth in this world may come about from a false commonality, which arises from distortions due to deception. This deception combines with what is different to produce eighty-four thousand kinds of predilections for making substitutions. The result is the development of beings whose understanding has a deficiency.[15] These are such beings as the potter wasps and other creatures whose bodies develop among those of a different species. In their multitudes, they have spread throughout the world.

[12] "Further, revolving in a cycle of death and rebirth in this world may come about from malice, which arises from distortions due to killing.

---

heptacarpus kincaidi and *lebbeus grandimanus* with sea anemones of the *Urticina* genus. In coral reefs the shrimp live well-protected within the circle formed by the sea anemone's venomous tentacles; the shrimp are immune to the venom. Unlike the anemones, the shrimp have highly developed eyes, and they alert the anemones to the approach of predators. They are among the beings "whose physical forms are not self-sufficient," presumably so-called because they are dependent on other beings.

[14] See part 8.2.

[15] The meaning seems to be that they do not understand what species they are because they are born among other species.

This killing combines with monstrousness to produce eighty-four thousand kinds of thoughts of devouring one's parents. The result is the development of beings which sometimes lack and sometimes do not lack a cognitive capacity. These are such beings as owls whose young are hatched on the ground and mirror-smashing birds that lay their eggs in a toxic fruit.[16] These offspring then feed upon their parents. In their multitudes, they have spread throughout the world.

"These are the twelve classes of beings."

---

[16] The owl referred to here may well be the grass owl (*tyto longimembris*), a cousin of the barn owl. It nests in tussocks of grass on the ground. It is found in both India and China, as well as in Southeast Asia and Australia. The "mirror-smashing bird" (Ch. *puo jing niao* 破鏡鳥) is another matter. Both Ven. Hsüan Hua (*Shurangama Sutra* VI, 180) and Ven. Yuanying (1133) mention a mythical animal that was said to incubate a fruit to produce its young, but these two commentators note that this animal was said to resemble a wolf and was therefore not a bird, and that the Chinese translators must have misunderstood the original. A further difficulty here is that, while there are animals that eat their young in certain stressed circumstances, the present translators were unable to discover any reference to species whose young eat their parents. Nevertheless, the principle of the passage is intact: that there are instances in which the natural cognitive tendency to cherish parents and offspring is suspended.

3
Three Gradual Steps

A. Avoiding the Plants of the Onion Group

"Ānanda, all twelve of these classes of beings are affected by all twelve of these distortions.[17] Like the disordered and elaborate images that appear when pressure is exerted upon the eye, these distortions completely obscure the wondrous, perfect, pure, true, and understanding mind with deluded and disordered mental activity. Now, however, you wish to practice and to master the samādhi of the Buddhas. You should take three gradual steps in order to eradicate the fundamental factors that are the source of this disordered mental activity.[18] Taking these steps will be like cleaning a pot that has held poisonous honey by scouring it with hot water mixed with the ashes of burnt incense. Once the pot has been cleaned in this way, it may be used to store even a celestial ambrosia.[19]

"What are the three steps? The first is the practice that eliminates contributing factors. The second is the practice of truly ending any violation of the fundamental rules of behavior. The third is the practice of vigorously turning away from intentional engagement with perceived objects.

"What are the contributing factors, Ānanda? Consider it this way: the twelve classes of beings of this world cannot sustain themselves without some kind of nourishment, which may be taken in one of four ways: by mouth, by touch, by thought, or by consciousness. That is why the Buddha says that all beings take nourishment in order to sustain themselves.

> Ghosts, spirits, and some gods eat by touching. In the Realm of Form, the gods get their nourishment by thinking. They take the bliss of meditation in stillness as their food. In the Planes of Formlessness, the formless gods are nourished by means of consciousness. (VII, 4)

[17] That is, each of the distortions named in the previous section applies not only to one class of being but to all twelve.

[18] The three steps are necessary if the practitioner is to enter the path of the Bodhisattva.

[19] Skt. amṛta, Ch. gan lu 甘露, the drink of the gods.

"All beings must take nourishing food to live, Ānanda, and if they consume a toxic substance, they may die. Beings who seek to enter samādhi must refrain from eating the five plants of the onion group.[20] When eaten cooked, these plants arouse sexual desire; when eaten raw, they increase anger.

> Eating meat has similar effects. If eaten cooked, it increases desire; eaten raw, it can cause people to lose their temper. This is one reason why people who follow the Path should not eat meat. (VII, 6)

"Gods and ascetic masters of the ten directions keep their distance from anyone who eats these plants, because the plants cause people to stink, including even people who can expound upon the twelve types of discourse spoken by the Buddha.[21] Hungry ghosts, meanwhile, will come to lick and kiss the lips of people who have eaten these plants. Such people will always be accompanied by ghosts, and their blessings will lessen day by day. They will experience no lasting benefit.

"When people who eat the plants of the onion group practice samādhi, the Bodhisattvas, gods, ascetic masters, and wholesome spirits of the ten directions will not come to protect them. Demon-kings of great power, however, will seize the opportunity to appear before these people in the form of a Buddha and will pretend to speak Dharma to them. These demons will denounce the precepts and will praise sexual desire, anger, and delusion. Such people, at the end of their lives, will inevitably join the retinues of demon-kings. Once they have exhausted the blessings that they may enjoy as demons, they will fall into the Unrelenting Hell.

"Ānanda, those who practice in pursuit of full awakening must forever refrain from eating the five plants of the onion group. This is the first step they should take in their practice in order to make progress on the Path.

> Why don't Dharma-protectors and good spirits guard such people? It's because people who eat these five plants smell bad. Preferring purity, the

---

[20] That is, onions, garlic, shallots, leeks, and chives, and by extension, any similar member of the *allium* (lily) family.

[21] See part 4, note 32.

Dharma-protectors avoid the stench. . . . However, protectors are essential to spiritual practice. . . . In the absence of protectors, powerful demon-kings are able to do as they please. They will appear in the body of a Buddha and speak to practitioners about what they claim is the Dharma. Seeing an unprotected practitioner, the demon-kings come on the scene to gather him into their retinue. They will enter when they catch you off guard. How great is their power? They can seem to turn into Buddhas! I've advised you that if in the future you open your Buddha-eye,[22] you may see Buddhas or Bodhisattvas or gods or spirits or ascetic masters come. If they are genuinely what they appear to be, they will have a light about them that is pure and cool, and when it shines on you, you will experience extreme comfort such as you have never known. That, then, is a true Sage. A demon, meanwhile, puts out heat. However, it requires a lot of wisdom to make this distinction. If you lack sufficient wisdom, you will not notice the heat and so may take the demon to be a Buddha. Another way you can tell the difference between a demon appearing as a Buddha and an actual Buddha is to look at the Dharma they teach. Demon-kings will denounce the precepts and praise sexual desire, anger, and delusion. They will say, "Don't follow precepts. That's a Lesser Vehicle practice. Followers of the Greater Vehicle may kill, but it's not really killing; they may steal but it won't count as theft. . . . Violations don't matter." . . . In fact, if you don't take the precepts and then follow them carefully, you will not be able to make any spiritual progress. . . . Recently a book was published in India praising the tantric practices, claiming that enlightenment can be reached through sexual practices. This is a book written by demons. (VII, 8–11)

B. Ending Any Violation of the Fundamental Rules of Behavior

"What is meant by the 'fundamental rules of behavior'? Ānanda, beings who wish to enter samādhi must strictly observe the pure precepts. They must rid themselves of sexual desire once and for all. They must not consume alcohol or meat. They may eat raw food only when it has been made allowable after it has been exposed to fire, to ensure the plant's

---

[22] One of the five spiritual eyes. See part 3, note 38.

vital energies are not consumed for nourishment.[23] Ānanda, if people who practice do not put an end to their sexual desire and do not refrain from taking life, it will be impossible for them to transcend the three realms.

> The text here refers to improper sexual desire. It is absolutely unprincipled to think that a lustful person could become a Buddha. . . . Love that is a loving regard for one's spouse and children is not what is meant here. Also, if special circumstances arise where one wishes to help someone else and one is not just seeking ephemeral bliss, that too would be a temporary expedient rather than a violation because one's wish is to help someone else, and one is basically doing something one would prefer not to do.
>
> What disadvantages are there in consuming alcohol and meat? Taking alcohol deranges one's nature. Once you drink alcohol, you lose your focus. And then you are likely to engage in confused behavior. . . . Another reason is that the odor of wine and other alcoholic drinks, which people and ghosts may consider to be fragrant, makes the good spirits upset, and they and the Bodhisattvas and Arhats do not like the smell. Bodhisattvas and Arhats regard the smell of wine as we regard the smell of urine. . . .
>
> Further, all foods should be cooked before they are eaten, because almost all raw foods will increase one's anger. (VII, 15–6)

"People of this world who are accomplished in following the precepts will be free forever of the mutual karma that arises when one kills in this life and so is killed in turn in a subsequent life. Further, people of this world who do not steal from one another will never become indebted to one another; they will incur no debts from the past.

---

[23] "Fruits and seeds that can germinate and roots (bulbs, tubers) that can be planted again should be made 'allowable' or kappiya for bhikkhus [monks]. An unordained person can do this by touching it with fire, by drawing a knife over it, or by marking it with a fingernail. . . . There is no need for the ceremony with seedless fruit, or with fruit if the seeds are unripe so that they cannot germinate. . . . Also, if the bhikkhu carefully eats certain sorts of fruits — for instance, mangoes, jackfruit, plums, peaches, etc. — without damaging the seeds, there is no offense." Bhikkhu Ariyesake, The Bhikkhus' Rules: A Guide for Laypeople (Kallista, Victoria, Australia: Sanghāloka Forest Hermitage, 1998), 133.

You control your physical behavior and avoid the offenses deserving of expulsion.[24] . . . Then you follow the Bodhisattva's pure regulations, the ten major and forty-eight minor Bodhisattva precepts, in order to control your mental activity. . . . This is the path that people who practice must walk. (VII, 16)

"When such pure people practice samādhi, they will very naturally be able to see the worlds of the ten directions while remaining in their bodies born of their parents and without needing the celestial eye.[25] They will see the Buddhas and hear the Dharma, and they will respectfully receive the sages' instructions in person. They will gain great spiritual powers, they will be able to roam playfully throughout the ten directions, and they will have clear knowledge of past lives. They will never encounter danger or difficulty.

"That is the second step they should take in their practice, in order to make progress on the Path.

C. Avoiding Intentional Engagement with Perceived Objects[26]

"What is meant by 'intentional engagement with perceived objects,' Ānanda? People who practice in this way — who observe the prohibitory precepts with purity and who have no sexual desire — allow themselves few outflows in response to the six kinds of perceived objects. Because their outflows are few, these people are able to redirect the attention of their faculties inward to the faculties' source. Since their faculties are no longer paying attention to objects of perception, the faculties and objects are no longer paired. Once the attention has been redirected inward, the faculties become one and cease to function in six separate ways. Then the lands throughout the ten directions will be as pure and as transparent as a bright moon appearing within a crystal. In their bodies and minds they will experience bliss, wondrous perfection, and their essential equality with all beings and all things. They will know peace and great tranquility.

---

[24] The pārājikas (sexual misconduct, killing, theft, and making false claims).

[25] Another of the five spiritual eyes.

[26] The Buddha here briefly reiterates the instructions given by the Bodhisattva Mañjuśrī and the Bodhisattva Who Hears the Cries of the World. See part 6.2.

In their midst all the Thus-Come Ones will appear — mysterious, perfect, pure, and wondrous. These people will soon develop patience with the state of mind in which no mental objects arise. Because they take these steps in their practice, they will, as a result of their practice, abide peacefully in the succession of stages on the path to become sages.

"That is the third step one should take in one's practice in order to make progress on the Path."

4

The Fifty-Seven Stages
of the Bodhisattva's Path

A. Arid Wisdom

"Ānanda,[27] when in good people emotional love and desire have dried up and their sense-faculties are no longer paired with sense-objects, their remaining habitual tendencies no longer arise. Their attachments are emptied out, and their minds are clear. What is left is pure wisdom, whose brilliant and perfect nature shines throughout the worlds of the ten directions. This pure wisdom exists because their desires have dried up, and so this stage is called 'Arid Wisdom.' Although their habits of desire have now dried up, they have not yet entered the stream of the Thus-Come Ones' Dharma.

B. Ten Stages of Stabilizing the Mind

[1][28] "When these people have reached the very essence of that stage,[29] they enter the stream of the Middle Way, where a wondrous perfection opens out before them. From this true and wondrous perfection, yet another true and wondrous perfection appears, and they experience a wondrous and unshakable confidence. All their deluded acts of mind are ended, and the Middle Way remains as the only truth. This stage of stabilizing the mind is called 'Confidence.'

> These people, by means of Arid Wisdom, which is the initial vajra-mind . . .
> reach the state where a wondrous perfection reveals itself and opens out in
> abundance. . . . From the truth of that wondrous perfection there repeatedly
> arise further wonders of truth. In the wondrous perfection of the suchness of
> reality within the mind's true nature, truths within truths come forth. . . . At that
> point, all deluded mental activity is ended, without exception. (VII, 28)

[27] The Buddha now undertakes to answer the question Ānanda raised at the beginning of part 9.

[28] The numbering has been added by the translators.

[29] That is, the stage of Arid Wisdom.

[2] "This true confidence brings about complete clarity so that all is fully understood, and the aggregates, the sites, and the constituent elements can no longer be a hindrance. These people are now able to see before them all the habits they cherished during their successive lives throughout countless eons in the past; they can even tell what habits they should expect to have in the future. These good people, then, can remember all their habits, forgetting none. This stage of stabilizing the mind is called 'Recollection.'

[3] "When only the true and wondrous perfection remains, the essence of this true perfection begins to transform these people's habits, which have accumulated over time without beginning, into a single essential clarity. By means of this essential clarity, these people advance into a true state of purity. This stage of stabilizing the mind is called 'Advancement by Means of Essential Clarity.'

[4] "As this essential clarity becomes more and more present to them, their minds function by means of wisdom alone. This stage of stabilizing the mind is called 'The Mind Residing in Functioning with Wisdom.'

[5] "As they become steadfast in this wisdom and its light, their minds extend everywhere in clarity and stillness — a stillness that is wondrously constant and unchanging. This stage of stabilizing the mind is called 'Abiding in Samādhi.'

[6] "As this samādhi becomes more luminous, their wisdom grows, and with this wisdom they enter yet more deeply into samādhi so that they only advance; they never retreat. This stage of stabilizing the mind is called 'Resolve.'

[7] "As they advance in this state of mind, they are ever more tranquil. They cherish this state and do not let go of it, and they become connected with the energy of the Thus-Come Ones of the ten directions. This stage of stabilizing the mind is called 'Protecting the Dharma.'

[8] "As they successfully protect their enlightened understanding, they use its wondrous power to become able to redirect the light of the Buddhas' compassion inward to the Buddhas' tranquil abode. It is as if light were being reflected between two mirrors and as if wondrous images of light were appearing in the mirrors in an infinite regress. This

stage of stabilizing the mind is called 'Redirecting One's Light Inward.'

[9] "As the light of their minds is thus mysteriously reflecting, they attain the steadfastness and the unsurpassed wondrous purity of the Buddhas. They abide in the unconditioned and will no longer lose ground. This stage of stabilizing the mind is called 'Steadfastness in Precepts.'

> With this secret interplay of light, they obtain the Buddhas' steadfastness and unsurpassed wondrous purity. There is a hidden connection between the light of the practitioner's mind and the light of the Buddhas' minds. Your mind's light reaches the Buddhas, and their light reaches you. After the Buddhas' light has entered your mind, it returns to the Buddhas. After the light of your mind has entered the Buddhas' minds, it returns to you. This mutual exchange of light goes full circle. (VII, 36)

[10] "Having mastered this steadfastness in precepts, they are able to roam playfully throughout the ten directions, going wherever they wish. This stage of stabilizing the mind is called 'Accomplishing What One Wishes.'

C. Ten Abodes[30]

[1] "Ānanda, these good people have entered these ten states of mind with true skill-in-means, and their minds' essence is radiant. The functions of these ten states of mind are now completely integrated. This stage is called 'The Abode of the Resolved Mind.'[31]

[2] "From within that state of mind, light shines forth like pure gold appearing from within a flawless crystal, and these good people rely upon that wondrous state of mind just described to discipline themselves

---

[30] For a more detailed explanation of the Ten Abodes, see *The Flower Adornment Sūtra, The Ten Dwellings, with the commentary of Tripitaka Master Hua,* trans. Buddhist Text Translation Society (Talmage, California: Dharma-Realm Buddhist University, 1981); also "Ten Abodes," Chapter 15 of *The Flower Ornament Scripture,* trans. Thomas Cleary (Boston: Shambhala, 1993), 384ff.

[31] This part of the Bodhisattva's spiritual progress, the Ten Abodes, is described with metaphorical reference to the process of a child being physically born into the Buddha's family. Accordingly, the first four abodes correspond to the conception of the child, the next four to the fetal stage, the ninth to birth, and the tenth to growth toward maturity.

as if they were leveling a piece of ground. This stage is called 'The Abode of Leveled Ground.'

[3] "On this level ground of the mind, their wisdom is integrated so that they attain a luminous understanding. Their travels throughout the ten directions are now without hindrance or obstruction. This stage is called 'The Abode of Practice on the Path.'

[4] "They walk the Buddhas' Path and share in the Buddhas' energy, and so — just as beings who seek new parents while in the passage between death and rebirth connect with their new parents without the parents' being aware of it — so these good people, as if at the moment of conception, enter into the Thus-Come One's family. This stage is called 'The Abode of Noble Birth.'

> The intermediate consciousness[32] is what is reborn. . . . After the old set of five aggregates has been left behind, the intermediate consciousness lives in a world as black as ink. There is no light for it at all. Though the sun and moon still appear, this intermediate consciousness dares not look at them. . . . But when its future parents engage in intercourse, then no matter how far away from them the intermediate consciousness may be, it perceives a bit of yin light, and in an instant, in response to this thought, it arrives at the place where its parents are. It is drawn to that place like iron filings drawn to a magnet, except that in this case the force of the magnetic field extends for thousands of miles. When the intermediate consciousness arrives at that place, conception occurs immediately, and so there is rebirth.
>
> The birth of the Bodhisattva of the Fourth Abode into the household of the Buddha is likened to the process just described, but only as an analogy. It merely suggests the force of attraction that brings these Bodhisattvas to birth in the household of the Dharma-King. . . . No matter how many thousands of miles away it may be, it is as if there is a mutual connection based on confidence and trust. The Bodhisattvas in this way enter the Thus-Come One's family. The Bodhisattva is born into an honorable and wealthy household, the Buddha's home. To say that the Buddha has a home and family is also just an analogy, since the Buddha long ago left the household for the monastic life. (VII, 39–40)

[32] Skt. *antarābhava*, Ch. *zhong yin shen* 中陰身.

[5] "They have now entered the Thus-Come One's family, so they inherit the attributes of the Awakened Ones, just as every human feature is already fully evident in the unborn child. This stage is called 'The Abode of Full Development of Expedient Attributes.'

[6] "Their outward appearance is like a Buddha's outward appearance, and their minds share the attributes of the Buddha's mind. This stage is called 'The Abode of the Right State of Mind.'

[7] "Mentally and physically resembling the Buddha, they grow day by day. This stage is called 'The Abode of Irreversible Development.'

[8] "Their ability to have their bodies appear in ten forms — each form endowed with spiritually efficacious attributes — comes to fullness at the same time. This stage is called 'The Abode of Childlike Purity.'

[9] "Once they are fully formed, they come forth from the womb as the Buddha's children. This stage is called 'The Abode of the Dharma-Prince.'

[10] "Having grown to adulthood, they are like a crown prince who has come of age. To him the king entrusts the affairs of state, and he is anointed as the Kśatriya lord's royal heir. This stage is called 'The Abode of Anointment.'

D. Ten Practices[33]

[1] "Ānanda, these good people, having become children of the Buddha, are fully endowed with the immeasurable and wondrous virtues of the Thus-Come Ones. They respond to the needs of all beings throughout the ten directions. They are at the stage called 'The Practice of Happiness.'[34]

The first of the Bodhisattva's perfections is the practice of giving, of which there are three kinds:

1) the giving of wealth,

2) the giving of Dharma,

---

[33] For a fuller explanation of the Ten Practices, see Cleary, 454 ff.

[34] The sequence of the Bodhisattva's Ten Practices correspond to the ten perfections (Skt. *pāramitā*). These are the six perfections (giving, following precepts, patience, vigor, mindfulness, and wisdom) together with four others: skill-in-means, vows, powers, and knowledge of expedients.

3) the giving of fearlessness.

Besides these three kinds of giving, there are also two aspects to giving that apply to the Practice of Happiness:

1) Giving makes us happy;

2) Our gifts make others happy. . . .

You should enjoy giving. It's not that you decide to give only under duress; it's not that on the one hand you want to give, but on the other hand you don't want to. It's not that you are hesitant, thinking, "I'd like to make a gift, but parting with my money is as painful as cutting off a piece of my flesh!" On the other hand, you know that if you do not practice giving, you will not generate any merit. So it's a real dilemma. . . .There may be some merit in making gifts even if it is because one feels constrained to do so, but that certainly is not the Practice of Happiness described here.

As to the second aspect of giving, your gifts should make other beings happy. When you practice giving, you should not act like someone tossing crumbs to a beggar. It shouldn't be that they have to come crawling to your door crying, "Dear uncle, dear auntie, can't you spare a little?" and you open the door a crack, throw out a dime or a quarter, and shout, "Take it and go away!" That can't be called giving. There's no merit in that kind of behavior. . . . People with any self-respect would not accept something that is offered in that way. They'd rather go hungry.

Also, you should be careful not to give in such a way that you expect gratitude in response. If you make people feel they must thank you, then you aren't giving in a way that makes people happy. (VII, 45–6)

[2] "They become skillful in doing good deeds for all beings. This stage is called 'The Practice of Beneficial Deeds.'

This practice corresponds to perfection in following precepts. It is called the "Practice of Beneficial Deeds" because it includes teaching others to follow precepts and thus rescuing them. If everyone were to follow the precepts, the entire world would benefit. (VII, 46)

[3] "In the process of awakening themselves and awakening others, they become skillful in not opposing and not resisting. This stage is called 'The Practice of Freedom from Resentment.'

Here the Bodhisattvas reach the point of not putting forth any resistance. This method of nonresistance refers to patience, the third perfection in the Bodhisattva's practice. When something pleasant happens, one is happy; when something unpleasant happens, one is still happy. One doesn't oppose the opinions of others. That requires patience. In all circumstances, one forebears . . . and doesn't get angry. (VII, 48)

[4] "Unto the farthest reaches of the future, they undergo rebirth freely and equally among the various kinds of beings in the three periods of time throughout the ten directions. This stage is called 'The Practice of Inexhaustibility.'

Undergoing rebirth among the various kinds of beings . . . represents the perfection of vigor. (VII, 49)

[5] "For them the various ways of practice merge into a single practice, and in these practices they are beyond error. This stage is called 'The Practice of Departing from Ignorance and Delusion.'[35]

This level of practice corresponds to perfection in meditation in stillness, a practice which aids those who are scattered and easily confused. (VII, 49)

[6] "Within what is identical, many different attributes appear, and these good people perceive the identity that exists among all these different attributes. This stage is called 'The Practice of Skill with Regard to What Manifests.'

"What is identical" is the general principle. What is different are the specific instances. At the noumenal level, there is identity; at the level of phenomena, there are differences. The noumenal is interfused without hindrance in the phenomenal, and the phenomenal is interfused without hindrance in the noumenal. Further, phenomena are interfused without hindrance in phenomena; both phenomena and noumena are mutually interfused. Within identity, difference appears, and within difference, identity is found. . . .This is the perfection of wisdom. (VII, 49–50)

---

[35] The translation here follows the interpretation of Ven. Zhenjiao (2079).

[7] "In the same way, these good people perceive that all the worlds in the ten directions appear in each and every mote of dust throughout space in the ten directions without any mutual interference. This stage is called 'The Practice of Nonattachment.'

Not only does difference appear within identity and identity within difference, but within the few the many can appear, and within the many the few are evident. Within the small the great can appear; within the great the small are evident. . . . Within every mote of dust, worlds appear; every world can fit within a mote of dust. But the world does not shrink, nor does the mote of dust expand. . . . The Bodhisattva at the stage of the Practice of Nonattachment experiences this. This is the seventh perfection, skill-in-means. (VII, 50–1)

[8] "They look upon each of these states of mind as the foremost among the perfections. This stage is called 'The Practice That Is Worthy of Veneration.'

This practice is brought to perfection by the power of vows, . . . the eighth perfection. (VII, 51)

[9] "When these good people perceive that all is perfectly interfused in this way, they are able to conform perfectly to the rules and regulations of all the Buddhas throughout all ten directions. This stage is called 'The Practice of Skill in the Dharma.'

This stage corresponds to the Bodhisattva's perfection of powers. (VII, 52)

[10] "Each and every one of these practices, in its fundamental nature, is pure and without outflows, such that all are a single unconditioned truth. This stage is called 'The Practice of Truth.'

This stage corresponds to perfection in the knowledge of expedients. (VII, 52)

E. Ten Dedications

[1] "Ānanda, now that these good people have gained full spiritual powers and have gained proficiency in doing the work of the Buddhas, they are entirely pure and true, and they are far from all hindrance and misfortune. They will now be able to rescue beings, and yet they have relin-

quished all attachment to their rescuing of beings. In rescuing them, they turn from the mental state that is apart from conditions towards the path that leads to nirvana. This is the stage called 'Dedicating[36] the Rescue of Beings while Remaining Unattached.'

> The myriad practices they cultivate are mere flowers in the air. The places for awakening where they sit are like the moon's reflection in water. The work of subduing the demonic armies is nothing more than a reflection in a mirror. They do the Buddhas' work while in the midst of a dream. That represents their nonattachment. Everything is an illusion; . . . nothing really exists. So don't be attached to anything. See through it all; let it go, and you can gain mastery over yourself. . . .
>
> The Diamond Sūtra has a similar explanation. The Buddha Śākyamūni says there that one should rescue all beings, and yet when all beings have thus been rescued, no beings will actually have been rescued. The meaning, again, is that you must not be attached. You must not think, "I did this, I did that." . . . It was your responsibility to do it in the first place, so why would you need to let anyone know it had been done? . . . Conversely, some people say, "I didn't steal anything or kill anyone, so why aren't things better for me?" This implies that it was their destiny to steal and kill but that they refrained from doing so and therefore should be rewarded! This is a mistaken point of view. (VII, 53–4)

[2] "They abandon what should be abandoned and leave behind what should be left behind. This stage is called 'Dedicating What One Has Not Abandoned.'

> "What should be abandoned" are our karmic obstacles, ignorance, and afflictions. "What should be left behind" are our faults. . . . What should not be abandoned are our good roots in the Dharma and our fundamental enlightened nature. (VII, 55–6)

[3] "Their inherent enlightenment, deep and clear, is equivalent to the enlightenment of the Buddhas. This stage is called 'Dedicating One's Identity with All Buddhas.'

---

[36] "Dedicating" in the sense of wishing that the positive results of one's practice will be enjoyed by other beings.

[4] "When the essential truth is fully revealed, these good people stand on the same ground as the Buddhas. This stage is called 'Dedicating One's Ability to Reach All Places.'

[5] "Having entered worlds and having become identical with the Thus-Come Ones, they now experience both of these as merged together without a hindrance. This stage is called 'Dedicating One's Inexhaustible Treasury of Merit.'

[6] "These good people have the same grounding in reality as the Buddhas have, and so at every stage along the path, they generate pure intentions. By means of these pure intentions, they radiate light, and they do not stray from the path to nirvana. This stage is called 'Dedicating One's Roots of Goodness That Are Grounded in the Same Reality as the Buddhas.'

[7] "Since their roots of goodness have now been grounded in reality, they each make this contemplation: 'All beings in the ten directions have the same fundamental nature that I have, and now that my nature is fully realized, I know that no being is excluded from it.' This stage is called 'Dedicating the Contemplation of One's Identity with All Beings.'

> Buddhas and Bodhisattvas see themselves and all beings as having the same nature. They are one with all beings. Therefore, for them to save beings is not really to save other beings but to save themselves. . . . To say that all beings have the same fundamental nature as oneself is to speak of beings who exist outside oneself. But we can also speak of internal beings, because there are boundlessly many beings within the body of each of us. Science . . . verifies that our bodies contain innumerable microscopic organisms. If you open your Buddha-eye and look into people's bodies, you will see an uncountable number of tiny forms of life, even to the point that when you exhale, you send a lot of beings out with your breath. . . . When you become enlightened and develop some skill, you become one with all the beings inside you and outside you. (VII, 59–60)

[8] "While experiencing oneness with all phenomena, they are nevertheless apart from the attributes of phenomena. Further, they are without attachment either to oneness with phenomena or to separateness from them. This stage is called 'Dedicating the Suchness of Reality within All Phenomena.'

[9] "When they have truly reached the suchness of reality, they meet no obstacles anywhere throughout the ten directions. This stage is called 'Dedicating on Behalf of Liberation from All Bonds.'

10] "When they have fully realized the virtue of their true nature, all limits to the Dharma-Realm are eradicated. This stage is called 'Dedicating the Boundlessness of the Dharma-Realm.'

F. Four Additional Practices

"Ānanda, when in each of these forty-one stages these good people have completely purified their minds, they next master four wondrous and perfect additional practices.

[1] "First, they are on the brink of being able to model their minds on the Buddha's enlightenment. They are like a piece of wood smoldering when it is drilled. This is called 'The Stage of Heating Up.'

> The analogy is of wood which is drilled to obtain fire; this stage of the Bodhi-sattva is compared to the point just before the wood ignites. . . . The igniting of the wood being drilled is like enlightenment. Here the wood is right on the point of bursting into flame. (VII, 63)

[2] "Next, in that their minds are about to complete the journey that the Buddhas have made, they are as if on the point of no longer being bound by the earth. They are like a person standing on a mountain summit, with his body in the air and hardly any solid ground beneath his feet. This is called 'The Stage of Standing at the Peak.'

[3] "Their minds and the minds of the Buddhas had been separate, but now they have become one. They gain true understanding of the Middle Way. They are like someone who endures something that cannot be repressed and yet cannot be expressed. This is called 'The Stage of Patience.'

[4] "When all delineations have melted away, these good people no longer distinguish between confusion and enlightenment and the Middle Way. This is called 'The Stage of Preeminence in the World.'

> At the level of the Tenth Dedication, all measurements in the Dharma-Realm ceased to be. Here, all delineations are gone. . . . When there are no such

designations as the Middle Way or as confusion and enlightenment, and when perfection is total and the light is brilliant, the situation is like a zero. There's nothing that can be said about zero, since it means the absence of everything. And yet everything outside the zero is contained within it. The zero is the mother of all things, yet . . . there isn't anything there. . . . Still, the mountains, the rivers, the vegetation, and all the other myriad phenomena in the entire world come forth from it. Since this state is like zero, there can be no designation for enlightenment or for confusion, or for the Middle Way. There's no name for this state, but we have to call it something, so we force the issue and call it the "Stage of Preeminence in the World." It is foremost in the world because there is no second. (VII, 65)

G. Ten Grounds[37]

[1] "Ānanda, these good people have fully understood the Great Enlightenment, and their awakening is much the same as the Thus-Come Ones'. They have fathomed the state of the Buddha's mind. This stage is called 'The Ground of Happiness.'

[2] "The different natures become identical, and that identity itself disappears. This stage is called 'The Ground of Freedom from Defilement.'

On the first of the Ten Grounds there was still happiness, and so an identity also existed. Although there were no designations, there was still an identity. Differences merged into identity and became one; that is, although the phenomena and the noumenon were united, the noumenon continued. Here at the second ground, identity disappears. This ground is called "Freedom from Defilement" because at this ground the Bodhisattva leaves ignorance behind; yet it is not completely ended, and a slight bit of attachment remains. (VII, 67)

[3] "At the point of ultimate purity, bright light appears. This stage is called 'The Ground of Shining Light.'

[4] "At the point of ultimate luminosity, there is full awakening. This stage is called 'The Ground of Wisdom Blazing Forth.'

---

[37] For a full explanation of the Ten Grounds, see *The Flower Adornment Sūtra: The Ten Grounds,* 2 vols. (Talmage, California: Dharma-Realm Buddhist Association, 1980).

[5] "All the previous grounds of identity and difference are now surpassed. This stage is called 'The Ground of Being Hard to Surpass.'

[6] "The pure nature of the unconditioned suchness of reality now becomes clearly manifest. This stage is called 'The Ground of Manifestation.'

[7] "They reach the very boundaries of the suchness of reality. This stage is called 'The Ground of Traveling Far.'

> The suchness of reality has no limit and no farthest point, so how can it have boundaries? The text is merely descriptive here, . . . an attempt to describe what is basically beyond comprehension. (VII, 70)

[8] "Everything is the true mind, the suchness of reality. This stage is called 'The Ground of No Movement.'

[9] "They now skillfully reveal the functioning of the suchness of reality. This stage is called 'The Ground of Using Wisdom Skillfully.' At this point, Ānanda, these Bodhisattvas' practices and merit have already been perfected. Therefore this ground may also be called 'The Stage at Which Practice is Perfected.'

> At the eighth ground, the suchness of reality and the mind became one; this is the Ground of No Movement. But to simply be unmoving, never to move, would be useless. Therefore, within the suchness of reality, one's functions manifest. That is . . . these Bodhisattvas always respond to circumstances, yet they do not move; not moving, they nevertheless always respond to circumstances. Since such functioning must be connected with wisdom, it is called "Using Wisdom Skillfully." (VII, 71)

[10] "The wondrous cloud of compassion covers the sea of nirvana with its shade. This stage is called 'The Ground of the Dharma-Cloud.'

H. Two Final Stages

"When Thus-Come Ones reverse their direction[38] and the Bodhisattvas advance towards them along the path of practice, they meet at the

---

[38] The meaning here is that the Buddhas come back along the Bodhisattva Path in order to teach beings, while the Bodhisattvas are advancing towards the state of the Buddhas (Zhenjiao, 2135).

threshold of the Buddha's enlightenment. This stage is called the 'Equivalent Enlightenment.' Thus, Ānanda, they have progressed from the stage of Arid Wisdom to the stage of Equivalent Enlightenment. Their ground of awakening is the wisdom that results from the drying up of ignorance within the Vajra-mind.

> The enlightenment of the Buddhas and the enlightenment of the Bodhisattvas merge at this point. It is therefore called "Equivalent Enlightenment." These Bodhisattvas are equal to Buddhas. But theirs is still not the Wondrous Awakening, still not entirely the same as the Buddhas' enlightenment, because at this stage, Bodhisattvas still have one bit of ignorance left. . . . Once they break through that, they will be Buddhas. (VII, 74)

"Thus, having passed through these various stages — twelve stages in all, some counted singly, some in groups[39] — they reach at last the stage of Wondrous Awakening, which is the unsurpassed enlightenment.

"At each of these stages, with their Vajra-mind, they have used ten profound analogies to make the contemplation that all is an illusion. They have stopped the flow of deluded thoughts in their minds, and by means of the Thus-Come Ones' contemplative insight, they have advanced step by step as they bring their pure practice to fulfillment.

> The ten profound analogies are as follows:
>   1) All karma is like an illusion.
>   2) All phenomena are like a mirage.
>   3) All physical bodies are like the moon in water.
>   4) All wondrous forms are like flowers in space.
>   5) All wondrous sounds are like echoes in a valley.
>   6) All Buddhalands are like cities of the gandharvas.[40]

---

[39] The fifty-seven positions along the Bodhisattva path may be thought of as a total of twelve in that there are seven positions listed singly (Arid Wisdom, Heating Up, Standing at the Peak, Patience, Preeminence in the World, Equivalent Enlightenment, and Wondrous Awakening) and five groups of ten positions (Ten Stages of Stabilizing the Mind, Ten Abodes, Ten Practices, Ten Dedications, and Ten Grounds).

[40] Celestial musicians, one of the eight kinds of spirit-beings.

7) All deeds of the Buddha are like dreams.

8) The Buddha's body is like a reflection.

9) The Reward-body[41] is like a shadow.

10) The Dharma-body is like a transformation.

Do not look upon any of these things as real. You should neither grasp nor reject these illusory states. That is because everything is empty, and so you should not regard anything as having any real and permanent existence. The meaning behind these ten profound analogies is that you should not be attached to anything at all. You have to let everything go. If you see through it and let it all go, then you will gain mastery over yourself. (VII, 77)

"Because they have taken the three gradual steps, Ānanda, these people are fully capable of reaching each of the fifty-five stages[42] along the true path to full awakening. The contemplations that have been described here are the right contemplations; all other contemplations are mistaken."

If you can look upon the three realms as if they were flowers in the air; if you can regard all deeds of the Buddha as if done in a dream; and if you rely on the three gradual steps in your practice, your contemplations are being made correctly. (VII, 78)

[41] Skt. *saṃbhoga-kāya*, Ch. *bao shen* 報身, a spiritual body that a Buddha perfects upon reaching full enlightenment. This body is visible only to Bodhisattvas and Buddhas.

[42] Included here are the five groups of ten, the four additional practices, and Equivalent Enlightenment.

5
Naming the Discourse

Then the Bodhisattva Mañjuśrī, Prince of Dharma, stood up in the assembly and bowed at the Buddha's feet. He said to the Buddha respectfully, "What shall this discourse be called? How shall we and other beings hold it in respect and rely on it in our practice?"

The Buddha said to Mañjuśrī, "This discourse may be called 'The Sutra of the Supreme and Magnificent Dharma-Imprint of the Mantra of the White Canopy, Which Is Spoken above the Crown of the Great Buddha's Head, and Which Is the Serene and Pure Oceanic Eye of the Thus-Come Ones of the Ten Directions.' It may also be called 'The Sutra Concerning the Rescue of the Buddha's Cousin Ānanda, the Teachings for Liberating Him, the Awakening of the Nun Named Nature in this Assembly, and Her Entry into the Sea of All-Knowing.'

"It may also be called "The Hidden Basis of the Thus-Come Ones' Practices and the Basis of their Verification of Ultimate Truth.' It may also be called 'The Sutra of the Wondrous Royal Lotus-Flower of the Expanded Teachings[43] and of the Dhāraṇī-Mantra That Is the Mother of All Buddhas Throughout the Ten Directions.' It may also be called 'The Sutra of the Consecrating Mantra Phrases and the Myriad Śūraṅgama Practices of the Bodhisattvas.'

"In this way you may you hold it in respect and rely on it in your practice."

The "Wondrous Royal Lotus-Flower" is the Śūraṅgama Sutra; the "Dhārāni-Mantra" is the Śūraṅgama Mantra. The "Myriad Śūraṅgama Practices of the Bodhisattvas" is another reference to the Śūraṅgama Mantra. If you recite this mantra, your karmic obstacles will very quickly be eradicated. Very soon you will gain wisdom. Earlier in the Sutra, Ānanda speaks in verse about the mantra:

---

[43] Skt. vaipulya, the "expanded" teachings; that is, the teachings of the Mahāyāna.

O deep and wondrous Honored One, all-knowing, pure, and still,

Śūraṅgama, the King of Mantras, rarest in the world,

Extinguishing distorted thoughts from countless eons past —

No need to wait forever to attain the Dharma-body.[44] (VII, 82–3)

When the Buddha had spoken these words, Ānanda and the others in the assembly — having heard the Thus-Come One's instruction concerning the meaning of the hidden Dharma-imprint of the Mantra of the White Canopy and the profoundly significant titles for this discourse — immediately understood the practices of meditation in stillness that lead to advancement through the stages of sagehood. They progressed in their mastery of the wondrous truth. Their minds became empty of all deliberation. They broke free of the six kinds of subtle affliction that, in the three realms, affect the practitioner's mind.

At this point, Ānanda becomes a second-stage Arhat.[45] (VII, 85)

[44] The verse concludes part 3 above.

[45] Skt. *sakṛdāgāmin,* one who must undergo only one more rebirth.

6
The Hells

A. Ānanda Requests Instruction

Ānanda stood up and bowed at the Buddha's feet. Placing his palms together reverently, he said to the Buddha: "World-Honored One, your great virtue inspires awe, and your compassionate voice reaches everywhere unhindered. You skillfully help beings break free of subtle and deeply buried delusions. Today you have brought me delight in body and mind. It has been of great benefit to me.

> Many beings are stubborn and obstinate. . . . They don't believe that there are causes and effects, they don't believe that there is a cycle of death and rebirth, and they don't believe that there is retribution. So the Buddha, as a skillful expedient, can subdue beings by causing them to feel awe. On the other hand, it is his virtue that attracts beings who have faith and are receptive. (VII, 86–7)

"World-Honored One, granted that, at the fundamental level, this true, pure mind, with its wondrous understanding, fully pervades all things. Granted that all things, from the entire planet, with its forests and plains, to the most minute forms of wriggling life, have as their foundation and source the suchness of reality, which is identical to the true essence of the Buddhahood realized by all Thus-Come Ones. Given all that, why are there still the destinies of hells, ghosts, animals, asuras, humans, and gods, since the essential nature of all Buddhas is the true reality? World-Honored One, do these destinies exist of their own accord, or do they come into being based on the deluded habits of living beings?

"World-Honored One, there was the case of the Bhikṣuṇī Precious Lotus-Fragrance, who had been following the Bodhisattva Precepts but then indulged her lust in secret and afterward made the false claim that sexual acts involve no retribution because they do not involve killing or stealing. Immediately after she said this, her reproductive organs burst into flame, and the fire spread through all her joints as she fell into the Unrelenting Hell.

346

Although the bhikṣuṇī Lotus-Fragrance had accepted the Bodhisattva Precepts, she not only broke her vow of celibacy, . . . she also praised sexual desire by claiming that sexual acts have no karmic retribution. She was a nun, and yet she was promoting sex. . . . Her retribution involved being burned, because sexual desire belongs to the element of fire. (VII, 89)

There are hells especially equipped for individuals with strong sexual desire. One of the implements is a copper pillar that is red-hot because a fire blazes within it. However, when one who is fond of sex looks at that hot pillar, he or she sees it as a former lover and rushes madly to it to embrace it. . . . Then the red-hot pillar burns the person to a crisp. As if that weren't enough, out of the corner of their eye they see a bed. Actually, it's a red-hot iron bed. But what the person sees is a former boyfriend or girlfriend on the bed. The person runs to the bed and is burned again. That's how severe the karmic retribution is for excessive sexual desire. (VII, 90–1)

In the Unrelenting Hell, there are no lapses in time and there is no unoccupied space. One person fills it, and many people fill it. . . . The extreme suffering is unintermittent. . . . In a single day and night, beings in the hells undergo thousands of deaths and rebirths. They die and are revived again and again, with no respite from their bitter suffering. (VII, 90)

"There were also King Virūḍhaka[46] and Bhikṣu Sunakṣatra. King Virūḍhaka exterminated the Gautama clan, and Sunakṣatra persisted in making false statements about the emptiness of phenomena.[47] These two also fell alive into the Unrelenting Hell.

"Do hells have a fixed location? Or do they come into being naturally, such that each being creates karma and each undergoes privately the

---

[46] King Virūḍhaka was the son and successor of King Prasenajit, who appears in part 2.3 of this Sutra. Virūḍhaka was ridiculed as a child by members of the Śākya tribe (to which the Buddha belonged), and when Virūḍhaka assumed the throne, he exacted his vengeance by annihilating not only the Buddha's Gautama clan but the entire tribe of Śākyans.

[47] The story of Sunakṣatra is found in chapter forty of the Mahāyāna Mahāparinirvāṇa Sūtra. Upon seeing a naked ascetic on the floor of a tavern, Sunakṣatra denied the existence of cause and effect and made the false statement that the naked ascetic was an Arhat. He later also taught that the Buddhas, Dharma, and nirvana have no real existence.

appropriate retribution? We younger disciples are uninformed about this matter, and we only hope that the Buddha, out of his great kindness, will explain it so that beings who are following the precepts will hear precisely what the teaching is, will joyfully and reverently accept it, and will take care to avoid error in order to maintain purity."

B. The Roles of Emotion and Thought

The Buddha said to Ānanda, "An excellent question! It will keep people from adopting wrong views about this matter. Listen carefully now; I will explain this matter to you.

"The fundamental nature of all beings is truly pure, Ānanda, but because of their wrong views, they develop deluded habit-patterns, which are of two kinds: those that are internal and those that are directed outward.

"Habit-patterns that are internal involve beings' internal autonomic processes. When they are influenced by emotional desire, Ānanda, and their feelings accumulate steadily, they generate fluids associated with emotion. Thus when beings think of delicious foods, their mouths water. When they think of others who are no longer alive, whom they may have cherished or may have hated, their eyes fill with tears. When they are seeking wealth, they experience intense craving, and when they encounter someone whose body is sleek and glowing, lust takes hold of their thoughts. When they think about sexual acts, their procreative organs, whether male or female, will secrete fluid in response.

"Emotions differ, Ānanda, but all are alike in that they are associated with secretions, which may be exuded or may remain within the body. Moisture does not rise; its nature is to flow downward. Such is the situation with internal habit-patterns, whereas habit-patterns that are directed outward, Ānanda, concern beings' aspirations. When they yearn for something higher, beings have uplifting thoughts, and when these thoughts accumulate steadily, they can generate a superior energy. Thus those who follow the precepts feel that their bodies are serene, and beings who hold mantras in their minds develop an heroic and fearless air about them. If they aspire to birth in the heavens, they will dream of floating or flying. If they are mindful of the Buddha-lands, sacred visions will appear to them privately. If they serve a wise and skillful teacher, they will consider their bodies and their lives to be of little importance.

> When beings follow the precepts, their bodies will be buoyant and feel light and clear. This can happen to anyone. . . . You almost feel like you're floating when you walk, and your mind will be extremely pure and clean. . . . If you specialize in holding a mantra in your mind, you will have an heroic air about you, and your glance will be powerful and determined. You will know no fear. . . . When you maintain a mindfulness of the lands of the Buddha, the realms of the sages will appear in a shimmering vision. . . . You will see it, but others won't be able to see it. . . . And when you have the chance to draw near to wise and skillful teachers, to respect them, and to make offerings to them, you will have total disregard for your former lifestyle. Your very life will seem unimportant compared to this opportunity. (VII, 98–9)

"Ānanda, these aspirations differ, but all are alike in that they lead beings to soar upward by conferring either lightness or upward motion. It is their nature not to sink but to take flight and to transcend. Such is the situation with habit-patterns which are directed outward.

"Ānanda, all beings in all worlds are caught up in an endless succession of births and deaths. While beings are alive, they follow their natural inclinations, and upon their deaths, they follow the various currents of their karma. At the moment of death, while some warmth remains in their bodies, all the good and all the evil that they have done during their lifetimes suddenly appear before them. Their inclinations are to shun death and to embrace life — two habitual emotions that complement each other and are felt at the same time.

> The place on the body from which the eighth consciousness departs will be warm to the touch. For instance, if the eighth consciousness leaves through the soles of the feet, that spot will be warm. If it leaves from the legs, the legs will be warm. . . . If it goes out the top of the head, the top of the head will be warm. . . . When a person is on the verge of death, the good and evil he or she has done is revealed and a reckoning is at hand. The person is rewarded

or undergoes retribution depending on what he or she has done. If you performed good deeds, you can be reborn in the heavens; if what you did was evil, you may fall into the hells. If you did more in the way of good deeds and meritorious acts, then you can leave from your head. If you did more in the way of committing crimes and creating offenses, then you'll leave from your feet. To leave from the upper part of the body signals that rebirth will be in the higher realms. (VII, 101–2)

If you have practiced well, you can become a Buddha. If you have not practiced well, you can become a ghost. You may ask whether there are really such things as ghosts. Ask yourself first if there are Buddhas. If so, then of course there are ghosts as well. If you are not sure that there are Buddhas or ghosts, ask yourself whether there are people. If you acknowledge the fact that there are people, then you will know that there are also Buddhas and ghosts, because they are all different aspects of the same thing. (VII, 101)

"If pure mental activity alone is present in their minds,[47] they will soar upward and will be certain to be born in the heavens. While in this soaring state of mind, if they have both blessings and wisdom, and if they have vowed to be reborn in a pure land, their minds will naturally open, and they will see the Buddhas of the ten directions. They will be reborn in any one of the pure lands in accordance with their wish.

The Buddha is known as "The One Whose Blessings and Wisdom Are Complete." It's not enough to gain wisdom; you must plant the seeds of future blessings as well. . . . Making offerings to the Buddha, Dharma, and Sangha and doing other good deeds bring blessings in the future. If you don't make offerings in this life, no one will make offerings to you when you become an Arhat in a future life. (VII, 103–4)

"If pure mental activity is dominant in their minds but some emotion is also present, they will still soar upward, but not as far. They may become flying ascetic masters[48] or ghost-kings of great power, or flying yakṣas, or rākṣasas that travel along the ground. Such beings roam

[47] That is, all thought and no emotion.
[48] See part 9.10 below.

unhindered in the Heaven of Four Celestial Kings. Further, beings may have made wholesome vows, or simply have a wholesome intent, to be protective of the Dharmas I have been teaching. They may have vowed to defend the precepts and to be protective of precept-holders. Or they may have vowed to be protective of mantras and to guard beings who recite mantras. Or they may have vowed to defend the practice of meditation in stillness and to be protective of beings whose practice is to meditate in stillness, and who are likely to encounter aspects of the Dharma that are new to them. Such beings will become close disciples who will sit at the feet of the Thus-Come Ones.

"If their pure mental activity and their emotions are equal in strength, beings will neither soar nor fall. They will be born in the human realm. The brighter their thoughts, the greater their intelligence will be; the darker their emotions, the duller their wits will be.

"If beings have more emotion than pure mental activity, they will be reborn in the realm of animals. If their emotions are of greater weight, they will become fur-bearing beasts, and if their emotions are of lesser weight, they will become winged creatures.

"If emotion is seventy percent of their mental activity and pure thoughts are thirty percent, they will fall beneath the disk of water[49] and will be reborn as hungry ghosts along the rim of the disk of fire. They will be buffeted by the raging fire, and they will be constantly burned by the blaze and scalded by the steam. For hundreds of eons they will have nothing to eat or to drink.

> The karma of hungry ghosts is such that when they see water, it turns into a raging fire. . . . As a hungry ghost one is burned to death, but after a while one revives and then has to go through being burned to death again. Because they see water as fire, they can't drink, and they can't eat, either. (VII, 111–2)

"If emotion is ninety percent of their mental activity and pure thoughts are ten percent, they will fall through the disk of fire and will be reborn between the disk of fire and the disk of wind. If their emotions are less

[49] See part 4.1 and note 11.

weighty, they will enter a hell where suffering is intermittent. If their emotions are of greater weight, they will enter either the Unrelenting Hell.[50]

"When they are ruled entirely by emotion, they sink into the Unrelenting Hell. If, in this submerged state of mind, they have spoken ill of the Mahāyāna teachings or of the Buddhas' precepts; if they have recklessly propounded false doctrines which they present as being in accord with Dharma; if they have greedily sought the offerings of the faithful under false pretenses; if they have shamelessly accepted undeserved reverence from others; or if they have committed the five unnatural crimes or the ten major offenses,[51] then they will be reborn in the Unrelenting Hell in one world after another throughout the ten directions.

"Beings undergo these retributions exactly in accord with the evil karma that they create. But though they have brought their retributions upon themselves, they will share the same fate in the same place with other beings who have created the same karma.

> People who are governed by emotion . . . are totally unreasonable. . . . Their motto is "Eat, drink, and pass the time. The Buddha is only a figment of the imagination, so don't follow the Buddha's moral precepts. What do you want to do that for? They'll just control you. If you don't follow precepts, see how free you'll be." In fact, if one does not follow moral precepts, one is very likely to end up in the hells. Is that what you'd call freedom? If you receive the Buddha's precepts and then use them to govern your behavior, it's not so likely that you'll fall into the hells, and even if you do, you'll get out much more quickly . So don't outsmart yourself. It's better to follow the precepts. (VII, 112–3)

C. Ten Causes and Six Retributions

"Ānanda, these retributions are the consequences of individual beings' intentional acts. For this karma there are ten causes based on beings' habits, and beings undergo in turn six kinds of retribution.

---

[50] "Lesser weight" indicates a proportion closer to eighty percent, and "greater weight" indicates a proportion of more than ninety percent (Yuanying, 1223).

[51] That is, violating the ten major Bodhisattva Precepts.

[1] "What are these ten causes, Ānanda? The first cause is the habit of sexual desire, which, when joined to physical contact, leads to intercourse. When the friction of contact is sufficiently prolonged, there is an inner feeling of a great raging fire erupting from within. It is like the warmth that arises when the hands are rubbed together.

"When the latent habitual energies of sexual desire erupt into the fires of habitual sexual activity,[52] the consequence in the hells will be the experience of the iron bed and the copper pillar. Therefore, when the Thus-Come Ones of the ten directions see evidence of sexual desire and the activity that results from it, they call these things the 'fires that arise from craving.' Bodhisattvas view sexual desire as something to be avoided, as one would avoid a fiery pit.[53]

[2] "The second cause is the habit of craving, which, when one is attracted to something, leads to plotting and planning. When the attraction and the grasping are incessant, there is an inner feeling of freezing cold and solid ice. It is like the experience of the air being cold when one inhales sharply through the mouth.

"When latent habitual energies of craving are compounded with habitual acts of craving, the consequence in the hells will be the experience of freezing, which causes babbling, chattering, and whimpering, and which cracks ice into shapes of blue and red and white lotuses, and other such

[52] The text says simply Ch. *er xi* 二習, "two habits." The present translation adds to the phrase in accord with the Ven. Hsüan Hua's commentary in order to make more accessible an already difficult passage.

[53] This very compact discussion of ten causes for birth in the hells follows a repeating rhetorical pattern. Each of the ten causes is described in seven steps, as follows: 1) To begin the first sentence of each of the ten, a habit is identified. 2) Next, in the same sentence, an emotion corresponding to that habit is identified (this step is omitted in the discussion of the first cause). 3) Still in the same sentence, acts that can result from the habit and emotion are identified. 4) The next sentence describes what the habit, emotion, and acts, when indulged to excess, cause the person to feel. 5) The next sentence explains the process just described by comparing it to a parallel situation in daily life, as in a syllogism. 6) In the second paragraph, the Buddha considers what will happen to the offenders once they reach the hells. 7) Finally, the Buddha suggests how extremely wary the sages are of creating such negative karma.

effects. Therefore, when the Thus-Come Ones of the ten directions see evidence of excessive greed, they call them 'the water of craving.' Bodhisattvas view craving as something to be avoided, as one would avoid a sea of pestilent poisons.

[3] "The third cause is the habit of arrogance, which, when compounded with haughty feelings of self-superiority, leads to competitiveness. When that arrogance continues unchecked, there is an inner feeling of a rushing torrent of leaping waves of water. It is like the mouth watering when a person tries to taste his own tongue.

"When the latent habitual energies of arrogance are expanded to include habitual arrogant acts, the consequence in the hells will be the experience of rivers of blood, rivers of ashes, burning sands, or seas of poison, or the experience of molten copper being poured over one's body or of being forced to swallow the copper. Therefore, when the Thus-Come Ones of the ten directions see instances of arrogance and arrogant acts, they call them 'taking a drink of stupidity.' Bodhisattvas see arrogance as something to be avoided, as one would wish to avoid drowning at sea.

[4] "The fourth cause is the habit of hatred, which, when joined to a predilection for defiance, leads to confrontations. When one's entanglement in habits of defiance is unrelenting, there is an inner feeling of the heart becoming so hot that it burns, and its fiery energy becomes like metal. Then this person will feel as if he is being exposed to mountains of knives, of iron clubs, of swords standing like forests or arrayed like spokes of a wheel, and of axes, spears, and saws. It is like a harbored grievance intensifying until it explodes into an urge to kill.

"When the latent habitual energies of hatred recklessly incite habitual acts of hatred, the consequence in the hells will be the experience of being castrated, dismembered, beheaded, abraded, pierced, flogged, clubbed, and so forth. Therefore, when the Thus-Come Ones of the ten directions see instances of hatred and hateful acts, they call them 'sharp swords.' Bodhisattvas view hatred as something to be avoided, as one would wish to avoid being executed.

[5] "The fifth cause is the habit of enticing others, which, when joined to a fondness for conniving, leads beings to the practice of entrapment.

When the setting of traps becomes too much, this person will feel as if he is being bound by ropes and immobilized in wooden stocks. It is inevitable, just as it is inevitable that trees and grasses in a field will shoot up when the field is saturated.

"When the latent habitual energies of enticing others become prolonged, leading to acts of entrapment, the consequence in the hells will be the experience of handcuffs and fetters, along with cangues and chains attached to cangues, whips and canes, clubs and cudgels, and so forth. Therefore, when the Thus-Come Ones of the ten directions see enticement and entrapment, they call them 'cunning thieves.' Bodhisattvas view defrauding others as something worthy of fear, as one would fear a pack of jackals.

[6] "The sixth cause is the habit of falsehood, which, when joined to deviousness, leads to insinuations and insults. When these insinuations rise to the level of treachery, such a person will feel as if he is being covered with dust and dirt and with excrement and urine and all manner of filth. It is like the dust that, when stirred up by the wind, obscures people's vision.

"When the latent habitual energies of lying are added to acts of deceit, the consequence in the hells will be the experience of sinking and drowning, first being hurled upward, then flying through the air, then falling, floating, and finally perishing. Therefore, when the Thus-Come Ones of the ten directions see instances of falsehood and insinuation, they call them 'robbery and murder.' Bodhisattvas view lying as something to avoid, as one would avoid stepping on a venomous snake.

[7] "The seventh cause is the habit of festering resentment, which, when joined to a propensity to nurse hatreds, leads to acts of vengeance. Such a person will come to feel as if he is being stoned, or being imprisoned in cells or in cages mounted on carts, or being confined in urns or in sacks that are then beaten. It is like the evil designs harbored and nurtured by venomous and secretive people.

"When the latent habitual energies of making false accusations merge with acts of making such accusations, the consequence in the hells will be such experiences as being hurled, seized, stabbed, and stoned. Therefore, when the Thus-Come Ones of the ten directions see instances of resentment and vengeance, they call them 'unscrupulous and harmful ghosts.' Bodhisattvas view making false accusations as equivalent to drinking liquor laced with a fatal poison.

[8] "The eighth cause is the habit of holding wrong views, which, when joined to a temperament that automatically rejects the opinions of others, leads to such mistaken understandings as the wrong view that the self is real,[54] wrong views concerning prohibitions, and wrong views concerning karma. Such a person will come to feel as if he has been brought before officials of the royal court[55] to determine what views he has held. Such scrutiny will be unavoidable, just as one cannot escape being scrutinized by people whom one meets when walking in the opposite direction on a road.

"When the latent habitual energies of holding wrong views are joined to acts that result from holding wrong views, the consequence in the hells will be the experience of being interrogated while subjected to devious tricks and to high-pressure questioning, so that all is eventually brought out into the open. The youths who keep track of good and evil deeds consult the evidence to counter the offenders' arguments and excuses. Therefore, when the Thus-Come Ones of the ten directions see instances of wrong views, they call them 'pit-traps.' Bodhisattvas consider attachment to wrong and biased views as equivalent to standing on the edge of a ditch full of pestilent water.

> The youths mentioned here are employees of the hells; they keep records of good and evil done in the world. When your turn comes, they read out your

---

[54] The wrong view that the self is real is the first of the five wrong views (Skt. *mithyādṛṣṭi;* Ch. *xie jian* 邪見). The second of these, not mentioned in the text, is the wrong view of endings (that is, the view that humans are always reborn as humans, or, at the other extreme, that there is no life after death). The third, which is mentioned in the text, consists of wrong views concerning karma; the fourth, not mentioned in the text, consists of stubborn attachment to one's views. The fifth, wrong views concerning prohibitions, refers to belief in the efficacy of unbeneficial acts of asceticism.

[55] That is, the court of King Yāma, the lord of death, who judges the karma of the dead and the corresponding retribution that the dead must undergo.

record. If you try to argue or rationalize, they merely find the page and place and read it out just as it actually happened. They have unimpeachable proof, and your protestations are useless. (VII, 128)

[9] "The ninth cause is the habit of blaming, which, when joined to a predilection for defamation, leads to making false accusations. Such a person comes to feel that he is being crushed between mountains or between boulders, or that he is being broken on stone wheels, or being ripped by plows, or being ground up by millstones. These are like the injuries visited on good people by a slanderous villain.

"When the latent habitual energies of blaming lead to habitual unjust acts, the consequence in the hells will be the experience of being pressed, pummeled, bagged, squeezed, and strained, then weighed and measured, and so forth. Therefore, when the Thus-Come Ones of the ten directions see false accusations being made, they call them 'vicious tigers.' Bodhisattvas view unjust acts as equivalent to claps of thunder.

[10] "The tenth cause is the habit of disputatiousness, which, when joined to a predilection for obfuscation and concealment, leads to vociferous court proceedings. Such a person will feel that in the end, everything will be revealed, as if reflected in a mirror by the light of a candle — just as no shadows can hide people when they are in full sunlight.

"When the latent habitual energies of disputatiousness are joined to engagement in disputes, the consequence in the hells will be the truth about one's acts being confirmed by evil companions, as if one's karma were illumined in a mirror. Therefore, when the Thus-Come Ones of the ten directions see instances of obfuscation and concealment, they call them 'shadowy villains.' Bodhisattvas view obfuscation to be as burdensome as the task of carrying a high mountain on one's head while walking in the ocean.

"Ānanda, these retributions are the consequences of individual beings' intentional acts. For this karma there are these ten causes based on beings' habits, and beings undergo in turn six kinds of retribution.

"How is it that there are six kinds of retribution, Ānanda? All beings create karma through their six consciousnesses, and they experience retribution through their six faculties. How is it that the various retributions are experienced through the six faculties?

[1] "First, there are the retributions that are the negative consequence of intentional acts of seeing. This karma of seeing affects the other five consciousnesses as well. When a being is about to die, he may first see fire raging throughout the worlds of the ten directions.[56] Upon his death, his spiritual awareness will ascend and then fall, riding downward on a wisp of smoke directly into the Unrelenting Hell. Then one of two things may happen. If there is light for the being to see by, he may perceive all manner of ferocious creatures, which cause him to experience the extremes of fear. Or there may only be darkness, and all will be silent; nothing can be seen. The being then feels a boundless terror.

> The text here describes how the ten causes lead to retributions through the six faculties. These retributions are interconnected. Although one of the six faculties may have been the predominant cause of a karmic offense, the other five are all involved to some extent. They act as accomplices. . . .
>
> In general, the reason we commit so many karmic offenses is that we are unable to control our faculties. We can't keep ourselves from being affected by the experience of the six kinds of perceived objects. Instead of redirecting our hearing inward to listen to our true nature so that we can experience the supreme awakening, we fly out through our six faculties in pursuit of perceived objects, and we commit a myriad of karmic offenses in the process. . . .
>
> If you have samādhi, then it doesn't matter what you look at every day. The more you see, the less you will be influenced by the beauty of the opposite sex. But if you don't have that kind of skill, then you need to be a little bit more careful. With a little more care, you won't have to hug the copper pillar or fall into some other hell. (VII, 134–5)

"Next, that raging fire that he saw may overload his ear-consciousness so that he is overwhelmed by the sounds of liquids and molten copper boiling in cauldrons. His nose-consciousness may also be overloaded

---

[56] Seeing and fire are associated because sexual desire often arises in response to what is seen.

so that he is overwhelmed by the smells of black smoke and purplish fumes. His tongue-consciousness may also be overloaded so that he is overwhelmed by the scorching taste of a gruel of hot iron pellets. His body-consciousness may be overloaded so that he is overwhelmed by the sensation of hot ashes and blazing embers burning his body. His mind-consciousness may be overloaded so that he experiences the processes of cognition as overwhelming spurts of flame and showers of sparks flickering and bursting in the air.

[2] "Second are the retributions that are the negative consequence of intentional acts of hearing. This karma of hearing affects the other five consciousnesses as well. First, when a being is about to die, he may hear the roar of gigantic waves as they inundate earth and sky. Upon his death, the being's spiritual awareness will sink downward, riding the waves directly into the Unrelenting Hell. Then one of two things may happen. If the being can hear, he may perceive a crashing din that causes him to become dull and deranged. Or, the being may be unable to hear, and the utter absence of sound causes him to sink into mental darkness.

> When a being is about to die, he may hear the roar of gigantic waves inun-
> dating heaven and earth. But does this phenomenon really take place? No,
> it merely appears that way to that particular being as his karmic retribution.
> The same is true when we see mountains, rivers, vegetation, buildings . . .
> and everything else in the world. They all are manifestations of our karma. . . .
> When our karma ends and our emotion is emptied out, we will realize that
> everything throughout the Dharma-Realm is empty. There isn't anything at all.
> But due to our attachment to phenomena, we see all kinds of colors, shapes,
> and forms. (VII, 139–40)

"That roar of the gigantic waves that he heard may now overload his ear-consciousness so that he hears voices accusing and interrogating him. Next, his eye-consciousness may be overloaded also so that he is overwhelmed by a vision of thunderclouds composed of noxious vapors. His nose-consciousness may also be overloaded so that he is overwhelmed by the stench of marsh-water infested with venomous bugs that swarm over his body as the water drenches him. His tongue-consciousness may be overloaded so that he is overwhelmed by the tastes of pus, blood, and all kinds of filth. His body-consciousness may be overloaded so that he is overwhelmed by the feeling that his body is covered with the feces and urine of beasts and ghosts. His mind-consciousness may be overloaded so that he experiences the processes of cognition as overwhelming lightning-strikes and pounding hail.

[3] "Third are the retributions that are the negative consequence of intentional acts of smelling. This karma of the nose-consciousness affects the other five consciousnesses as well. First, when a being is about to die, he may perceive toxic vapors thickly filling the air far and near. Upon his death, his spiritual awareness will try to rise above the vapors, but instead he will fall into the Unrelenting Hell. Then one of two things may happen. If the being's nasal passages are open, he will inhale so much of the noxious vapors that his mind becomes deranged. Or, if his nasal passages are blocked, he will suffocate, lose consciousness, and fall to the ground.

"The vapors that he smelled may overload his nose-consciousness, and he will feel that he is being subjected to interrogations concerning his character and past behavior. Next, the vapors may overload his eye-consciousness so that he is overwhelmed by visions of flames and torches. The vapors may also overload his ear-consciousness so that he is overwhelmed by the cries of beings drowning in cauldrons filled with boiling liquids. The vapors may also overload his tongue-consciousness so that he is overwhelmed by the taste of rotten fish and rancid stews. The vapors may overload his body-consciousness so that he is overwhelmed by an experience of being split open and of putrefying into a great mountain of flesh with a hundred thousand open wounds like so many open eyes, and these wounds are fed upon by countless maggots. His mind-consciousness may also become overloaded so that he experiences the processes of cognition as ashes and fumes and as sand and gravel flying though the air to pound and shatter his body.

[4] "Fourth are the retributions that are the negative consequence of intentional acts of tasting. This karma of the tongue-consciousness affects the other sense-consciousnesses as well. First, when a being is about to die, he may perceive a net of red-hot iron that covers the whole world

with intense heat. Upon his death, the being's spiritual awareness will fall into the net and be suspended there, hanging upside down until he falls into the Unrelenting Hell. Then one or two things may happen. He may breathe a vapor in through his mouth, and this vapor may cause his tongue and his whole body to freeze solid and crack. Or, if he tries to spit the vapor out, he will be engulfed by a raging fire which burns him to the marrow of his bones.

"As his tongue-consciousness undergoes these experiences, he will feel that he is being forced to make confessions and to suffer punishments. Next, his eye-consciousness may have the experience of overwhelming visions of being burned by hot metal and hot stones. His ear-consciousness may undergo an overwhelming experience of sounds seeming to stab him with sharp blades. His nose-consciousness may undergo an overwhelming experience of his nose becomng a gigantic cage of iron that encompasses everything around him. His body-consciousness may undergo an overwhelming experience of being pierced by arrows and darts. His mind-consciousness may be overwhelmed by the experience of the contents of his mind seeming like flying bits of hot iron raining down on him from the sky.

[5] "Fifth are the retributions that are the negative consequence of intentional acts of touching. This karma of the body-consciousness affects the five other consciousnesses as well. First, when a being is about to die, he may perceive great mountains closing in on him on all sides so that he cannot escape. Upon his death, the being's spiritual awareness will perceive a great iron city teeming with fire-dogs and fire-snakes and with tigers, wolves, and lions. Ox-headed guards of the hells and horse-headed rākṣasas, armed with spears, drive the being through the city gates and into the Unrelenting Hell. Then one of two things may happen. If the being's body is still capable of sensation, he will feel his body being crushed between mountains so that his blood spurts forth from his squashed flesh and bones. Or, if the being's body is no longer capable of sensation, swords will pierce his body and slice up his heart and liver.

"As his body-consciousness undergoes these experiences, it will seem to him that he is being clubbed, caned, stabbed, or pierced with arrows.

Next, his eye-consciousness may have an overwhelming vision of being engulfed in flames. His ear-consciousness may undergo an overwhelming experience of hearing cries of distress on the road to the hells or in the holding cells, courtrooms, or prisoners' docks. His nose-consciousness may undergo the overwhelming experience of suffocation due to being confined to a sack, or else by the experience of restricted breathing when he is tied up and beaten. His tongue-consciousness may undergo the overwhelming experience of his tongue being plowed up, or clamped and pulled out, or chopped up, or cut out. His mind-consciousness may undergo the overwhelming experience of the contents of his mind falling or flying, or frying or roasting.

[6] "Sixth are the retributions that are the negative consequence of intentional acts of cognition. This karma of mind-consciousness affects the five other consciousnesses as well. First, when the being is about to die, he may encounter a violent wind that lays waste to the lands. Upon his death, the being's spiritual awareness may be conscious of being swept high up into the air and then of plummeting down along the winds straight into the Unrelenting Hell. Then one of two things may happen. If the being lacks clear awareness, his extreme confusion may lead to panic, and he will run about ceaselessly. Or, if he is conscious and not confused, he will be fully aware of his suffering as he feels that he is being endlessly fried and burned. The excruciating pain will be beyond bearing.

"These perversities in his mind-consciousness may now become so overwhelming that it will seem to him that he is being confined. Next, his eye-consciousness may experience overwhelming visions of people interrogating him and confronting him with testimony. His ear-consciousness may undergo an overwhelming experience of what seems to him to be the din of great rocks clashing together or else of what seem to be storms of ice or of dust that cloud his hearing. His nose-consciousness may undergo an overwhelming experience of what seems to him to be a great burning, whether of a chariot or a ship or a prison. His tongue-consciousness may undergo an overwhelming experience of sensations that are felt by the tongue when it is uttering great shouts, cries, groans of regret, and sobs. His body-consciousness may undergo an overwhelming experience of being expanded or shrunk, or of lying face-down while he undergoes ten thousand deaths and rebirths within a single day.

"Ānanda, these are the ten causes and six negative consequences of being reborn in the hells. All these experiences are created by beings' confusion and delusion.

> Many different hells have just been described, and all result from the ten habitual causes. They are sexual desire, craving, arrogance, hatred, enticement, falsehood, resentment, wrong views, blaming, and disputatiousness.
>
> These habitual causes result in the six interconnected retributions that involve the eyes, ears, nose, tongue, body, and mind as they react to visible objects, sounds, odors, flavors, objects of touch, and objects of cognition. All these hells are created by beings' own confusion and delusion. . . . Once ignorance arises, it leads to various karmic manifestations. From karma, various offenses are created. However, if we can return our hearing inward to hear our true nature, then all this karma will become empty. (VII, 153–4)

"If a being's six consciousnesses all create evil karma at the same time, he will enter the Unrelenting Hell, where he will undergo an immeasurable amount of suffering for uncountable eons. However, if the negative consequences arise from intentional acts that were committed at separate times by the faculties' engagement with their objects, the being will enter one of the Eight Cold Hells. If a being commits acts of killing, stealing, and sexual misconduct with body, speech, and mind — all three — then he will enter one of the Eighteen Hells.

"However, if a being has committed only two of the three major offenses — for example, if he has killed and has stolen — then he will enter one of the Thirty-Six Hells. And if he has committed only one of the three major offenses with only one of the three creators of karma, then he will enter one of the One Hundred and Eight Hells.

"Therefore, individual beings create their own karma by their own acts, but if their karma is the same as other beings' karma, they will all fall into the same hells in this world. These hells are created by their deluded acts of mind. Apart from those acts, the hells have no independent existence."

7
The Destiny of Ghosts

"Next, Ānanda, after these beings have passed through eons of fire to pay the debts they incurred for committing these offenses — such offenses as violating and vilifying the precepts and the rules for deportment, violating the Bodhisattva Precepts, slandering the Buddha's teachings about nirvana, and all the other various offenses — then these beings will become ghosts.

> These individuals denounce the idea of precepts and rules of deportment by saying things such as . . . "People should be free to do as they please. After all, this is a democratic country, and everyone is free and independent. So there shouldn't be any prohibitive rules in Buddhism, either." These people commit even more karmic offenses by claiming that one can become a Buddhist monk or nun without taking the necessary precepts. (VII, 158)
>
> Ten kinds of ghosts are discussed below in connection with the karma created by their habitual craving. However, there are many more kinds of ghosts. The ones described here are merely representative. (VII, 159)

"If it was a craving for possessions that led a being to commit offenses, then once the debt incurred for committing those offenses is paid, the being will encounter some object, assume its form, and become a bizarre shape-shifting ghost.

"If it was craving for the opposite sex that led a being to commit offenses, then once the debt incurred for those offenses is paid, the being will encounter a wind, assume its attributes, and become a drought-ghost.

"If it was a craving to mislead people that led a being to commit offenses, then once that debt is paid, the being will encounter an animal, assume its form, and become an animal-possessing ghost.[57]

---

[57] Ch. *mei gui* 魅鬼, a ghost that possesses animals, as mentioned here. It may also possess a person. The Sanskrit name is not known.

"If it was the cravings and emotions of hatred that led a being to commit offenses, then once that debt is paid, the being will encounter a venomous creature, assume its form, and become a hex-poison ghost.

"If it was the cravings and emotions of long-cherished enmity that led a being to commit offenses, then once that debt is paid, the being will encounter some enfeebled creature, assume its attributes, and become a plague-ghost.

"If it was the cravings and emotions of arrogance that led a being to commit offenses, then once that debt is paid, the being will encounter some source of vital energy, assume its attributes, and become a hungry ghost.

"If it was a craving to indulge in slander that led a being to commit offenses, then once that debt is paid, the being will encounter some source of dark energy, assume its attributes, and become a nightmare-ghost.

"If it was a craving to indulge in perverse uses of intelligence that led a being to commit offenses, then once that is paid, the being will encounter some source of intense vital energy, assume its attributes, and become a malicious shape-shifting ghost.[58]

> Although this person may consider himself to be extremely intelligent, in fact he is totally confused in what he does. He may be smart, but he misuses his intelligence and ends up by outsmarting himself. For example, he clearly knows that murder is wrong, but he commits murder anyway. . . .
>
> Shape-shifting ghosts sometimes take the form of a child, but with only one leg. Sometimes this ghost will appear as an adult . . . with its head growing out from between its legs. (VII, 165–6)

"If it was a craving for selfish advancement that led a being to commit offenses, then once that debt is paid, the being will encounter someone who has light and will assume the attributes appropriate for becoming an attendant ghost.

"If it was a craving to form factions that led a being to commit offenses, then once that debt is paid, the being will encounter some human, assume that person's attributes, and become an oracle-ghost.

---

[58] Skt. *vyāḍa,* Ch. *wang-liang* 魍魎.

This kind of ghost can possess people and speak through them, saying such things as "I am the Buddha so-and-so," or "I am the Bodhisattva such-and-such." . . . Among these people are oracles who predict auspicious and inauspicious events . . . with complete accuracy. They can foretell the future. This is an example of the need to distinguish between what is proper and what is not. The proper way to gain the ability to predict the future is to practice in accord with the Dharma. Relying on a ghost is not correct. (VII, 169)

"Ānanda, their cravings are the sole reasons for these beings' having previously fallen into the hells. Once they have burned away their debts in the hells, they ascend to be reborn as ghosts. This too is a consequence of their own delusion. If they were to become fully awakened, then with their wondrous and perfect understanding, they would know that, fundamentally, these retributions are not real at all."

8
The Destiny of Animals

"Ānanda, once a being has made full payment on that part of his karmic debt which he was due to pay as a ghost, his mind will empty itself of the emotions and thoughts that brought him to the ghostly destiny. Now he must come to this world to face the enmity of his original creditors and in person repay what he owes them. Thus he is born in the body of an animal to repay his debts from his previous lives.

> Such a being has to repay the debts that he accumulated during countless past eons, and these debts need to be repaid in kind. For example, if you have killed someone, you will have pay with your own life. If you owe someone a pig, you will become his pig in order to repay him. . . . We can see how improper actions can lead to a lot of trouble. (VII, 171–2)

"Suppose a being has been a bizarre shape-shifting ghost and has assumed the attributes of an object. When the object disintegrates, then the being, having undergone its retribution as a ghost, is reborn into this world, usually as an owl.

"Suppose a being has been a drought-ghost and has assumed the attributes of a southeast wind. When the wind dies down, then the being, having undergone its retribution as a ghost, is reborn into this world, usually among the various kinds of animals that are considered to be ill omens.

"Suppose a being has been an animal-possessing ghost and has assumed the attributes of an animal. When the animal dies, then the being, having undergone its retribution as a ghost, is reborn into this world, usually as a kind of fox.

"Suppose a being has been a hex-poison ghost and has assumed the attributes of a venomous creature. When that venomous creature dies, then the being, having undergone its retribution as a ghost, is reborn into this world, usually as an animal that is venomous itself.

"Suppose a being has been a plague-ghost and has assumed the attributes of an enfeebled creature. When that creature dies, then the being, having undergone its retribution as a ghost, will be reborn into this world, usually as a kind of parasitic worm.

"Suppose a being has been a hungry ghost and has assumed the attributes of some vital energy. When that energy disperses, then the being, having undergone its retribution as a ghost, is reborn into this world, usually among the kinds of animals that are eaten by people.

"Suppose a being has been a nightmare-ghost and has assumed the attributes of some dark energy. When that energy disperses, then the being, having undergone its retribution as a ghost, is reborn into this world, usually among the animals that serve people or that are a source of people's clothing.

"Suppose a being has been a malicious shape-shifting ghost and has assumed the attributes of some intense vital energy. When that energy is exhausted, then the being, having undergone its retribution as a ghost, is reborn into this world, usually as a migratory bird.

"Suppose a being has been an attendant ghost and has assumed the attributes of someone who has light. When that person's light is extinguished, then the being, having undergone its retribution as a ghost, is reborn into this world, usually among one of the many kinds of animals that are considered to be good omens.

"Suppose a being has been an oracle-ghost and has assumed the attributes of a human. When that human dies, then the being, having undergone its retribution as a ghost, is reborn in the world, usually among animals who serve people as companions or as messengers.

"In this way, Ānanda, when the fires of their karma have caused their lives as ghosts to wither away, these beings are reborn as animals in further repayment of the debts they incurred during their previous lives. This too is the consequence of their own delusion. If they experience a full awakening, then with their wondrous and perfect understanding, they will know that, fundamentally, these retributions are not real at all.

"You spoke earlier[59] of Bhikṣuṇī Lotus-Fragrance, King Virūḍhaka and Bhikṣu Sunakṣatra. They themselves created their evil karma. It did not

---

[59] In asking for instruction at the beginning of part 9.6 above.

descend upon them from the heavens, nor did it emerge from the earth. No other human being imposed it on them. Their own delusion brought their karma about, and they themselves must undergo the retribution for it. Yet all this consists merely of illusions and delusions that manifest within the fully awakened mind."

9

The Destiny of Humans

"Moreover, Ānanda, suppose these beings, having been born as animals to pay the debts they incurred in previous lives, live longer as animals than their debts have required. On that basis, these beings can now return to their original status as humans, and provided that their strength, their blessings, and their merit are sufficient, they can retain their human bodies as compensation for their overpayment of their karmic debt.[60] But if their blessings are not sufficient, they will fall back into the realm of animals in order to make a direct payment of any other debts they owe.

"Ānanda, beings should realize that they should settle their debts, whether with money, goods, or labor, so that their indebtedness can naturally come to an end. But if, during this process, beings take each other's lives or eat each other's flesh, then they may well continue through countless eons killing each other and eating each other as if they were turning ceaselessly on a wheel, now on top, now beneath. The wheel may never stop unless they undertake the practice of calming the mind or unless a Buddha appears in the world.

> There are only two ways to escape the cycle of karmic debts. One is by stopping the mind until one realizes the great Śūraṅgama Samādhi. The other occurs when a Buddha appears in the world and explains people's karmic debts to them. Then both the debtor and the creditor understand that they should not continue to incur such debts, and in this way they can stop the endless cycle of mutual indebtedness. (VII, 182)

"Now you should understand that when beings who have been owls have paid their debts, they will regain their human form and will be born among people who are pig-headed and stubborn.

"When beings who have been animals that are considered to be ill omens have paid back their debts, they will regain their human form and be reborn among people who are deformed.

---

[60] That is, when an overpayment was made during their long lives as animals.

> We often see mention of this type of rebirth in the newspapers. A child may
> be born with two heads, or with two bodies but only one head. Sometimes the
> child's faculties of perception will be out of place. Perhaps the eyes will be
> where the ear should be and the ears where the eyes belong. . . . Often such
> individuals die as soon as they are born. (VII, 183)

"When beings who have been foxes have paid back their debts, they will regain their human form and will be reborn among people who are of lowly status and low intelligence.

'When beings who have been venomous animals have paid back their debts, they will regain their human form and will be reborn among people who are vicious.

> Although these beings manage to be reborn in the human realm, they still
> have not changed their bad habits. They are extremely fierce and cruel. . . .
> They pay no attention to whether their actions are justifiable or not. If you get
> in their way, and even if you don't, they will kill you without hesitation. (VII,
> 184)

"When beings who have been parasitic worms have paid back their debts, they will regain their human form and will be reborn among people who are menial workers.

"When beings who have been animals of the kind that are eaten by people have paid back their debts, they will regain their human form and will be reborn among people who are weak-willed and dependent.

"When beings who have been animals of the kind that serve people or of the kind that are a source of people's clothing, have paid back their debts, they will regain their human form and will be reborn among manual laborers.

"When beings who have been migratory birds have paid back their debts, they will regain their human form and will be reborn among people of refinement.

"When beings who have been animals serving as good omens have paid back their debts, they will regain their human form and will be reborn among people who are intelligent.

"When beings who have been domesticated animals have paid back their debts, they will regain their human form and will be reborn among people who are accomplished.

> People like this comprehend what's going on. They understand social graces. But they don't have a genuine and comprehensive understanding that allows them to see into the past and comprehend the present. . . . They simply attain a superficial kind of success in dealing with the world. (VII, 187)

"Ānanda, all these people have paid their debts from previous lives and have regained their human form. Since time without beginning, they had been creating the karma that results from deluded scheming, and they had been taking turns killing and being killed. If they do not encounter a Thus-Come One or if they do not hear the true Dharma, then in the midst of the stress of entanglement with perceived objects, they will repeat this cycle of karma indefinitely, as the Dharma explains. These people are to be deeply pitied."

10
The Destiny of the Ascetic Masters

"Ānanda, there are also people who practice kinds of samādhi that do not follow the path that leads to true awakening. Instead, their practices are based on a mistaken intent to fortify the physical body. They seclude themselves in mountain forests beyond the reach of people. These are the ascetic masters, of which there are ten kinds.[61]

"Some of these beings, Ānanda, in their effort to fortify themselves, tirelessly devote themselves to a diet of medicinal potions. When they have perfected this dietary practice, they become ascetic masters who are earth-bound.

"Some of them, in order to fortify themselves, tirelessly devote themselves to a diet of medicinal herbs. When they have perfected this practice, they become ascetic masters who can fly.

"Some of them, in order to fortify themselves, tirelessly devote themselves to ingesting precious metals and minerals. When they have perfected their alchemical practice, they become ascetic masters who are adept at roaming freely.

"Some of them, in order to fortify themselves, tirelessly devote themselves, whether they are moving or still, to bringing their spirit and their vital energies to perfection. When they have perfected this practice, they become ascetic masters who are adept at astral travel.

[61] In this section on ascetic masters, the Chinese is so extremely terse that the meanings are hardly intelligible without the aid of the commentarial tradition. Yet difficulties exist even with the commentaries, since the Chinese commentators, at least before modern times, were not generally familiar with the Indian practices described in the text. The tendency was to interpret these practices in terms of Daoist practices, which were well known in China. Here, Daoist influence seems to be present in the Chinese text. The Chinese *xian* 仙 (which is translated here as "ascetic master," but which is more often rendered into English as "immortal") usually referred to the recluses and alchemists of the Daoist tradition. However, the original Sanskrit was probably *ṛṣi*, a class of pre-Buddhist ascetics who were considered to be different from both ordinary humans and gods.

"Some of them, in order to fortify themselves, tirelessly devote themselves to transforming their saliva. When they have perfected this practice, they become ascetic masters who can travel to the heavens.

> When the tongue is placed on the roof of the mouth, saliva accumulates. Some non-Buddhist practitioners call this "ambrosia," "water from heaven," and other such names. The process is complete when the saliva is swallowed. . . . The faces of these ascetic masters take on a glow from this practice, and although they may be very old, their faces have a child-like appearance. (VII, 194)

"Some of them, in order to fortify themselves, tirelessly devote themselves to absorbing the essences of celestial bodies. When they have perfected this practice, they become ascetic masters who can travel everywhere freely.

> These ascetic masters practice breathing in the essence of the sun and the moon. . . . For example, in the morning, they face the sun and inhale three hundred and sixty times. In the evening, they face the moon and inhale another three hundred and sixty times. . . .
>
> Actually, some of the ascetic masters' practices are similar to Buddhist practices. One major difference is that the ascetic masters' practices involve attachments, whereas Buddhist practices do not. The kind of skill that the ascetic masters develop is basically all right, but they become attached to it. . . . Due to this attachment, they cannot completely transcend the cycle of death and rebirth. (VII, 194–5)

"Some of them, in order to fortify themselves, tirelessly devote themselves to reciting mantras and observing prohibitions. When they have perfected their skill in these practices, they become ascetic masters who adhere to a specific path.[62]

"Some of them, in order to fortify themselves, tirelessly devote themselves to mental control of their vital energies. When they have perfected

---

[62] The first six groups of ascetic masters gain skill in various modes of travel; the last four gain skill in various practices.

this practice so that they can bring it to mind at will, they become ascetic masters who practice by means of contemplative illumination.

> When these ascetic masters have perfected their practice, they have a kind of light. In thought after thought, they imagine that they are transformed into a golden light. When they hold this thought for a long time . . . they may eventually have some success. Because of the way these masters gain some light, they are referred to as "ascetic masters who practice by means of contemplative illumination." (VII, 196)

"Some of them, in order to fortify themselves, tirelessly devote themselves to an internal union of energies. When they have perfected this practice, they become ascetic masters who are adept at a practice that is based on their inner essences.

"Some of them, in order to fortify themselves, tirelessly devote themselves to following the principles of internal change. When they have perfected their understanding of this practice, they become ascetic masters who are without peer.

"Ānanda, all these are people who, in training their minds, do not follow a path that leads to a correct awakening. Instead, they seek to know the secrets of living a long life, and they may live for thousands of years. They retire deep into the mountains or onto an island in the ocean, cutting themselves off from human contact. However, because of their deluded thinking, they too are bound to the cycle of death and rebirth. They do not practice the correct samādhi, and therefore, although they have lived long lives as a result of their practices, they too must die and enter one of the various destinies."

11
The Destiny of the Gods

A. The Gods of the Six Heavens of Desire

[1] "Ānanda, some people in this world do not seek what is everlasting and cannot yet renounce their love and affection for their spouses. But if their minds do not turn to thoughts of sexual misconduct, they will develop a certain purity and radiance. After their lives have ended, they will ascend to the vicinity of the sun and moon. Such people become gods in the Heaven of the Four Kings.

> Not to "seek what is everlasting" can mean that these people don't seek eternal life in this world, but it can also mean that they don't seek the everlasting true mind. . . . These individual are not interested in sexual misconduct. Sexual misconduct means engaging in sexual activities with someone other than one's spouse and does not apply to sexual activities between married couples. However, even in marriage, such activities should not be excessive. When you practice in accord with Dharma, no matter how much merit and virtue you may have, you must not engage in sexual misconduct; otherwise, all your hard work will be in vain. . . . When one does not engage in sexual misconduct, one will be pure, and out of that purity comes light — the natural light of virtue. (VII, 201–2)

[2] "Some others have only a small amount of desire for their spouses, but they do not manage to live in complete purity. After their lives have ended, they will ascend beyond the sun and moon to dwell at the summit of Mount Sumeru. Such people become gods of the Heaven of the Thirty-Three.

> Those who become gods in the Heaven of the Four Kings did not engage in sexual misconduct, but they still desired their spouses. . . . The text discusses people with very little regard for sexual activity even within their marriage. . . . With little emotional desire, the light of their true nature comes forth and enables them to be reborn in the heavens. But because they don't know how to practice in accord with Dharma, they do not attain complete purity. (VII, 203–4)

> Why do some people have such strong sexual desires? It's because of the formidable obstacles that their karma places in their path. . . . Such obstacles cause people to think of nothing but sex from morning till night. . . . However, it's precisely in the midst of these obstacles that we must wake up and realize the need to reduce their power over us. If we simply accept our karmic obstacles, we will continue to fall, and we will be reborn as an animal in the future. The stronger our desires, the farther we will fall. (VII, 203)
>
> On the other hand, if you want to be reborn in the heavens, just have few desires and be content. (VII, 207)

[3] "Some others will succumb to desire when an occasion arises, but after an indulgence they give the matter no further thought. While they are in the human realm, their desire is quiescent more than it is active. After their lives have ended, they abide peacefully, shining with their own radiance, in a realm of space that is so far above the sun and the moon as to be beyond the reach of sunlight and moonlight. Such people become gods in the Heaven of Self-Restraint.

[4] "Some others are always still, except when they are unable to resist the stimulus of contact. After their lives have ended, they ascend to a refined place that is isolated from the lower heavens and from the human realm. Here they are untouched even by the three great disasters that come at the end of an eon.[63] Such people become gods of the Heaven of Joyous Contentment.[64]

[5] "Some others have no desire themselves but will respond to the actions of their spouses. For them the act itself has no more flavor than wax. After their lives are ended, they ascend still higher to a realm of creativity. Such people become gods in the Heaven of Delight in Creating.

[6] "Yet others have no mundane thoughts. Although their actions seem no different than the actions of ordinary people, their minds transcend the acts that they engage in. After their lives are ended, they ascend

---

[63] Disasters caused by fire, wind, and water.

[64] Skt. Tuṣita. This heaven consists of an inner court, presided over by the Bodhisattva Maitreya and populated by Bodhisattvas, and an outer court, populated by the gods here described.

beyond all the lower heavens, including the Heaven of Delight in Creating. Such people are born in the Heaven of Pleasure Derived from What Others Create.

> Nothing in the environment of this heaven originates there. The gods here take delight in the offerings made by beings from other heavens. The bliss is vast here, and there's no work to be done. (VII, 208–9)

"Ānanda, these six kinds of gods have transcended the physical act of mating, but their minds are not free of it. Because of this, they have had to return to these heavens, which belong to the realm of desire.

B. The Gods of the Eighteen Heavens of Form: The First Dhyāna[65]

[1] "Ānanda, some people in this world, in refining their minds, do not avail themselves of the practice of meditation in stillness, and so they do not develop wisdom. Nevertheless, if they can refrain from sexual activity and if their minds are free at all times of any thought of sexual desire such that they are undefiled by sexual passion, they will not remain in the realm of desire. These people, if they wish, may be reborn as one of the companions of Brahma in the Heaven of Brahma's Retinue.

[2] "These people have cast out their habits of desire, and with their minds free of desire, they delight in following the precepts and the rules of deportment. At all times, they are able to practice the virtue of purity, and so they become gods in the Heaven of the Ministers of Brahma.

[3] "When in body and mind these people have attained a wondrous perfection such that their flawless deportment inspires awe, they will not only follow the prohibitory precepts in complete purity but will gain a clarity of understanding as well. They become great Brahman kings in the Heaven of the Great Brahma, and at all times they are able to govern their retinues of gods.

"Ānanda, the gods at these three levels are free of the burdens of suffering and affliction. Although their samādhi is not the genuine samādhi

---

[65] "Dhyāna" elsewhere has referred to the practice of meditation in stillness or to states of mind achieved through meditation; here, however, "dhyāna" refers to the states of mind of the gods in the eighteen heavens in the realm of form.

that results from correct practice, their minds are nevertheless pure, and their outflows are not active. These are the gods of the heavens of the first dhyāna.

> If you practice in accord with Dharma, your pulse may stop when you reach the level of the first dhyāna. . . . However, this is not a lofty state; it's just a first step in one's practice. (VII, 214)

C. The Gods of the Eighteen Heavens of Form: The Second Dhyāna

[4] "Next, Ānanda, above the gods of the Brahma Heavens are gods who govern them and who have perfected the practice of purity. The minds of these higher gods are lucid and still. From their deep tranquility, light comes forth. They abide in the Heaven of Lesser Light.

[5] "Next are gods who emit light and who — as they shine upon one another with an inexhaustible brilliance — illumine their realm throughout the ten directions, turning it all to crystal. They abide in the Heaven of All-Permeating Light.

[6] "Next are gods who take full control of their light, having mastered the essence of the teaching about it. They are able to emit and to respond to many kinds of pure light, and they use this light to convey countless meanings. They abide in the Heaven of Speech by Means of Light.

> In this heaven, the gods communicate by sending pulses of light to each other. Their ideas are transmitted by means of their light. (VII, 216)

"The gods of these three heavens, which are higher than the heavens of the first dhyāna, are freed from the burdens of worry and anxiety. Although their samādhi is not the genuine samādhi that results from correct practice, their minds are nevertheless pure, and their coarse outflows have been subdued. They are the gods of the heavens of the second dhyāna.

> When practitioners meditate and enter the second dhyāna, their breath comes to a halt, and just as in the first dhyāna, their pulse stops. . . . If someone's pulse stops, doesn't it mean that he or she is dead? Not in this case, because even though the external evidence of a pulse is gone, the pulse of one's

essential nature is active. The same applies to the breath. In other words, the true breath and pulse of one's essential nature awaken and take over, so the coarse forms of the pulse and the breath can stop. (VII, 217)

D. The Gods of the Eighteen Heavens of Form: The Third Dhyāna

[7] "Ānanda, to the gods who have perfected light as a medium of communication, the wondrous secrets of this medium are now revealed. They refine their practice until they succeed in opening their minds to the bliss of stillness. These are the gods of the Heaven of Lesser Purity.

[8] "Next they experience a state of purity and emptiness which expands until it becomes boundless. Their bodies and minds are serene and are filled with tranquil bliss. These are the gods of the Heaven of All-Permeating Purity.

[9] "After their bodies and minds have become completely pure, the world itself is purified due to the virtue of their perfected purity. This purified state becomes a superior place of refuge in which they can rest in the bliss of tranquility. These are the gods of the Heaven of Universal Purity.

"Ānanda, in these three heavens, which are above the heavens of the second dhyāna, the gods experience perfect harmony, and their bodies and minds are peaceful and secure. They enjoy all-permeating bliss. Their samādhi is not the genuine samādhi that results from correct practice, but because their minds are peaceful and secure, they are filled with bliss. These are the gods of the Heavens of the third dhyāna.

> Before you reach the third dhyāna, your thoughts are still active. For instance, when your pulse stops, you may think, "Why has my pulse stopped?" and with that one thought, the pulse starts again. When your breath stops, you may think, "I'm not breathing!" and as soon as you have that thought, the breath starts again. This is what happens before your thoughts stop. Now, in the third dhyāna, . . . thoughts no longer arise. You pay no attention to your pulse or to your breath. . . . When no thoughts arise, you realize the genuine bliss of stillness. (VII, 222)

E. The Gods of the Eighteen Heavens of Form: The Fourth Dhyāna

[10] "Moreover, Ānanda, there are gods whose bodies and minds are no longer creating the causes for future suffering. They realize that the bliss of the heavens is impermanent and must eventually decay, and they thereupon renounce both suffering and bliss. Because they have put an end to all coarse and burdensome mental attributes, the essence of pure blessing is created. These are the gods of the Heaven of the Creation of Blessings.

[11] "Once they have wholly renounced those mental states,[66] they gain a superior understanding and purity. In their state of unlimited merit, they experience a wondrous harmony that is everlasting. These are the gods of the Heaven of Cherished Blessings.

[12] "From that heaven, Ānanda, the path divides. On one path, some gods of the Heaven of Cherished Blessings are able to shine with a pure and infinite radiance such that the light of their blessings and their merit is perfected. They will be secure in the results of their practice and will become gods of the Heaven of Great Fruition.

[13] "On the other path are gods who, while dwelling in the Heaven of Cherished Blessings, reject both suffering and bliss and intensely and unrelentingly investigate the practice of renunciation. When they have thoroughly understood that practice and have completely mastered it, their bodies disintegrate, and for five hundred eons their minds are utterly still, like cold and compacted ashes.[67] But because they have based their practice on the mind that comes into being and ceases to be, they are unable to discover the true nature that neither comes into being nor ceases to be. Their cognitive processes cease but then revive during the last half of the final eon.[68] These are the gods of the Heaven of the Cessation of Cognition.

When these gods' cognitive processes revive, their lives enter a period of decline, and they begin to speak ill of the Buddha, the Dharma, and the Sangha. They say, "The Buddha said that an Arhat at the fourth stage has ended death

---

[66] That is, suffering and bliss.

[67] That is, their sixth consciousness is inactive.

[68] That is, the five-hundredth eon.

and rebirth. I am an Arhat at the fourth stage, so why am I on my way to undergo death and rebirth again? Probably the Buddha lied about this." . . . In
fact, reaching the level of the fourth dhyāna definitely does not mean that one
has become a fourth-stage Arhat or even a first-stage Arhat. (VII, 226)

"Ānanda, the gods of these four heavens, which are above the heavens
of the third dhyāna, can no longer be influenced by any worldly states
of suffering or bliss. However, they do not base their practice on the
unmoving and unconditioned mind, and they still harbor intentions to
attain something. Yet their spiritual skill is pure and perfected. These are
the gods of the heavens of the fourth dhyāna.

F. The Gods of the Eighteen Heavens of Form: The Pure Abodes

"Also within this dhyāna, Ānanda, are the five Heavens of Pure Abode.
The gods in these heavens have by this time completely eliminated the
nine stages of habitual delusion.[69] Here both suffering and bliss have been
forgotten. These gods will never again live at any lesser celestial level.
They dwell together in a place of peace, each of them at an equal level of
renunciation.

These five higher heavens may be considered to be among the heavens of
the fourth dhyāna, but these heavens are the dwelling places of sages, and so
they are different from the other heavens of the fourth dhyāna. (VII, 228)

[14] "First, Ānanda, are gods for whom both suffering and bliss have
ended so that they no longer have to struggle with contrasting experiences. These beings are the gods of the Heaven Beyond Affliction.[70]

[15] "Next are the gods who, having focused their practice exclusively
on renunciation, no longer harbor any basis for even the thought of suffering and bliss. These are the gods of the Heaven Beyond Heat.[71]

---

[69] The nine kinds of habits refer to the first nine categories of the eighty-one categories
of cognitive delusion.

[70] Ch. *wu fan tian* 無煩天. The Sanskrit. name of this heaven is unclear. The translation
here is of the name as it is given Chinese text, but this name may be a descriptive choice
by the Chinese translators.

[71] Skt. *atapas* — the heat generated by distress.

[16] "Next, throughout the worlds in the ten directions, their wondrous vision becomes so flawlessly clear that no perceived object can defile it. These are the gods of the Heaven of Refined Vision.

[17] "Next, their skill in envisioning becomes yet more refined, like the skills of a master potter. These are the gods of the Heaven of Clear Envisioning.

[18] "When their contemplation of the myriad subtleties of the nature of form and the nature of space reaches its ultimate point, they enter a state of boundlessness and become gods of the Highest Heaven of Form.

"Ānanda, the gods of the lower heavens of the fourth dhāyna — and even their kings — cannot see the gods of these five higher heavens. They only hear about them with admiration, just as ordinary dull-witted people in the world cannot see Arhats dwelling in the wilderness or deep in the mountains, where they keep up their practices in their sacred places for awakening.

"Ānanda, the gods of these eighteen heavens practice in solitude, free of entanglements. But they have not yet set down the burden of their bodies. Thus all these heavens comprise the Realm of Form.

G. The Gods on the Four Planes of Formlessness

"Moreover, Ānanda, at the very summit of the Realm of Form, the path again divides. On one path are those who in their practice of renunciation develop to perfection the full light of their wisdom. These gods will transcend all three realms and will become Arhats who will board the Vehicle of the Bodhisattvas.

[1] "On the second path are gods who, having been successful in their practice of renunciation, realize that their bodies are an obstacle to further progress. They cause their bodies to vanish and to become like space. Then they become gods on the Plane of Boundless Space.

[2] "Next are gods who, having caused the obstacle of their bodies to vanish, now find that there are no further obstacles of form for them to put an end to. Only their storehouse-consciousness and half of the subtle functions of the individuating consciousness remain. These are the gods on the Plane of Boundless Consciousness.

At this point, these gods don't have bodies; they only have consciousness. That consciousness is the *ālaya-vijñāna,* or storehouse-consciousness, also known as the eighth consciousness. Every move we make, every word we speak, everything we do and encounter in the course of our daily lives is stored in this consciousness. It is actually within the Matrix of the Thus-Come One, but at this point, the distinction between the eighth consciousness and the Matrix of the Thus-Come One has not completely disappeared.

In these gods on the Plane of Boundless Consciousness, in addition to their storehouse-consciousness, there remains half of their individuating consciousness, their seventh consciousness, which is also known as the defiling consciousness. Although it is true that ignorance arises in the eighth consciousness, . . . it is only when the information stored in the eighth consciousness passes through the seventh consciousness that it becomes defiled. For these gods, the seventh consciousness is functioning only at half of its capacity, so the defilement that remains is extremely subtle. (VII, 234)

[3] "When both form and space have come to an end for these gods, and when their conscious minds[72] have disappeared entirely, then there is stillness throughout the ten directions. Nothing remains, and there is no place to go. These are the gods on the Plane on Which One Has Nothing.

[4] "When their storehouse-consciousness is completely inactive, these gods can make use of this cessation of activity to contemplate deeply, so that within the endlessness of that consciousness, the nature that lies at its ending nevertheless becomes known to them. That consciousness now seems to exist and yet not to exist; it seems to have disappeared and yet has not. These are the gods on the Plane on Which Cognition Is Absent Yet Not Absent.[73]

"The gods in these heavens have deeply contemplated their emptied consciousness and yet have failed to understand its true nature.[74] This is

[72] What has disappeared here is the other half of the individuating consciousness (Yuanying, 1332).

[73] Cognition in the sense of the distinction-making consciousness.

[74] Quoting Zhenjiao, the Ven. Yuanying explains that the gods of the first of the formless planes seek to put an end to form; those of the second, to space; those of the third, to the seventh consciousness; and those of the fourth, to the eighth consciousness (1324).

the end of the sages' path that led from the Heavens of Pure Abode. These gods now become Arhats of inferior ability who turn away from the Vehicle of the Bodhisattvas.

"Other gods, who have come from the Heaven of Cessation of Cognition[75] and from other heavens that are not on the right path, never return from their deep contemplation of their emptied consciousnesses.[76] Because they lack the knowledge they need, they become lost in these heavens. As gods who have outflows, they eventually will fall back into the cycle of death and rebirth.

"Ānanda, the gods of these heavens[77] are not enlightened. Having enjoyed the rewards that were the results of their good karma, they must again be bound to the cycle of death and rebirth. But the kings of these heavens are Bodhisattvas. They play this role while in samādhi, and thereby they gradually progress in their practice towards the level of the Sages.[78]

"With regard to the gods on these four planes of formlessness, Ānanda, the activities of their bodies disappear and their mental activities cease so that they abide in samādhi. They are no longer burdened by any form that is the result of karma.[79] These four heavens comprise the realm of formlessness.

"None of the gods of these heavens fully comprehend the wondrous enlightened mind that understands. Such accumulated delusions as theirs bring about the illusory existence of the three realms. In the midst of these realms, each individual[80] in his delusion sinks into the seven destinies to join other beings whose karmas are similar."

---

[75] The fourth heaven of the fourth dhyāna.

[76] The text here refers back to the first divergence, at the pinnacle of the Heavens of Form, where some gods become great Arhats, while others, including those referred to in the present passage, enter the planes of formlessness.

[77] Excepting the gods who chose at one of the two divergences to follow a path to sagehood.

[78] That is, of Buddhas.

[79] "Any form" refers both to a body and to the external forms of the realm of desire and the realm of form.

[80] Skt. *pudgala*.

12
The Destiny of Asuras

"Moreover, Ānanda, in the Three Realms there are also the asuras, who are of four kinds.

[1] "Asuras who take the path of ghosts, devoting their strength to protecting the Dharma, have the spiritual power to live in the air. These asuras are born from eggs, and are included in the destiny of ghosts.

[2] "Some asuras, because their merit is insufficient, fall from the heavens and are fated to dwell beneath the sun and the moon.[81] These asuras are born from wombs and are included in the destiny of people.

[3] "Some asuras are world-commanding kings, both powerful and fearless. They contend for mastery with King Brahma, with Śakra, Lord of the Heavens, and with the Four Celestial Kings. These asuras are born by metamorphosis and are included in the destiny of gods.

[4] "Some asuras — a baser kind, Ānanda — are born in deepwater caves in the middle of the ocean. By day they emerge to fly about in the air, and at night they return to their watery abodes. These asuras are born in the presence of moisture and are included in the destiny of animals."

---

[81] That is, on earth.

13
The Seven Destinies Are the Result of Karma

"Ānanda, such is a detailed explanation of the seven destinies — of beings in the hells and of ghosts, animals, humans, ascetic masters, gods, and asuras. In their confusion, all are submerged in the attributes of the conditioned world. Their deluded mental activity leads them into rebirth in accordance with their karma. Within the wondrous perfect understanding that is the fundamental unconditioned mind, these destinies are like mirages of flowers seen in the sky. These destinies do not actually occupy any location; they are simply illusions. Even less do they signify anything real.

"These various beings fail to recognize the fundamental mind, Ānanda, and so they are bound to the cycle of death and rebirth. They pass through countless eons without ever attaining genuine purity, all because they indulge in killing, stealing, and sexual misconduct. If they break the precepts against these three, they will be born into the destiny of the ghosts and the other inauspicious destinies. If they avoid these offenses, they will enter the destinies of the gods and the other auspicious places of rebirth.[82] Because these beings are constantly torn between their tendency to commit offenses and their tendency to refrain from committing offenses, they continue to be bound to the cycle of death and rebirth.

"When beings are able to enter this wondrous samādhi,[83] they abide in a wondrous and everlasting stillness. That stillness is beyond the duality of existence and nonexistence, and that negating of duality is also ended. Since they have gone beyond the state in which there is killing, stealing, and sexual misconduct, how could they possibly commit those offenses?

"Ānanda, each being who has not put an end to these three intentional acts creates his own individual karma. Although each being's retribution is his own, beings may undergo a common retribution together in a definite

---

[82] The Chinese text mentions only "the destiny of gods" and the "destiny of ghosts"; these stand respectively for all the higher and lower destinies.

[83] That is, the Śūraṅgama Samādhi.

place. Their intentional acts arise from delusion, which itself has no cause. No matter how exhaustively you search for a cause, you will not find one.[84]

"You should advise practitioners that if they wish to realize full awakening through their spiritual practice, they must no longer engage in these three deluded acts. If they do not cease engaging in them, then even if they should develop spiritual powers, their skills will be limited to the circumstances of the conditioned world. If they cannot put an end to their habits of killing, stealing, and sexual misconduct, they will take the path that leads to existence as a demon.

"Even if they want to cease committing these offenses, they will end up engaging in falsehood and making the offenses worse. The Thus-Come One says that such beings are pathetic and greatly to be pitied. You all should understand that you are responsible for your own deluded actions. Your true nature that is capable of full awakening is not to blame.

> People start out by telling a lie, but later they say that they hadn't lied — which is another lie. If you tell a lie and then admit it, there's just one lie. But someone who denies the first lie he told ends up by telling two. In this way he compounds his offenses. (VII, 251)

"What has been spoken here is the right teaching. To teach otherwise is the work of the demon-king."

---

[84] That fundamental delusion has no cause is the subject of part 4.1 above.

X

Fifty Demonic
States of Mind

1
Dangers May Arise with Advanced Practice

Then the Thus-Come One prepared to leave the Dharma seat. Rising from the Lion's Throne, he placed his hand on the table before him, which was wrought of the seven precious things.[1] But then, moving his body, which was the color of purple-golden mountains, he sat down again, and he said to Ānanda and to the rest of the great assembly, "You who still need instruction, you Hearers of the Teaching and you Solitary Sages, have now dedicated yourselves to attaining a great awakening — the supreme and wondrous enlightenment. I have now taught you the right method for practice. But you are still not aware of the subtle demonic events that can occur when you undertake the practices of calming the mind and contemplative insight. If you do not purify your mind, you will not be able to recognize demonic states as they arise. You will not find the right path, and you will fall into the error of wrong views.

"Demons may arise within you from the five aggregates. Or a celestial demon or a ghost or a spirit — perhaps a mountain spirit or an animal-possessing ghost — may come to possess you. If your mind is not clear when this happens, you may well take a burglar to be your own child. Or you may feel satisfied with a small accomplishment, as did that monk who was ignorant of the Dharma. Having only reached the level of the fourth dhyāna, he made the false claim that he had become a sage. When his reward of celestial life had run its course and the signs of decay had appeared, he vilified the Arhats' enlightenment, and so he was reborn in the Unrelenting Hell. Listen carefully while I explain this matter in detail."

Earlier, Ānanda asked the Buddha how to practice; he asked for teaching on behalf of the beings of the future. He now understands the principle of self-cultivation, the theory, but since he lacks experience, he doesn't know what can occur while in the midst of practice. So the Buddha said, "You are still not

---

[1] See part 5, note 28.

aware of the subtle demonic events that can occur when you undertake the practice of calming the mind and contemplative insight." Here "calming the mind" refers to the practice of the great Śūraṅgama Samādhi. (VIII, 2–3)

The Buddha says that if your mind has not been fully purified, and if your motivation is not correct, then the slightest improper thought can make you vulnerable to being caught by a demon. . . . If you encounter a demonic state and fail to recognize it and understand it, you will end up "taking a burglar for your own child," . . . and then all the priceless treasures in your house will be stolen. What is your priceless treasure? . . . It is your very own Matrix of the Thus-Come One. . . . It is your own vital energy, which penetrates heaven and earth, to the point that all Buddhas and Bodhisattvas are fundamentally the same as us, because our vital energies are interconnected. This energy is like our breath; it can be detected. What is within our vital energy and what controls it is the Dharma. Therefore, it is essential that we nurture our energy; for example, we should not lose our temper . . . or talk too much. (VIII, 4–6)

Ānanda and the others in the assembly who still needed instruction stood up, bowed to the ground joyfully, and then quieted their minds in order to be ready to receive the Buddha's compassionate teaching.

The Buddha said to Ānanda and the rest of the great assembly, "You should know that although the twelve classes of beings in this world have outflows, they are, nevertheless, fundamentally identical to the Buddhas of the ten directions, in that they all are fundamentally endowed with the wondrous enlightened understanding — with the awakened, perfect, essential mind. But their thinking is deluded and they have a confused view of the truth, and so they stubbornly cling to emotional attachments.

"As a result, space appears, and as they become more and more confused, worlds come into being. In the lands in the ten directions, numerous as motes of dust, beings who have outflows are created out of confusion, obstinacy, and deluded thinking. You should know that space is created within the mind. It is like a wisp of cloud in the vastness of the sky. The worlds in the emptiness of space are even less significant. If you discover true reality by returning to the source, space throughout the ten directions will disappear. How could all the lands not cease to be as well?

Earlier the Sutra said that the space created within the great enlightenment is like a single bubble in all the sea.[2] Now it says that the space created in our minds is like a wisp of cloud in the vastness of the sky. Since the scope of empty space is so small compared to our minds, how vast our minds must be! . . . This passage describes how our enlightened nature pervades all places. . . . To "discover true reality by returning to the source" is to become a Buddha, or at least a fourth-stage Arhat. (VIII, 13)

"When you practice meditation in stillness and enter samādhi,[3] the essence of your mind merges with the minds of the Bodhisattvas of the ten directions and with the minds of all the great Arhats, who have ended outflows. You abide in a place of profound purity. Then the kings of demons, ghosts, and spirits and the general population of gods see their palaces collapse inexplicably. Their lands quake. Terror strikes the creatures who move through water, on land, and in the air. Ordinary people, in the darkness of their confusion, know nothing of these events.

"All these demonic beings have five spiritual powers; they lack only freedom from outflows because they are still attached to the stress of entanglement with perceived objects.[4] How could they be happy with seeing their palaces destroyed? Celestial demons, shape-shifting ghosts, and succubus-demons will all come to disturb your samādhi. But despite their furious rage, they are subject to the stress of entanglement with perceived objects, while you abide within wondrous enlightenment. Therefore they can do you no harm any more than wind can blow light away or a knife cut water. You are like water at the boil, and they are like ice frozen solid; as they come close to your warmth, they will melt. They have only their

---

[2] See part 2.4.

[3] That is, the Śūraṅgama Samādhi.

[4] The six types of spiritual power are the power of celestial vision, which sees what is ordinarily invisible, including the past and the future; the power of celestial hearing; knowledge of previous lives; knowledge of others' thoughts; extraordinary bodily powers; and the ending of outflows. Only enlightened beings have ended outflows; the other powers are available to the unenlightened. See Buddhist Text Translation Society, trans., *The Buddha Speaks of Amitābha Sūtra: A General Explanation with Commentary by the Ven. Master Hsüan Hua,* 2nd ed. (Burlingame, CA: Buddhist Text Translation Society, 2003), 7–8.

spiritual powers, so they can visit you only briefly. They cannot disturb you except through your mind, which is the host of the five aggregates. Only when the innkeeper is befuddled can his guests do as they please.

"When you are absorbed in meditation, fully awake and free of delusion, how will the deeds of these demons be able to affect you? For you, the five aggregates will have dissolved, and you will have entered into the light of understanding. These deviant hordes rely upon dark energy, and your light will overcome their darkness. If they come near you, they will be destroyed. How will they dare to linger and try to disrupt your samādhi? But if you have not awakened to the light of understanding and are confused by the five aggregates, Ānanda, you yourself could become a disciple of demons and could turn into a demon yourself."

Fifty demonic states are described in this section of the Sutra, but in fact there are countless numbers of these states. . . . These demonic states are basically nothing but a mass of yin energy, which comes from our yin thoughts. Yin thoughts include thoughts of desire, anger, and delusion. They give rise to the aggregates of form, sense-perception, cognition, mental formations, and consciousness; and in each of these aggregates, various kinds of yin phenomena naturally appear when your skill reaches a certain level. If your skill hasn't reached that level, then you won't encounter these demonic states even if you want to. They will manifest only when your skill has reached a certain level. Don't worry when they appear. There's no need to fear being possessed by demons. When these yin phenomena appear, you should remain calm, as if they didn't exist. See them as if not seeing them; hear them as if not hearing them. . . . If you don't let your attention be diverted by sights, sounds, odors, flavors, objects of touch, and objects of cognition, then the demonic states will have no way to harm you. If you are without desire, anger, and delusion, you will subdue these states. . . . The demons that you encounter in your practice are illusions produced from the yin thoughts and yin energy in your own nature. If you can remain unmoved by these illusory appearances, then there will be no problem. . . . No matter what level you reach in your cultivation, do not become happy or afraid. That is the essence of what is needed to overcome demonic obstacles. (VIII, 21–2)

"Your encounter with the Mātaṅga woman was an exception, and it turned out to be a minor incident. Though she tried to make you break the Buddha's rules, all she was able to do was to cast a spell on you. In the end, you only broke one among all the eighty thousand rules of conduct. Because your mind was pure, you did not fall. But if the demons of the aggregates had been able to destroy your precious Dharma-body, you would have become like a member of the family of a government minister whose property has been confiscated. The family is uprooted and scattered, with no one to pity them or come to their aid.

2
Ten Demonic States of Mind
Associated with the Aggregate of Form

"You should know, Ānanda, that when you sit in a place for awakening, all your thoughts may melt away. When your thoughts come to a halt, only an essential awareness will remain. Movement outside your mind will seem the same as stillness, and the presence of thoughts in your mind will seem the same as the absence of thoughts. When you abide in this state, having entered samādhi, you will be like someone who ordinarily can see clearly but who finds himself in a dark place. His essential nature will be wonderfully pure, but his mind does not yet emit light. He is in the region of the aggregate of forms.

"When his mind's vision does become bright, then ten directions will open out before him, and the darkness will be dispelled. Having come to the end of the aggregate of forms, he will now transcend the turbidity of time.[5] His contemplations show him that the illusion of solid matter is the basis of this aggregate.[6]

[1] "However, Ānanda, in the midst of his mental darkness,[7] this person's intense scrutiny within his wondrous awareness may reveal that the four primary elements are not ultimately interwoven into the body. Then in an instant he will be able to leave his body. This state is called 'the essential awareness being able to emerge into one's surroundings.' What the practitioner has gained is temporary. It does not indicate that he has become a sage. There is nothing unwholesome about his state un-

---

[5] See part 5.2 above.

[6] This is a a description of what happens if the practitioner does not overrate or otherwise misconstrue any of the following ten demonic states. These states are separate situations that may or may not arise and that the practitioner may or may not succumb to — an array of alternatives, of possible pitfalls, rather than a fixed list of tests to be passed through in sequence. The same is true of the other four sets of ten demonic states described in the sections that follow.

[7] That is, the darkness described above, experienced by the practitioner whose thoughts have come to a halt.

less he thinks that he is now a sage. If he does think he is a sage, he will be open to a host of deviant influences.

[2] "Further, Ānanda, in the midst of his mental darkness, this person's intense scrutiny within his wondrous awareness may allow him to see inside his own body. Suddenly he may find that he can pull intestinal worms out of his body without harming himself or the worms. This state is called 'the essential awareness being able to reach deep into the physical body.' What the practitioner has gained is temporary. It does not indicate that he has become a sage. There is nothing unwholesome about his state unless he thinks that he is now a sage. If he does think he is a sage, he will be open to a host of deviant influences.

> When you have made some progress in your practice, you will have accumulated some treasure, and that's what these demons are after. What should you do when they come? You have to remain in a state of unmoving suchness and clear understanding. Do not become attached to appearances. Have no attachments at all. Do not think, "Ah, what a fine state this is! I'd love to experience that again!" Don't welcome these states and don't reject them. Just continue as if nothing were happening. . . . Don't start seeing yourself as a sage, thinking, "Hey, wow! I'm incredible! I can pull parasites out of my body!" . . . With that one thought of arrogance, the demons will come. They will bore into your mind and take over. They can manipulate you until you have no samādhi left. (VIII, 30)

[3] "Further, in the midst of his mental darkness, this person's intense scrutiny may be directed both inward and outward. Then his will and the vital energies of his individual spirit may merge or become dissociated or exchange roles. His body will be unaffected. Suddenly he may hear the sound of someone teaching the Dharma in the middle of the air, or he will hear voices throughout the ten directions proclaiming identical esoteric teachings. This state is called 'essential mental elements becoming dissociated and reintegrated as the result of the sprouting of wholesome seeds.'[8]

---

[8] The words heard in the air are actually spoken by dissociated elements of the practitioner's mind. While this may seem to describe a psychotic state, it can also be a symptom of the dismantling of the false, constructed ego.

What the practitioner has gained is temporary. It does not indicate that he has become a sage. There is nothing unwholesome about his state unless he thinks that he is now a sage. If he does think he is a sage, he will be open to a host of deviant influences.

[4] "Further, in the midst of his mental darkness, a brilliant light may appear within this person's mind and then shine forth to imbue everything throughout the ten directions with the purple-golden color of the River Jambu. He may see creatures of every kind becoming Thus-Come Ones. At that moment, he will see Vairocana Buddha[9] seated upon a dais of celestial light and surrounded by a thousand Buddhas. Each of these Buddhas, while seated on a lotus-flower, will appear in a hundred million lands at once. This state is called 'the mind and spirit becoming imbued with a spiritual awakening while the mind illuminates all worlds clearly and in detail.' There is nothing unwholesome about his state unless he thinks that he is now a sage. If he does think he is a sage, he will be open to a host of deviant influences.

[5] "Further, in the midst of his mental darkness, as this person continues these contemplations within his wondrous awareness, he may be unable to bring them to a halt. When he tries to subdue his mind so that these visions do not become overwhelming, all of space throughout the ten directions may suddenly take on the colors of the seven precious things or perhaps the colors of a hundred precious gems. Each of these colors will pervade all of space, but without interfering with each other. The practitioner will see the blues, yellows, reds, and whites with perfect clarity. This state is called 'restraining the mind so that its contemplations do not become excessive.' What the practitioner has gained is temporary. It does not indicate that he has become a sage. There is nothing unwholesome about his state unless he thinks that he is now a sage. If he does think he is a sage, he will be open to a host of deviant influences.

[6] "Further, in the midst of his mental darkness, this person's awareness may shine constantly with a brilliant light. Then in the middle of the night and in darkened rooms, he may be able to see as clearly as if it

---

[9] The body of a Buddha that is equivalent to the Dharma-Realm.

were broad daylight. Objects that would ordinarily be hidden[10] may be clearly visible to him. This state is called 'refining the mind and purifying the vision to reveal what is hidden so that one can see in the dark.' What the practitioner has gained is temporary. It does not indicate that he has become a sage. There is nothing unwholesome about his state unless he thinks that he is now a sage If he does think he is a sage, he will be open to a host of deviant influences.

> Some practitioners, when they reach this level, will suddenly see all kinds of things because they have opened their Buddha-eye. However, not everyone is able to open the Buddha-eye, and even if it does open, it may not stay open indefinitely. In the state described here, the Buddha-eye opens temporarily, enabling one to see all of the objects in a dark house as if the house were illuminated. . . . Another possibility is that one may see a spirit, a ghost, a Bodhisattva, or a Buddha coming into a dark house from outside. . . . People who have practiced according to the Dharma for a long time may open the Buddha-eye permanently . . . provided that their minds are constantly pure and that they have practiced the Dharma of great compassion in their previous lives. (VIII, 39–40)

[7] "Further, in the midst of this person's mental darkness, what is external and what is internal may become mutually interfused within his awareness. In this state, this person may suddenly become incapable of sensation. It may seem to him that his limbs are made of grass or wood. If he is burned, he will feel nothing. If he is stabbed, he will feel that his body is like a piece of wood that is being carved. This state is called 'rejecting the four primary elements so that sense-objects disappear and only awareness remains.' What the practitioner has gained is temporary. It does not indicate that he has become a sage. There is nothing unwholesome about his state unless he thinks that he is now a sage. If he does think he is a sage, he will be open to a host of deviant influences.

[8] "Further, in the midst of his mental darkness, this person's awareness may become pure, and as a result, his skill will be perfected. Then he

---

[10] That is, objects that would ordinarily be unseen even in daylight.

suddenly may see the whole world throughout the ten directions being transformed into a Buddha-land. This land will be filled with the seven precious things and will be suffused with light. In his vision the sky will be filled with magnificent and beautiful multistoried palaces and with Buddhas — with as many Thus-Come Ones as the sand-grains in the River Ganges. Nothing will obstruct this person's vision of the hells below and of the palatial abodes of the gods above. This state is called 'thoughts of pleasure and displeasure gradually being transformed and purified as day by day one's concentration deepens.' This state does not indicate that the practitioner has become a sage. There is nothing unwholesome about his state unless he thinks that he is now a sage. If he does think he is a sage, he will be open to a host of deviant influences.

[9] "Further, in the midst of his mental darkness, this person's mind may explore distant places. In the middle of the night, he may suddenly see marketplaces, or public wells, or streets and lanes. He may see relatives or friends, and he will be able to listen to them conversing. This state is called 'the mind, having been restrained to an extreme, flying outward to see much that has been blocked from view.' This state does not indicate that the practitioner has become a sage. There is nothing unwholesome about his state unless he thinks that he is now a sage. If he does think he is a sage, he will be open to a host of deviant influences.

[10] "Further, in the midst of his mental darkness, as he pushes his mental explorations to their limit, this person may have a vision of himself as a good and wise teacher. He may be able to change his appearance from moment to moment, quickly taking on different forms one after another. This state is called 'a vision arising from a deviance in the mind, leading to possession by a nightmare-ghost, a mountain spirit, or a celestial demon.' While he is possessed, the practitioner may speak spontaneously of what he supposes to be the Dharma, and he may claim to have discovered wondrous truths. The practitioner has not become a sage. There is nothing unwholesome about this state unless he thinks that he is now a sage. If he does think he is a sage, he will be open to a host of deviant influences.

"These ten states, Ānanda, may manifest when these beings practice meditation in stillness and interact with the aggregate of form. They may be dulled and confused by these experiences, and they will no longer be capable of taking a proper measure of themselves. When faced with these circumstances, they will become further confused, and in their failure to know themselves, they will make the claim that they have reached the level of a sage. This egregious falsehood will cause them to fall into the Unrelenting Hell.

"After my nirvana, you must explain my teachings and transmit them to beings of the time of the Dharma's ending so that all beings everywhere will understand what I have taught. Do not allow the celestial demons to have their way. Protect these practitioners and lend them support so that they can realize the supreme enlightenment."

3

Ten Demonic States of Mind Associated with the Aggregate of Sense-Perception

"Ānanda, as this good person practices samādhi and as his mind becomes still, he no will longer experience the aggregate of form. He may see the mind of the Buddhas appear to him as if in a mirror. But he may not know how to make use of that mind. He may undergo what seems to him to be a kind of paralysis. It is as if a deviant being has come into contact with his mind and has prevented him from moving, even though his hands and feet are intact and his vision and hearing are unimpaired. He is now in the region of the aggregate of sense-perception.

"If the paralysis subsides, his mind will be able to leave his body, and he will be able to look back and see his own face. He will be able to stay or go as he pleases, without further hindrance. Having reached the end of the aggregate of sense-perception, he will now transcend the turbidity of perception. He contemplates how this aggregate arises, and he sees that its basis lies in illusion and deluded thinking.[11]

[1] "Ānanda, in this situation, this good person experiences an inner light of great brilliance. If he has been restraining his mind too severely, then wherever he sees beings illuminated by the light that shines forth from his mind, he may immediately be overwhelmed by a boundless sorrow. He will look upon even mosquitoes and worms as he would look upon a newborn child. His mind will be filled with pity, and he will frequently burst into tears without knowing why. This state is called 'an excess of severity in one's practice.' If he understands this state, he will

---

[11] This paragraph describes a successful completion of an encounter with the aggregate of sense-perception. The paragraphs that follow describe ten demonic states of mind that practitioners may experience and that may put their spiritual progress in jeopardy. This pattern is repeated in the sections below on the aggregates of cognition, mental formations, and consciousness. In this section on the aggregate of sense-perception, the text does not state explicitly whether these states involve possession by external demons or by demonic inner afflictions. The translation is based on the second interpretation. By exception, the tenth state involves an external demon.

not suppose that he has become a sage, and he will not become confused. Eventually the state will disappear of its own accord. But if he thinks that he has become a sage, then a demonic sorrow will enter into the depths of his mind. Whenever he sees someone, he will feel such sadness that he will break into uncontrollable sobs. Having lost his ability to enter correct samādhi, he is certain to fall.

[2] "Further, in this samādhi,[12] once this good person has seen the aggregate of form disintegrate, he will see the aggregate of sense-perception appear. He may then have a vision of his own superiority, for which he feels an overwhelming gratitude. Immediately a boundless courage and intensity may arise within him so that he comes to believe that his resolve is equal to the resolve of all Buddhas. He will announce that he can accomplish in a single moment of thought what others need three quadrillions of eons[13] to accomplish. This state is called 'an excessive and improper haste in trying to excel in one's spiritual practice.' If he understands this state, he will not suppose that he has become a sage, and he will not become confused. Eventually the state will disappear of its own accord. But if he thinks that he has become a sage, a demonic insanity will enter into the depths of his mind. He will boast about himself to everyone he meets. In his boundless arrogance he will acknowledge neither Buddhas nor ordinary people. Having lost his ability to enter the correct samādhi, he is certain to fall.

---

[12] With two exceptions, the ten states of mind the practitioner may encounter upon engagement with the aggregate of sense-perception are not a sequence but a set of possible alternatives. Thus "this samādhi" here refers to the practitioner's state of mind when he first sees the aggregate of forms disintegrate and the aggregate of sense-perception appear. It is not implied that the state can appear only subsequently to the state described in the previous paragraphs. The two exceptions to this pattern are the ninth and tenth states of this group. The tenth builds upon the ninth.

[13] Skt. *asamkhyeya*, one of several Sanskrit words for very large numbers. The translation "quadrillion" suggests the vastness of the amount rather than giving a precise numerical equivalent. It is said to take three asamkhyeya of eons for a practitioner to become a Buddha, but this overconfident practitioner believes he can become a Buddha immediately.

At this stage of his practice, because the practitioner thinks that he can transcend three asamkhyeya of eons in a single moment of thought, he claims
that he is a Buddha. . . . Such a person has fallen prey to wrong beliefs and
viewpoints. It's true that everyone has the potential to become a Buddha, but
to achieve that, one has to practice for a long time. . . . The time can be shortened if one understands the Buddha's Dharma and if one practices in accord
with the Dharma, but one still can't become a Buddha in a single moment of
thought. . . .

Because of his intense overexertion, the practitioner becomes courageous
and vigorous, and there is nothing wrong with that state if it is used to advance
one's practice in accord with the Dharma. But one must not become conceited
and claim to be a Buddha. (VIII, 55–6)

Excess is as bad as insufficiency. There is little difference between going
too far and not going far enough. Neither is in accord with the Middle Way. For
example, while traveling, if you go beyond your destination, it's the same as if
you had not gone the full distance. (VIII, 54)

[3] "Further, in this samādhi, once this good person has seen the aggregate of form disintegrate, he will see the aggregate of sense-perception
appear. He may then see nothing further to accomplish, while being
unable to return to his previous state. He no longer has the wisdom to
understand what is happening to him, and he enters a state in which it
seems he is in a land that is desolate as far as the eye can see. Suddenly
he will experience an overwhelming feeling of inner aridity and longing.
He will be plunged at all times into memories that will not fade. He will
mistake his situation for evidence that he is being diligent and vigorous.
This state is called 'losing one's way by practicing without sufficient wisdom.' If he understands this state, he will not suppose that he has become
a sage. But if he thinks that he has become a sage, then a demonic longing
for things past will enter into the depths of his mind. Day and night this
longing will grasp hold of his mind, and he will not be able to let go of it.
Having lost his ability to enter correct samādhi, he is certain to fall.

In this state, the practitioner feels that everything is meaningless and bor-
ing, and he is thirsty because he needs the refreshment of the water of the

Dharma. He feels he is drying up and withering away because for him there is nothing at all. Something similar happens with ordinary people who don't have a spiritual practice, when they start to feel lonely and bored. This loneliness and boredom are certain to lead them into trouble — the same old trouble of thinking about members of the opposite sex — until they feel very anxious and restless. (VIII, 58)

[4] "Further, in this samādhi, once this good person has seen the aggregate of form disintegrate, he will see the aggregate of sense-perception appear. He may have developed his wisdom more strongly than he has developed his samādhi, and as a result he may lose himself in a fierce boldness. He will cherish a belief in his own superiority, and he will make the mistake of supposing that he has become Vairocana Buddha. He will be content with what he believes he has achieved, although in fact he will have accomplished very little. This state is called 'mental effort leading to a loss of steady discernment upon becoming immersed in a wrong understanding of one's state of mind.' If he understands this state, he will not suppose that he has become a sage. But if he thinks that he has become a sage, then his contentment with an inferior accomplishment will become demonic and will seize hold of his mind. Under its influence he will announce, 'I have discovered the supreme and ultimate truth.' Having lost his ability to enter correct samādhi, he is certain to fall.

[5] "Further, in this samādhi, once this good person has seen the aggregate of form disintegrate, he will see the aggregate of sense-perception appear. But he may feel that he has not accomplished anything new, as he feels he should have. Yet he cannot resume his previous state of mind, nor can he move forward to a new state. In both what is behind him and what is ahead of him he will sense that he is in peril. Immediately he will become extremely despondent. It may seem to him that he is lying on a bed of hot iron or that he has swallowed a dose of poison. He will have no wish to go on living, and he will persist in asking people to take his life so that he can escape his anxiety with an early death. This state is called 'losing sight of what method is suitable to one's practice.' If he understands this state, he will not suppose that he has become a sage.

But if he thinks that he has become a sage, then his chronic despondency will become demonic and will take over his mind. He may seize a sword and slash his own flesh, happy to give up his life, or driven by his chronic despondency, he may flee into the mountain forests because he cannot bear the company of other people. Having lost his ability to enter correct samādhi, he is certain to fall.

> Now that you've read this passage, take care not to be unhappy all the time. Don't be weepy and melancholy. If you keep feeling worried and depressed, this demon will take possession of you. Both the demon and you are equally responsible for sustaining this state, for the demon avails itself of your energy. . . . If it tells you to worry, you can become so worried that you flee from the company of other people. (VIII, 66)

[6] "Further, in this samādhi, once this good person has seen the aggregate of form disintegrate, he will see the aggregate of sense-perception appear. He may come to abide in a state of purity, and his mind will be at peace. A feeling of boundless joy may suddenly well up within him. He will take such pleasure in this state of mind that he loses control of it. This state is called 'feeling what one takes to be serenity but lacking the wisdom to exercise self-control.' If he understands this state, he will not suppose that he has become a sage. But if he thinks that he has become a sage, then his fondness for joy will become demonic and will take hold of his mind. He will laugh whenever he meets someone, and he will sing and dance in the streets. He will claim to have attained an unimpeded liberation. Having lost his ability to enter correct samādhi, he is certain to fall.

[7] "Further, in this samādhi, once this good person has seen the aggregate of form disintegrate, he will see the aggregate of sense-perception appear. Now he may tell himself that he has done enough, and immediately an unreasonable and intense arrogance will well up within him.[14]

---

[14] Skt. *māna*, Ch. *man* 慢 Of seven kinds of arrogance listed in the Abhidharmakośa, five are named here. The two not mentioned are Ch. *wo man* 我慢, arrogantly considering oneself master of the five aggregates, and Ch. *xie man* 邪慢, arrogantly supposing one is possessed of virtues that one lacks. See *Abhidharmakośabhaṣyan*, v. 13, 784–5.

He will feel pride in his actual status, and further, he will arrogantly consider himself to be the equal of people whose status is in fact above his. He may also have the arrogance to think that he is not merely equal to but superior to people whose status is above his. He may cherish the arrogant belief that he is already enlightened. Finally, he will come to the arrogant conclusion that he is almost the equal of people who are greatly superior to him. These feelings arise in him all at the same time. He will think disparagingly even of the Thus-Come Ones throughout the ten directions, not to speak of the sages at the lower levels of realization — the Hearers of the Teaching and the Solitary Sages. This state is called 'having the view that one is superior and lacking the wisdom to free oneself of this view.' If he understands this state, he will not suppose that he has become a sage. But if he thinks that he has become a sage, then a demonic arrogance will enter the depths of his mind. He will refuse to bow when he visits stupas[15] or temples, and he will destroy sutras and images of the Buddhas. He will say to those who give him alms, 'These images are nothing but gold or bronze, nothing but clay or wood. The sutras consist of nothing but palm-leaves or layers of cloth. What is everlasting and real is my physical body, yet you do not revere it. Instead you venerate clay and wood. That is to get it backwards.' Some people will believe in him so strongly that they follow him in smashing images or in discarding sutras in refuse pits. He will raise doubts in people's minds and lead them straight into the Unrelenting Hell. Having lost his ability to enter correct samādhi, he is certain to fall.

[8] "Further, in this samādhi, once this good person has seen the aggregate of form disintegrate, he will see the aggregate of sense-perception appear. He may perfect an even more subtle basis for his already refined understanding. He may reach a state in which everything is in accord with his wishes. Immediately a feeling of infinite serenity[16] may arise in his mind. He may tell himself that he has become a sage and has achieved

---

[15] A free-standing mound-like structure built to house the relics of an enlightened master.

[16] Skt. *prasrabdhi*, Ch. *qing an* 輕安, one of the seven constituents of enlightenment.

complete mastery of himself.[17] This state is called 'becoming pure and serene on the basis of wisdom.' If he understands this state, he will not persist in supposing that he has become a sage. But if he continues to think that he has become a sage, then a demonic pleasure in serenity will enter into the depths of his mind. The good person will tell himself that he has done enough, and he will no longer try to make progress. In this he will be acting much like that ignorant monk.[18] He will lead people into delusion and error, and as a result they will fall straight into the Unrelenting Hell. Having lost his ability to enter correct samādhi, he is certain to fall.

[9] "Further, in this samādhi, once this good person has seen the aggregate of form disintegrate, he will see the aggregate of sense-perception appear. Within what has been his clear understanding, an illusory understanding may arise, and immediately he may come to the conclusion that there is no existence after death. His preoccupation with this wrong idea of emptiness may cause him to deny the existence of causation. He will be convinced by this wrong idea so much so that he will come to the further conclusion that after death there is nothing at all.[19] If he understands this state, he will not suppose that he has become a sage. But if he thinks that he has become a sage, then a demonic wrong view of emptiness will enter into the depths of his mind. He will speak ill of keeping the precepts, saying that precepts are the province of the Lesser Vehicle. He will say that since Bodhisattvas have understood emptiness, how could there be any keeping or breaking of precepts where Bodhisattvas are concerned? In the presence of almsgivers who have faith in him, he will often drink alcoholic beverages, eat meat, and defile himself with lustful promiscuity. His demonic power will keep his followers from doubting him and questioning his doctrines. When this ghostly state of mind has possessed him for a long time, he may even drink urine and eat excrement, saying that these

---

[17] Skt. *paramaheśvara*, Ch. *da zi zai* 大自在.

[18] This personage is mentioned at greater length on p. 391.

[19] The expected sentence offering a name for this state of mind is missing, and according to the Ven. Master Hsüan Hua "it must have been left out of the text when it was first copied." In his commentary, he suggests that this state of mind may be called "the mental state of samādhi dissolving so that one loses sight of what is right" (VIII, 73–4).

things are the same as emptiness. Because he himself will feel free to violate the Buddha's regulations, he will induce others to commit offenses. Having lost his ability to enter correct samādhi, he is certain to fall.

[10] "Further, in this samādhi, once this good person has seen the aggregate of forms disintegrate, he will see the aggregate of sense-perception appear. Now his previous illusory understanding[20] may become so strong that it fills his mind and permeates his bones. Then a boundless craving may suddenly arise in his mind and may become so extreme that he goes mad with sexual desire. This state is called 'being in a samādhi in which one's mind seems filled with contentment and making the mistake of succumbing to desire because one lacks the wisdom needed for self-control.' If he understands this state, he will not suppose that he has become a sage. But if he thinks that he has become a sage, a demon of desire will enter the depths of his mind and possess him. He will constantly speak of desire as the Bodhisattvas' path. He will teach his white-robed followers[21] that those who indulge in indiscriminate promiscuity will be the ones who will inherit his Dharma.[22] Because in the time of the Dharma's ending credulous people will be easily swayed by the power of ghosts and spirits, he will be able to attract a following of one or two hundred or perhaps five or six hundred people, or even a thousand or ten thousand people. But when the demon that has possessed him becomes weary of possessing him, it will abandon him. Then his charisma will vanish, and as a result he will become entangled in legal difficulties with the royal government. He will confuse his followers and lead them straight into the Unrelenting Hell. Having lost his ability to enter correct samādhi, he is certain to fall.

"These ten states, Ānanda, may manifest when these beings practice meditation in stillness and interact with the aggregate of sense-perception. They may be dulled and confused by these experiences, and they will no longer be capable of taking a proper measure of themselves. When faced

---

[20] That is, the wrong understanding arrived at in the previous (ninth) state of mind.

[21] That is, his disciples among the laity.

[22] That is, those whom he chooses to represent his teachings after his death.

with these circumstances, they will become further confused, and in their failure to know themselves, they will make the claim that they have reached the level of a sage. This egregious falsehood will cause them to fall into the Unrelenting Hell.

"After my nirvana, you must explain my teachings and transmit them to beings of the time of the Dharma's ending so that all beings everywhere will understand what I have taught. Do not allow the celestial demons to have their way. Protect these practitioners and lend them support so that they can realize the supreme enlightenment."

4
Ten Demonic States of Mind
Associated with the Aggregate of Cognition

"Ānanda, when a good person who has been practicing samādhi no longer experiences the aggregate of sense-perception, he will be able to leave his body as if he were a bird escaping from a cage, although he will not have put an end to his outflows. He retains his ordinary human body, but he already has the potential to ascend through the sixty stages of a Bodhisattva.[23] He is now able to use his mind to create a spiritual body[24] that can travel about freely just as he wishes. He will be like a man who talks while sound asleep but who does not realize he is doing it. His voice will be clear enough and his words will make sense enough to be understood by others who are awake. He is now in the region of the aggregate of cognition.

"Now, if the movement of thought in his mind ceases such that all superfluous cognition dissipates, then his awakened mind will cease to be defiled. He will understand with complete clarity the deaths and rebirths of all the classes of beings, without exception. He has reached the end of the aggregate of cognition and will now be able to transcend the turbidity of affliction. He will contemplate how this aggregate arises, and he will see that its basis is the pervasive influence of deluded mental activity.

[1] "Ānanda, in the wonder that ensues when this good person no longer experiences the aggregate of sense-perception, he will not give rise to any harmful anxiety.[25] As he perfects his concentration, he will experience light, and within his samādhi he may come to crave a more ample

---

[23] The fifty-seven stages explained in part 9.4 above, together with the three gradual steps described in part 9.3.

[24] Skt. *manomayakāya*, Ch. *yi sheng shen* 意生身.

[25] According to the Ven. Master Hsüan Hua, this sentence means that the practitioner is no longer subject to anxieties that arise from within his own mind. However, because he has not put an end to his own desires, his concentration is not strong enough to withstand influences that come from outside himself. See the Ven. Master Hsüan Hua, *The Śūraṅgama Sūtra: Fifty Skandha-Demon States: A Simple Explanation by the Ven. Master Hsüan Hua*, bilingual edition (Burlingame, CA: Buddhist Text Translation Society, 1996), 545.

illumination. He will intensify his concentrated thought as he seeks avidly to develop his skill.

"Then a celestial demon, seizing the opportunity it has been waiting for, will descend upon some other person and possess him.[26] This other person will not realize that he has been possessed, and so when he is speaking about the sutras, he will claim that he himself has entered the supreme nirvana. He will then seek out the good person who has avidly desired to develop his skill. Then the possessed person will arrange a seat and begin to teach his methods.

> Demons can discern what it is that you crave, and they can use that to tempt you. Therefore, practitioners don't need to ward off demons by reciting a particular mantra or by engaging in a special practice. They need simply to be honest and true. They need to avoid contention and greed; they need to avoid craving and selfishness. If you practice diligently with all your effort, no demon can bother you. But as soon as you become greedy or you start scheming how to gain some personal benefit or how to take a moral shortcut, it's easy for demons to possess you. They can see what level of practice you've reached and know what methods to use in order to lure you. They can easily find some other person to possess and use as an intermediary in order to entice and delude you. That's the case here in this passage. (VIII, 93–4)

"He will be able to instantly change his appearance, causing his listeners to see him as a monk or as Lord Śakra, or as a precepted laywoman or a nun. He may cause his body to emit light while he is reclining in a darkened room. His listeners[27] will have such confidence in him that they

---

[26] The accounts of the ten demonic states associated with the aggregate of cognition may be interpreted in two ways: that the practitioner is himself possessed by a demon, or that someone else is possessed by the demon and the practitioner becomes one of that possessed person's disciples. In his commentary, the Ven. Master Hsüan Hua explained the text according to the second of these two interpretations, and the present translation follows this interpretation. However, Master Hua later stated that the first of these two interpretations is also valid. Ibid., 549.

[27] The "good person," that is, the practitioner, is part of the group of followers whom the possessed person has attracted, and he is misled along with the possessed person's other followers.

will be fooled into thinking that he is a Bodhisattva. He will disturb their minds profoundly. As a result, their sexual desires will overwhelm them, and their lusts will lead them into illicit and clandestine liaisons in violation of the Buddha's moral guidelines.

> If you encounter people who are manifesting spiritual powers as described in this passage, don't get carried away by what you see, no matter what it is. . . . Rather, look on the situation as if it didn't exist. . . . Be neither elated nor disgusted. If you do become elated or disgusted, you will have responded to the influence of what you've seen. (VIII, 93)

"This possessed person will also take pleasure in predicting extraordinary occurrences, whether calamitous or auspicious. He may announce that a Thus-Come One has appeared in the world in a certain place. He may speak of fires at the end of eons; he may predict war. In this way he will frighten people into recklessly squandering their families' wealth.

> If you want to determine whether someone is genuine or phony, whether he is a Bodhisattva or a demon, you can look for the following two things. First, see whether he has any sexual desires; and second, see whether he is greedy for money. If he cheats people in order to satisfy his lust and avarice, then he is not genuine. (VIII, 95)

"This is called 'being troubled and confused by an uncanny ghost that in its old age has become a demon.' When the demon has wearied of troubling and confusing the person it has possessed, it will abandon him. Then he and his followers will run afoul of the law of the royal domain.

"You should be aware of all this in advance so that you will not be reborn among these celestial demons. If you do not recognize what is happening to you, you will become confused, and you will fall into the Unrelenting Hell.

[2] "Further, Ānanda, in the wonder that ensues when this good person no longer experiences the aggregate of sense-perception, he will not give rise to any harmful anxiety. As he perfects his concentration, he will experience light, and within his samādhi he may come to crave the

experience of roaming far and wide by letting his concentrated thought fly forth. He may avidly seek such experiences.

"Then a celestial demon, seizing the opportunity it has been waiting for, will descend upon another person and possess him. This other person will not realize that he has been possessed, and so when he is speaking about the sutras, he will claim that he himself has entered the supreme nirvana. He will then seek out the good person who avidly wishes to roam far and wide. Then the possessed person will arrange a seat and begin to teach his methods.

> In this state, the practitioner is greedy for adventure. He wants his spirit to leave his body so he can go everywhere, see the sights, and have some fun.
> . . . As soon as he entertains this thought of roaming, it gives a celestial demon the chance to disturb him. If the practitioner had not had these thoughts, the demon wouldn't have come. (VIII, 99–100)

"He himself will not change his appearance, but he may cause the people who are listening to him to suddenly see themselves sitting on magnificent lotus-flowers, with their entire bodies transformed into masses of purple-golden light. They all will feel that they have experienced something entirely new. They will be fooled into thinking that the possessed person is a Bodhisattva, and as their minds are weakened by lust, they will enter into illicit and clandestine liaisons in violation of the Buddha's moral guidelines.

"The possessed person will like to say that Buddhas are appearing in the world. He will claim that in such and such a place, such and such a Buddha has appeared as a particular person. Or he will claim that such and such a person is some particular Bodhisattva who has come to teach people and transform them. Those who witness all this will be filled with admiration. Their wrong views will imperceptibly grow into a dense profusion, while the seeds from which wisdom grows will be destroyed.

"This is called 'being troubled and confused by a drought-causing ghost that in its old age has become a demon.' When the demon has wearied of troubling and confusing the person it has possessed, it will abandon him. Then he and his followers will run afoul of the laws of the royal domain.

"You should be aware of this in advance so that you will not be reborn among these celestial demons. If you do not recognize what is happening to you, you will become confused, and you will fall into the Unrelenting Hell.

[3] "Further, in the wonder that ensues when this good person no longer experiences the aggregate of sense-perception, he will not give rise to any harmful anxiety. As he perfects his concentration, he will experience light, and within his samādhi he may come to crave the experience of a sustained merging of minds. He will purify his mind at its subtlest levels in his avid search for that merging.

> In this state, the practitioner seeks to join his mind with the minds of all the sages. . . . His avid search for that merging gives the celestial demon a chance to come and disturb him. (VIII, 105)

"Then a celestial demon, seizing the opportunity it has been waiting for, will descend upon another person and possess him. This other person will not realize that he has been possessed, and so when he is speaking about the sutras, he will claim that he himself has entered the supreme nirvana. He now will seek out that good person who craves a merging of minds. Then the possessed person will arrange a seat and begin to teach his methods.

"He himself will not change his appearance, nor does he cause people who have come to hear him to change their appearance. But even before they begin listening to him, he will make them undergo a series of constantly changing mental experiences. He may enable them to remember their past lives, or to read other people's minds, or to see into the hells, or to be aware of all the good and evil events that are occurring in the human realm. Or he may enable them to speak spontaneously in verse or to recite sutras.[28] They all will rejoice in their belief that they have just experienced something entirely new and extraordinary. They will all be fooled into thinking that the possessed person is a Bodhisattva. He will make them feel inexhaustible cravings, and they will enter into illicit and clandestine liaisons in violation of the Buddha's moral guidelines.

---

[28] That is, to recite as if from memory sutras that they have not actually memorized.

"This possessed person will delight in saying that some Buddhas are greater and some lesser, or that some Buddhas are senior and some junior, or that some are genuine and some are false, or that some are male and some are female. He will say the same of Bodhisattvas. Hearing all this will erode his listeners' connection with their fundamental minds so that it becomes easy for them to adopt deviant ideas.

"This is called 'being troubled and confused by an animal-possessing ghost that in its old age has become a demon.' When the demon has wearied of troubling and confusing the person it has possessed, it will abandon him. Then he and his followers will run afoul of the laws of the royal domain.

"You should be aware of this in advance so that you will not be reborn among these celestial demons. If you do not recognize what is happening to you, you will become confused, and you will fall into the Unrelenting Hell.

[4] "Further, in the wonder that ensues when this good person no longer experiences the aggregate of sense-perception, he will not give rise to any harmful anxiety. As he perfects his concentration, he will experience light, and within his samādhi, he may crave knowledge of ultimate origins. He may wish to make a thorough investigation of beginnings and endings as he contemplates the changing natures of all things. He may seek to refine his understanding of things, and he avidly seeks analytical explanations.

"Then a celestial demon, seizing the opportunity it has been waiting for, will descend upon another person and possess him. This other person will not realize that he has been possessed, and so when he is speaking about the sutras, he will claim that he himself has entered the supreme nirvana. He now will seek out the good person who craves knowledge of ultimate origins. Then the possessed person will arrange a seat and begin to teach his methods.

"His body will have an overwhelming spiritual presence that will allow him to intimidate those who seek him out. Even before he has begun to speak, he will effortlessly subdue the minds of the people who sit at his feet. He will say to all of them, 'This physical body of mine that you see before you is none other than the Dharma-body of the Buddhas' full awakening, which is nirvana. This everlasting Dharma-body has been passed down from father to son in uninterrupted succession. What you see at this moment is nothing else but the land of the Buddha. The pure abode is nowhere else, and no other body has the hallmark of golden light.' His listeners, accepting his words on faith, will abandon their former intentions. They will offer up their lives to him in the belief that they have obtained something new and extraordinary. They will be fooled into thinking that the possessed person is a Bodhisattva. Striving slavishly to anticipate his wishes, they will enter into illicit and clandestine liaisons in violation of the Buddha's moral guidelines.

"The person who has been possessed will delight in saying that the eyes, ears, nose, and tongue are the Pure Land and that the male and female genital organs are the real locus for full awakening to nirvana. Ignorant people will believe such degrading words.

"This is called 'being troubled and confused by a surpassingly evil hex-poison ghost that in its old age has become a demon.' When the demon has wearied of troubling and confusing the person it has possessed, it will abandon him. Then he and his followers will run afoul of the laws of the royal domain,

"You should be aware of this in advance so that you will not be reborn among these celestial demons. If you do not recognize what is happening to you, you will become confused, and you will fall into the Unrelenting Hell.

[5] "Further, in the wonder that ensues when this good person no longer experiences the aggregate of sense-perception, he will not give rise to any harmful anxiety. As he perfects his concentration, he will experience light, and within his samādhi, he may begin to crave psychic responses from afar. He will make an intense and wide-reaching investigation as he avidly seeks responses that ordinary people cannot perceive.

> At this stage of his practice, the practitioner may crave knowledge of distant events. . . . For example, as soon as he begins to meditate while in San Francisco, he may be able to see clearly what his friends and relatives are doing

in New York and to hear clearly what they are saying. Later, he finds out that what he saw and heard is exactly what was truly happening at the time. That's the kind of psychic response he would like to experience. (VIII, 117–8)

"Then a celestial demon, seizing the opportunity it has been waiting for, will descend upon another person and possess him. This other person will not realize that he has been possessed, and so when he is speaking about the sutras, he will claim that he himself has entered the supreme nirvana. He now will seek out that good person who craves psychic responses. Then the possessed person will arrange a seat and begin to teach his methods.

"This possessed person will be able to briefly appear to his listeners as a man who is a hundred years old or even a thousand years old. Their minds will be infected with such devotion to him that they cannot bear to be parted from him. They will act as his personal attendants and never weary of making four kinds of offerings to him.[29] Each wishes to sit at his feet, and he makes them all believe that he was their teacher in previous lives, their good and wise mentor. Out of a singular infatuation for his teachings, and in the belief that they have experienced something new and extraordinary, his followers will cleave to him as if they have been adhered to him with glue. They will be fooled into thinking that he is a Bodhisattva. Seduced by his teachings, they will enter into illicit and clandestine liaisons in violation of the Buddha's moral guidelines.

"The person who has been possessed will delight in saying that in the past, during such and such a previous lifetime, he had brought the teachings to a certain group of people, who in their previous lives had been his wives or concubines or his older or younger brothers. He will say, 'Now we are together again so that I can come to your rescue. We will all return to such and such a world and make offerings to the Buddha there.' Or he may speak of another place, a heaven filled with brilliant light, a place where a certain Buddha dwells and where all the Thus-Come Ones find rest and repose. People who have no wisdom will believe his mendacious ravings, and they will forget their original intent to practice in accord with Dharma.

---

[29] That is, food, clothing, bedding, and medicine.

"This is called 'being troubled and confused by a plague-ghost that in its old age has become a demon.' When the demon has wearied of troubling and confusing the person it has possessed, it will abandon him. Then he and his followers will run afoul of the laws of the royal domain.

"You should be aware of this in advance so that you will not be reborn among these celestial demons. If you do not recognize what is happening to you, you will become confused, and you will fall into the Unrelenting Hell.

[6] "Further, in the wonder that ensues when this good person no longer experiences the aggregate of sense-perception, he will not give rise to any harmful anxiety. As he perfects his concentration, he will experience light, and within his samādhi he may crave deep mental concentration. He will diligently exercise self-control, and he will enjoy silent and secluded places as he avidly seeks stillness and quietude.

> In this case, a demon comes because the practitioner is too greedy for peace
> and quiet. In our practice, we should not be greedy for good things or bad
> things. The Path is found within the everyday mind. (VIII, 124)

"Then a celestial demon, seizing the opportunity it has been waiting for, will descend upon another person and possess him. This other person will not realize that he has been possessed, and so when he is speaking about the sutras, he will claim that he himself has entered the supreme nirvana. He now will seek out that good person who craves states of deep mental concentration. Then the possessed person will arrange a seat and begin to teach his methods.

"He will enable his listeners to know the karma they created in their previous lives. He may say to one follower, 'Although you have not yet met your death, you have already become an animal.' He may order another follower to stand behind the first follower, saying, 'Step on his tail.' And immediately that first follower will be unable to stand up when he is ordered to do so.[30] At this, all who are present are filled with admiration for the person who has been possessed.

---

[30] The text here is not explicit as to whether the possessed person had made the disciple actually grow a tail that the rest of the disciples cannot see, or whether he has

"The possessed person will be able to discern immediately the thoughts that arise in people's minds. He will require extreme ascetic practices that go beyond what is permitted by the Buddha's precepts and rules for deportment. He will slander monks and scold his followers. He will expose people's private affairs such that they cannot escape ridicule and contempt. He will take pleasure in foretelling events that bring disaster or good fortune, and when the time comes, it will turn out that his predictions were accurate in every respect.

"This is called 'being troubled and confused by a ghost of great power that in its old age has become a demon.' When the demon has wearied of troubling and confusing the person it has possessed, it will abandon him. Then he and his followers will run afoul of the laws of the royal domain.

"You should be aware of this in advance so that you will not be reborn among these celestial demons. If you do not recognize what is happening to you, you will become confused, and you will fall into the Unrelenting Hell.

[7] "Further, in the wonder that ensues when this good person no longer experiences the aggregate of sense-perception, he will not give rise to any harmful anxiety. As he perfects his concentration, he will experience light, and within his samādhi he may come to crave knowledge that he alone will possess. With diligence and toil, examining and probing, he will avidly seek to know about previous lives.

"Then a celestial demon, seizing the opportunity it has been waiting for, will descend upon another person and possess him. This other person will not realize that he has been possessed, and so when he is speaking about the sutras, he will claim that he himself has entered the supreme nirvana. He will now seek out that good person who craves exclusive knowledge. Then the possessed person will arrange a seat and will begin to teach his methods.

"At the place where he has been teaching his methods, the possessed person will inexplicably come into possession of a large pearl. Because a

---

simply caused the disciple to believe he has a tail. In any case, a second disciple is made to see a tail, or to think he sees one, and his stepping on it is sufficient to keep the first disciple from standing up.

demon has possessed him, he may be able to transform himself into an animal that carries the pearl in its mouth. Or the animal carries other jewels, or letters and other documents, or bamboo tablets, or tallies or talismans, or other peculiar objects. Anyone who takes one of these objects from the animal will be possessed by the demon.

"He may beguile his listeners into believing in him by saying that the place where they are is illuminated by a pearl that is buried underground and yet emits the light of the moon. All who witness this feel that they have experienced something entirely new and extraordinary.

"The possessed person may restrict his diet to medicinal herbs, or he may simply refrain from eating fine foods. Or he may eat only one sesame seed and one grain of wheat a day, and yet his body will remain sleek and robust, sustained by the power of the demon. He will slander monks, scold his followers, and expose people's private affairs such that they cannot escape ridicule and contempt. He will delight in speaking about treasures to be found in other places or in speaking about remote locations where sages from the ten directions dwell in seclusion. Those who accompany him in his wanderings will encounter strange and remarkable people.

"This is called 'being troubled by a ghost or spirit that has become a demon in its old age.' It may be a ghost or spirit of a mountain forest, or of the earth, or of a walled town, or of a river or a mountain peak. The possessed person may publicly advocate lustful behavior in violation of the Buddha's precepts, while privately he and his attendants indulge themselves in the objects of the five desires.[31] Perhaps he may adhere strictly to a diet of wild plants and the bark of trees, but he will not exert himself to practice samādhi. When the demon has wearied of troubling and confusing the person it has possessed, it will abandon him. Then he and his followers will run afoul of the laws of the royal domain.

"You should be aware of this in advance so that you will not be reborn among these celestial demons. If you do not recognize what is happening

---

[31] The five desires may be explained as the desires for wealth, sex, fame, food, and sleep, or as desires for the objects of the eyes, ears, nose, tongue, and body.

to you, you will become confused, and you will fall into the Unrelenting Hell.

[8] "Further, in the wonder that ensues when this good person no longer experiences the aggregate of sense-perception, he will not give rise to any harmful anxiety. As he perfects his concentration, he will experience light, and within his samādhi he may come to crave spiritual powers, including extraordinary bodily powers.[32] He will seek to know the source of these powers and capabilities. He will desire to possess these powers for himself.

"Then a celestial demon, seizing the opportunity it has been waiting for, may descend upon another person and possess him. This other person will not realize that he has been possessed, and so when he is speaking about the sutras, he will claim that he himself has entered the supreme nirvana. He now will seek out that good person who avidly seeks to acquire spiritual powers, and he will arrange a seat and begin to teach his methods.

"This possessed person may take hold of some fire, and holding the fire in his hands, he may place a portion of it on top of the head of each of his listeners among the four assemblies. The flames on top of the listeners' heads may rise several feet, but they will not be hot, and no one will be burned. Or the possessed person may walk on water as if he were walking on dry land; or he may sit tranquil and unmoving in the middle of the air; or without the slightest difficulty, he may enter into a large jar or bag, or he may pass through closed windows or through walls. Only in the presence of weapons will he feel ill at ease.

"He will say that he is a Buddha, and wearing the clothes of a layperson, he will accept reverential bows from monks. He will vilify the practice of meditation and the keeping of precepts. He will scold his followers and will expose their private affairs such that they cannot escape ridicule

---

[32] There are said to be eighteen extraordinary bodily powers, and together they count as one of the six types of spiritual power. Of the eighteen kinds of extraordinary bodily powers, six are mentioned here in the text: walking on water, sitting in lotus posture in mid-air, passing through walls, disappearing, reappearing, and traveling great distances in the space of an instant.

and contempt. He will speak often of spiritual powers and mastery of the self. He may cause people to see visions of Buddha-lands, but these visions will not be of anything real. Rather, they will be created by the demon's power to delude people. He will praise lustful acts, and instead of condemning such coarse behavior, he will use these indecencies to transmit his teachings.

"This is called 'being troubled by a powerful goblin who has become a demon in its old age.' It may be a mountain-goblin either of the heavens or of the earth, or it may be a goblin of the seas or of the winds, or a river-goblin, or an earth-goblin, or a forest-demon that over a period of eons has absorbed the vital essences of trees and grasses. Or it may be an evil dragon or an ascetic master who at the end of a long life has been reborn as a forest-demon. It may be an ascetic master whose toll of years has reached its end and whose death should come, but who lives on with his body unchanged while he is possessed by some other uncanny demon. Any one of these may possess the person, but when it has wearied of troubling and confusing him, it will abandon him. Then he and his followers will run afoul of the laws of the royal domain.

"You should be aware of this in advance so that you will not be reborn among these celestial demons. If you do not recognize what is happening to you, you will become confused, and you will fall into the Unrelenting Hell.

[9] "Further, in the wonder that ensues when this good person no longer experiences the aggregate of sense-perception, he will not give rise to any harmful anxiety. As he perfects his concentration, he will experience light, and within his samādhi he may come to crave a state of mental cessation. He may seek to understand how subtle mental transformations occur, and he will avidly seek the depths of mental vacuity.

"Then a celestial demon, seizing the opportunity it has been waiting for, will descend upon another person and possess him. This other person will not realize that he has been possessed, and so when he is speaking about the sutras, he will claim that he himself has entered the supreme nirvana. He now will seek out that good person who craves mental vacuity. Then the possessed person will arrange a seat and begin to teach his methods.

"Before his audience, the possessed person may suddenly make his body disappear into the air, and then suddenly reappear. He will show that he has such mastery over himself that he can control whether he is visible or invisible. Or he will be able to make his body seem as transparent as crystal. Or it may be that when he shakes his hands or feet, they emit the fragrance of sandalwood. His urine and feces may be as sweet as candy.

"This person will vilify the precepts, and he will be contemptuous of people who have entered the monastic life. He will often deny the existence of cause and effect, saying that there is no life after death — that there is no rebirth into another body. Further, he will make no distinction between sages and ordinary beings. Though he can enter into a state in which he experiences a kind of vacuous stillness, he nevertheless secretly indulges in acts of desire. People who are the objects of his lusts will also have an experience of vacuous stillness. They too will deny the existence of cause and effect.

"This is called 'being troubled by a demon that began as a vital energy generated by eclipses of the sun or moon.' Such energy may have been incubated within a piece of gold or jade, or in a medicinal fungus or herb, or else in a one-horned beast, a spirit-raptor, a tortoise, or a crane. Having passed undying through thousands of years, this vital energy will develop its own sentient life and will be reborn into this world. In its old age it will become a demon. It will possess the person just mentioned, and when it has wearied of troubling and confusing that person, it will abandon him. Then the possessed person, together with his followers, will run afoul of the laws of the royal domain.

"You should be aware of this in advance so that you will not be reborn among these celestial demons. If you do not recognize what is happening to you, you will become confused, and you will fall into the Unrelenting Hell.

[10] "Moreover, in the wonder that ensues when this good person no longer experiences the aggregate of sense-perception, he will not give rise to any harmful anxiety. As he perfects his concentration, he will experience light, and within his samādhi he may come to crave a long

life. Then he will labor to understand the mental process involved in becoming immortal. He will hope for immediate escape not only from the physical death and rebirth of the body but also from the coming into being and perishing of mental hindrances.[33] He wishes to abide forever in a subtle form.

> Ordinary people undergo the cycle of death and rebirth of the body. A fourth-stage Arhat has ended this kind of death and rebirth but still has to suffer the coming into being and perishing of mental hindrances. This refers to the continual passage of thoughts — the ever-changing thought process, in which one thought is produced as another perishes in an endless flow. (VIII, 153)

"Then a celestial demon, seizing the opportunity it has been waiting for, will descend upon another person and possess him. This other person will never realize that he has been possessed, and so when he is speaking about the sutras, he will claim that he himself has entered the supreme nirvana. He will seek out that good person who craves immortality, and he will arrange a seat and begin to teach his methods.

"He will like to say that he can travel unhindered to and from other places, or that he can travel a thousand miles and more and then return in the time it takes to blink an eye. He will say that he can bring things back from the places he has traveled to. Or when he is in a dwelling, he may tell someone to walk from the east wall to the west wall of a room — a distance of a few paces — and yet no matter how quickly that person walks, he will not be able to cross the room. He would not be able to do so even over a period of years. For such reasons as these, people will believe in the possessed person and make the mistake of thinking that he is a Buddha who has appeared before them.

"He will often tell them: 'All beings throughout the ten directions are my children. It is from me that all Buddhas come into being. I created the

---

[33] Skt. *pāriṇāmikī cyutiḥ*, Ch. *bian yi sheng si* 變易生死, literally "the death and rebirth of what has been transformed" — so called because only the fourth-stage Arhats, the Solitary Sages, and the Bodhisattvas can transcend the birth and death of the physical body and, if they so choose, can be reborn transformed into a rarified bodily form. They are not yet entirely free, however, of the rise and fall of thoughts and other mental hindrances.

world and did it effortlessly. I am the original Buddha and always have been; I did not become a Buddha through some spiritual practice.'

"This is called 'being troubled by the king of the Heaven of Pleasure Derived from What Others Create.'[34] This king will send down to earth a member of his retinue — perhaps a goddess[35] from his own heaven or a young energy-eating demoness[36] from the Heaven of the Four Kings, but not one who has made a resolve to practice in accord with the Dharma. This being will take advantage of the good person's vacuous clarity, and it will devour his vitality. The possessed person who acted as the practitioner's teacher may not be involved at this point. The demon will appear directly to the practitioner, taking the form of a vajra-wielding spirit. It will tell the practitioner that it has come to grant him immortality. It will appear to him in the form of a beautiful woman, and together they will engage in such a frenzy of lust that before a year has passed, the practitioner's physical vitality will be depleted. To those who can hear him, he seems to be having conversations with himself in the gabbling language of ghosts. They will not understand what is happening to him. He is likely to run afoul of the laws of the royal domain. If he does, his vital energies will have already been so greatly depleted that he will die before his punishment can be meted out to him. Thus by troubling and confusing him, the demon will have brought about his death.

"You should be aware of this in advance, so that you will not be reborn among these celestial demons. If you do not recognize what is happening to you, you will become confused, and you will fall into the Unrelenting Hell.

"You should know that in the time of the Dharma's ending, Ānanda, these ten kinds of demons will join communities of monastics who practice in accord with my Dharma. These demons may possess people or may

[34] The sixth and highest of the heavens of desire. Māra, king of demons, lives there. The Heaven of the Four Kings mentioned in the next sentence is the first of the heavens of desire.

[35] Skt. camuṇḍā, one of the seven "divine mothers" associated with the worship of the god Śiva.

[36] Skt. piśāca.

appear in a body that they have created for themselves, but in either case they will make the claim that they have already attained the right and universal awakening of a Buddha.[37] They will praise sexual desire and will violate the Buddha's regulations. These evil and demonic teachers that I have just described will transmit their teachings to their followers by engaging in sexual acts with them. In these ways, depraved demons will take control of practitioners' minds, and for the practitioners' next nine lives, or for as many as a hundred lives, the practitioners will join the retinues of demons, although they may have wished to be true to their former practices. At the end of those lives, they will inevitably become demons themselves. Having failed to realize their claim to right and universal awakening, they will fall into the Unrelenting Hell.

"There is no need for you to seek the nirvana of the Arhats. When you reach the level at which no further instruction is needed, you should still hold fast to your vow to be reborn during the time of the Dharma's ending.[38] Let your great compassion come forth. Rescue beings whose minds are true and whose faith is deep. Make sure that they are not possessed by demons and that their knowledge and viewpoints are correct. The Buddha is rescuing you now from the cycle of death and rebirth. By respectfully carrying out the instructions that the Buddha has given you, you will requite the kindness that he has shown you.

"These ten states, Ānanda, may manifest as these beings practice meditation in stillness while they are engaged in interaction with the aggregate of cognition. They may become dulled and confused by this experience, and they may no longer be able to take a proper measure of themselves. When faced with these circumstances, they may become further confused, and in their failure to know themselves, they will make the claim that they have reached the level of a sage. This egregious falsehood will cause them to fall into the Unrelenting Hell.

These ten states are changes that occur while experiencing the aggregate of cognition as a result of effort one applies in one's practice. When you are

---

[37] Skt. *samyak-sambodhi.*

[38] Ānanda makes this vow in the verse he speaks at the end of part 3.

practicing with maximum effort, such states will manifest. If you encounter these states, . . . don't be confused by them. When you meditate, your mental effort interacts with the aggregate of cognition; they engage in a battle. . . . If your samādhi is strong enough, the aggregate of cognition will be conquered. But if not, your samādhi may disintegrate, and you may become ensnared in a demonic state and experience the phenomena described in the text. (VIII, 168)

"After my nirvana, you must explain my teachings and transmit them to beings of the time of the Dharma's ending so that all beings everywhere will understand what I have taught. Do not allow the celestial demons to have their way. Protect these practitioners and lend them support so that they can realize the supreme enlightenment."

5
Ten Demonic States of Mind Associated with the Aggregate of Mental Formations

"Ānanda, when a good person who has been practicing samādhi has reached the end of the aggregate of cognition, the usual cognitive processes involved in dreaming will disappear from his mind. For him there will no longer be any difference between waking and sleeping. His awareness will be as luminous, as empty, and as still as a cloudless sky. Images of gross external objects will no longer appear before him as objects of cognition. He will view all the phenomena in the world — the mountains, the rivers, and everything else — as mere reflections that briefly appear in a clear mirror, leaving nothing behind, disappearing without a trace, receiving and reflecting, nothing more. He has done away with his habitual and long-cherished karmic impressions. Only the true essence of consciousness remains.

"As the source of the coming into being and ceasing to be is exposed to him, he may have a clear vision, which extends throughout the ten directions, of all the kinds of beings in their twelve classes. Although he cannot yet discern the thread of causes that is unique to each individual life, he will be able to perceive the origin that is common to all lives. This origin will appear to him as a subtle, glimmering, vibrating mirage. This is the ultimate point, the pivotal point, at which the faculties and their objects meet. He has reached the region of the aggregate of mental formations. If he is able to see the subtle, glimmering vibrations, which are the origin of beings, revert to the clarity that is their original nature, then his habitual karma will become still, just as clear waters become calm when waves are stilled. He will have reached the end of the aggregate of mental formations. He will be able to transcend the turbidity of individual beings. He will contemplate how this aggregate arises, and he will see that its basis lies in mental distortions in the deep recesses of the mind.[39]

---

[39] In this paragraph, the practitioner is described as one who has succeeded in putting an end to his attachments to the aggregate of mental formations. The paragraphs that

The aggregate of cognition is like a raging torrent, whereas the aggregate of mental formations is like a series of ripples on the water. When the only aggregate remaining is the aggregate of consciousness, there are no more waves and the water is clear and calm. (VIII, 178)

[1] "Ānanda, you should know that this good person has gained right knowledge and has calmed his mind such that he is firmly settled into the light generated by his correct mental state. None of the ten kinds of celestial demons will have any chance to influence him.[40]

At this point, external demons can no longer use their tricks to disturb the practitioner's samādhi. However, sometimes transformations take place in his own aggregate of mental formations, causing him to have wrong ideas. These are demons of one's own mind. (VIII, 188)

"He may now focus intently on a thorough investigation of the origins of the lives of all the classes of beings. He will observe the subtle movement that is the origin of all beings in each of their twelve classes. As the source of their lives becomes apparent to him, he may begin to speculate about all that he has observed concerning these origins. In so

follow describe practitioners who instead run into difficulty. They make errors that involve wrong views. The Sutra describes fifty-four of these wrong views, which are arranged into ten groups. The first five of the groups include various erroneous speculations about the origins of beings in the past, while the last five groups involve speculations about the future, specifically about what beings may encounter after their death. Further, within each of the groups involving speculation about the past, some of the wrong views arise when the practitioner, by means of his spiritual power, looks into previous eons. Other wrong views arise not in association with observations but simply from logical reasoning. All these experiences involve use of the seventh consciousness (the individuating or manas consciousness), not the cognitive activities of the sixth consciousness, since when this practitioner is in samādhi, the aggregate of cognition is no longer present.

The fifty-four wrong views described here roughly correspond to the sixty-two wrong views described in the *Brahmajāla Sutta*. See *The Discourse on the All-Embracing Net of Views: Brahmajāla Sutta*, trans. Bhikkhu Bodhi (Kandy, Sri Lanka: Buddhist Publication Society, 1998).

[40] In contrast to the vulnerability to demonic influences described in the previous section.

doing, he may fall into the error of adopting either of two theories that deny causation.[41]

"First, this person may not discern any causes for the origin of life. How might this be? This person will have already completely eliminated the means for the arising of cognitive distortions.[42] Employing his eye-faculty, with its eight hundred degrees of efficacy,[43] he will now be able to see all beings caught in the swirling flux of their karma during the previous eighty thousand eons, as they meet their death in one place and are born again in another. But he will not be able see beyond eighty thousand eons, and therefore he will suppose that eighty thousand eons ago, all beings in the worlds throughout the ten directions came into being of their own accord, independently of any cause. Because of this speculation, he will lose all the ground that he has gained in his quest for right and universal wisdom. In his confusion about the nature of full awakening, he will fall and take a wrong path.

"Or second, this person may not discern any cause for the ending of life. How might this be? This person has already observed the origins of all beings. He has discerned that some humans are reborn as humans, and he has been aware of birds being reborn as birds. He may therefore conclude that black crows are inevitably reborn as black crows, while swans are inevitably reborn as white swans. He may conclude that people and gods are always reborn among beings who walk upright and that animals are always reborn as beasts that walk on four legs, and also that washing is not what makes white swans white, nor dyeing what makes crows black. He will therefore conclude that for the last eighty thousand eons until the present moment, no being has been reborn into a different class. He further concludes, 'In all this time I have observed no instance of full

---

[41] Skt. *asatkāryavāda*, Ch. *wu yin lun* 無因論, the theory that causes do not exist or that causes cannot be found in effects. The analysis of wrong views begins here with two theories that deny causation, the first arising from observations of past eons, the second from speculation.

[42] That is, he has been successful in ending his attachment to the aggregate of cognition.

[43] See part 5.2 above.

awakening. How then could a being who is not awake change into a being who has awakened? I can only conclude that to this very day all creatures have existed without any special cause for their being what they are.'

> Although the text says that this person can see for eighty thousand eons, this practitioner is actually under the influence of a delusion. . . . This individual may feel that eighty thousand eons have passed by, but it actually may not be that long. . . . Controlled by his own deluded thinking, he experiences a totally unreal state in which he sees birds being reborn as birds. . . . If he had really seen as far back in time as eighty thousand eons, he would have seen those birds being reborn as something else. It's clear that the experience of eighty thousand eons is only a false perception of his mind. (VIII, 182)
>
> In addition, he has no idea of what occurred longer ago than eighty thousand eons, and so he mistakenly concludes that there is no cause of the existence of anything, because he has no knowledge of events that occurred previously. (VIII, 187)

"Because of this speculation, the practitioner will lose all the ground that he has gained in his quest for right and universal wisdom. In his confusion about the nature of full awakening, he will fall and take a wrong path. These two theories that deny causation constitute the first group of wrong paths.

[2] "In his practice of samādhi, Ānanda, this good person's mind has settled into the light generated by his correct mental state. No demon will have any chance to influence him. He may now focus on a thorough investigation of the constant and subtle movement at the origin of the lives of all the classes of beings. He may begin to speculate about all that he has observed about the constancy of this movement, and in so doing he may fall into the error of adopting one of four theories concerning universal everlastingness.

"First, as this person fully investigates the nature of his mind and what it experiences,[44] he may conclude that there is no cause either for the mind or for what it perceives. His practices may enable him to discern the

---

[44] That is, the first six of his consciousnesses and their objects.

deaths and rebirths that all beings throughout the ten directions have suffered during the previous twenty thousand eons. He may observe that throughout that period of time, as these beings have clung to the cycle of death and rebirth, their minds and their minds' experiences have not been lost. On that basis he may speculate that the mind and its experiences are everlasting.

"Second, as this person fully investigates the origins of the four primary elements, it may seem to him that these primary elements never change. His practices may enable him to discern the cycle of death and rebirth that all beings throughout the ten directions have undergone during the previous forty thousand eons. He may observe that throughout this period of time, there has been no alteration in the nature of the primary elements. On that basis he may speculate that it is the nature of the primary elements to be everlasting.

> Actually the four primary elements — earth, water, fire, and air — are created from beings' deluded mental activity. They don't have an independent existence of their own. Therefore, how can they be everlasting? (VIII, 189)

"Third, as this person fully investigates the perceptual functions of the sixth consciousness, the individuating consciousness,[45] and the storehouse consciousness,[46] it may seem to him that, from their very origins, it has always been the nature of these consciousnesses to be everlasting. His practices may enable him to discern the cycle of death and rebirth undergone by all beings throughout the ten directions during the previous eighty thousand eons. It may seem to him that throughout this period of time, beings' consciousnesses have maintained their original natures. On that basis he may speculate that the inherent nature of these consciousnesses is everlasting.

"Fourth, as this person comes to the end of the aggregate of cognition, it may seem to him that the source of coming into being and ceasing to be has stopped functioning. Since he has put a stop to the activity of the

---

[45] The manas or seventh consciousness.
[46] The eighth consciousness.

aggregate of cognition, he may reason that there can be no resumption of that activity. On that basis he concludes that the coming into being and ceasing to be of cognition, with its ebb and flow, have come to a permanent end. He will therefore conclude that this state in which there is neither coming into being nor perishing must be everlasting.

"Because of this speculation, the practitioner will lose all the ground that he has gained in his quest for right and universal wisdom. In his confusion about the nature of full awakening, he will fall and take a wrong path. These four theories about what is everlasting constitute the second group of wrong paths.

[3] "Further, when in his practice of samādhi this good person's mind is firmly settled in his correct mental state, no demon will have any chance to influence him. He may now focus on a thorough investigation of the constant and subtle movement at the origin of the lives of all the classes of beings. He may begin to speculate about self and other, and in so doing he may fall into error by adopting one of four deluded theories that consider some entities to be everlasting and others not to be everlasting.

"First, as he observes the above,[47] this good person may speculate that his mind's wondrous understanding pervades all the worlds throughout the ten directions. He may take his mind in its profound stillness to be the ultimate cosmic self,[48] and he may speculate that this unmoving cosmic self, with its focused understanding, pervades the ten directions. He may suppose that within his cosmic mind, all beings die and are reborn. Therefore he may conclude that his mind, which he takes to be the cosmic self, is everlasting, while the beings that upon their death are reborn within his mind are not everlasting.

"Second, instead of observing his mind, this person may observe the worlds everywhere throughout the ten directions, as many as the sandgrains in the River Ganges. He may see worlds that are in the declining eon of their life cycle, and he may conclude that these worlds must ulti-

---

[47] That is, the constant and subtle movement at the origin of life (Yuanying, 1470).

[48] Skt. *puruṣa*, Ch. *shen wo* 神我, in the Sāṅkhya school of Indian philosophy, the cosmic self.

434

mately be impermanent. He concludes that worlds that are not in a declining eon must belong to a category of worlds that are everlasting.

"Third, this person may instead focus his observations on the refined, subtle, and hidden aspects of his mind, which may seem to him like the tiny motes of dust that float and swirl about throughout the ten directions, their nature never changing. He may speculate that this subtle aspect of his mind controls the death and rebirth of his body. He may conclude that this subtle aspect of his mind is an indestructible and everlasting self, whereas he as a person who repeatedly dies and is reborn from that permanent self must be impermanent.

"Fourth, as this person becomes aware of the ending of the aggregate of cognition, and as he observes the wave-like flux of the aggregate of mental formations, he may speculate that the constant flux of the aggregate of mental formations is everlasting. Since at that point, the aggregates of form, sense-perception, and cognition have already ceased functioning, he may conclude that these three aggregates are not everlasting.

"Because of these speculations, the practitioner will lose all the ground that he has gained in his quest for right and universal wisdom. In his confusion about the nature of full awakening, he will fall and take a wrong path. These four theories about what is everlasting and what is not everlasting constitute the third group of wrong paths.

[4] "Further, when in his practice of samādhi, this good person's mind is firmly settled in his correct mental state, no demon will have any chance to influence him. He may then fully investigate the origins of the lives of all the classes of beings. If he speculates about the existence of certain distinctions, he may fall into error by adopting one of four deluded theories concerning what is finite and what is not.

"First, this person may speculate that the wave-like flux that is the source of life continues to function without cease. He may conclude that both past time and future time are finite, while the mind functioning in the present moment continues indefinitely and so is infinite.

"Second, in his samādhi this person may be able to see beings throughout eighty thousand eons of the past. When he attempts to perceive earlier eons, he does not see or hear anything there. The expanse of time in which he sees and hears nothing he supposes to be infinite, while the expanse of time in which he perceives beings he supposes to be finite.

"Third, this person may speculate that his own awareness is infinite and that all other people appear within his awareness. However, he is not aware of other people's awarenesses, and therefore he may conclude that their awarenesses are merely finite, not infinite, as he supposes his is.

"Fourth, this person may thoroughly investigate the aggregate of mental formations in his wish to bring this aggregate to an end. Based on what he has observed of the pathways of his mind, he speculates that a portion of the mind of each and every individual being is subject to coming into being and ceasing to be, while another portion is not subject to coming into being and ceasing to be. Thus he concludes that everything in this world is half finite and half infinite.

"Having made these suppositions about what is finite and what is infinite, he will fall and take a wrong path. He has become confused about the nature of full awakening. These theories about what is finite and what is infinite constitute the fourth group of wrong paths.

[5] "Further, when in his practice of samādhi, this good person's mind is firmly settled in his correct mental state, no demon will have any chance to influence him. He may now focus on a thorough investigation of the constant and subtle movement at the origin of the lives of all the classes of beings. Then he may begin to speculate about his own knowledge and viewpoints, and in so doing he may fall into error by adopting one of four baseless and distorted theories involving conceptualizations[49] of immortality.

"First, this person may observe the source of the fluctuations within the aggregate of mental formations. If he perceives variation in the patterns of the flux, he will call that variation 'change.' If he perceives continuity in the patterns, he will call that continuity 'constancy.' He will say that what he sees is what has come into being, and if he sees nothing, he will say that whatever had been there has perished. If there is continuity in the patterns of flux, he will say that it is 'caused by augmentation'; and

---

[49] Skt. *parikalpita*, Ch. *bian ji* 遍計.

436

if at some point the continuity in the patterns of flux is interrupted, he will say that it is 'caused by diminution.' All the places in which he has observed things come into being he will call the 'totality of what exists,' and all the places in which he has observed nothing he will call the 'totality of nonexistence.' In this way, by observing everything in the light of the aggregate of mental formations, he forms various conclusions about what he has seen. If someone seeking to learn his methods should come to ask him about his theories, he will reply: 'I both come into being and cease to be. I exist and yet do not exist. I both grow and diminish.' What he says is so confusing that no one can understand what he means.

"Second, this person may look intently into his mind, and he may not see any beings anywhere. On this basis he will draw his conclusions. When people come to him with questions, he will answer with one word: 'No.' He will say no more than the single word 'no.'

"Third, this person may look intently into his mind, and he may see all beings in their various places. On this basis he will draw his conclusions. When people come to him with questions, he will answer with one word. 'Yes.' He will say no more than the single word 'yes.'

"Fourth, this person, when looking into his mind, may sometimes see beings in their various locations, and at other times he may see no beings at all. Because of this inconsistency in his experience, he may become confused. When people come to him with questions, he will answer, 'Both yes and no. But if it is "no," then it isn't "yes."' His confused sophistries will not stand up to scrutiny.

"Having made these muddled suppositions about the existence and nonexistence of beings, he will fall and take a wrong path. He has become confused about the nature of full awakening. These four baseless theories concerning muddled ideas about immortality constitute the fifth group of wrong paths.

[6] "Further, when in his practice of samādhi this good person's mind is firmly settled in his correct mental state, no demon will have any chance to influence him. He may now focus on a thorough investigation of the constant and subtle movement at the origin of the lives of all the classes of beings. He may begin to speculate about the endless flux that

he has observed, and in so doing he may make the mistake of committing himself to confused ideas about the attributes of forms that exist after death.

"Perhaps he is strongly attached to his body, and so he will say that his body, which is composed of attributes of form, is his true self. Or perhaps his view is that all worlds are contained within himself, and so he will say that his true self contains the totality of all forms. Or perhaps he concludes that all perceived objects are dependent for their existence on his perceiving them, and so he will say that all the attributes of form belong to his experience. On the other hand, he may conclude that the existence of his true self is dependent on the constant flux of mental formations, and so he will say that he belongs to the attributes of form.

In general, these theories are illogical and make no sense. (VIII, 214–5)

"All four of these speculations propose that the attributes of form continue after death. Cycling through these four speculations, he may apply them to each one of the four aggregates,[50] so that there are sixteen propositions concerning the attributes of form. He also proposes that afflictions will always be afflictions, that full awakening will always be full awakening, and that the two continue to exist together without ever coming into contact.

"Because he has made these suppositions about the existence of attributes of form after death, he will fall and take a wrong path. He has become confused about the nature of full awakening. This belief in wrong-headed theories concerning the existence after death of attributes of all five aggregates is the sixth of these wrong paths.[51]

[7] "Further, when in his practice of samādhi this good person's mind is firmly settled in his correct mental state, no demon will have any chance to influence him. He may now focus on a thorough investigation of the constant and subtle movement at the origin of the lives of all the classes

---

[50] Four because the aggregate of consciousness is not included.

[51] All five are mentioned here because the practitioner assumes that since attributes of the first four aggregates exist after death, it applies to the fifth also.

of beings. He may speculate about the aggregates of form, sense-perception, and cognition — all of which have already ceased to function within his samādhi — and in so doing, he may make the mistake of adopting confused ideas about the nonexistence of those aggregates after death.

"Having seen that the aggregate of form has ceased to function within his samādhi, it may seem to him that his own body exists without a cause. Since he is aware that the aggregate of cognition has ceased to function within his samādhi, he may suppose that his mind has no connection to anything. Having observed that the aggregate of sense-perception has ceased to function within his samādhi, he may suppose that his cognitive faculty has no connection with objects that he perceives.

"Since these three aggregates have all vanished — even though the fourth aggregate is still functioning — he may suppose that, without sense-perception or cognition, he is the same as a blade of grass or a piece of wood. He may conclude that the attributes of the aggregates do not continue after death. Cycling through these speculations, he will conclude that there are eight instances of their nonexistence.[52] Based on these instances, he may speculate that nirvana and causation ultimately do not exist but are mere names that do not refer to anything real.

"Because he has made these suppositions about nonexistence, he will fall and take a wrong path. He has become confused about the nature of full awakening. This belief in wrong-headed theories concerning the nonexistence after death of the attributes of the five aggregates is the seventh of these wrong paths.

[8] "Further, when in his practice of samādhi this good person's mind is firmly settled in his correct mental state, no demon will have any chance to influence him. He may now focus on a thorough investigation of the constant and subtle movement at the origin of the lives of all the classes of beings. Within his samādhi, the aggregate of mental formations continues, while the aggregates of form, sense-perception, and

---

[52] Eight because he has concluded that each of the first four aggregates has these two attributes: they do not function while the practitioner is alive, and they cease to exist after his death.

cognition have ceased, and so he entertains contradictory notions about whether the aggregates exist or do not exist. Thus he will fall into error by proposing wrong-headed and incorrect theories about existence and nonexistence after death.

"Looking beyond the aggregates of form, sense-perception, and cognition, he sees that although the aggregate of mental formations seems to exist, it does not really exist. As he observes the flux of the aggregate of mental formations, he may see that although the aggregates of form, sense-perception, and cognition seem not to exist, they actually do exist. As he explores the aggregates in depth, he cycles through his speculations and proposes eight instances concerning the existence and nonexistence of attributes of the four aggregates after death. Following this line of reasoning, he concludes that the attributes of the four aggregates neither exist nor do not exist after death.

"Further, based on these speculations — that the nature of all mental formations is that they are in flux and that their reality is deceptive — he believes that he has made a breakthrough in his understanding. But although he has concluded that the attributes of the aggregates neither exist nor fail to exist, he is in fact still at a loss as to what is real about them and what is not real. Despite his suppositions that deny both the existence and the nonexistence of attributes of aggregates after death, he cannot in fact see into the future and ought not to speak of it. As a result of these errors, he will fall and take a wrong path. He has become confused about the nature of full awakening. This belief in wrong-headed theories concerning the existence and nonexistence of the attributes of all five aggregates after death is the eighth of these wrong paths.

[9] "Further, when in his practice of samādhi this good person's mind is firmly settled in his correct mental state, no demon will have any chance to influence him. He may now focus on a thorough investigation of the constant and subtle movement at the origin of the lives of all the classes of beings. He may then begin to speculate that there is no existence beyond the aggregate of mental formations. He may adopt any of seven wrong-headed theories concerning the cessation of individual existence after death.

"He may speculate about where within the realm of desire the bodies of individual beings might perish;[53] or about where beyond the realm of desire the bodies of individual beings might perish;[54] or about where beyond the reach of suffering the bodies of individual beings might perish;[55] or about where, within the bliss that is beyond joy, the bodies of individual beings might perish;[56] or about where, within the renunciation of cognition, the bodies of individual beings might perish.[57] Cycling through these speculations, he will fully investigate each of these seven locations and conclude that in each, individual beings perish and that, having perished, they will not be reborn.

"Because he has made these suppositions concerning the cessation of individual existence after death, he will fall and take a wrong path. He has become confused about the nature of full awakening. This belief in wrong-headed theories concerning the cessation of individual existence after death within the realm of all five aggregates is the ninth of the wrong paths.

[10] "Further, when in his practice of samādhi this good person's mind is firmly settled in his correct mental state, no demon will have any chance to influence him. He may now focus on a thorough investigation of the constant and subtle movement at the origin of the lives of all the classes of beings. He may speculate that beyond the aggregate of mental formations, there is existence after death. He may adopt any of five wrong-headed theories concerning nirvana.

"He may in his contemplations observe a radiance that suffuses the heavens of the realm of desire.[58] Longing for this radiance, he may specu-

---

[53] The first two of these seven theories concern the perishing of beings in the human realm and in the six heavens of desire.

[54] The third theory concerns the perishing of beings in the three heavens of the first dhyāna.

[55] The fourth theory concerns the perishing of beings in the three heavens of the second dhyāna.

[56] The fifth theory concerns the perishing of beings in the three heavens of the third dhyāna.

[57] The sixth and seventh theories concern the perishing of beings in the nine heavens of the fourth dhyāna and on the four planes of formlessness.

[58] In the heavens there is no nocturnal darkness.

late that in those heavens he will be able to transform his future deaths and rebirths into a future entry into nirvana. Or he may speculate it is in the heavens of the first dhyāna that he will be able to enter nirvana, because in the first dhyāna beings have no anxiety. Or he may speculate that it is in the heavens of the second dhyāna that he will be able to enter nirvana, because in the second dhyāna beings do not suffer. Or he may speculate that it is in the heavens of the third dhyāna that he will be able to enter nirvana, because in the third dhyāna beings know the extremes of the bliss that is beyond joy. Or he may speculate that it is within the heavens of the fourth dhyāna that he will be able to enter nirvana, because in the fourth dhyāna both suffering and joy are transcended, and as he supposes, beings there are no longer bound to the cycle of death and rebirth.

"He will make the mistake of supposing that these dhyāna heavens are unconditioned states, although in fact the beings in them are still subject to outflows. Since beings in these five locations are able to experience an inner serenity, he will suppose that these are places where he will be able to abide in a supreme purity. Cycling through these suppositions, he will conclude that it is in these locations that ultimate nirvana may be found.

"Because he thought that he could enter nirvana if he could manage to abide in these five locations, he will fall and take a wrong path. He has become confused about the nature of full awakening. This belief in wrong-headed theories that, in these five locations, he could enter nirvana within the realm of the five aggregates is the tenth of these wrong paths.

"While they are practicing meditation in stillness, Ānanda, these beings may adopt these ten wildly wrong interpretations of the dhyānas as a result of their interaction with the aggregate of mental formations. They may become dulled and confused by this experience, and they may no longer be able to take a proper measure of themselves. When faced with these circumstances, they may be even more confused, and in their failure to know themselves, they will make the claim that they have

442

reached the level of a sage. This egregious falsehood will cause them to fall into the Unrelenting Hell.

> Before you have broken through the aggregate of mental formations, your practice of samādhi does battle with it. If your own correct knowledge and viewpoints are victorious, you can leap over this hurdle. If not, you end up with . . . these wildly mistaken interpretations. (VIII, 231)

"After my nirvana, you must explain my teachings and transmit them to those who will live during the time of the Dharma's ending so that all beings everywhere will understand what I have taught. Then they will not allow their own demonic views to lead them into egregious offenses. Protect and support my Dharma so that wrong beliefs are dispelled. Instruct practitioners so that they are thoroughly convinced of the true meaning of my teachings, lest they stray from the supreme path and content themselves with insignificant attainments. You should all become leaders who are greatly enlightened. Become the pure ones who show others the Path."

6
Ten Demonic States of Mind Associated with the Aggregate of Consciousness

"Ananda, when a good person who has been practicing samadhi has reached the end of the aggregate of mental formations, he may observe, within the clear light in the deep recesses of his mind, the vibrations which are the shared foundation of the nature of all beings in the world. Then suddenly the tiny hidden knot that holds together the intricate net of karma of his individual being during his many lifetimes will burst open, and he will lose his connection to the vibrating resonances of that karmic net.

"He will now be on the verge of experiencing a great illumination in the sky of nirvana. It is as if he is gazing at the pale light of dawn in the eastern sky just as the rooster has finished crowing. His six faculties will be quiescent; they will have ceased to hurry outwards toward their objects. His faculties and their objects will merge into a single deep and luminous clarity. The duality of observer and observed will have ceased. He will have a deep understanding of how the twelve classes of beings throughout the ten directions enter into life. However, though he may take an interest in how beings are born into their various classes, in no case will he be drawn in to the process. His consciousness will merge with everything in the worlds throughout the ten directions. The pale light that he observed will not fade, and it will illuminate what has heretofore been hidden. This is the region of the aggregate of consciousness.

> The fluctuations of the aggregate of mental formations have now subsided, and . . . at this point, when only the aggregate of consciousness remains to be broken through, there is a brilliant light both within and without. . . . The six faculties and the six kinds of perceived objects have united, and there is no further duality between the faculties and their objects. (VIII, 235)

"He will attain a state of unified consciousness with the classes of beings, but he does not comply when they call him to follow them into

444

rebirth. He has erased the distinctions among his six faculties, and he has succeeded in enabling each of the six to perform the functions of all of the others. For example, his faculties of seeing and hearing will become connected to one another and will function both separately and together and with complete clarity. The worlds throughout the ten directions and his own body and mind will be suffused with light, like a crystal. This state is the ending of the aggregate of consciousness. This person will now be able to transcend the turbidity of lifespans. He will contemplate how this aggregate arises, and he will understand that it neither exists nor does not exist — that its existence and nonexistence are both unreal. It is based on the distortions of deluded mental activity.

[1] "You should know, Ānanda, that this good person, having completely eliminated the mental formations aggregate, must now return the aggregate of consciousness to its source. At this point, although he has already done away with the coming into being and perishing of mental formations, he has not yet completed the journey to the wonder of his essential nature, which is nirvana. However, he will be able to merge his perceptual faculties so that they can function as one or function interchangeably.

He may have encountered many demonic states, caused by demons from the heavens, by demons of his own mind, or by other kinds of demons, but they did not weaken his samādhi. When he encountered them, he recognized them for what they were and did not become confused by them. Or he may not have experienced any demonic states at all. Now he has to break through the aggregate of consciousness, and when he does, he will return to the Matrix of the Thus-Come One. (VIII, 238)

"Since his consciousness is connected to all the classes of beings in the ten directions, he and they become as if one body. He may assume that he is himself the entire source of all of them. Based on that assumption, he will conclude that he is the true and permanent cause of everything. He will believe that in this he has discovered the ultimate truth. Thus this person will become attached to a mistaken notion concerning what acts as a cause and what is the effect of that cause. He will become an adherent of the doctrines of Kapila, who taught that one should return to what he called the 'truth of the unmanifested nature.' The practitioner is confused about the nature of the full awakening of the Buddhas, and as a result, the Buddhas' right knowledge and correct views are no longer accessible to him.[59]

"This first theory is called 'concluding that one has fully achieved one's goal.' Instead of breaking through to enlightenment, this person proceeds far in the opposite direction. He turns his back on the city of nirvana and plants a seed that will result in his rebirth as a follower of a wrong path.

[2] "Further, Ānanda, although this good person has completely eliminated the aggregate of mental formations — although he has already done away with the coming into being and perishing of mental formations — he has not yet completed the journey to the wonder of his essential nature, which is nirvana. Once he has entered the consciousness aggregate, he may take that consciousness to be his own body, and he may have a vision of his body extending to the ends of space. He may have the experience of seeing all beings in all twelve classes being born from within his own body. He will believe that in this he has discovered the ultimate truth. Thus this person makes the mistake of believing that he has an ability[60] that no one else has. He becomes one of the adherents of the doctrines of Maheśvara, who appears in an infinite body.[61] The practitioner is confused about the nature of the full awakening of the Buddhas, and as a result, the Buddhas' right knowledge and correct views are no longer accessible to him.

"This second theory is called 'concluding that one has a special ability and believing that one has succeeded in exercising it.' Instead of breaking through to enlightenment, this person proceeds far in the opposite

---

[59] In this and the other nine states of mind encountered during meditation and associated wiith the aggregate of consciousness, the practitioner's progress is derailed when he adopts one or another of the schools of thought prevalent in India during the Buddha's time. Here he adopts the theories propounded by Kapila, the founder of the Sāṅkhya school.

[60] That is, an ability to create all beings out of his own body.

[61] Maheśvara is often identified with the Hindu god Śiva.

direction. He turns his back on the city of nirvana and plants a seed that will result in his rebirth as a god who, in his great arrogance, considers his self to be all-pervading and to include everything within it.

[3] "Further, although this good person has completely eliminated the aggregate of mental formations — although he has already done away with the coming into being and perishing of mental formations — he has not yet completed the journey to the wonder of his essential nature, which is nirvana. Once he has entered the consciousness aggregate, he may become attached to abiding there. Then he may wrongly suppose that his body and mind are born from there and that everything in the ten directions throughout empty space arises from there. Because he supposes that both his body and mind well up from the consciousness aggregate, he may conclude that this supposed source constitutes an immortal body which neither comes into being nor ceases to be. In fact, he is still subject to death and rebirth. He has come to the unjustified conclusion that his consciousness is immortal. Already deluded about what is beyond coming into being and ceasing to be,[62] he is also confused about what is subject to coming into being and ceasing to be. Having sunk into confusion, he is content to abide in that state of mind, considering it to be the ultimate truth.

"Thus this person becomes attached to the mistaken view that the consciousness aggregate is permanent and that everything else is impermanent. He becomes one of the adherents of the doctrines of the god Īśvara. He is confused about the nature of the full awakening of the Buddhas, and as a result, the Buddhas' right knowledge and correct views are no longer accessible to him.

"This third theory is called 'concluding that one has an origin and making deluded speculations about what arises from there.' Instead of breaking through to enlightenment, this person proceeds far in the opposite direction. He turns his back on the city of nirvana and plants a seed that will result in his rebirth in a place that he has wrongly taken to be perfection.

---

[62] That is, the enlightened mind.

[4] "Further, although this good person has completely eliminated the aggregate of mental formations — although he has already done away with the coming into being and perishing of mental formations — he has not yet completed the journey to the wonder of his essential nature, which is nirvana. If he becomes aware that his consciousness is all-pervading and includes all things, then based on that awareness, he may theorize that all the vegetation throughout the ten directions is no less sentient than people are. He may suppose, further, that a plant can be reborn as a person and that, after death, a person can go anywhere in the ten directions to be reborn as a plant. Believing that awareness is universal in this way, and supposing that this belief is the ultimate truth, this person makes the mistake of ascribing awareness to what in fact is not aware. He becomes one of the adherents of the doctrines of Vaiśiṣṭa and Senika,[63] who were convinced that everything is endowed with awareness. The practitioner is confused about the nature of the full awakening of the Buddhas, and as a result, the Buddhas' right knowledge and correct views are no longer accessible to him.

"This fourth theory is called 'supposing that all things are aware and drawing erroneous conclusions from that supposition.' Instead of breaking through to enlightenment, this person proceeds far in the opposite direction. He turns his back on the city of nirvana and plants a seed that will result in his rebirth into a state of distorted awareness.

[5] "Further, although this good person has completely eliminated the aggregate of mental formations — although he has already done away with the coming into being and perishing of mental formations — he has not yet completed the journey to the wonder of his essential nature, which is nirvana. When, in the perfect interfusing of his faculties, he has completely mastered their interchangeable functioning, he may theorize that all perceived objects come forth from that perfectly interfused functioning. This supposition will lead him to crave the brilliant light of

[63] Vasiṣṭha was a Brahmin mentioned in the Mahāyāna-Mahāparinirvāṇa Sūtra. The name is sometimes given as Vāsiṣṭha. The Senika or Sainika were a non-Buddhist class, perhaps Jain.

fire, to delight in the purity of water, to cherish the ubiquitous motion of wind, and to enjoy contemplations of the earth, upon which all things depend. He will hold these primary elements in reverence, supposing that they are fundamental causes and are everlasting. Thus he makes the mistake of believing that the primary elements bring into being what in fact they do not bring into being. He becomes one of the adherents of the doctrines of Kāśaypa and of other Brahmins who, through mental diligence and physical asceticism, seek to escape death and rebirth by reverently making ritual offerings to water and to fire. The practitioner is confused about the nature of the full awakening of the Buddhas, and as a result, the Buddhas' right knowledge and correct views are no longer accessible to him.

"This fifth theory is called 'mistaken speculations and misplaced reverence that cause one to be so confused as to worship the primary elements.' Having come to false conclusions concerning fundamental causes, this person seeks a wrong result. Instead of breaking through to enlightenment, he proceeds far in the opposite direction. He turns his back on the city of nirvana and plants a seed that will result in his rebirth among beings with distorted beliefs.

> From morning to night, this person bows to water, fire, wind, and earth, worshiping the four primary elements. He makes offerings to them. Each of the four primary elements is associated with spirits, and soon this person is as reverent to these spirits as he might be to his own ancestors. The elder monk Mahākāśyapa had been a member of the fire-worshiping sect, and he used to bow in homage to fire.
>
> The practitioner described here takes these mundane elements to be the cause of his very existence, and he believes that they are everlasting. It is true that at the fundamental level, wind, earth, fire, and water are identical with the Matrix of the Thus-Come One. However, the Thus-Come Ones, not the primary elements, are the proper objects of reverence. (VIII, 252)

[6] "Further, although this good person has completely eliminated the aggregate of mental formations — although he has already done away with the coming into being and perishing of mental formations — he

has not yet completed the journey to the wonder of his essential nature, which is nirvana. It may seem to him that his consciousness illuminates everything, and he may speculate that within this illumination there is a void. He may wish to negate any of the various forms that arise and to abide forever in permanent cessation. He will believe that his understanding of this place of abiding is the ultimate truth. Thus he makes the mistake of believing that what is not a place of permanent abiding nevertheless is such a place. He adopts the doctrines of the dwellers in the empty void of the Heaven of No Cognition.[64] He is confused about the nature of the full awakening of the Buddhas, and as a result, the Buddhas' right knowledge and correct views are no longer accessible to him.

"This sixth theory is called 'making suppositions about a void and drawing various conclusions concerning that void.' The person speculates that this void is the basis of his consciousness and that the result is permanent cessation. As a result, instead of breaking through to enlightenment, he proceeds far in the opposite direction. He turns his back on the city of nirvana and plants a seed that will result in his rebirth into a void in which everything has ceased to be.

[7] "Further, although this good person has completely eliminated the aggregate of mental formations — although he has already done away with the coming into being and perishing of mental formations — he has not yet completed the journey to the wonder of his essential nature, which is nirvana. If his consciousness seems to him to be all-pervading and permanent, he may attempt to fortify his body in the hope that it will become immortal — as long-lasting, as refined, and as all-pervading as his consciousness. He will conclude that his quest for immortality of the body is the ultimate truth. Thus this person makes the mistake of craving something that should not be an object of craving. He becomes one of the adherents of the doctrines of Asita[65] and of others who seek a long life. He

---

[64] Here the phrase Ch. *wu xiang tian* 無想天, the heaven of no cognition, is presumably an abbreviated form of Ch. *fei xiang fei fei xiang chu* 非想非非想處, the Heaven in Which Cognition Is Absent and yet Not Absent. See part 9.11g.

[65] Asita was an ascetic master, a teacher of the Buddha Śākyamuni in a previous life, and in the Buddha's present life, an advisor to the Buddha's father, Śuddhodana, King of

is confused about the nature of the full awakening of the Buddhas, and as a result, the Buddhas' right knowledge and correct views are no longer accessible to him.

"This seventh theory is called 'becoming attached to a belief concerning the source of life and drawing the erroneous conclusion that fortifying the body will result in a long life.' Instead of breaking through to enlightenment, this person proceeds far in the opposite direction. He turns his back on the city of nirvana and plants a seed that will result in a long life of delusion.

[8] "Further, although this good person has completely eliminated the aggregate of mental formations — although he has already done away with the coming into being and perishing of mental formations — he has not yet completed the journey to the wonder of his essential nature, which is nirvana. Having contemplated the interconnectedness of the lives of all twelve classes of beings, he will retreat into a reengagement with his own stressful inner world of perceived objects. In this situation, fearing that this world will come to an end, he will cause himself to be seated in a palace made of lotus-flowers and the seven precious things, where he is surrounded by beautiful women.[66] Concluding that this is the ultimate truth, he will abandon himself to luxurious enjoyments. Thus he makes the mistake of believing that what is not genuine is in fact genuine. He becomes one of the adherents of the doctrines of the lord of celestial demons. He is confused about the nature of the full awakening of the Buddhas, and as a result, the Buddhas' right knowledge and correct views are no longer accessible to him.

"This eighth theory is called 'perverse thoughts arising and leading to the erroneous conclusion regarding the raging fire of the world of perceived objects.' Instead of breaking through to enlightenment, this person proceeds far in the opposite direction. He turns his back on the city of nirvana and plants a seed that will result in rebirth as a celestial demon.

Kapilavastu. It was Asita who predicted upon the birth of the Prince Siddhārtha that the child would grow up to be either a sage-king or a Buddha.

[66] The palace is created through his own spiritual power.

[9] "Further,[67] although this good person has completely eliminated the aggregate of mental formations — although he has already done away with the coming into being and perishing of mental formations — he has not yet completed the journey to the wonder of his essential nature, which is nirvana. In his understanding of the source of individual lives, he will distinguish between the fine and the coarse, and he will discern what is true and what is false, based on the interplay of cause and effect. He seeks an awakening in response to his efforts, thereby turning his back on the path to the highest purity.[68] That is to say, he perceives the unsatisfactoriness of life, eliminates the accumulation of afflictions, and realizes cessation as he practices in accord with the Path.[69] But once he comes to abide in cessation, he stops there and goes no farther in his practice. He considers cessation to be the ultimate meaning of life. In this way he makes the mistake of becoming a Hearer of the Teaching who is restricted to a single lineage.[70] His companions will be ignorant members of the Sangha and supremely arrogant practitioners. He is confused about the nature of the full awakening of the Buddhas, and as a result, the Buddhas' right knowledge and correct views are no longer accessible to him.

"This ninth theory is called 'perfecting the essence of the mind and so realizing the goal of cessation.' But instead of breaking through to enlightenment, this person proceeds far in the opposite direction. He turns his back on the city of nirvana and plants a seed that will result in his becoming restricted by emptiness.[71]

---

[67] While the first eight of these theories have been associated with rebirths in an unenlightened state, the ninth and tenth theories are associated with enlightenment as an Arhat (the ninth) or as a Solitary Sage (the tenth). These are sages of the Lesser Vehicle who do not aspire to the enlightenment of a Bodhisattva or a Buddha.

[68] That is, the proper path to becoming a Buddha.

[69] The Four Noble Truths.

[70] That is, he wishes to remain an Arhat, believing that to be the highest spiritual accomplishment; he has no intention of undertaking the Bodhisattva path, Ch. *ding xing sheng wen* 定性聲聞.

[71] This emptiness is not the true emptiness, but rather the emptiness experienced by sages of the Lesser Vehicle, whereas the "city of nirvana" is the nirvana of the Buddhas.

[10] "Further, although this good person has completely eliminated the aggregate of mental formations — although he has already done away with the coming into being and perishing of mental formations — he has not yet completed the journey to the wonder of his essential nature, which is nirvana. If he inquires into the deep wonder of the pure and perfectly interfused illumination of his awakening, he may come to the conclusion that this deep wonder is the final nirvana. He then may cease to make progress, believing that he has already realized the ultimate meaning of his life. In this way this person will make the mistake of becoming a Solitary Sage who is restricted to a single lineage. His companions will be Solitary Sages — both those who have become enlightened through contemplation of the conditioned world and those who have become enlightened on their own. These sages do not turn their minds toward the Great Vehicle.[72] Thus this person becomes confused about the nature of the Buddhas' full awakening, and for him the Buddhas' right knowledge and correct views are no longer accessible.

"This tenth theory is called 'completely merging the mind with a perfected awareness and so realizing the goal of gaining a profound understanding.' But instead of breaking through to perfect enlightenment, this person proceeds far in the opposite direction. He turns his back on the city of nirvana and plants a seed that will result in his continuing in the all-pervading but still imperfect illumination of a Solitary Sage.

"In these ways, Ānanda, these ten states are experienced while practicing meditation in stillness, and they are caused by confusion that leads to derangement. Because of their confusion, these practitioners will believe that they have completely attained what they have not completely attained. Each of these mental states is the result of the interaction of meditation practice and unwarranted speculation while within the realm of the aggregate of consciousness.

In these ten states of mind that appear during the practice of meditating in stillness, the practitioner becomes confused and claims to have attained complete

---

[72] That is, the path of the Bodhisattvas.

realization before actually having done so. . . . He claims that he is now a
Buddha, but . . . if someone asks how he became a Buddha, it will become
apparent that he doesn't know. A Buddha who doesn't know how he became
a Buddha is certainly a confused Buddha — except that there are no confused
Buddhas. (VIII, 264–5)

All these states are the result of interactions between the consciousness
aggregate and the mental effort of the practitioner. . . . When you work hard,
the consciousness aggregate battles against your skill. If you have the slightest bit of greed, lust, or deluded thinking, you will enter a demonic state. If
you become attached to this state, then you will be possessed by a demon.
(VIII, 265)

"In their obtuseness and confusion, these beings will not take proper
measure of themselves. When they encounter these states — each one
according to what he craves, each one confused by his long-cherished
habits — they will choose to abide in one of these states, which they
will suppose is the final and serene place of refuge. They will make the
claim that they have completed a full and supreme awakening. This is an
egregious lie, and because of it — once the karma of their present state
has been exhausted — those whose karma has led them to be followers
of wrong paths, or to be disciples of perverse demons, will fall into the
Unrelenting Hell. As for the Hearers of the Teaching and the Solitary
Sages, they will make no further progress on the Path.

"You all must devote yourselves to the Path of the Thus-Come Ones.
After my nirvana, you must explain my teachings and transmit them to
beings of the time of the Dharma's ending so that all beings everywhere
will understand what I have taught. Then they will not allow their own
demonic views to lead them into egregious offenses. Protect them, give
them comfort, compassionately rescue them, and free them of their perverse tendencies, so that in mind and body they may enter the path to
the wisdom and vision of the Buddhas. Then from the beginning to the
end of their journey, they will not stray from the Path.

"For as many past eons as there are sand-grains in the River Ganges,
Thus-Come Ones as many as motes of dust have entered the gateway of

this Dharma, have opened their minds, and have traveled along this supreme path.

"Once you have come to the end of the aggregate of consciousness,
your faculties will function interchangeably, and then on the basis of
that mutual functioning, you will be able to reach the Bodhisattva's level
of vajra-like wisdom. When you experience the full illumination of that
refined state of mind, you will undergo a transformation. Your mind
will become like a resplendent moon enclosed within a pure crystal, and
then you will leap over all the stages of the Bodhisattva's Path — the Ten
Stages of Stabilizing the Mind, the Ten Abodes, the Ten Practices, the Ten
Dedications, the Four Additional Practices, the vajra-like Ten Grounds,
and Equivalent Enlightenment, in which understanding is finally perfected. You will enter into the wondrous and magnificent multitude of all
the Thus-Come Ones, vast as the sea. You will attain the perfection of full
awakening, in which there is nothing that is attained.

"All the Buddhas, World-Honored Ones of the past, while calmly abiding in samādhi and while practicing contemplative insight, applied their
contemplative insight to all these states. By means of their enlightened
understanding, they analyzed these subtle demonic activities. Once you
can clearly recognize these demonic states when they occur, you will be
able to cleanse your mind of those defilements, and you will not fall prey
to wrong views. Then the demonic states associated with the aggregates
will be eradicated, and the celestial demons will be utterly defeated.
Ghosts and spirits of great power will be frightened out of their wits and
will run for their lives. Animal-possessing ghosts and nightmare-ghosts
will no longer dare to show themselves. You will reach your goal of full
awakening without having experienced the slightest weariness, and you
will all progress directly to full awakening. Even those whose roots in the
Dharma are inferior will be able to make progress toward nirvana without becoming confused or discouraged.

"In the time of the Dharma's ending, some beings who like to practice
samādhi may not have sufficient intelligence to practice meditation in
stillness correctly or to explain the Dharma correctly. You should be concerned lest they fall under the influence of the kind of wrong views that I

have been describing. Devote yourselves to teaching these beings how to hold in their minds the dhāraṇī-mantra spoken at the crown of the Buddha's head.[73] If they cannot learn to recite it from memory, teach them to write it out and to place it in their meditation halls or else to wear it close to their bodies. Then no demon will be able to disturb them.

"You should hold in the greatest reverence all the teachings of the Thus-Come Ones of the ten directions. These are my final instructions."

You should respect and honor the wonderful Śūraṅgama Samādhi and the method of breaking through to enlightenment by directing the hearing inward to listen to your inherent nature. You should also revere the Dharma of the Śūraṅgama Mantra, which is the supreme and most honored dhāraṇī of the Buddhas. . . . The Śūraṅgama Samādhi is the Dharma of the nature of all the Thus-Come Ones of the ten directions; it is the mother of all Buddhas. It is the ultimate, most thorough, and subtly wonderful Dharma for progress in self-cultivation, the most important method, the most important instruction about the road you should take to attain the wisdom and vision of the Buddhas. (VIII, 280)

[73] The Śūraṅgama Mantra.

7
The Five Aggregates Arise from Delusion

Then Ānanda once again stood up amidst the great assembly and bowed reverently, having fully retained in his memory the instructions he had heard the Buddha give. He said respectfully to the Buddha, "The Buddha has said that the five categories of delusion which characterize the five aggregates are the basis of the deluded activity of the mind. We have never before received from the Thus-Come One such a detailed explanation. Now, when these five aggregates disappear, do they do so all at once, or do they disappear in sequence, one after the other? And if they do disappear in sequence, what are the defining characteristics of each of the five aggregates? I only hope that the Thus-Come One, out of his great kindness, will explain this, so that all of us in this great assembly can purify our minds and make our vision clear. In this way we will be able to act as guides for beings in the future time of the Dharma's ending."

> Don't get the wrong idea here. When Ananda speaks out again in the assembly, it's certainly not the case that he is showing off. It's not that he wants everyone to notice him. He is seeking the Dharma on behalf of all beings, . . . including you and me, who are his fellow practitioners from a different time. (VIII, 282)

The Buddha said to Ānanda, "In the subtle, true, wondrous understanding, in the fundamental, awakened, perfect purity, no death or rebirth remains, nor any defilement, not even space itself. All these arise out of deluded mental activity. From within the true essence which is the fundamental, original, awakened, wondrous understanding, delusion arises and brings about the world of perceived objects. We might compare the situation to Yajñadatta's confusion about the face he saw in the mirror.[74] His delusion did not arise from any cause. People's deluded thinking leads them to conclude that what is subject to causes and conditions must have an independent existence. Others, not even understanding

---

[74] See part 4.4 above.

about causes and conditions, assert that things come into being on their own. The nature of space itself is that it, too, arises from illusion. The notion that things come into being due to causes and conditions and the notion that they come into being on their own are mere speculations born of beings' deluded minds.

> The Buddha says that in the essential, true, wondrous understanding and complete purity of fundamental enlightenment, neither death nor rebirth exists, nor do worldly defilements and even space itself. This is the Matrix of the Thus-Come One, the fundamental suchness of reality that is inherent in us all. It's not that some people have it and other people don't. We are all endowed with the essential, true, and wondrous understanding — the complete purity of fundamental enlightenment. Within it there is not a single defilement, not a single phenomenon; there isn't anything at all. If you can return to this source, you will be free of ignorance, lust, greed, stupidity, and delusion. . . . The aim of our practice is to return to that place that is within us all. (VIII, 284–5)

"Ānanda, one who understands where delusion comes from will say that it comes about due to certain causes and conditions. One who understands that there can be no place of origin for delusion will know that there is no place where causes and conditions can arise. We hardly need to mention the people who know nothing of causes and conditions and who say that all phenomena come into being on their own. Therefore, based on what the Thus-Come One has already shown you, you should understand that the fundamental cause for the coming into being of the five aggregates is the deluded activity of the mind.

"Your body came into being because of mental activity on the part of your parents, but if there were no such activity in your mind as well, you would not have been born. It is through such mental activity that life is perpetuated. I already mentioned to you that thinking about something sour can cause the mouth to water, and that merely thinking about climbing up to the edge of a precipice can cause your feet to ache.[75] In fact, there is no precipice under your feet, nor is there anything sour in

---

[75] See part 3.1.

your mouth. If there were no connection between your body and deluded thinking, what would cause your mouth to water when there is mention of something sour? From this you should know that the body which you now have is an instance of the illusion of solid matter. This is the first of the delusions of the mind.[76]

"As we have said, merely the thought of approaching a precipice can cause your feet actually to ache. In this way even a sense-perception caused by deluded mental activity can affect your physical body. You now experience what is pleasing and beneficial and what is displeasing and harmful. These two kinds of experience, which affect you in rapid succession, are an instance of the illusion of sense-perception. This is the second of the delusions of the mind.

> If you could stop the activities of your mind completely, . . . the Matrix of the Thus-Come One would manifest. It is your own inherent treasure; it is the landscape of your homeland; it is your original countenance. But at the slightest movement of your faculties of perception, your true nature will be obscured by a covering of clouds. (VIII, 300)

"Thus your thoughts and concerns exert control over your physical body. Suppose there were no relation between your body and your thoughts; what then would be the agency that exerts control over your body? In fact, your body tries to obtain various things that you have been thinking about. In other words, when the thought of a perceived object arises in the mind, that thought evokes the body's response, which is to seek to obtain or to avoid that object. This is true not only when you are awake and thinking but also when you are asleep and dreaming. These are instances of the activity of cognition creating an illusory understanding. This cooperative functioning of mind and body constitutes the third delusion of the mind.

"Then there are the systematic changes in your body which never stop — such incessant and imperceptible changes as the lengthening of

---

[76] That is, the first aggregate, that of form. The ensuing paragraphs concern the other four aggregates in sequence.

your fingernails, the growth of your hair, the lessening of your vitality, and the wrinkling of your face. Each of these continues as day and night succeed one another. Yet you fail to be aware of them. If these systematic changes are not part of you, Ānanda, then why does your body undergo them? If in fact they are truly a part of you, how is it that you are not aware of them? The uninterrupted succession of thought after thought characterizes the aggregate of mental formations. This subtle and hidden mental activity constitutes the fourth delusion of the mind.

"Further, if you were to attain a permanent state of refined mental clarity that is pure and unmoving, you would no longer be able to experience seeing, hearing, tactile awareness, and cognition.[77] If your mind were in fact to attain this refined level of reality, it would no longer contain any traces of those habitual distorted mental activities. How then is it that you may have entirely forgotten about some strange sight that you once saw years ago, and yet the memory has not entirely disappeared, because when you suddenly see something very like that same strange sight, you recall perfectly the first time you saw it? This place of refined clarity that you wrongly suppose to be pure and unmoving is in fact permeated with an endless succession of countless mental impressions.

> Although you have temporarily forgotten about it, the memory is stored in your eighth consciousness, . . . where it is stored as a natural process. There isn't anyone keeping track. (VIII, 305)

"You should know, Ānanda, that this subtle clarity is not the true mind. It is, rather, like a rapidly flowing stream that seems at first glance to be calm and still. Although you do not see it, there is nevertheless a current. Similarly, if in your consciousness aggregate there were no source of deluded mental activity, what else could be the repository of your deluded mental activities? Until your six faculties merge and become interchangeable, you will never be able to put an end to your deluded mental acts. That is why at present this subtle clarity of mind is still bound up with subtle habits belonging to seeing, hearing, tactile awareness, and mental

---

[77] Smelling and tasting are understood to be included.

awareness.[78] In the same way, these false mental impressions lying within what seems to be the clarity of the consciousness aggregate seem to exist and yet not to exist. This extremely subtle and barely discernable activity constitutes the fifth kind of distortion of the mind.

"The five aggregates, Ānanda, are simply the development of these five kinds of deluded mental activity.

"Now you also wish to know what the defining attributes of each of the aggregates are and how coarse or refined they are. Form and emptiness are the defining attributes of the aggregate of form. Contact and separation are the defining attributes of the aggregate of sense-perception. What is recorded and what is not recorded are the defining attributes of the aggregate of cognition. Coming into being and perishing are the defining attributes of the aggregate of mental formations. Entering into the state of deep clarity and being stored in that deep clarity are the defining attributes of the aggregate of consciousness. These five aggregates arise in successive layers, beginning with the coming into being of consciousness. Their perishing begins with the ceasing to be of the aggregate of form. You may suddenly reach an understanding of the principle of the aggregates, and on that basis you may presume the aggregates will all vanish together. But, in fact, they do not all vanish at once; they must be ended in sequence.

> The five aggregates arise in layers. . . . They arise first in the aggregate of consciousness, and to eliminate them one must begin with the aggregate of form. (VIII, 308)

"I have already explained this to you with the example of untying my scarf.[79] What is it that you did not understand, so that you ask me about it again? You should thoroughly understand the source of deluded acts of mind, and then you should transmit this teaching to future practitioners during the time of the Dharma's ending. Lead them to recognize their delusion so that they come to abhor the fact that it arises within

---

[78] The nose-consciousness and tongue-consciousness are understood to be included.
[79] In part 5.4.

themselves. Let them know of nirvana so that they cease to long for further existence in the three realms."

8
The Merit of Teaching the Śūraṅgama Dharma

"Suppose, Ānanda, that someone gathered together as many of the seven precious things as would fill the realm of space to its farthest reaches in all ten directions. Suppose that this person then offered all these precious things to as many Buddhas as there are motes of dust, with his mind intent in every moment on reverently serving these Buddhas. What do you think? By making such an offering to the Buddhas, would this person merit many blessings?"

Ānanda replied, "The reaches of space are infinite, and so these precious things would be beyond counting. Yet someone once gave the Buddha a mere seven coins, and as a result, at the end of his life, he was reborn and became a universal monarch. How much greater must be the reward of blessings that would come to this other person who offers to the Buddhas as many of the seven precious things as would fill the Buddhas' lands everywhere to the ends of space. Even if one were to ponder this for countless eons, one could not conceive of the extent of his reward."

The Buddha said to Ānanda, "The Buddhas, the Thus-Come Ones, never speak falsely. Imagine then the situation of some other person who has committed the four grave offenses and the ten offenses that merit expulsion. He deserves to fall immediately into the Unrelenting Hell and then gradually to pass through the Unrelenting Hells of all the other worlds throughout the ten directions. Now, suppose this same person were to explain this Dharma, even for just a moment, to beings who in the time of the Dharma's ending had not learned about this teaching. Then as a consequence of that one moment of explanation, this person's offenses would vanish, and the hells in which he had deserved to suffer would be transformed into lands of peace and delight. In fact, the blessings merited by such a person would exceed by hundreds of thousands of tens of millions of billions of times the blessings merited by the other person I just mentioned, the one who made those offerings of precious things. The difference would be so great that no calculation or example could express it.

"Ānanda, even in an infinite number of eons I could not fully describe the benefit that beings will gain from reciting this Sutra and from holding this mantra in their minds. By relying on this teaching that I have given you, and by practicing just as I have instructed you, you will go directly to full awakening without creating any more karma that would lead to entanglement in the demonic."

The Buddha had now finished speaking this Sutra. Monks, nuns, precept-holding laymen, and precept-holding laywomen, as well as gods and asuras from all the worlds, and also Bodhisattvas, Arhats, and Solitary Sages from other worlds, together with sages, ascetic masters, pure young people, and ghosts and spirits of great power who had made the initial resolve to attain full awakening — all who were there felt great joy. They bowed in reverence and departed.

Appendix

A Brief Account of the Life of
the Venerable Master Hsüan Hua

One of the most eminent Chinese Buddhist masters of the twentieth century, the Venerable Master Hsüan Hua (Xuanhua) was a monastic reformer and the first Chinese master to teach Buddhism to large numbers of Westerners. During his long career he emphasized the primacy of the monastic tradition, the essential role of moral education, the need for Buddhists to ground themselves in traditional spiritual practice and authentic scripture, and the importance of respect and understanding among religions. He focused on clarifying the essential principles of the Buddha's original teachings, on establishing a properly ordained monastic community, on organizing and supporting the translation of the Buddhist Canon into English and other languages, and on the establishment of schools, religious training programs, and programs of academic research and teaching.

Born in 1918 into a peasant family in a small village south of Harbin in northeast China, the Venerable Master was the youngest of ten children. His father's surname was Bai, and his mother's maiden name was Hu. His mother was a vegetarian, and throughout her life she held to the practice of reciting the name of the Buddha Amitābha. When the Venerable Master formally became a Buddhist in his mid-teens, he was given the Dharma name Anci ("Peace and Compassion"), and after becoming a monk, he was also known as Dulun ("Liberator from the Wheel of Rebirth"). Upon granting him the Dharma-seal of the Weiyang lineage, the Elder Chan Master Xuyun (1840–1959) bestowed upon him the Dharma-transmission name Hsüan Hua (Xuanhua — "To Proclaim and Transform").

When the Venerable Master was a child, he followed his mother's example, eating only vegetarian food and reciting the Buddha's name. When he was eleven years old, upon seeing a dead baby lying on the ground, he awakened to the fundamental significance of death and rebirth and the impermanence of all phenomena. He then resolved to become a monk and practice on the Buddhist Path, but he acquiesced to his mother's request that he not do so until after her death. When he was twelve, he obtained his parents' permission to travel extensively in search of a true spiritual teacher.

At the age of fifteen, the Venerable Master went to school for the first time, and when he was sixteen, he started lecturing on the Buddhist sutras to help his fellow villagers who were illiterate but who wanted to learn about the Buddha's teachings. He was not only diligent and focused but possessed a photographic memory, and so he was able to memorize the Four Books and the Five Classics of the Confucian tradition. He had also studied traditional Chinese medicine, astrology, divination, physiognomy, and the scriptures of the great religions. When he was seventeen, he established a free school in which, as the lone teacher, he taught some thirty impoverished children and adults.

At the age of eighteen, after only two and a half years of schooling, he left school to care for his terminally ill mother. He was nineteen when she died, and for three years he honored her memory by sitting in meditation beside her grave in a hut made of sorghum stalks. During this time, while reading the Avataṃaska Sūtra, he experienced a deep awakening. Subsequently, while seated in deep meditation, he had a vision of the Sixth Chan Buddhist Patriarch Huineng (638–713 C.E.). In his vision Master Huineng came to visit him and to give him the mission of bringing Buddhism to the Western world.

At the end of his period of mourning, the Venerable Master took as his teacher Chan Buddhist Master Changzhi, and he entered Three Conditions Monastery as a novice monk. Chan Master Changzhi subsequently transmitted to him the Dharma of the Pilu Chan lineage. During this time, the Master devoted himself not only to meditation but also to the study of the Buddhist scriptural tradition and to the mastery of all the major schools of Chinese Buddhism.

In 1946 the Master began the long journey to the south of China. In 1947, he received full ordination as a monk at the Buddhist holy mountain Putuoshan. In 1948, after over two thousand miles of travel, the Master arrived at Nanhua Monastery and bowed to Chan Master Xuyun,

China's most widely revered enlightened master. From him the Master received the mind-seal transmission as verification of his awakening, and later a more formal transmission of the Dharma of the Weiyang lineage of the Chan school.

In 1949 the Master left China for Hong Kong. There he taught meditation, lectured on the Buddhist sutras, and sponsored their printing. He also commissioned the making of images of Buddhas and Bodhisattvas, and he aided monastic refugees from mainland China. He also built Western Bliss Garden Monastery, established the Buddhist Lecture Hall, and rebuilt and renovated Flourishing Compassion Monastery.

In 1962, he traveled to the United States at the invitation of several of his Hong Kong disciples who had settled in San Francisco, and he began lecturing at the San Francisco Buddhist Lecture Hall, which had been previously established as a branch of the Buddhist Lecture Hall in Hong Kong. As the community at the Buddhist Lecture Hall in San Francisco grew both in size and in diversity, the institution's name was changed, first to the Sino-American Buddhist Association and then to the Dharma-Realm Buddhist Association. In 1976 the Venerable Master established the organization's first branch monastery – Gold Wheel Temple in Los Angeles – and he established a new headquarters as well, the City of Ten Thousand Buddhas, in Talmage, California.

In the summer of 1968, the Master began the intensive training of a group of Americans, most of them university students. In 1969, he astonished the monastic community of Taiwan by sending there, for complete ordination, two American women and three American men whom he had ordained as novices. They were the first Americans of that period to become fully ordained Buddhist monks and nuns. During subsequent years, the Venerable Master trained and oversaw the ordination of hundreds of people, both Asians and Westerners, from among the multitudes who came to California from every part of the world to study with him. These monastic disciples now teach in the twenty-eight temples, monasteries, and convents that the Venerable Master founded in the United States, Canada, and several Asian countries.

The Venerable Master was determined to transmit to the West the original and correct teachings of Buddhism, and he categorically rejected what he considered to be corrupt practices that had become widespread in China. He guided his disciples in distinguishing between genuine, scripture-based practices that were useful and in accord with common sense, as opposed to ritual superstitions that were unwholesome cultural accretions.

Among the many reforms in monastic practice that he instituted was his insistence that his monastic disciples accord with the ancient practice of wearing the monastic robe or precept-sash (kaṣāya) as a sign of membership in the monastic Sangha. He himself followed, and he required that his monastic disciples follow, the prohibition against eating after noon. He considered a vegetarian diet to be of paramount importance. He encouraged his disciples among the Sangha to join him in following the Buddha's beneficial ascetic practices of eating only one meal a day and of never lying down. Of his monastic disciples he required strict purity, and he encouraged his lay disciples to adhere to the five precepts of the Buddhist laity.

Although he understood English well and spoke it when necessary, the Master almost always lectured in Chinese. His aim was to encourage his Western disciples to learn Chinese so that they could help fulfill his wish that the Buddhist Canon be translated into other languages. So far, the Buddhist Text Translation Society, which he founded, has published well over a hundred volumes of translations, including several of the major Mahāyāna sutras with the Master's commentaries.

As an educator, the Venerable Master was tireless. At the City of Ten Thousand Buddhas, he established formal training programs for monastics and laity, elementary and secondary schools for boys and girls, and Dharma Realm Buddhist University. From 1968 to the early 1990s he himself gave lectures on sutras at least once a day, and he traveled extensively on speaking tours. Responding to requests from Buddhists around the world, the Venerable Master led delegations to Hong Kong, Taiwan, India, Southeast Asia, and Europe to spread the Dharma. He also traveled to Burma, Australia, and South America. His presence drew a multitude of the faithful everywhere he went. He was also often invited to lecture at universities and academic conferences.

The Venerable Master was a pioneer in building bridges between different Buddhist communities. Wishing to heal the ancient schism between Mahāyāna Buddhism and Theravada Buddhism, he brought distinguished Theravada monks to the City of Ten Thousand Buddhas to share the duties of full ordination and transmission of the monastic precepts, which the two traditions hold in common.

He also insisted on interreligious respect and actively promoted interfaith dialogue. He stressed commonalities in religious traditions, above all their emphasis on proper and compassionate conduct. Together with his friend Paul Cardinal Yubin, who had been archbishop of Nanjing and who was the chancellor of the Catholic Furen University in Taiwan, he established the Institute for World Religions, now located in Berkeley.

In 1990, at the invitation of Buddhists in several European countries, the Venerable Master led a large delegation on a European Dharma tour, knowing full well that, because of his ill health at the time, the rigors of the trip would shorten his life. However, as always, he considered the Dharma more important than his very life. After his return, his health gradually deteriorated, yet while quite ill, he made another major tour, this time to Taiwan, in 1993.

In Los Angeles, on June 7, 1995, at the age of 77, the Venerable Master entered nirvana. When he was alive, he craved nothing, seeking neither fame nor wealth nor power. His every thought and every action were for the sake of bringing true happiness to all sentient beings. In his final instructions he said: "After I depart, you can recite the Avataṃaska Sūtra and the name of the Buddha Amitābha for however many days you would like, perhaps seven days or forty-nine days. After cremating my body, scatter all my remains in the air. I do not want you to do anything else at all. Do not build me any pagodas or memorials. I came into the world without anything; when I depart, I still do not want anything, and I do not want to leave any traces in the world. . . . From emptiness I came; to emptiness I am returning."

Index